Advertising Design by Medium: A Visual and Verbal Approach

Conceived to give readers the principles and the tools to create successful advertisements in a variety of mediums, this book is a detailed exploration of how visual and verbal elements of design work together to solve a business goal.

Effective visual and verbal design solutions are more than just a good idea; they are purposeful, on-target, on-strategy, and recognizable no matter where, or in what form, they appear. Success depends on creative teams' understanding of ideation, layout, type, color, varied image formats, copywriting, media advantages and limitations, and production procedures for varied media formats. The step-by-step approach of this book goes beyond broad theoretical discussions on copy and design. Instead, the book dissects the creative process into individualized and detailed discussions both creative and non-creative students alike can understand and employ. This book is ideal as a textbook for design courses within programs in advertising, graphic design, integrated marketing communication, strategic marketing, entrepreneurship, business, and mass communication.

Accompanying the text are online materials for instructors: lecture slides, a testbank, and an instructor manual. www.routledge.com/9781032183596

Robyn Blakeman received her bachelor's degree from the University of Nebraska in 1980 and her master's degree from Southern Methodist University in Dallas, Texas, in 1990. She began teaching advertising and graphic design in 1987 with the Art Institute of Dallas. As an assistant professor of advertising, she taught both graphic and computer design at Southern Methodist University. As an assistant professor at West Virginia University in Morgantown, Blakeman held several positions, including advertising program chair and coordinator of student affairs and curriculum, in addition to developing the creative track in layout and design. She was responsible for designing and developing the first online integrated marketing communication graduate program in the country. She is the author of seven other books, including *The Bare Bones of Advertising Print Design*, *Integrated Marketing Communication from Idea to Implementation* (3rd edition), *The Bare Bones Introduction to Integrated Marketing Communication*, *Strategic Uses of Alternative Media*, *Advertising Campaign Design*, and *Nontraditional Media in Marketing and Advertising*, and is the coauthor of *The Brains Behind Great Ad Campaigns*. She is currently a full professor at the University of Tennessee, Knoxville, where she teaches advertising design and creative strategy.

Advertising Design by Medium

A Visual and Verbal Approach

Robyn Blakeman

Routledge
Taylor & Francis Group

NEW YORK AND LONDON

First published 2022
by Routledge
605 Third Avenue, New York, NY 10158

and by Routledge
2 Park Square, Milton Park, Abingdon, Oxon, OX14 4RN

Routledge is an imprint of the Taylor & Francis Group, an informa business

Library of Congress Cataloging-in-Publication Data
Names: Blakeman, Robyn, 1958– author.
Title: Advertising design by medium: a visual and verbal
approach / Robyn Blakeman.
Description: New York, NY : Routledge, 2022. |
Includes bibliographical references and index.
Identifiers: LCCN 2021045113 | ISBN 9781032185552 (hardback) |
ISBN 9781032183596 (paperback) | ISBN 9781003255123 (ebook)
Subjects: LCSH: Advertising copy. | Advertising layout and typography.
Classification: LCC HF5825 .B5325 2022 |
DDC 659.13/2–dc23/eng/20220103
LC record available at https://lccn.loc.gov/2021045113

ISBN: 978-1-032-18555-2 (hbk)
ISBN: 978-1-032-18359-6 (pbk)
ISBN: 978-1-003-25512-3 (ebk)

DOI: 10.4324/9781003255123

Typeset in ITC Officina Sans
by Newgen Publishing UK

Access the Support Material: www.routledge.com/9781032183596

To Buckley, my creative inspiration.
And to every student who ever told me
"I can't do this."

Contents

Contents

Figures

List of Figures

Tables

Templates

Introduction

To be creative doesn't mean you have to have great hand skills, as those seen in, for example, painting or sculpture; it can also mean you have and/or recognize a great idea when imagined, or presented to you. Understanding what makes a great idea and what to look for when studying creative can be helpful when trying to decide how to promote your own business, developing ads, or constructing a portfolio.

Advertising Design by Medium: A Visual and Verbal Approach will help guide you through the varied skills you will need to strategically and creatively interpret good design and write for advertising across multiple media platforms.

The detailed exploration will focus on how all visual and verbal elements of design must work together to solve a business problem for diverse mediums. The step-by-step approach will go beyond broad theoretical discussions on copy and design. Instead this combined look will dissect the "creative" process down into individualized and detailed discussions both creatives and non-creatives alike can both understand, and employ.

For creatives, effective visual and verbal design solutions are more than just a good idea; they are purposeful, on-target, on-strategy, and recognizable no matter where, or in what form, they appear. Each piece of copy, each design element chosen, must represent the brand and its image. Success depends on creative and account management teams, clients, and small business owners alike, having a thorough understanding of the roles of ideation, layout, type, color, varied image formats, copywriting,

media advantages and limitations, and production procedures for varied media formats.

Each chapter will take an extensive and exclusive look at the intricacies that surround both advertising copy and layout, and how each must adapt to multiple media vehicles without altering its visual and verbal voice. The problem-solving discussions will break down copy and design, beginning with strategic conceptual development, moving through the creation process with all its diverse options and steps, and dissecting the often dreaded approval process. After laying the detailed foundation for type, copy, and design, each will be further broken down into its use within the varied media vehicles discussed.

Not everyone is creative, but this text will help you to better understand the "creative process." For those of you interested in art direction and copywriting, who already know the thrill of design, you will learn how to become better at your craft by studying the ins and outs of what it takes to move an idea through varied mediums.

Creative is a fantastical journey into the unknown, and few knew its ins and outs better than William Bernbach who wrote, "Let us blaze new trails. Let us prove to the world that good taste, good art and good writing can be good selling."

Bibliography

Bernbach, William. *Bill Bernbach Said* ... New York: DDB Needham Worldwide Books, 1989, p. 87.

DOI: 10.4324/9781003255123-1

CHAPTER 1

Where Does the Creative Process Fit in Advertising? The Business Behind Advertising Creative

Chapter 1 Objectives

1. The reader will understand the role the marketing plan and creative brief play in creative.
2. The reader will understand the role research plays in the development of the visual/verbal message.
3. The reader will be introduced to the varied creative roles found in advertising.

The Business Behind the Creative Idea

Art direction in advertising is the movement from sales objectives to creative solutions. Advertising is considered "creative" according to Gestalt psychology because it inspires new and unique ideas and offers insights that result in a solution using imagination rather than logic or reason. Advertising creative can also be defined less imaginatively, as a unique visual and verbal idea that must creatively camouflage a client's business goals.

Because business decisions drive the development of advertising creative, it cannot be subjective, or imaginative without foundation. Great advertising requires a strong business plan that assists with the development of strong visual/verbal solutions.

The results seen on television or in digital or print media are just a small part of the business of advertising. Wrapped up in the final creative solution is an in-depth study of the product or service to be advertised, the competition, and the audience to be reached. Additional steps include ensuring the visual and verbal message can be coordinated across multiple media channels without losing meaning, will stand out from competing brands, and reach the right target with the right message in the right medium at the right time. No small job.

Before consumers see or interact with any advertising, the creative direction must unearth a unique way to sell a product or promote a service. Creative teams or "creatives" most often will have very strict parameters they must work within, rarely if ever getting to do whatever they want creatively. Budget and a client's marketing initiatives will drive creative development. It is important to always remember you do not design for yourself; you design to sell a product or service to a predetermined set of individuals or target audience.

Before the creative team puts marker to paper or fingers to keys, there are multiple business steps that must first be prepared to ensure the creative team has enough information to successfully solve the client's advertising problem; these include 1) research, 2) the development of a marketing plan, and 3) the construction of a creative brief. Let's take a very brief look at each one.

The Visual and Verbal Message Is Grounded in Research

Surprisingly, all creative solutions have a foundation in research. Before coming up with that great idea that entices the target to buy the client's product or use their service, the creative team must thoroughly understand what the client needs to accomplish with their advertising efforts. The type of research undertaken will vary by brand, the life-cycle stage the brand is in, the target audience's overall knowledge about the brand and the current competitors in the brand category.

There are two basic types of research: Qualitative and quantitative. *Qualitative* data employs the use of open-ended questions that can be distributed and collected through interviews or convenience polling. Another popular data-gathering option is the use of focus groups. A *focus group* assembles together a small group of demographically similar members of the potential target to use, discuss, or try the brand in a controlled environment. Conversely, *quantitative* data uses closed-ended or controlled surveys, where participants must choose their answers from a preselected set

DOI: 10.4324/9781003255123-2

of responses. Surveys can be conducted over the phone, in any preset location, or from panel studies. Once gathered, research is organized in a document known as a marketing plan.

The Marketing Plan Is the Client's Business Plan of Attack

The *marketing plan* organizes and analyzes the overall environment in which the brand will be seen and used. Its job is to take a comprehensive look at a business's place within its brand category. Before any creative executions are undertaken, the *client* or *marketer* must first determine what they want to do—financially, strategically, and competitively.

A marketing plan is a brand's strategic business plan; it identifies how a company will market a brand, or brands, to its customers. It will define both the marketing and advertising strategy for a set period of time, often a year. Size and overall content will depend on the client and brand, but will typically include a target market profile, sales objectives, analysis of marketing opportunities and threats, as well as brand strengths and weaknesses as compared to competitors within the brand category, and will determine implementation and evaluation tactics.

Without the research in the marketing plan, the client cannot ensure their advertising efforts are unique and will reach the correct target with features they care about. Ultimately, the goal is to find out as much as possible about any current trends and/or attitudes in the brand category, and overall target needs. Any problems that need to be addressed or favorable trends that might be exploited will need to be researched further.

Developing a comprehensive plan that incorporates research efforts is the foundation for creative direction. If the client wants to increase sales, profits, and brand equity, he must have a plan that will talk to the right audience, define the brand and the competition, and offer a product that is unique and consistently reliable. The next business step is the construction of the creative brief.

The Creative Brief: The Communication Plan of Attack

The *creative brief* evolves from the client's marketing plan. Its job is to lay out for the creative team the communications plan of action. It is a detailed document that outlines the product or

service and keeps the creative team on-target or talking to the right audience, and on-strategy, or accomplishing the creative or strategic goals.

A small but informative internal agency document (usually no more than one page), created by the account manager assigned to the brand or in conjunction with the client, the brief serves as a guide for initial brainstorming. A good brief, according to creative legend Jackie End in a 2009 *Adage* article by Howard Margulies entitled, "What are you packing into your (creative) briefs?" is "when you can read it without missing lunch and dinner." The equally legendary Leo Burnett, quoted in the same article defined a brief as "single minded ... logical and rooted in a compelling truth ... [incorporating a powerful human insight]."

The brief is not a document that theorizes, simplifies, or outlines the visual/verbal message; it should be concise, focusing only on the information the creative team needs to develop a creative solution for the client's advertising problem.

It is a compact version of the client's marketing plan that assists the creative team to understand the client's advertising goals. The team will use the information to develop the visual/verbal message. It is not a creative outlet—it does not determine copy, or define or determine what creative solutions should show. It is a guide for what creative needs to accomplish only. Like advertising, a creative brief must inspire the target audience to action. The target for a brief, is the creative team. It becomes the skeletal structure the creative team will use to flesh out the final creative idea. A well-crafted brief is thought out and thoroughly researched. An informative brief requires culling through the research and reporting only on the insights that matter most. Its job is simple and singular, educate the creative team to assist them in the development of a unique, informative visual and verbal solution.

Account managers use the brief to keep all the stakeholders (the account and creative teams and the client), on the same page, avoid directional ambiguity, save time, avoid waste, and help to eliminate confusion and risk. Beyond being informational, it also helps to enhance collaboration between the account and creative teams to ensure efficiency and integration between the teams. By working together, there is less chance for errors, surprises, and endless rounds of revisions.

Secondly, creative briefs are the initial inspiration for the brainstorming of ideas and the final, strategically driven, creative solution that ultimately solves the client's advertising problem. It is a type of "living" document that can, and often does, change at almost any point along the way as needed.

Finally, it should help answer questions and solve any misunderstandings anyone involved with the creative product—copywriters, designers, digital developers, illustrators, and especially the client—may have before the creative team starts brainstorming.

A well-written brief should define the target audience and the communication objectives, analyze the target's knowledge about the brand, describe individual brand features and corresponding consumer benefits, address the competition, introduce the key consumer benefit and support statement, and determine the appropriate creative strategy and tone as well as layout any relevant promotional options. In my book *Integrated Marketing Creative Strategy From Idea To Implementation*, I show what needs to be included in a brief. See Template 1.1 for a sample creative brief template.

Template 1.1 Sample Creative Brief

Creative Brief Template

1. **Target Audience**
   Primary:
   Demographics:
   Psychographics:
   Behavioristics:
   Geographics:

   Secondary: (If needed)
   Demographics:
   Psychographics:
   Behavioristics:
   Geographics:

2. **Communication Objectives**
   * To create awareness about ...
   * To convince the target that ...
   * To persuade the target ...

3. **Target Analysis**
   What does the target currently think about my brand?
   1.
   2.
   3.
   What would you like them to think?
   1.
   2.
   3.
   Why should they believe it?
   1.
   2.
   3.

4. **Brand Features and Benefits**
   * Feature:
     Benefit:
   * Feature:
     Benefit:
   * Feature:
     Benefit:
   * Feature:
     Benefit:
   * Feature:
     Benefit:
   * Feature:
     Benefit:
   * Feature:
     Benefit:

5. **Positioning**
   (Place competitor name here)
   * Short description of competing brand.
   * Description of the brand's similarities and differences as compared to the client's brand.
   * Their current advertising. What does it say and/or show?
   * What is their key consumer benefit (KCB)?
   * Logo design: What colors, symbols, typefaces are used?
   * Are they using a tagline or slogan?
   * Any unique colors or graphics used in advertising?
   * Current packaging.

6. **Key Consumer Benefit (KCB)**
   USP or Big Idea (Choose only one)
   Feature:
   Benefit:

7. **Support Statement**
   Feature:
   Benefit:

8. **Creative Strategy**
   Approach
   Product and/or Consumer
   Focus:

   Appeal
   Rational and/or Emotional
   Focus:

9. **Tone**
   Rational and/or Emotional
   Focus:
10. **Tagline or Slogan** (Placement can appear either above or below the logo)

11. **Logo**
12. **Detail Copy Points** (This information can appear above or below the logo)
13. **Coupon or Other Promotional Information**

There is no one format for a creative brief; however, most will contain some or all of the following:

1. Target audience profile
2. Communication objectives
3. Target analysis
4. Product or service features and benefits
5. Positioning of the product or service
6. Key consumer benefit
7. Support statement
8. Creative strategy
9. Tone
10. Slogan or tagline
11. Logo
12. Detail copy points
13. Promotional information

Target Audience Profile

The *target audience*, also known as target market, consists of those individuals that research has determined will most likely buy or in some way interact with the brand. First, as defined in the marketing plan, the more the creative team knows about who will be using the brand the better they can target the message to them. Research initiatives will break the target down into four distinct categories: Demographics, psychographics, behavioristics, and geographics. *Demographics* can be broken down into *primary audiences* or those most likely to buy the product or use the service, and *secondary audiences* or that group that has the greatest potential to buy in the future or influence the primary audience to buy. Both primary and secondary audiences will need to be further defined by sex, age, income, marital and professional status, education, and number of children, to name just a few categories. *Psychographics* outline lifestyle and how the brand will enhance or be integrated into their lifestyle and their attitude about the brand category overall. *Behavioristics* defines why a person buys. *Geographics* segregates out where the target lives by country, state, region, city, or even by zip code. Understanding how the target thinks, interacts, and digests the visual and verbal message can be further isolated by whether they are more visually or verbally driven.

Understanding How the Target Thinks: A Brain Teaser
The more the creative team knows about how the target thinks, acts, feels, and processes information, the easier it will be for them to better match the visual/verbal message to meet their individual needs. These unique needs are governed by the brain, which is divided into two distinct halves, the left and right sides.

The left, or more conservative, side of the brain is responsible for language and speech, judgment, reasoning and sequencing, math and science skills, and controls logical and rational thoughts. It is also the side that helps with memorization skills. The more active or left-brained individual needs facts, and will often respond to a message by researching a brand more thoroughly through customer service calls or by surfing the Web for example, making copy more important.

The right, or more liberal, side of the brain is responsible for all types of creativity. Right brainers typically process information in pictures and patterns. These more passive individuals tend to rely on the visual aspects of an ad more heavily than on the verbal, and before taking any type of action, need to see a message repeatedly, and preferably in multiple media vehicles.

The majority of us tend to use abilities from both sides of our brain. For example, we all know there are consequences to our actions, but the level to which we care about them will vary. And some of us trust our intuition more than others when making decisions.

The overall creative message needs to appeal to both kinds of individuals within the target audience. The left brainers within the target will be attracted to verbal facts, while the right brainers will be attracted to the visual representations of those facts. It's not that right brainers don't care about the written word or left brainers don't care about seeing the brand, it's just that right brainers and left brainers are attracted to different elements in the ad. Because of this, it is important the creative team develop a strong interrelated visual/verbal message. The more the creative team know about the brand category, relevant competitors, and the target, the better they can create a meaningful and informative message.

All advertising needs to inform. The goal is to find a creative way to inspire the target audience to act. All creative efforts must be developed around the intended target. The more that is known about them, the better the visual/verbal solution will address their needs and be more clearly tied to their overall lifestyle and interests. The target is why the advertised message is ultimately being developed. Success depends on understanding how they will react to and engage with the message. Understanding what the target thinks about the brand or brand category, how they see it fitting within their lifestyle, and how the client's brand can fulfill their immediate needs makes it easier to imagine the right message. Any visual/verbal message will fail when incorrectly targeted with a vague message. Success relies on delivering a customized, consumer-focused message.

Communication Objectives

Communication objectives define what advertising needs to accomplish. Very basically, objectives lay out what the target needs to know about the brand and how to purchase after exposure to advertising efforts.

Typically, no advertising campaign will have more than one to three attainable objectives. Objectives focus on communication-related goals, not sales-related goals. Communication objectives concentrate on giving the target valuable yet personalized lifestyle-enhancing information. The goal is for the visual/verbal message(s) to push the objectives in a way that informs and educates the target about the brand. Objectives are developed around how much the target knows about the brand. A look at the brand's life-cycle stage will help with deciding what needs to be said and shown, introduced, maintained, or beefed up, and what needs to be reimagined. Taking the brand's life-cycle stage into consideration will help ensure objectives can be accomplished, over the short or long term.

The Age of the Brand

There are three stages to a brand's life cycle: New, mainstream or mature, and reinvention.

When introducing a new product into the market, it will need a visual and verbal message that focuses on developing an image that matches the target audience's self-image and reflects their lifestyle. *New products* have no existing identity and no brand loyalty. Hard-won loyalty will need to be earned over time thanks to well-targeted messages. In order to stand out and away from competing brands, a new product must quickly focus attention on its individualized characteristics.

Mainstream or mature brands are ones that have been established over time. Communication efforts must work to remind and

reinforce quality and reliability, and not only maintain but continue building a relationship with the target.

Reinvention can occur when a brand has been improved, updated, or fighting back from a damaged reputation. Reinvention means owning past mistakes, or reimaging an outdated image that directly affects image and target perception. Any time a brand is in need of reinvention, no matter the reason, consumer loyalty will have to be rebuilt.

Target Analysis

This section, using either qualitative or quantitative research efforts, asks the target:

1. What do they currently think about the brand?
2. What would you like them to think about the brand?
3. Why should the target believe it? Analysis of the above responses determines the answers displayed here.

Like the objectives, assessing the target's brand knowledge helps determine what the visual and verbal message needs to do to attract their attention, educate them further, and encourage action.

Product Features and Benefits

This section looks at brand characteristics and assigns them a benefit based on the target's lifestyle or needs. It is common to try and push only a brand's features and ignore its benefits. A *feature* is a specific attribute unique to the brand, such as colors or sizes, or implied attributes such as the status or image of a brand—for example, Tesla—which can affect the consumer's self-image or lifestyle. A *benefit* lets the target clearly know what they will get out of purchasing the brand. Let's use over-the-counter cold medicine as an example; see Table 1.1.

Features are informative, but without a corresponding benefit to the target, are ineffective. Advertising efforts need to push what the feature can offer the target. Finding a benefit for each of the brand's features is not only attractive to the target but helps the creative team better focus the visual and verbal message.

For example, one feature for over-the-counter cold medicine, might be that it covers a wide range of symptoms and conditions. It's important that one or more feature and benefit combinations inform the creative team about all available options. Research might point out the target suffers from yearly allergies and is looking for a stronger more reliable over-the-counter option. Perhaps the target is tired of always having to use more than one product in pill form to alleviate all their symptoms. Based on this

Table 1.1 Feature and benefit example, using an over-the-counter cold medicine product.

Feature	The cold medicine covers multiple conditions: cold and flu, cough, stuffiness, sinus, and allergy.
Benefit	Whatever your symptoms, relief is available.
Feature	Comes in multiple formulations: liquid gels, effervescent tablets, hot drink mixes, and extended release tablets.
Benefit	No matter your dose preference, there is a viable option to ease your symptoms.

information, the visual/verbal message might push a *feature* that highlights the diverse options available and the resulting *benefit* is that relief is available for all symptoms. Another *feature* might push the different options beyond pills available. The resulting *benefit* is that no matter how you like to take your medicine, there is an option.

Positioning of the Product

Positioning looks at the brand that represents direct competition to the client's brand. The main competitor should be broken down into eight basic sections that include:

1. A short description of the competing brand.
2. A description of the brands similarities and differences as compared to the client's brand.
3. A short description of their current advertising, specifically what is currently being said and shown.
4. Their key consumer benefit.
5. A short description and overall appearance of their current logo, such as type, colors, shape.
6. A description of their current slogan or tagline if using one.
7. A description of any unique graphics or color combinations used and finally.
8. A description of what their packaging looks like.

Understanding what competitors are saying and showing helps the creative team from duplicating their advertising efforts and helps find an interesting way to ensure the brand stands out within the brand category.

Key Consumer Benefit

The *key consumer benefit (KCB)* is what will be featured both visually and verbally in all advertising efforts. Research has determined this feature and benefit combination, found in the "Features and Benefits" section discussed above, is important to the target.

This section will also determine whether the visual and verbal solution should employ a *unique selling proposition (USP)* or a *big*

idea. The big idea or USP is determined by dissecting the target audience and establishing which feature/benefit combination can achieve the stated objectives, differentiates itself from competitors, and talks to the target about something they are interested in or need. It will be the visual/verbal tie that unites all advertising and promotional efforts under a single idea.

To determine which one is employed, the account manager must know what makes the brand special or unique to the target and the brand category and what competitors are doing. The feature/benefit chosen must not only scream creative stardom but also address each of the target's concerns.

A USP can either have a feature/benefit combination that is unique to the brand, or one that will promote a commonplace feature/benefit combination as unique.

Whether to use a USP or a big idea depends on what the brand wants to promote as different from the competition, and how the target audience thinks the benefits will enhance their lives. This can be done with a creative idea that touches on a known target interest, fulfills a known need, or creates a status symbol. Brands with little or no differentiation from competing brands will need a big idea.

A big idea is all about unique and innovative solutions that set the brand off from competitors. The feature/benefit combination used may not be unique to your brand, but no competitor is pushing it as unique or important in their advertising efforts.

Finding creative solutions for a big idea can be more difficult than determining a USP. This is due to the fact that big ideas will typically have to create something inspirational and informative out of nothing, to capture the target's attention. Ideas that focus specifically on the target, and their needs and wants, can make even a brand in a generic product category seem exciting and relatable to the target. Brands that set out to look and sound like competing brands rather than unique within the category, will always appear second-best to consumers. A brand must have both an individualized personality and offer individualized benefits that the target can relate to and is interested in, and a creative message that offers the target a reason to interact with the brand.

Support Statement

The *support statement* features one additional feature/benefit combination that further explains or advances the key consumer benefit.

Creative Strategy

The *creative strategy* tells the creative team how they will talk to the target. The tactics employed need to accomplish the objectives, and determines the best way to feature the key consumer benefit and set it apart from competing brands.

The creative strategy is broken down into two parts: The approach and the appeal.

The *approach*, or how the brand will be positioned, can focus on whether advertising efforts will focus on either the product or the consumer, or use a combination of both.

A *product approach* focuses on one or more feature(s)/benefit(s) of the brand. This type of approach can focus all advertising and promotional efforts on one or more different approaches: Generic claim, product feature, USP, or positioning.

- Generic claim: Focus is on a specific product category rather than an individual brand.
- Product feature: Focus is on one specific "feature" of the brand, ideally one unique to the brand.
- Unique selling proposition (USP): Focus is on a single brand "benefit" the target is known to value.
- Positioning: Focus is on how the target compares the brand to competitors.

A *consumer approach* works to shape the target's attitude about the brand and demonstrate how the brand can solve a problem the target has. This type of approach can concentrate on any of three distinct options: Brand image, lifestyle, and attitude.

- Brand image: Develops an image and/or creates a personality for the brand.
- Lifestyle: Ties the brand directly to the target's lifestyle.
- Attitude: Ties brand attributes to feelings, attitudes, and overall benefits of use.

Strategies under each type of approach can be used individually or combined together.

The Appeal of the Message

The *appeal*, or feel, determines the best way to reach the target and whether the product or service will fulfill an emotional or lifestyle enhancement need, or a rational or life-sustaining need, such as food. As with choice of approach, it is not unusual to see many advertising efforts employing multiple types of appeals.

Emotional appeals will typically focus on product or consumer image and are most often seen with status-related products or those brands that have no differentiating features from competing brands. These types of ads are typically more creative and appeal to the target's need to be a part of the in-crowd, a trendsetter, or a need to stand out as unique.

Rational appeals are informational and typically use facts, charts, or expert opinions to back up claims. Rational ads are used to attract the target's attention and influence the perception of need for a brand and/or how it will affect their lifestyle.

To visually and verbally project the correct rational or emotional "feel," you must determine how you will strategically interpret that appeal for the target. There are seven basic appeals: Generic, preemptive claim, unique selling proposition (USP), brand image, positioning, resonance, and affective. Choice will depend on the approach chosen, the key consumer benefit, the competition, the objectives, and the target. Let's take a look at each one.

1. Generic appeal: This appeal type makes no effort at differentiation; any competitor in the brand category could make claims.
2. Preemptive appeal: Focus is on the use of a feature and benefit common to all brands in the category but advertises it first, forcing competitors into "me too" positions; this approach is used in categories with little differentiation, or in new product categories.
3. Unique selling proposition appeal: Focus is on creating a distinct differentiation between brand features that create a meaningful consumer benefit; it is appropriate in categories with relatively high levels of technological improvements.
4. Brand image: Focus is on claims of superiority or distinction based on extrinsic factors, such as psychological differences in the minds of consumers; this is used with homogeneous and low-technology goods and services with little physical differentiation.
5. Positioning appeal: Focuses on establishing a unique place in the consumer's mind relative to the competition, and is suited to new or small brands that want to challenge the market leaders.
6. Resonance appeal: Focus is on situations, lifestyles, and emotions that the target audience can identify with; this is used with highly competitive, non-differentiated product categories.
7. Affective appeal: Focuses on the use of an emotional, sometimes even ambiguous, message to break through indifference and change perceptions; this is used where competitors are making an honest appeal.

Many creative strategies are a *combination* of these basic strategic approaches and appeals, although any one of them can be used individually. Appeals are used to attract consumer attention and influence the perception of need for a product. The point to remember is that the creative team uses a combined approach and appeal to determine the concept, or the overall visual and verbal focus of the ad. The focus is most often placed on the consumer's need for, or use of, the product and/or how it will affect their lifestyle.

Tone

The *tone*, also referred to as tone of voice, determines the personality and the overall visual/verbal voice and/or style of the advertised message. Like the creative strategy appeal, this personality can be conceptually represented with either a rational or emotional message or with a combination of both. Consider some of the following techniques.

Rational tones are straightforward, focusing only on facts that can be proven and typically include one or more of the following types of messaging: Straight sell, technical, demonstration, comparison, testimonial, news event, authoritative voice, reminder, teaser, instructional, talking head, conversation or dialogue, lifestyle, reminder, or price.

Emotional tones focus on the target's needs and wants and might include one or more of the following types of messaging: Humor, fantasy, animation, slice-of-life (scenes or stories taken perhaps from current users), fear, sex, and brand scarcity.

Whichever tone or combination of tones are chosen, it should be the tie that binds the creative strategy approach and appeal together, pushes the key consumer benefit, addresses the objectives, talks to the target in a style they will respond to, and works to create, build, or maintain, the brand's image.

Slogan or Tagline

Often used interchangeably, both a slogan and a tagline are tied to the logo and can be placed either above it or below it. A *slogan* expresses a company or corporate philosophy, and a *tagline* highlights the campaign direction or ad philosophy.

Logo

The logo is the identifying symbol for the brand to be advertised.

Detail Copy Points

Here is where the creative team will find any details the target audience needs to help with purchase, such as social media used, any maps needed, address(es), phone number(s), Web address, the hours a brick-and-mortar store is open, credit cards accepted, any applicable 1–800 numbers, any relevant parking information, and so on. The media employed will determine what needs to be displayed.

Coupons or Other Promotional Information

If applicable, any information the creative team needs to promote a sale, contest, or sweepstakes, will be outlined here.

In summary, the job of this very important document is the skeletal framework the creative team will use to construct the visual and verbal message. Now that the business knowledge that drives the visual and verbal solution is complete, let's take a quick look at just who the creative team is.

Creatives Create the Words and Images Seen in Advertising

A *creative* is a person who is involved in the writing and designing of all types of advertising. Creative can also refer to the advertising material that is produced by creatives. The *creative team* is typically made up of a creative director and one or more art directors (the visual idea people) and copywriters (the verbal idea people) and a production artist (the construction people). Job titles are not static, and will depend on the agency's culture, where you are in the country, and even on the size of the agency. Our discussion here will talk only about the most commonly used titles.

Creative directors are usually the team leaders and determine what ideas should be trashed and developed further. They are the final voice as to which ideas will ultimately advance to the client. The *art director* is responsible for strategically executing the idea in varied visual forms. Art directors are often mistaken for designers; however, a designer's job is to focus solely on the execution of a design idea. *Copywriters* write the copy that will be read or heard. They work closely with art directors to ensure strategically that what is said relates to what is being shown.

Together, these creative, imaginative individuals will dissect the business-oriented brief into visual and verbal ideas that solve the client's advertising problem. Beyond talent, the creative team must be open-minded enough to:

* Give new meaning to common brand attributes. If a brand comes in multiple sizes, what does that represent: A trend or fad, a mountain, an ant, or an exciting set of options? What can it be made to mean to the target?
* Look for multiple solutions. Do not linger on one idea too long. Overworked ideas can become stale. The more diversified the options whether good or bad, the more solid the final idea. When inspiration is lacking, consider staring off into space, playing charades, or borrowing mannerisms, attitudes, and

even speech patterns from an office mate or favorite uncle to help jumpstart your imagination.

- Understand the role of visual/verbal messaging. For an idea to be truly great, it must sell.
- Understand the history of media. Step out of your comfort zone, watch diverse types of television and digitally produced shows; go to movies; pick up a book or magazine and dissect current political issues; know what is currently in or out of fashion and understand why what is in and out of fashion; listen to the radio, read a newspaper and interpret historical versus current events. The more you know will not only help to position or reposition the brand, it will also assist with opening up multiple options and opportunities for creating new uses or a reinvented image.
- People watch. There is no end to the inspiration to be found in basic human nature.
- Know the brand and the competition. In order to understand the importance and uniqueness of your brand, use it. If you haven't tried the competitor's brand, do so and compare features; personal knowledge will always be more inspirational. Knowledge is the first step in separating your brand from competing brands and attracting target interest.
- Remember, advertising is a business. Creative is based on a business plan and must be adhered to with few exceptions. Creatives only get to do what they want in the movies.
- Excellence defines the job. If you can't tell a stimulating, fact-based story or have strong spelling and grammatical skills, copywriting may not be the career for you. If you get easily frustrated with the burden of brainstorming and find it a challenge to come up with more than two or three ideas, art direction may not be the best career path for you. Clients expect and pay for the creative expertise advertising is famous for. Because of this, expectations are high, the hours long, the competition fierce, and the stress high. It's what makes being a creative aspirational and sought after.
- Change is advertising design's first name. Ideas are fleeting. All ideas are changeable at any time along the design and production highway. Changes are an inevitable part of any creative position. Because of this, it can be frustrating when your best idea is dismantled and reimagined. Get over it. There are a multitude of ideas ahead waiting to soar.

Once the creative team finalizes the creative direction and the client has signed off on it, it is handed off to the production department. A *production artist* works closely with the creative or art director assigned to the project, on finalizing the design or production stages. These meticulous "finishers" review final copy and layout and are responsible for editing and putting the final design touches on print, digital, or video. They are the watchdog for brand standards and overall production quality.

Seeking Help or Expertise In-House or through Independent Contractors

Are advertising agencies better than in-house agencies? Well, that depends on whom you ask. Each has a very diverse personality and culture. Creative is about the only trait both share. Where advertising agencies can be located locally, nationally, or regionally, they typically are fast moving, often require long hours, and offer a diverse array of products and services to work on. In-house agencies, on the other hand, are connected to the brand's corporate headquarters, are focused on fewer brands, and have better control over deadlines and thus hours worked. Which you choose depends on whether brand diversity and working at a lightning pace is preferred over the comfort of working with a known brand in a somewhat more controlled environment.

Traditionally, in-house design was most often used for smaller, one-off projects that need to be done immediately or that don't happen on a regular basis. But this is changing. More and more brands are disengaging from using traditional agency creative departments to creating or enlarging their in-house creative departments. Internal or in-house agencies have been around a long time, but only recently have we seen greater emphasis placed on these once-small departments grow in importance as brands question the validity of agency-made decisions. Cost, the need for greater control of the creative product, and the demand for increased transparency are a few more reasons for the move.

Additionally, in-house agencies also offer 1) a strong brand and corporate connection to the brand, 2) an in-depth knowledge of the brand, 3) time dedicated to working only on internal brands, 4) better budget control, and 5) the control of deadlines.

The pros to working with an outside advertising agency include 1) the ability to offer a new and unique view of the brand, 2) experienced multi-media creative and production teams, 3) broader skill sets, and 4) enough employees to finish jobs on a set timeline.

Today, many brands are using a blended approach, where agencies often collaborate with in-house teams. This blending of strengths helps to 1) offset cultural and corporate biases, 2) eliminate or at least minimize any weaknesses a single perspective may have, 3) encourage the sharing of experience and knowledge between teams, 4) better share and negotiate cost, and 4) maximize timelines or deadlines, always a problem no matter who sits at the design table.

When additional help is needed, it is not unusual for both marketers and advertising agencies to hire independent contractors known as *freelancers* when (1) the marketer or agency has a limited staff, (2) area specific experts are needed, or (3) the amount of work cannot be handled by the current number of staff members.

Hired on a project-by-project basis, freelancers typically specialize in creative, media, or research. When freelance creatives working in copywriting, art direction, illustration, photography, and/or graphic and digital design set up a shared business, it's known as a *creative boutique*.

Advertising and the Need-To-Know Terminology

Before you can work in any area of advertising, you need to first become familiar with the terminology that defines it. Typically, the jargon and acronyms used seem to be in a constant state of change, as new technology and media options emerge and old technology and media options evolve. But there are some terms that have cemented their place in the profession. Let's take a quick look at a couple.

All terms begin with a brand in mind. The American Marketing Association defines a *brand* as a "name, term, sign, symbol, or design, or a combination of them intended to identify the goods and services of one seller or group of sellers and to differentiate them from those of other sellers." Quite simply, a brand is the product or service. The opinion, favorable or otherwise, the target has about a brand is known as *brand image*. Image is created through advertising efforts and maintained by the target based on product quality and performance. *Brand loyalty* refers to the relationship between the brand and the target. If the brand delivers the same user experience with each purchase, the target no longer considers another brand. This reliability and reputation leads to *brand equity* or a company's or a brand's reputation within the brand category.

The *promotional mix* refers to the communication options that will be used to reach the target with the advertised message. They include public relations, advertising, out-of-home, direct marketing, sales promotion, digital, guerrilla marketing, and alternative media. Determining which options to employ will depend on the target's media preferences and overall knowledge about the brand.

The *media mix* dissects the promotional mix down into individual media vehicles, such as magazine, direct mail, mobile, Facebook, the Web, and so on. The choice of mix employed is based primarily on the budget, the objectives for the ad or campaign, and on the target's knowledge and loyalty to the brand.

Positioning refers to how the consumer thinks about a product or service and/or rates it against the competition. Positioning requires highlighting the target-relevant benefits of the brand's features. Benefits must be tied to uses that will enhance the target's lifestyle or image. The position of a brand is sometimes confused with brand image; a brand's positioning in the mind of the consumer is created via advertising and promotion, whereas brand image is created based on experience.

A strong position is a direct result of a strong brand. This position is built up over a period of time and based on reliability of performance. Branding gives a product or service an air of exclusivity and a unique identity, differentiating it from its competitors within the product category. Successful, memorable advertising begins with an established position.

A brand is *repositioned* when there is a need to alter the way the target views the brand. This could result from a damaged reputation, declining sales, the need to update or alter the target to be reached, if the brand has changed in a significant way, if new competitors are emerging, or if the brand is looking outdated. Changing consumer perception can be more difficult than working with an existing position or creating one from scratch. Repositioning should help the target reimaging the brand's role in their life by giving it a new meaning or by introducing a new or previously un-thought of use.

Now that the business of advertising is out of the way, let's tackle creative.

Bibliography

Blakeman, Robyn. 2018. *Integrated Marketing Communication: Creative Strategy from Idea to Implementation*. 3rd ed. Lanham, MD: Rowman and Littlefield Publishing, p. 58.

Margulies, Howard. 2009. "What are you packing into your (creative) briefs?" AdAge.com (May 18). Retrieved from: www.adage.com/article/small-agency-diary/creative-briefs-simple/136711/.

CHAPTER 2
Conceptual Development

Chapter 2 Objectives

1. The reader will understand the role of conceptual development.
2. The reader will understand the diverse ways to find a visual/verbal solution.
3. The reader will learn how the age of a brand affects its visual/verbal voice.

Conceptual Development: The Story of the Idea

Conceptual development, also known as *brainstorming*, is all about uncovering the unimagined. Advertising executive Alex Osborn coined the phrase in his book *Your Creative Power* in the late 1940s, describing it as a way to "[use] the brain to storm a creative problem, and do so in commando fashion with each stormer attacking the same objective." He believed that "it is easier to tone down a wild idea than to think up a new one." More simply, brainstorming is your imagination at work on a creative solution to a marketing problem. Brainstorming sessions are used to generate as many interesting, imaginative, and innovative ideas as possible, all within a limited time period, that will ultimately solve the client's advertising problem. At this point, no idea is immediately rejected, no direction is absolute except the promotion of the key consumer benefit, to avoid limiting the number of ideas the session may generate. Dozens, maybe hundreds, of good and bad ideas will be discussed and dissected; most will eventually be tossed, but some will hang around longer than others and be reimagined further.

Leading the creative charge in brainstorming sessions, as defined in Chapter 1, is the creative team that includes at least one art or creative director and a copywriter. Attendees may also include an account planner and/or an account manager and even occasionally the client. More rarely, the creative team may work independently, quietly gathering ideas to be presented and/or reworked at a later time.

The creative team is responsible for strategically developing the idea, writing copy, and designing ads that seamlessly integrates the brand into the consumers' life. They must ensure that all creative efforts focus on the key consumer benefit, speak directly to the target audience both visually and verbally in a relatable way, about problems or situations they can relate to; and that the visual and verbal idea can successfully be employed across multiple media vehicles without losing its identity or corrupting the visual or verbal message. When copywriters and art directors work together, visual and verbal communication are joined into a powerful problem-solving combination.

Being a member of the creative team requires more than a creative imagination. It also requires enough business savvy to solve a business problem in a creative and memorable way. The development and eventual execution of an idea is the last phase in a business-driven process that often started months earlier with the gathering and analyzing of research, and the development of a marketing plan, creative brief and media plan. It's the creative team's job to bend and twist the creative brief into a creative idea that attracts attention, is memorable, and that ultimately sells.

Each brainstorming session will begin with a discussion of the creative brief. Once the creative team understands what needs to be accomplished, the next step is to isolate the brand's *inherent drama*. What brand characteristics will talk directly to the target? How can those characteristics be made distinct or dramatically shown and talked about? Brainstorming targets that drama and ties it to the target's lifestyle in diverse and unique ways the target can relate to.

There are several ways the team might explore and then define that drama for the target. The first step might simply outline what the brand does, what it looks like, or how it is used. Once exhausted, if still looking for inspiration, the next step might focus on the unexpected or unusual, for example, how many of

DOI: 10.4324/9781003255123-3

you would have used a gecko to sell insurance (Geico), or a pink bunny to sell batteries (Energizer)? It's too easy to use a talking head that redundantly focuses on problems the target already knows they have, it's another for the problem to creatively talk solutions. Everyone is frustrated with dead batteries, but giving longevity a symbol and a noise is memorable. It is not unusual for young designers to often take the easiest way out. The result is ideas that are at best redundant and uninspiring and, most often, immediately forgettable. The more memorable and relatable the message, the more targeted and successful a truly great idea can be.

It's important to understand, whether conceptualizing, writing, or designing, that consumers will not work to understand abstract ideas; they want messages that can be easily understood since they will probably be multitasking while listening, scrolling, or reading the advertising message. The goal is easy and relatively repetitive, find ways the brand can solve their individualized problem or satisfy a specific need. To do this successfully, the visual/verbal message must adhere to information found in the creative brief. So before any brainstorming session begins, before any one creative direction is pursued, the creative team needs to be thoroughly immersed in the parameters set down in the brief.

The Creative Brief Is the Foundation Behind Imaginative Ideas

Fortunately, there is no business document that determines creative direction. The documents discussed thus far—the marketing plan and creative brief—look only at the research done on the brand, target, competitors, overall marketplace, and communication needs.

Creative, its interpretation, and its ultimate ability to inspire the target to the desired action are critical to the success of any ad or campaign. Modern advertising messages must stop attention, talk to the target in a language they can understand, about situations they care about. If creative efforts that are on-target and on-strategy fail, it is because the marketing plan lacked clarity, and the creative brief lacked informative and interpretive substance.

The brief's job is to 1) outline both brand and consumer needs and wants, 2) clearly define what communication efforts need to accomplish, and 3) be the foundation for the visual/verbal direction. The brief supplies the creative team with an informational starting point. It summarizes the target audience profile by outlining how the target feels about the brand, or even the brand category, and how the target might incorporate

the brand into their lifestyle. The objectives will pinpoint what creative efforts need to accomplish, and positioning will help the team avoid brand parity. The key consumer benefit will drive the tone and direction of the ad or campaign, and must strongly influence all creative executions, both visually and verbally. And the strategy and tone will assist with determining message focus, overall tone of voice, and how all visual and verbal components will talk to the target and distinguish the brand from the competition.

Once the creative team understands what needs to be accomplished, the next step is determining a visual/verbal solution that will bring the brief to life. Coming up with that all-encompassing idea is never easy, no matter how well the communication parameters are laid out in the brief. It involves using both sides of the brain. As the left side sorts out the business direction, the right side begins the ideation process.

The Black Hole of Art versus Business

The creative team will need to use both sides of their brains to solve the business/creative problem set before them. Believe it or not, the tighter the brief, the more emancipating and energizing brainstorming sessions can become. Less defined briefs are more open to interpretation and can impede the team's progress as they get lost in a deluge of ideas with no strong ties to the brand or target. When given a metaphorical straight line to problem solving, ideas tend to be explored to the point that some are exhausted, which produces not only more creative ideas, but also more strategic ones.

Every word should help the creative team to see the brand in a new way. The more informative the brief, the more distinctive the final visual/verbal identity will be, helping the brand to step out and away from its competitors. Unique ideas are the first steps to developing a memorable brand image that defines the brand's position of quality in the mind of the target.

To do this, every visual/verbal characteristic of a campaign must spotlight the brand and inspire the target. Creatively, brand attributes must be not only tied to solutions but must also represent the target's lifestyle and self-image, as well as solve a relevant problem or fulfill a need.

Most brand categories are crowded, and a lot of advertising is repetitive. A good creative recognizes this and looks for an innovative and memorable way to make their brand stand out amongst the clutter. In order to position a brand as a solution to the target's problem, it cannot mimic solutions communicated by other competitors within the brand category. The first time the target experiences a visual/verbal message, it's seen as new, unusual, educational, or inspirational, and becomes part of the brand's image. When copied by a competitor, it's relegated to second place in the target's mind, and seen as "me too" advertising or visual/verbal advertising noise. Teams that successfully invent visually memorable advertising like the Chic-fil-A cows, or verbal phrases that can become a part of our day-to-day lexicon like McDonald's "I'm Lovin' it," Guinness' "Good things come to those who wait" phrase, and the Las Vegas tourism tag "What Happens Here, Stays Here" are not only memorable, but advertising gold.

Memorable solutions to the client's advertising problem begin with ideas that creatively and imaginatively solve a problem for the target. To do both successfully, it takes a multitude of creative scheming to successfully solve both sets of problems.

Finding the Elusive Visual/Verbal Solution

All great ads begin and end with a strategically sound idea. Finding this is not only fun but also almost always a bit frustrating. Good ideas can come from imaginative musings, life experiences, personal interests, and some good old-fashioned luck. A good idea will never come from dull, inexperienced imaginations. Anyone interested in working as a copywriter or art director needs to have an open mind, and be experimental and culturally diverse, in order to define and build ideas.

In my book *Strategic Uses of Alternative Media*, I talk about how

> all designers need a medley of experiences and interests to draw from. They should be open-minded, adventurous, and receptive to others' opinions and ideas. A solid creative direction will stem from interesting observations of human nature, a well-honed sense of curiosity, and no small amount of witty cynicism. Ideally, the creative team will be composed of students of human behavior and people who know a little about psychology, economics, art, and music and history. They cannot always expect to find inspiration in everyday situations. Designers typically venture beyond the bounds of everyday monotony in their search for inspiration. They must be able to employ historical references and use movies, television, and radio references from today and yesterday to represent a brand's image and set the visual/verbal tone for creative direction. (p. 13)

Inquisitive minds see and hear everything and know a little about a lot. Know the world your brand and target lives in. Experience art old and new, note how it reflects history, cultures, and attitudes. Watch television, immerse yourself in both old and current television and radio programming. Go see a movie genre outside your comfort zone or interests. People-watch no matter where you are; location will determine dress, attitude, demeanors. Silence your prejudices, just experience it. If you want your message to engage the target, you have to experience it through their eyes and circumstances.

As well as problem/solution role-playing, inspirational daydreaming and acting out are something creatives excel at. Unacceptable in most job positions, both these activities are critical to the conceptualization process. Don't be afraid to call on your inner child where ideas were abundant and uninhibited and every experience had a story to tell. These are the imaginings that as a creative adult can inspire award-winning campaigns.

Unfortunately, these inspirational traits are discouraged as children when our imaginations are at their super-charged creative height. Jumpstart your imagination and tap into your musings because, to succeed, creativity requires a peculiar and avant-garde thinker. Instead of rejecting those foolish thoughts, tap into them and explore.

Lastly, when possible, personally experience the brand. Use it in a different way than is intended, use it in the way intended, smash it, reimage its look or shape, compare it to the competition, show before and after comparisons, give it a unique voice based on your thoughts and experiments. When you finally see the idea-vs.-solution light go on, you will be ready to pounce on it.

Beginning the Conceptual Process: Visual and Verbal Solutions

The creative team initiates the creative process with a lot of daydreaming, talking, and doodling. You need to erase any preconceived notions about the brand before you can see new solutions and directions. Somewhere between here (imagination) and there (blank page), a good idea is waiting to jump to life. Next, the creative team needs to anticipate what questions the target may have about the brand, and write and design out the answers. Start simply with the basics of who, what, when, where, why, and how. Each question asked and answered should result in one or more visual and verbal solutions.

Constructive discussions are the first step towards developing a memorable idea, concept, or theme. In my book *Strategic Uses of Alternative Media*, I talk about

> *the goal of a conceptual development session is to illuminate the obvious and search for a new and innovative direction. At the root of innovation lie clichés and stale ideas. Innovation grows from the unfettered discussion of hundreds of ideas—many of which could be called weird, slightly off-strategy, or just down right ridiculous. But, successful design is not really about great ideas; it's about selling or promoting a product or service in a memorable way that sets the brand apart from competitors' messages. (p. 74)*

Good ideas are elusive but plentiful, great ideas are much less abundant, and successful and memorable ideas could be put in the once-in-a-blue-moon category. A successful idea is certainly not defined as something you've seen before, or that can be tweaked to fit an existing mold. This kind of advertising usually carries what I call a "been there, seen that" unimaginative label. That means the idea often mimics advertising used by another product in the brand category. Basically, if you've seen it done before, it's no longer creative and screams "second best." When you've seen something once, it captures your attention; once it becomes mainstream, it's boring. Once your target is bored, they're no longer paying attention to anything the brand has to say.

Because of this oft-repeated parity, there is a lot of repetitive advertising in all brand categories out there that have lost their creative way. Missing is a strong brand identity, and a brand-loyal target audience. Finding an innovative creative direction takes a lot of work, and once one is unearthed that will appeal to the target and solve their problem, the team will continue to flesh it out and perfect it. You will know you have a solution, because the idea checks off all the right boxes laid out in the brief. In other words, the creative direction screams out the key consumer benefit, speaks to the target audience about a problem they have, and offers a viable solution. Advertising that is off-target or off-strategy can be very entertaining, even cutting-edge, but if it doesn't increase sales, and encourage brand loyalty, it's useless.

Great Visual and Verbal Identities Are Hard to Come By

It is important to understand that developing a unique visual and verbal identity for a brand doesn't happen on cue. It takes long hours and a lot of reworking before an idea takes on the visual/verbal voice needed to solve the client's advertising problem. Once solved, only then can it be presented to the account management

team and eventually externally to the client. No matter how big or small the job, the amount of time needed to find a visual/verbal solution is always limited. A creative spark may have as little as a few hours to ignite, or as much as three to four weeks to smolder a bit. The job requires the art director and copywriter to be creative on demand and often for long hours at a time. Stress is often used for inspiration, not as an excuse or deterrent.

Nothing the creative team does is stagnant, repetitive or easily discovered in research documents. It is ever-changing and new everyday, even every hour. To nurture these creative minds, they are pretty much allowed to use whatever methods it takes to inspire them creatively.

But even the right environment doesn't ensure immediate creative success. Every great solution begins as a series of bad ideas that will be reimagined, restated, and reinvented in multiple ways before one great idea will rise to the top and successfully accomplish the initiatives laid out in the creative brief. It is rare for any viable solution to be your first idea, or found in a single idea; most are combinations of several ideas. All great ads/campaigns begin as a (possibly) bad idea that will be reworded and reshaped dozens of times before a final great idea emerges. That doesn't mean a few mediocre ideas might live longer than they should, before being unceremoniously trashed. It can be painful sometimes to see your great idea die a slow death as other, better, ideas emerge. Because of this, it can sometimes be difficult to see new directions while holding on to a stale idea. But if you keep pushing, you will find more expressive, more informative, more on-target, on-strategy alternatives. Don't be possessive or lazy; keep pushing for a new and more unique perspective. If the arrival of a final resolution was painless, where is the continual challenge needed to drive motivation?

The main goal of all brainstorming sessions is to get the off-target, off-strategy ideas out of your head quickly so you can move on to more interesting, diverse, and creative solutions. It is these innovative ideas that will ultimately set your brand apart from competing brands. Each solution can be an important building-block to the development of the brand's image, and constructing a unique and ultimately, a solid position in the consumer's mind.

Fighting for the Idea: Everyone Will Hate an Idea at Some Point within the Creative Process

It's true, at some point, someone will hate some part of the final creative solution. Going back to the idea drawing board can be frustrating, time consuming, and expensive, and should be avoided when possible. To circumvent this, creatives must not only be staunch advocates for their ideas but also be willing to repeatedly battle for the integrity of their words and images. However, you must also know when to let go of those ideas that are flat-out bad.

If you don't know when to let go, there is always the client, account manager, or even another creative team member happy to offer constructive, opinionated, and often downright dismissive criticism. Change is a major part of the design process. Even after the final creative direction is found, it will be repeatedly tweaked in small but discernible ways before being presented to the client and ultimately produced or uploaded. The final outcome must promote the right message, to the right target, in the right media. Stressing over the minutiae is a lesser-known part of the creative process, but a big part of the creative team's unwritten job responsibilities.

As far as the creative team is concerned, there will never be enough time, money, or blind acceptance of the creative solution to go around. To the creative team, a final idea will always be elusive. No matter how successful the idea, the team's inner creative voice will continue to dissect it, wondering if the idea would have been better, stronger and more memorable, if the headline had been phrased differently, a visual made larger, or a different color combination used. See Figure 2.1.

Computers versus the Brainstorming Process on Paper

Brainstorming is not a technology function; it is still traditionally done the old-fashioned way, on paper. In a Spring 2017 *Journal of Advertising Education* article entitled "Technology in the Idea Generation Process: Voices from the Agency," by Robyn Blakeman and Maureen Taylor, an art director from Atlanta described the ideation process this way:

I always like to have a pen and paper during the beginning phases of a brief—there's something about being able to scratch stuff down that just feels right. When you write something physically it has a way of sticking in your mind. Your mood comes across. Your photographic memory responds to the quality of the line, doodles and thumbnails are paired with your thinking. And, it will better jog your memory when you go back to it. Plus, it's as portable as can be and doesn't require a battery. Pencil and paper is still the best way to conceptualize ideas. I see young creatives carrying around laptops like it's a security blanket. Put it down and you'll be able to stretch out your ideas. (p. 8)

Basically, computers and brainstorming are two incompatible words that should never be used in the same sentence together. Idea generation is spontaneous and original; it is not about moving the same, no longer original, ideas around the screen,

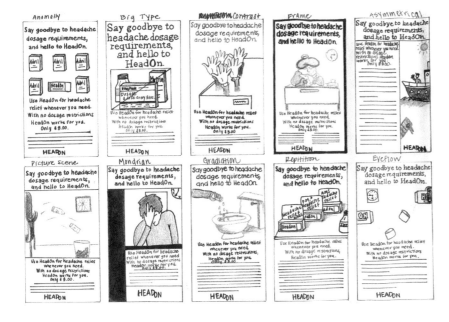

Figure 2.1 Example of concepting, using different layout styles. Images courtesy of Heather Burke, University of Tennessee.

or repeatedly using the same stock photos or illustrations as placeholders. The computer is a design tool; it is not a not an ideation tool. In the article cited above, an art director from New York City states that "Ideas aren't in the computer. If you can't put your idea on paper, you can't make it in the computer. Idea is everything. Paper first. Be loose. Be fast. Make more work, and fail fast. It's the only way to get to great work" (p. 9). Another art director from Chicago adds, "I begin the process with pen and paper. This allows me to step away from the computer and just focus on potential ideas for a project. This is important, since not every idea has legs (meaning that it can't be used for multiple mediums, and can't be expanded to larger campaigns, etc.). This ensures that I am spending the most amount of time working on an idea that can work well, instead of one that won't" (p. 9).

The point here is, you don't want to lose a single idea if you can avoid it, so doodle, write, or even record it, but just get it down. Consider keeping a notepad near you at all times: "You never know when inspiration will strike," says the Chicago art director. "I can

pretty much guarantee that brilliance won't wait for you to get home and boot up the computer. When ideas come, they explode in your head" (p. 9).

It is important to understand that the computer reproduces ideas; it does not create them. The computer cannot dream or imagine; it reproduces, period. Once the idea is solidified, then you can move it to the computer for finishing touches.

In design, creativity, interpretive insight, and engagement are what separate us from machines. Our ability to use our senses while daydreaming gives us the power to create or even exploit reality. So imagine it, see it come alive in varied forms on paper, and reproduce it on the computer. See Figure 2.2.

Great Ways to Jump-Start the Ideation Process

If you asked a hundred creative teams how they came up with their great ideas or overcame a creative blockade, you would get as many different answers. Each team's approach will be uniquely theirs. Let's take a look at some possible brainstorming techniques that creative teams might use to test out varied ideas during the conceptual development stage.

Words and Graphics as Brainstorming Devices

Talking It Out
Although the most simple, this is how most brainstorming sessions begin. This initial exploration might begin with a copywriter throwing out a headline that creatively pushes the key consumer benefit while the art director, with drawing pad and marker in hand (no computer), quickly roughs out one or more visuals that support the headline. It is not unusual for a creative team to easily come up with dozens and dozens of ideas per session. Not surprisingly, very few of these ideas will be usable. Some ideas are just bad, some too complicated, others just plain ridiculous, but each one builds toward another more unique direction, some may even be combined together. Once the supply of ideas seems exhausted, the team can employ more advanced forms of brainstorming techniques.

Word Lists
As previously discussed, to find that perfect idea in a dry business document like a creative brief, you often have to look at how a brand and its benefits are used, or how the brand is described for inspiration. Isolating visually descriptive words is one of the

Figure 2.2 Example of concepting graphic options. Images courtesy of Allison Schepman, University of Tennessee.

easiest ways to jump-start the ideation process. It is also the first step in interpreting how the target will react to what is said and shown, and how the idea will stand up when placed in different types of media. A typical word-association list should be anywhere from 15 to 25 words long, to creatively generate as many options as possible.

Ideas tend to start out as fragments, good words, possible images, etc., with few having any tangible direction. By developing a word list, you can get both your left and right brain working to solve the current problem. A typical list is comprised of three separate columns or parts. The first column lists as many words as you can think of to describe what the product looks like, how it is used, tastes, feels, and so on. This is not a column for creative thoughts. This column contains facts, not imaginative interpretation. Let's take a look at what an abbreviated list for cotton might look like in Table 2.1.

The second column requires the use of a thesaurus or synonyms book. Choose descriptive or more visual words to represent the blander, less inspiring brand facts used in Column 1. Across from each fact, list one or more colorful or descriptive words (see Table 2.2). This column should inspire new directions, and is where old, tired ideas go to die.

Table 2.3 shows the third column that requires you to write one or two sentences about how these words could be visually and verbally used in an ad. Now is the time to ask yourself questions. Always start with the five Ws: Who, What, When, Where, Why—and How. Create a solution for use visually and/or verbally. This column should create something the target can experience and/or relate to.

Set up the word list so the words are aligned across the page from left to right as seen in Table 2.4; one or more ideas can be expressed in any column for any word.

Remember, the best ads need to contain visual/verbal elements that resonate to both left- and right-brain consumers.

The final step: Toss out the ridiculous ideas (and there will be many), and further develop the ones that have promise.

Table 2.1 Shows the words in Column 1, that might be used to describe cotton.

Fact Column 1:	
	White
	Soft
	Fluffy
	Absorbent

Table 2.2 Shows a words list's Column 2, depicting multiple more creative options to describe cotton.

Descriptive Column 2:	
	Alabaster
	Ivory
	Pasty
	Comfortable
	Silky
	Pliable
	Downy
	Creamy
	Dry
	Penetrate
	Porous
	Thirsty

Table 2.3 Shows Column 3's multiple visual and verbal solutions taken individually from the words in Column 2.

Visual/Verbal Column 3:	
	White is not the absence of color, it's elegance.
	Show a variety of white items that feel unique and upscale.
	There is nothing more luxurious and inspiring than comfort.
	Show diverse types of soft materials.
	The taste of creamy milk chocolate.
	Show soft and creamy traits associated with the brand.
	How much can one piddle pad hold? It better be a lot.
	Show a St. Bernard puppy not wanting to go outside in the rain.

Using a visual/verbal word-association technique to solve a creative problem helps to simplify complex ideas. It can also help creative teams see how copy and images might work together, and how the visual/verbal solution might adapt to multiple media vehicles.

Table 2.4 Shows all three columns of a words list and how ideas can be expanded from diverse descriptive words.

White	Alabaster	White is not the absence of color, it's elegance.
	Ivory	
	Pasty	Show a variety of white items that feel unique and upscale.
Soft	Comfortable	There is nothing more luxurious and inspiring than comfort.
	Pliable	
	Silky	Show diverse types of soft materials.
Fluffy	Downy	The taste of creamy milk chocolate.
	Creamy	Show soft and creamy traits associated with the brand.
Absorbent	Dry	How much can one piddle pad hold? It better be a lot.
	Penetrate	
	Porous	Show a St. Bernard puppy not wanting to go outside in the rain.

Laddering

Another good idea-generating technique using words is "laddering." This exercise involves early preparation for the session by all team members. To begin, a moderator, or each team member transfers all ideas, good and bad, to Post-it notes, that are pasted to a flip chart or random piece of paper that can be taped or pinned up to expose every idea. Like brainstorming exercises, the laddering exercise involves building off each successive post to stimulate as many diverse ideas as fast as possible. Once idea saturation is met, each posted idea is critiqued. Ideas that are off-target or off-strategy are trashed, similar ideas are combined, and so on, creating multiple extended ladders of contrasting solutions to the advertising problem. Each ladder will go through a second round of ideation building and possibly elimination until three to five solid ideas are left standing.

180-Degree Brainstorming

In their book *Pick Me: Breaking into Advertising and Staying There*, Nancy Vonk and Janet Kestin offer another good brainstorming technique they call "180-degree thinking." This reverse creative exercise is a great one to use at the end of a long day when a breakthrough idea has yet to emerge. It requires the team to think of the worst possible way to sell the product ("These white strips are guaranteed to turn your teeth a grunge brown," "This smart car can't help a stupid driver"). This type of brainstorming technique forces the team to interpret the brand in new and atypical ways, ensuring the elimination of been-there-done-that ideas.

Exaggerations, Interruptions, and Rejections

In their book *Bang! Getting Your Message Heard in a Noisy World*, Linda Kaplan Thaler and Robin Koval suggest that the use of exaggeration, interruption, and building on creative mistakes and disasters can help ignite good ideas. Exaggeration is a great way to compare your brand to the competition. Interruption allows people who are not working on the creative problem, such as the account management team, to interrupt a meeting, often bringing in fresh thinking. Fresh ideas often come from fresh perspectives. Rejection is the starting place for newer, better ideas. Typically, there will be more rejected ideas than "ah ha" moments in any brainstorming session. Think of them as a rejected line of thinking, not a closed door. All bad ideas provide the foundation for the first tentative steps toward the final visual and verbal solution.

Another technique Kaplan Thaler and Koval integrate into sessions includes improvisation. This technique temporarily ignores the problem set before the team and allows them to interpret the solution in less acceptable ways, similar to the 180-degree technique. Once an idea is thrown out, another team member builds upon it by tossing out any idea that comes to mind to move the story forward. By temporarily forgetting the problem to be solved, you can open up a new line of creative thought, hopefully jump-starting the session once it begins again.

On the Flipside

Similar to the improvisation technique above, flipping your business line of thought to a more ridiculous line can ease some of the tension and hopefully get the session moving again. If you find you're just rehashing old and bad ideas from new, but still bad perspectives, don't trash them; run with them instead. What can you come up with to make a bad idea even worse? Sometimes having a little fun can be resuscitative for the entire team. For example, instead of asking the team to come up with an imaginative way to sell cat litter, consider instead what harm could a little poop around the house or apartment do? After having a little fun exhausting all the unacceptable possibilities, the team can flip back to the more "sellable" solutions.

Mindmapping or Cluster Writing

This technique uses a wheel to display ideas around a central hub that defines the key consumer benefit in one to two words. Varied idea themes are built out from the word(s). Each idea, or spoke of the wheel should take the team in a new direction. Like the laddering technique, each spoke can be continually built upon until a final direction is found.

Starbursting

Asking the right questions and delivering the best answers is at the core of starbursting. Like cluster writing, starbursting uses a graphic to organize both the session and the ideas. The session begins by drawing out a six-pointed star on a flip chart or other large piece of paper with the key consumer benefit strategically placed in the middle. On each point of the star write "who," "what," "when," "where," "why," and "how." Questions are posted next to the corresponding label. Hold off answering any of the questions until Round 2, when you repeat the exercise.

Charades

Getting interactive with an idea can help wake up a less than stellar creative session. Once a few or even a hundred ideas have been discussed, take three to five of the best ideas and let the team members act them out. This is a great time to bring in the account management team, or creative teams on other brands, to see if they can guess the idea direction. If they can, the idea is clear and direct. If they can't, the direction needs more work. It is helpful if a moderator writes down the responses to the actors' interpretive actions.

No matter what technique or combination of techniques is used, each will help the creative team to keep pursuing and then reimagining varied ideas. The more often the team goes through the ideation stage, the closer they will get to a viable visual/verbal solution that is both on-target and on-strategy, and that will successfully stand out and away for competitive brands.

Reasons Behind Mediocre Creative

There are many reasons behind mediocrity, but the biggest enemy to creativity is laziness. You did not fully research both your client's brand and the competition, and did not adhere to the creative brief, and did not exhaust the conceptual phase, so your ideas are off-target or off-strategy.

Young creatives will often believe their first ideas are the best overall solutions to their advertising problem. Unfortunately, when you do not repetitively exercise and explore creative options, it's only the best idea because it is the only idea. Many individually weak ideas when combined together, with a little tweaking, can emerge as a strong direction. Some of the best solutions will

materialize thanks to bizarre imaginations, warped senses of humor, and/or keen observations.

In the end, the key to a good ideation session is to never be afraid to voice your opinion, or share an idea that is less than stellar. Big misses are humbling, but are necessary to keep the session moving: One really stupid idea shared can and will spark another idea in someone else. It is important to never criticize or outright reject an idea before it is thoroughly dissected; the fear of ridicule often stifles creativity, and limits ideas. It isn't impossible that some small piece of an initially bad idea might be worth saving, or even retrieving from the junk pile and reusing with a new idea.

The Life Cycle of the Brand Affects the Message

Another consideration when conceptualizing is to know the life-cycle stage the brand is in. With a new product launch comes a new target audience that needs to be researched. When possible, advertising efforts should focus more on the consumer and less on brand features. Nielson, in their 2013 innovation report, as detailed in an online July 2013 *AdAge* article entitled, "14 Product Launches that Rocked and Why" by E.J. Schultz, describes this "as 'demand-driven insight,' or identifying the 'unarticulated desires, partially expressed needs and recurring frustrations in consumers' lives." This form of advertising is less tangible, anyone interested in finding out more about specific features will do the research.

It is important that the brand stands out within the brand category, especially if it is not unique in any clear and definable way. One way is to do something other brands have not done before, take a position creatively that is bold and memorable, and develop a world that your target wants to visit because of your brand. When possible, take the brand to the target in some new and unique way, if not in person, then online.

Mature or mainstream products usually have a dedicated target, so advertising efforts are used mostly as reminders. There are times when the advertising challenges another almost identical brand within the category. That will require an older brand to employ a few new launch tactics.

Brands that need to be reinvented, especially if due to a scandal, will have an uphill battle to alter consumer perception. Still others look at change as a way to appear fresh, new, and relevant to a new or existing target audience. A brand that is reinventing or rebranding a tired or damaged image, or one that is facing new challengers, within the brand category will need to adopt a new way of thinking. This kind of change usually starts with updating the logo and any spokesperson or character representatives they may be using. But to change perceptions, a rebranding campaign must have a visual and verbal voice that convinces consumers the brand has in fact changed for the better. The pace of change will depend on your target. If change happens too quickly, you can alienate your brand-loyal consumers; too slow, and you could lose those very consumers to new, more progressive, brands. Brands that are attempting to recover from some form of scandal must be transparent about what happened and own it. Today's consumer can recognize a comb-over pretty quickly. This type of campaign can take years to rebuild a damaged reputation and/ or convince the target that the brand is in fact an improvement over the original. Volkswagen is currently attempting a comeback in the United States after the emission scandal reported in 2015, where they falsely promoted certain models as environmentally friendly. The reveal was that the cars actually emitted high levels of nitrogen oxides.

Anytime a brand must rebuild a broken image, money and creative effort will need to be thrown at the problem, making reinvention a very expensive proposition.

No matter where the brand is in its life-cycle stage, concept development is only the first step in the creative process. Execution is the second and most detailed and time-consuming element of design. A great idea poorly designed and/or produced will fail as quickly as an idea that is off-target or off-strategy. Great creative teams must understand how to use every tool, both visual and verbal, in the design toolbox. Beyond that, it also requires the ability to organize, problem-solve, negotiate, pitch,

and have knowledge of multiple media vehicles and their creative options and limitations, and a thorough knowledge of technical or production techniques.

We have learned what it takes to come up with good ideas and solutions that are both on-target and on-strategy. And that coming up with a great idea not only takes a creative imagination and a lot of hard work but also business savvy. Once a viable direction is agreed upon, it's time to begin searching for quality in the quantity. The strongest ideas will continue to be reworked until a strong creative direction reveals itself. Before any idea goes any further, we have to understand what makes a good design beyond the idea.

Bibliography

Blakeman, Robyn. 2011. *Strategic Uses of Alternative Media: Just the Essentials*. Armonk, NY: Sharpe, 13, 74, and 75.

Blakeman, Robyn, and Maureen Taylor. 2017. "Technology in the Idea Generation Process: Voices from the Agency." *Journal of Advertising Education*, Spring, 21(1), 6–12.

Nelson, Roy P. 1989. *The Design of Advertising*. 6th ed. Dubuque, IA: Wm. C. Brown Company.

Osborn, Alex. 2007. *Your Creative Power*. Read Books.

Schultz, E.J. 2013. "14 Product Launches That Rocked and Why." *AdAge* (July 25). Retrieved from: http://adage.com/article/ news/14-product-launches-rocked/243273.

Thaler, Linda K., and Robin Koval. 2005. *Bang! Getting Your Message Heard in a Noisy World*. Currency.

Vonk, Nancy, and Janet Kestin. 2005. *Pick Me: Breaking into Advertising and Staying There*. Chichester: Wiley.

CHAPTER 3

Getting Attention and Delivering an Informative Message

Chapter 3 Objectives

1. The reader will learn the basic language of advertising design.
2. The reader will learn how the principle and elements of design are used in advertising design.
3. The reader will understand the reasons behind the placement of components within an ad.

Understanding the Language of Advertising Design

Before you recreate those brainstorming ideas, before you boot up the computer, you must first know what makes advertising design work. So before we dissect the next steps behind idea development, let's get a few terms under our belt. The vocabulary behind design is not exclusive to advertising. For example, many young designers may wonder what the difference is between art, design, and creativity? *Art* is meant to arouse an undefined response, while *design* has a predetermined purpose and response. *Creativity*, the foundation of all advertising design, is the imaginative or brainstorming stage. All art and design can be viewed either one-, two-, or three-dimensional.

In design, as in art, the term *dimension* is used to describe the overall shape or the roundness or flatness of an object. As we move through life, we interact everyday with three-dimensional objects. When we read or view visuals on paper or our computer screens, we see them in two dimensions. But images can be simplified even further into one single dimension. Let's take a brief look at each one.

Designs that are *one-dimensional* have only one dimension length. A simple line segment is the best example to explain one-dimensional design. Simple geometric shapes such as squares, rectangles, triangles, or circles are examples of *two-dimensional*

design or shapes having both length and width. Designers would use perspective to achieve a *three-dimensional* appearance on a two-dimensional page or screen. Three-dimensional design, or shapes having three dimensions—length, width, and depth (or volume)—are sculptural and can be viewed from multiple sides. Simple visuals such as cubes, spheres, cones, and pyramids are examples of three-dimensional images.

All advertising designs are comprised of two attributes: Content and form. *Content* refers to the varied visual and verbal components seen in the ad, and *form* refers to how those visual and verbal components will be organized within the design. The aesthetically pleasing arrangement of these components requires knowledge about the principles and elements of design.

Effective design is methodical and focused; an art director uses both the elements and principles of design to orchestrate the visual and verbal presentation of any advertised message.

The Elements and Principles of Design

As we have already learned, no aspect of advertising design is arbitrary. A good ad requires more than a great imagination and a few good ideas. To do its job, each component must be carefully chosen and placed to ensure the message clearly and imaginatively represents the idea. The elements and principles of design are the plan behind the idea that ensures visually attractive designs. The designer employs these principles and elements in the same way a copywriter employs grammar. Mastery of these visual guidelines lays the groundwork for understanding what makes a good design work. Though any of these foundational guides can be broken and manipulated, they should never be entirely abandoned, nor should they limit an art director to any one look, solution, or interpretation.

The elements and principles of design teach the designer how to organize the page and communicate effectively by using those

DOI: 10.4324/9781003255123-4

techniques that ensure the layout is effective, creative, and easy to read and understand. In advertising design, the elements are the visual and verbal components the designer uses to create an ad, such as headlines, body copy, and visual images. The principles of design are how the designer uses the elements. All of the principles and elements interact on the page, but some can be interdependent depending on the message.

The Elements of Design

The *elements* are the visual things we see in a design and include line, shape, volume, texture, value, and color.

Line

Lines are a one-dimensional or flat directional stroke that have a defined beginning and end and is considered the most basic element of design. Although simple, lines can express a range of emotions depending on thickness or shape. Using lines in an ad should take the viewer's eye to a predetermined destination. A seemingly simple line can be drawn or implied; it can be straight, twisted, curved, be uniform in width or taper off, be zigzagged, create texture, literally go in any direction, or can be used to point out details. Beyond visual variations in appearance, lines can depict varying emotions. For example, a straight line can depict balance or tradition; a curvy line may appear relaxing or fluid, while a jagged line can represent high energy or excitement. See Figure 3.1.

Shape

Shape in design is used to break up the page and/or stress a particular area. Comprised of both length and width, shapes are considered two-dimensional boundaries and can be created using lines, color, value, or texture. Very diverse in appearance and emotions, shapes can be either *geometric*, such as circles, squares, triangles, or rectangles, or *organic* in nature, that is, any shape that is not geometric. Or shape may be created through the use of positive/negative space. Emotionally, angular shapes such as triangles have a masculine feel, while curvy shapes like circles have a more feminine and unified feel. Designs with a square

Figure 3.1 Line examples showing different emotions. Drawing courtesy of Robyn Blakeman, University of Tennessee.

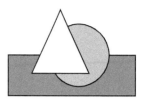

Figure 3.2 Example of different geometric shapes and screen tints. Drawing courtesy of Robyn Blakeman, University of Tennessee.

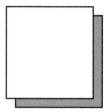

Figure 3.3 A simple example showing the design element of volume. Drawing courtesy of Robyn Blakeman, University of Tennessee.

appearance project security, trustworthiness, and stability. Any shape can be filled or surrounded by type or color. See Figure 3.2.

Volume

Visuals that project volume have a three-dimensional appeal consisting of length, width, and depth. Volume can be accomplished by simply adding shadows, or you can also give the illusion of volume by extending a portion of an object beyond a border. This could be accomplished by placing a border around a small inset photograph; a portion of the figure within the photograph could extend beyond or over the border. This also gives the appearance of movement in shape and form. See Figure 3.3.

Texture

Texture is the representative surface or feel of a visual. There are two basic types of textures: *Tactile* such as used in three-dimensional design where you can actually reach out and feel the texture, or *implied* where you can only see texture and not feel it. Texture can be depicted by using lights and darks, as well as by grouping repetitive shapes such as lines or triangles. Texture can also be portrayed with everyday objects such as rocks, sand, or glass. Whether gritty or silky, texture informs the viewer about the brand and/or its intended use. Using texture as a design tool helps to add additional accents to a particular area of a visual, making it more dominant on the page. See Figure 3.4.

Value

Value highlights details or textures through the use of contrast, or lights and darks. Value helps create the illusion of distance. Objects that are nearest to the viewer appear larger, darker, and richer in color. Because of this, all textures will appear more detailed. Objects farthest away from the viewer will appear smaller

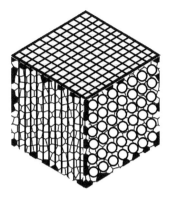

Figure 3.4 A cube showing the design element of texture. Drawing courtesy of Robyn Blakeman, University of Tennessee.

Figure 3.5 A cube showing the design element of value. Drawing courtesy of Robyn Blakeman, University of Tennessee.

and have less saturated colors and have little or no observable detail or texture. See Figure 3.5.

A design with a high contrast of values projects a sense of happiness, boldness, and clarity. Designs sporting similar values are darker, more subtle, and dramatic. Offering the viewer varied values creates interest in specific areas within a visual. Not everything in a photograph or illustration is of equal importance. The darkest or most colorful areas will attract the viewer's eye first. A color's value can create a mood, depth, or texture.

Color

Color, or the lack thereof, creates a mood and can be interpreted differently by different people. Depending on the hue and saturation, color can be bright, bold, soft, minimalist, or dull. It can alter the viewer's emotions and boldly represent a brand's identity. Color can be an attention-getter and/or used to set a mood. Bright colors project a youthful feel, while darker colors such as navy or black can be perceived as elegant or subdued. Bold colors both attract attention and appear to advance on the page, while light colors tend to soundlessly recede into the background. A design may use many colors, or just one or two strategically placed. A brand's image can be defined through the use of color.

The Principles of Design

The *principles* of design are the standard visual guidelines that govern the way the elements are used within the layout or the arrangement of the elements as a whole. Like the elements of design, the number of principles depends on whom you ask. Most artists or art directors could not actually name the most basic elements and principles, but they use them instinctively. Knowledge of the principles assists in managing both the order and variety of images found within a design.

Although rarely agreed upon, the most commonly recognized principles of design include balance, white space, eye flow, alignment, dominance, structure, gradation, contrast, negative/positive space, and unity.

Balance

An ad is in balance if it has visual equilibrium. In other words, if all components within the ad are distributed evenly. Balanced designs do not look like they could tip over; they instead look stable or aligned. There are basically two types of balance: Formal or symmetrical and informal or asymmetrical. *Formal* balance imagines a line that runs down the center of the ad where every element that appears on one side of the ad is duplicated in size or shape on the other. *Informal* balance also deals with optical weight but each side uses different-sized images to reach balance. For example, picture a teeter-totter, where a small child sits on one side and a larger teenager sits on the other; for the teeter-totter to balance, the older, larger teenager will have to move in closer to the center. Typically, informal balance is more interesting to look at as it causes the eye to move from element to element, whereas formal balance can be taken in with a quick glance. See Figures 3.6 and 3.7.

White Space

Every well-designed ad will use white space, or the white of the page, to emphasize and organize the elements within it, as well as bring order to chaos. White space refers to negative space, or the space around and between elements. However, despite

Figure 3.6 A simple example of the principle of balance. Drawing courtesy of Robyn Blakeman, University of Tennessee.

Figure 3.7 A simple example of the principle of informal balance. Drawing courtesy of Robyn Blakeman, University of Tennessee.

its descriptive name, white space does not have to be white. It's basically an area that is free of text or images that can be any color, pattern, texture, or even a background image. White space can be used to frame an ad, as well as bring elegance and order to a design. Ads lacking white space appear more cluttered and unbalanced, leaving the eye nowhere to land. When used effectively, white space ensures not only an organized design but makes it easier to read and understand. White space gives the eye a clear stopping place, making reading faster and bringing order to the page.

Ads that lack a strategic use of white space can inadvertently indicate the quality of the store and the products it sells. When the target sees clutter, it projects low budget. An abundance of strategically placed white space on the other hand can project elegance. It is not always about what you say, but how the viewer perceives it.

Since the number of items that the client wants to place in the ad is beyond the creative team's control, the team *can* control placement. Group items together when possible, or consider separating them by confining them into some type of drawn or implied grid pattern.

Margins, or the area that appears between the inside edges of an ad and where the visual/verbal elements are placed, is important to framing, or drawing the eye into the design. These areas of white space can be almost any size but should be no less than one-fourth inch on all four sides for larger pieces, and one-eighth inch for smaller designs. When using the white of the page as a design element, margins must be balanced. For example, if the top and bottom of the ad have a one-inch margin, the left and right sides could have three to four inches.

White space can also be used as an accent around type and visuals. For example, smaller text that wraps around visuals should create a relationship, not fight for attention. Text and visuals should look cozy, but not indifferent; one is being used to explain the other. To ensure clarity, there should be at least one-fourth inch of space between columns of text or between text and visuals.

Finally, large text such as headlines and subheads can also use white space to break up the appearance of a copy-heavy page. Longer headlines and subheads can become blocky. To create a more pleasing shape, breaking the lines into irregular lengths, such as long-short-long, or short-long-short, can open or lighten up an ad. Additionally, when text is centered one line over another, this creates a balance of white space on either end of

the line. Each of these suggestions are only starting points; there are no definitive rules to applying white space, but consistency is imperative to ensure a strongly structured design. The goal is to avoid allowing your reader to fall into any haphazardly placed large white holes that disrupt the appearance and flow of the ad.

If using large amounts of white space, it must be used judiciously around text and visuals and not haphazardly between or beside them. When applied uniformly, the reader will not fall into a white hole. This dead space is created when headlines or visuals are incorrectly sized, when there is only a small amount of body copy, or when the headline or logo has been pushed off to one side. Never push type to one side or stagger it, unless you have a visual(s) to fill the resulting hole(s) or are repeating the pattern used elsewhere.

Any type of hole is a sure sign that something is wrong with the design. To alleviate the problem, consider breaking the headline into additional lines, enlarging it, or both. Visuals can also be enlarged, or even added to the body copy. Holes can also appear when ads are not balanced, such as when logos are left to float alone at the bottom right of an ad. The resulting hole to its immediate left leaves the ad unbalanced. Consider filling it with either additional body copy, balancing depth with the logo in the right column, or by centering the logo at the bottom of the page.

Eye Flow

Eye flow involves arranging the ad's components in such a way as to create a predetermined path for the reader to follow. All designs should seamlessly lead readers through the ad (top to bottom and left to right) by creating a trail of components that flows from the opening headline or visual to the closing logo. Options for creating eye flow might include using a gradation of sizes or colors, such as moving from large elements to smaller ones, or from color to non-color, or through the use of lines or other components that travel from one concentrated spot across the page, such as with dripping water or spilled cereal.

Alignment

Alignment refers to the placement or alignment of components in an ad along the top, bottom, center, or sides of the design. Aligning components, usually along the side margins, creates consistency throughout the design. Incorporating photographs, illustrations or graphics that "bleed" beyond the edges or size of the ad, can break the resulting linear alignment.

Dominance

Not all elements within the ad are created equally. Only one element can dominate or be emphasized in the ad: The visual or the headline. Which one takes center stage will depend on the key consumer benefit. If it is easier to show than tell, focus on a single visual or a group of visuals. If the headline can push the key consumer benefit in a catchy or informative way, focus on it. Emphasis can happen in several ways, such as isolating the image from other elements on the page, or simply making it bigger, bolder, more graphic, or more colorful.

Structure

A design with structure means the placement of each component within the ad has a controlled or thought-out appearance. Nothing is randomly placed and all layout qualities are consistent. A design lacks structure, for example, when all components within the ad are centered, except for a subhead in the middle that is set flush left, which goes against the ad's structure. Everything has a purpose. Purpose can be created through repetition of layout qualities.

Gradation

Gradation is about a gradual and orderly step-by-step change. It can be accomplished with color, shades of gray, or through the use of thick to thin lines or large to small shapes. This stacking of large and small shapes creates weight or even instability. Add a dark color or tones, and the instability is magnified. Gradation of tones, colors, and sizes, can show movement, distance, shadows, highlights, or the passage of time. We see the concept of gradation daily. For example, through the use of perspective, things closer to us are larger and brighter in color than those seen at a distance.

Contrast

Contrast is occasionally considered an element rather than a principle of design. No matter where you place it, contrast creates visual interest and must be created between the components on the page. Items can be differentiated based on size, value, tone, color, shape, or texture. Using the design principle of contrast is a great way to make similar items placed together appear unique or independent. The liberal use of contrasting objects within a design creates eye flow and a harmonious, or unified look between components. The more obvious the contrasts between objects, the easier the ad is to read and understand. See Figure 3.8.

Negative/Positive Space

Negative/positive space refers to occupied and unoccupied spaces. Negative or unoccupied space refers to the white of the page or the area surrounding visuals and text. Positive space is the occupied portions of the page.

Judicious use of these unoccupied spaces, more commonly known as white space, increases both readability and legibility.

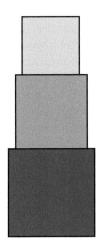

Figure 3.8 A simple geometric example of the principle of contrast. Drawing courtesy of Robyn Blakeman, University of Tennessee.

Unity

Also known as harmony, unity ensures all visual and verbal elements in the ad work together, to send a cohesive single message. Unity glues the visual and verbal components together. In other words, unity is created when each element not only works together but also is arranged so that they get along or do not compete with each other. This can typically be accomplished when elements have the same basic size, shape, color, mood, and texture. Type can also unify an ad by mimicking the character of the art. For example, if the art is thin, the type would have thin lines. The strategic use of borders and white space can also help to create unity within an ad.

The elements and principles of design should be considered as the guidelines for good design. By incorporating one or more of the principles or elements in any ad, you will help the design flow and visually assist the reader through the ad.

Placement of Components on the Page: What Goes Where?

Now that we have the elements and principles of design under our belt, it's time to dissect the types of components you will run into and how to best arrange them on the page or screen. Unfortunately, advertising design is so diverse that there is really no right or wrong answer to the question of what goes where in an ad. For example, a simple reminder ad may show nothing more than a visual and a logo, while new product launches may require a more copy-heavy layout with multiple visuals. To help solidify direction, there are some solid rules of thumb to get you started.

No matter how easy or complicated the design, never forget an ad has a lot to do. Not only does it need to employ a combination of design-relevant elements and principles, but it must push the key consumer benefit, be informative, advance the brand's image, and create interest in the minds of consumers. If it does, you're on the right track to finding an informative and creative solution. To ensure success as young designers, you'll want to stack the deck with a few absolutes and some safety nets.

Typically, a print or digital ad can be made up of any of the following five components, in varied order: Headline, subhead(s), visual(s), body copy, and logo. Not every component needs to be present in every ad; however, order is somewhat predetermined, especially for young designers. You want to show potential employers that you know how to use all five components, and that you know when—and when not—to use them.

The ultimate placement of components on the page will depend on your concept. If the headline can informatively and creatively scream out the key consumer benefit, then place it at the top of the design. If the visual says more than words can, then place it first. Ultimately, your decision will help you to determine whether the headline, or visual(s) should be the most dominant component on the page. Controlling the order and overall size of what the target sees and reads assists in understanding the advertised message.

See Table 3.1 for a list of the most common layout options that can help logically organize your design on the page.

Table 3.1 Shows the varied options for laying out components within a design.

Column 1	Column 2	Column 3	Column 4
Head	Head	Visual	Head
Subhead	Visual	Headline	Visual
Visual	Subhead	Subhead	Subhead
Body Copy	Body Copy	Body Copy	Visual
Logo	Logo	Logo	Body Copy + Visual(s)
			Logo

These layout options are neither static nor inclusive, but they are a good place to start. Each option allows the creative team to push the key consumer benefit by either featuring it in the headline or the visual.

In the end, it is important to remember that advertising design is all about how the visual and verbal components work together to deliver a message. The arrangement of these components should take the reader or viewer through an organized sequence to ensure they understand the message. The design is a package that contains the information the target audience needs to make an informed buying decision. How well these components are organized, will determine not only if the ad will capture the target's attention, but also hold it.

CHAPTER 4
Visuals and Their Voice in Advertising

Chapter 4 Objectives

1. The reader will learn what types of visual imagery are used within advertising.
2. The reader will understand the role varied imagery plays in an ad.
3. The reader will learn the difference between literal or symbolic imagery.

The Visual Voice of an Ad

The creative and strategic use of visuals and symbols in advertising can visually say as much about a brand as a paragraph of copy. The type of image employed will strategically depend on the media to be used, the product or service to be advertised, the target audience to be reached, and the key consumer benefit promoted.

Visuals speak faster than words, they are more memorable, persuasive, and credible, and allow the art director to bring an idea to life in dynamic and emotional ways. The imagery chosen to visually deliver the advertised message is an important one. As a storytelling device, they must not only attract attention and be informative about quality and use, but should create an experience that successfully integrates the brand into the target's lifestyle. Their job is to show the key consumer benefit in action.

It is up to the art director to decide how to visually tell the brand's story, whether through the reality of photography or the artistic expression of an illustration or graphic. A more simplistic or stark approach can be achieved through the use of black-and-white line art, or if the budget is tight, through the use of free or existing clip or stock art.

No matter how the image is expressed, good visuals have their own vernacular, or visual language, that reflects how the image should be interpreted. For example, models that gaze directly at the reader or viewer not only attract attention, but also imply a form of social interaction and communication. Content can reflect practicality, focus on specific details, or be representational or abstract. More complex images can place the target into situations they can relate or aspire to, creating a type of bond or positive association with the brand, or make a statement through body language for example, to successfully project any number of appropriate emotions.

The goal is to lead the reader or viewer to a specific meaning or conclusion, whether assisted by text or not. Today's overstimulated consumer sees a lot of content but reads very little of it and remembers even less. If you can show the brand in a unique way or demonstrate how a feature works and point out the benefits it brings, you have a better chance of grabbing the target's attention. A brand's visual identity, whether lifesaving, classical, sophisticated, or whimsical, can be expressed through diverse types of visual imagery.

Ultimately, whatever image becomes the visual voice of the client's brand, be sure it 1) reaches the correct target audience 2) creates interest in an often disinterested audience by focusing on the key consumer benefit, 3) reflects the target's lifestyle, 4) builds on or develops the brand's image, 5) ties the brand's image to the target's lifestyle, 6) reflects the brand's life-cycle stage, 7) highlights the brand's current positioning, 8) strategically reflects the appropriate strategy and tone, 9) is attention grabbing, 10) is impactful in some meaningful way, 11) stimulates curiosity, 12) demonstrates specific features and benefits, 13) gives any text a visual context, 14) reflects what the headline is saying, and 15) creates a powerful and memorable brand identity.

How the image is shown or the placement of imagery is also diverse. The brand can be featured alone, shown in use, placed in a unique setting or within body copy, be compared to another brand, show before and after results, interact with the headline, be grouped together with other images, appear large or small, be literal or

DOI: 10.4324/9781003255123-5

abstract in appearance, or be a simple black-and-white or full-color image. Finally, it is important that the brand's visual and verbal identity be able to move seamlessly between diverse media vehicles, no matter the format, without a loss of clarity or detail.

Visual Imagery Needs A Strong Verbal Voice

All imagery has its own visual language or reflects how the image should be interpreted. Advertising's ability to communicate an informed meaning or experience visually increases the viewer or reader's visual literacy about the brand and its use(s). If an image does not build visual literacy amongst the targeted readers or viewers, or promote some type of informed meaning through the images employed, then it should not be used.

Visuals dominate all forms of advertising for some very important reasons. Statistics show that visuals are processed 60,000 times faster by the brain than text. This is backed up the 20/80 memory rule that tells us that consumers typically recall only 20 percent of what they read compared to 80 percent of what they see and experience. Memorability is important since the average consumer is bombarded with over 3,000 advertised messages a day, ensuring many messages go unnoticed. So to stand out and quickly reach today's advertising-avoidant consumer, show the brand's story rather than tell it when possible. In the book *Nonverbal Communication in Advertising* edited by Hecker and Stewart, we learn that "Visual recall is becoming increasingly important and corporate symbols and advertising will need to be stronger and eye-catching to capture consumer attention. Nonverbal communication will not only become a means for drawing attention to a verbal message, but it will also become the message itself in many instances."

How Literal or Symbolic Do You Want to Get?

Very basically, there are two distinct types of visuals used in advertising: Realistic or literal, and symbolic. *Realistic* imagery is educational focusing on specific facts, uses, or lifestyle enhancements. *Symbolic* imagery, on the other hand, uses a more indirect approach to connect the brand with the meaning given them by the advertising.

Realistic or literal images consist of images such as logos and packaging, and might employ images that shows how the product

looks, or that compares before and after results, demonstrates product use, or points out specific details. Realistic visuals are used to show facts and details associated with the brand and/or use. Typically, realistic imagery will employ the use of illustrations or photographs, with the exception of logo design that often uses graphic imagery.

Symbolic visuals use association, abstractions, or metaphors to tell a visual story. Visually they are more diverse and can be seen in photographs and illustrations or graphics of all types. Visuals as symbols are more interpretive and can use more abstract associations to make a point. As a message strategy, either form can be used specifically for visual or artistic impact, as well as being an informative vehicle.

Mary Stribley offers up a few creative examples in an online article entitled "30 Advertisement Design Tips That Turn Heads: Brilliant Case Studies":

1. Simplicity Can Say a Lot. Most ads scream the brand benefits both visually and verbally, hawk the benefits of ownership and the reason(s) to own. A good informative visual can tone down the sales pitch and tune up image. Simple is great for a well-known brand like Coke for example, where brand loyalty and overall knowledge is high. Simplicity is a little harder especially for tech brands that have to be explained to be understood. Imagine the introduction of Alexa without copy.
2. Get Your Target up and Moving. Advertising is all about trying to get the target to do something, such as visit a brick and mortar store, go online or call for more information. Known as calls to action (CTA), these ads often scream "Limited Quantities" or push "Buy One Get One" promotions. Those with a more understated appeal encourage the importance of "Being The First To Own." These types of old-school approaches are still used but if you can get your message across more visually it has more impact. For example, the Monarto Zoo ran an ad that shows stripes painted on the street with the copy "come and see our baby zebra" plus the logo. That is how a visual and verbal message work together.
3. Talk Directly to the Target Audience. Ads that reflect what your target looks like, their lifestyle, or their specific needs attracts attention. If you are selling eyeglasses for example, showing how one person looks in different styles, or how your diverse target has a large and diverse selection to choose from, shows and tells with multiple visuals and of course, a logo.
4. Visual Metaphors Can Stop a Viewer. A written metaphor compares one thing to another, frequently unrelated, thing. Often startling, this can be done visually as well. Absolut Vodka put their iconic bottle on a mannequin stand and placed it in a sewing room. The headline underneath read

"Absolut Fashion," followed by a subhead "Proud sponsor of New Zealand Fashion Week." Ford ran a public service ad for Halloween that featured a gigantic orange construction cone that had the top tip folded over to look like a witch's hat. The small copy underneath reads "Treat kids to a safe Halloween" followed by the logo. Visual metaphors must be obvious to work. The goal is to create a clever and unique visual solution that is both immediately recognizable and understandable.

5. Search for Hidden Visual Relationships. The visual solution requires a detailed brainstorming session that thoroughly dissects the problem to be solved. The key is to find hidden visual relationships that deal with your brand. Stribley tells us to "try to brainstorm concepts related to your message that have similar shapes, lines, or contours, and try to think of a way to bring the two concepts together." For example, an ad dealing with mental health issues shows an image of an ear that completely dominates the ad. The hidden relationship appears in the front portion of the outer ear or the side nearest the face where we see the cartilage molded into the profile of a nose and mouth that looks like it is whispering into the ear. The headline underneath reads "Hearing voices? Felling paranoid? Talk to someone." Another ad features a large three-quarter view of a young girl staring out of the ad wearing a bike helmet and sporting a large black tire track across her face. The headline underneath reads, "Bicycles don't come with bumpers. Give cyclists room to ride."

6. Size Matters. Ads that focus on the visual usually go big to make an easily understandable point. Large visuals create drama and allow the viewer to focus on detail. But remember only one element can be dominate on the page, so if text or another visual is present, size down to make the details look more intricate or to focus attention.

7. Surrealism Is Catchy and Beautiful in Its Simplicity. Merriam-Webster defines surrealism as "the principles, ideals, or practice of producing fantastic or incongruous imagery or effects in art ... by means of unnatural or irrational juxtapositions and combinations." Basically, it's all about manipulating a common image and turning it into an unthought-of image. One good example of this is an ad for orange chocolate tea that found an interesting and simple way to show taste. The orange-tinted ad shows a steaming teapot made out of an orange. The lid is slightly askew allowing the viewer to see the orange fruit below. Next to the "pot" are squares of chocolate and hanging from under the "lid" is a tea bag with the logo.

8. Show, Don't Tell. If you can make your point visually without a lot of cumbersome copy do so—remember, it's more memorable. If you didn't believe Heinz uses real tomatoes in their ketchup, this bold ad will prove they do. The red ad shows a bottle of Heinz Ketchup made out of cut tomato slices. You can see the cut-up label stuck to the slices of tomatoes. The copy underneath reads, "No one grows Ketchup like Heinz."

9. Interactive Options Are Engaging and Memorable. Give your target something to do while looking at your ad. How can you get them to actually interact with it? Think print is dead? Consider some of these interactive options. Motorola put technology in their magazine ad by not only showing their phone but also placing buttons in the ad that readers could push to change the color of the phone. Peugot used print to focus attention on their airbags. The one-page magazine ad pictures a front view of one of their cars that asked readers to hit the ad with their fist. The two-page corresponding spread on the following pages included a mini airbag that inflated when hit, automatically turning the page to show the dashboard and the inflated bag.

10. Color Sets a Mood or Tone. Ads that use non-traditional colors for traditional images is eye-catching. Imagine the Coke logo in yellow or the Golden Arches in well, any other color than yellow. Not only does the unusual use of color attract the eye. it causes the viewer to pause and wonder why the change? What is the point?

11. Give Your Ad White Space. As previously discussed, white space in advertising helps set off details and ensures the ad is both readable and legible. When white space dominates an ad, it speaks simplicity and boasts an orderly and uncluttered look.

12. Eye Flow, as an Accent. Use images, shapes, or graduating colors to lead the viewer's or reader's eye across or down the ad to a predetermined location such as to the logo or packaging.

13. Customize It. If you have a brand that has little or no discerning features from other brands in the category, try to visually show it in a new way. Extra Gum for example, wanted to show that gum was good for your teeth between brushes. This is not a new idea, but the way they showed the idea is. On a blue background, they stood up seven pieces of gum in a row to simulate the bristles in a toothbrush. To complete the illusion, the resulting shadow from the sticks of gum created the brush's handle. The resulting eye flow leads directly to the packaging.

14. Negative Space Is a Positive Visual. As we previously discussed, negative space is the unused space around an image. Although never easy to imagine, this very visual technique requires brainstorming how the brand and the target will interact in the abstract. You need to think shapes—and how two or more shapes can be merged together to demonstrate your concept. To make the diverse images stand out, use contrasting colors to draw the reader's or viewer's eye to each image separately. One of the most commonly seen "negative positive" images is the Federal Express logo. The Fed portion of the logo is blue and the Ex is

in red. If you look closely you will see a white arrow created between the Ex. To remind consumers to have a Coke while dining, designers created a poster using Coke's signature red. Reversed out in white, we see a fork on the left and knife on the right. Together the utensils create the shape of a Coke bottle complete with logo.

15. Design a Typeface to Deliver Your Message. Nutella for example wanted an ad to look like the words were created using the spread. This example focuses on text. The headline dominates three-quarters of the ad saying "PLEASE DO NOT LICK THE PAGE." The period is punctuated with an angled knife that leads the eye seamlessly down to the very small jar of Nutella.

The take-away here is that powerful images can imaginatively and informatively speak for themselves. Knowing how to give them a voice requires not only knowledge of the rules of design, but also how to manipulate them. Visually dominate ads work best for mature brands looking to find a clever way to stand out in the brand category and as a creative reminder for the consumer. New brands or ones that require reinvention can use highly visual ads but will require a series of ads to cement the key consumer benefit in the target's mind.

To bring a concept visually to life, art directors have a deep and rich palette to choose from, including photographs, illustrations, line art, clip or stock art, graphics, and borders. Let's take a quick look at each one.

The Expressive and Detailed Photograph

Photographs are believable and full of details that can help the target imagine the brand in their life and the benefits of ownership. The decision to include a black-and-white or color photograph instead of an illustration or line art depends on the concept being used, the image of the brand, the budget, and the medium.

Photographs can be used alone to tell a visual story or as visual support for text. They can visually speak in an authentic voice, show realistic or graphically manipulated imagery, be interactive, capture a unique moment, and tag an emotion in both print and digital media. Whether dramatic or fantastical, photography is used in advertising to solicit a reaction either rooted in relatable and real-life experiences or exaggerated to highlight a specific point or use, the ultimate goal is to entertain and educate in a visually memorable way that will assist with building brand loyalty and enhance both the target's and brand's image.

The choice of image, no matter where it will be seen, must be chosen purposefully to solve a business problem, not an artistic one. It has to not only attract and hold the target's attention by creating some type of emotional or rational response, but must also scream out the key consumer benefit, and strategically ensure the correct tone is employed. Photography's role in modern advertising is multidimensional. It must 1) attract and hold the target's attention, 2) often deliver a message with no words, 3) ensure it visually supports what the copy is saying, 4) simultaneously support and/or enhance the brand's and target's self image, 5) have viral potential, 6) project both credibility and quality, 7) create some type of emotional response, 8) motivate the target to action, 9) inspire engagement, 10) build brand loyalty, and 11) ultimately produce a sale.

Photographs help to build a brand's image and informational aesthetic. Whether literal or symbolic, their job is to incite a response from the target. The goal of building trust and thus loyalty can often occur on an intangible level after repeated exposure. The choice of image should be considered an opportunity to communicate with the target on an emotional and/or intellectual or rational level. By educating and/or entertaining the target, you can introduce them to your company, your brand, and how the two can make their lives better.

The Choice to Use Photographs

Photographs are realistic and relatable. Because of that they offer an intimate viewing and storytelling opportunity. Consumers are exposed to diverse types of patterns, textures, qualities, and sometimes colors, as if the product were sitting before us. Photographs are a great choice if you need to highlight brand details, portray emotions, create an interactive link, or want to digitally and/or graphically manipulate the image to make a point.

Thanks to the visual reality photographs bring to the advertised message, certain types of brands will often use them in ads promoting services such as construction/remodeling, investing, or food products sold in restaurants. They are a great option for immersing the brand in the target's lifestyle, projecting their interests, controlling their eye movement across the page in a preset pattern, projecting status; they can even tap into the targets' senses by making their mouth water, or vicariously hear the activity shown, or even taste or smell the image.

Image composition and content is never arbitrary. Include only what is needed to push the key consumer benefit. Too much content can look tacky and cluttered; too little and your target may not understand the message. To ensure credibility, be sure the models used in all imagery reflect the target and their lifestyle. Be sure they are dressed similarly to the target, as well as the right age and/or sex.

Some images are guaranteed attention getters. Consider the following options:

- Infants
- Young animals
- Brides
- Celebrities of all types
- Graphically or digitally enhanced images
- Romance
- Slice of life
- Outrageous situations
- Outrageous costumes
- Current events.

Additionally, gender will play a small but notable role in the choice of visual images used; for example, men are attracted to all types of animals, whereas women are attracted to images of infants or children. But no matter the gender of the target, if visual content is not relatable to them, the ad will fail to both capture and hold their attention.

The Ins and Outs of Photographs

No matter the medium in which photography will be used, it is unfortunately expensive, especially color photography. Before an image hits the page or screen, a photographer must be hired, a date and time for the photo shoot arranged and finally, photo editing to be completed.

An art director needs to take into account the medium in which the visual will be seen. In order for the target to clearly see what the brand looks like and/or how it is used, the art director must pay close attention to the paper quality and any printing issues. An incorrectly used screen resolution can adversely affect overall quality. For example, when working on uncoated paper stocks like those found in newspaper and packaging, a larger visual as opposed to smaller ones will hold details better. Uncoated paper stocks absorb the ink causing it to move on the page, effecting quality by causing small visuals with minute details to blend together or fill in. Shiny or coated paper stocks like those used in magazines, direct mail, or any number of alternative media vehicles eliminates ink movement, preserving both detail and quality, and making the use of both larger and smaller visuals a great choice.

An art director also needs to know before the photo shoot whether a photograph will bleed off the page or screen, in order to ensure the photograph is big enough, or enough visual is present, to be used in varied media. Bleed is present when any visual, background color, or graphic element extends at least one-eighth to one-quarter inch beyond the trim size, or the size of the ad, on one or more sides. This means the photograph or illustration will extend to the edge of the page or screen; no white space will be showing on one or more sides. Bleed allows for more of the visual to be seen. When used in print, it is often more expensive to employ.

Getting the Photograph Just Right: The Photo Shoot

The photographer, the art director, the account manager, and often the client will attend the photo shoot. Photo shoots are expensive. You are paying for more than the final images, and wrapped up in the overall cost is time, equipment, and the reputation of the photographer. Depending on the brand and the number and type of images needed, a photo shoot can take anywhere from a couple of hours to a couple of days.

If the shot requires working with food, the assistance of a good food stylist will be needed. Stylists painstakingly work at making food look more appetizing by making it look crisper, juicier and fresher—basically, more edible.

Photo shoots can take place at any time, but are most commonly done once the client has approved the visual/verbal direction. The photographer will work closely with the art director arranging broth props and the brand to match the art director's vision. Oftentimes, in order to get the exact shot a little creative ingenuity is required. In order to match the photograph grouping to the ad, props are often required. It is not uncommon to see duct tape, bricks, string, or wire make a brief but important appearance to get the desired shot, but none of these types of props will show in the final photographs.

Getting the lighting just right is also critical during any shoot. In order to increase contrast, in any visual, it is important to pay attention to both highlights and shadows. These will help create depth and eye flow. It is important to play close attention to lighting during the entire shoot. Even though almost all issues can be corrected or retouched in Photoshop, the client will need to pay for any corrections the photographer or art director will make at a later date.

Black-and-White Photographs versus Color

Why use a black-and-white image when you can use color? One, it's an anomaly and two, it's price. Cost is always an issue especially for small businesses, and black-and-white photographs, known as *halftones*, offer an opportunity for high-contrast imagery. Just because black-and-white images are rare doesn't mean a great idea will suffer. The less mainstream the design choices, the more unique and memorable the idea can be.

The difference between a color and a black-and-white photograph may seem obvious, but there are some strong reasons to choose black-and-white over color. According to Amy Touchette in an online June 2017 article entitled, "Color vs. Black-and-White Photography: How Palette Affects What We See—And Feel," black-and-white images have reductive simplicity telling us:

- "Black-and-white photographs comprise only highlights, shadows, and the shades of gray between. In contrast, each hue in a color photograph adds an element to the image, which can distract viewers from the subject. By reducing an image's elements with black-and-white, there's less for photographers—and viewers—to contend with.
- Composition can be seen more readily in a black-and-white image because structure and spatial relationships take precedence. A silhouette, for example, can be particularly powerful in a black-and-white image if it's clearly separated from other shapes in the composition.
- Similarly, shapes, lines, textures, and contrast within a black-and-white image are prominent. As a result, black-and-white is more likely than color to create an abstract visual.
- The more complete the tonal range, the more dynamic the image. Black-and-white photographs with a deep black, a pure white, and lots of varying grays in between can engage the eyes and draw viewers in."

Additionally, researchers have found that consumers view black-and-white images differently than color ones. Black-and-white images tend to make viewers focus on basic product features and overall brand function or use, whereas color images tended to focus attention on secondary or more idiosyncratic or image-based aesthetics—for example, the comfort level of a pair of shoes (a basic feature) versus the fashion statement surrounding the height of the heel (a secondary feature). In short, black-and-white images tend to focus viewer attention on more rational uses, whereas color tends to highlight more emotional (and sometimes more superficial) brand aspects. Both could be useful, depending on your concept.

Finally, black-and-white photographs are timeless and are excellent mood or attitude setters. For example, issues such as animal abuse, or the need for additional care and rehabilitation, are more isolating in black-and-white adding to the desired mood. Sadness, natural disasters, even the passing of time, can be highlighted especially if surrounding ads are in color.

Many charitable organizations do not want to appear wasteful when recruiting volunteers or donations, making the choice to use black-and-white photographs an affordable and practical option. Black-and-white high-contrast imagery can also appear luxurious. Wherever, or however they appear, they will attract attention.

Color Photographs Offer a Dose of Reality

The obvious reason to choose color photographs is they project reality. We see the world in color and as pointed out above, we respond differently to it. Color is eye-catching and plays a big part in how the image will be viewed and the emotions it will conjure up. Representative colors appearing in a photograph can suggest time of day or year. Bright blues and yellows can suggest water and fun in the sun. Darker shades of yellow and orange make the viewer think of crisp fall days. Color can also be used to highlight a key detail or highlight packaging. A bright hue for example, will attract the viewer's attention first, while a darker color will recede and not stand out.

Choose color images to project emotion or set a mood, or when it must be used, for example, to expose a diverse palette of lipstick shades.

Black-and-White Images Pop with Spot Color

If you can't decide on whether to use color or black-and-white images, *spot color* is an excellent alternative to combine the two together. Spot color is an excellent way to spice up a black-and-white photograph by calling attention to a small area that has been singled out to receive color. Adding color to a single element is a very creative way to not only highlight the brand by giving it a three-dimensional feel but helps it to pop off the page by immediately drawing attention to itself. The addition of even a small amount of color can help create eye flow, drawing the viewer's eye to a predetermined spot such as the logo, or the packaging. The key is to keep the color section small. The use of photographs, especially color photographs, requires a large budget. Even a small spot of color will add cost to a black-and-white image, but it will always be worth the price. It attracts attention and gives the design a personality as well as adds a colorful accessory to the visual/verbal message creating consumer interest and involvement.

Cropping What's Not Important

Cropping is the removal of any unnecessary section(s) of an image; it is used when the art director wants to call attention to a specific area of an image by removing any imagery that is not needed to push the key consumer benefit and visual/verbal message. Too much extraneous imagery takes focus away from the brand or its use. If you don't need all the background around an image, remove it. By placing the focus only on what you need to show to deliver the message, you can zoom in on emotions and details.

All cropped images need to be either placed within a box or attached to one or more of the edges. The "attachment" grounds the partial images so detached body parts do not float on the page. Confining cropped images to borders, graphic lines, or to the edge of the page, such as with a bleed photograph, gives the illusion they are just entering our view or there is more than meets the eye to investigate.

Duotones: Two Colors Are Better Than One

Rarely seen in advertising these days, I include duotone because I hope to see it revived one day rather than lost to design history. When budgets are tight, think duotone. A *duotone* gives a black-and-white photograph a wash of a second color. Very basically, the second color, usually a Pantone color or a specific color choice, attaches itself in varying shades to the tones in the black-and-white image.

By adding a wash of color, you can give the ad a bit more eye appeal. If you're trying to get an aged or charred appeal with brown, it would be a great time to consider using a duotone.

Black-and-White Line Art

A simple line drawing with no tonal qualities is known as *line art*. Having a light and airy feel, a line drawing is a great choice when you want to keep your visual message simple. They are an unexpected and under-utilized visual device that can be used in both print and digital mediums. Drawings simplify a design and create a strong black-and-white contrast on the page or screen, as opposed to black-and-white photographs, which can cause the ad to recede by graying down the design. Tones are created with stippling (dots), crosshatching, or the addition of solid areas of black. By varying the drawing's line weights, the illustrator can create strong black-and-white contrasts for emphasis, depth, and interest.

Line art works well in many mediums when you need to highlight brands that have small delicate details, or if you need simply rendered character representatives that can be photographed or animated.

Rendered line art drawings are even a great choice if you need to group multiple images together without losing clarity through the strategic use of diverse contrasts, to highlight varying details and textures. When using line art, it is important your illustrator knows where, and how, the drawings are going to be used. Like some typefaces, line art often has delicate details; if they get too fine, they can blend together or disappear altogether on uncoated paper stocks during printing.

The Style of Illustrations

Photographers can capture a brand in a setting, in use, and alone; they work in showcasing reality. The art director will choose a photographer based on their experience and expertise in varied categories such as product specialization, creative use of highlights and shadows, interesting angles and even price. Illustrators are chosen based on style and can ignore reality, or even reinterpret it.

In advertising, an *illustration* can be defined as a drawing, painting, or digitally created image that uniquely informs and visually represents a brand or concept.

Illustrations, unlike line art, have tonal qualities, to give them depth and dimension. The choice between using an illustration or photograph is an interpretive one. Perception is based on the manner of illustration used. Think of the diverse styles of Peter Max, Andy Warhol, Toulouse-Lautrec, Marc Chagall, Henri Matisse, Pablo Picasso, Beatrix Potter, and Norman Rockwell. A very imaginative visual option, illustrations can bring a design to life with creative distinctiveness and individuality.

Strategically, choice will also depend on the brand, the target, and the overall concept. For example, photographs are a great choice if your concept needs to spotlight customer service, showcase any type of food item or you are using an emotional appeal. But to create personality, or to capture or represent something intangible, think illustration. Cheaper than hiring a photographer, an illustrator only needs inspiration and a computer, whereas a photographer needs props, a set, stylists, make-up artists, models, and traveling money if the shoot is on location somewhere.

Visually, as a part of the creative problem solving process, illustrations can expand the number of possible conceptual solutions, thanks to its ability to fantastically portray a diverse amount of abstract concepts and ideas. Illustrations can portray abstract concepts and ideas more imaginatively because they are not constricted by reality; illustrations bring a sense of individuality to a concept and thus to a brand. As a visual device they can 1) bring a character representative, like the Keebler Elves, to life, 2) show fantastical images and scenes often unavailable in photography, such as placing the brand on the moon complete with alien consumers, or by reincarnating a long-dead historical figure, 3) easily reflect any historical or future time period, 4) attract attention, and 5) are unique, and individualistic to the brand, making it more difficult for competitors to emulate, thanks to the fact that not everyone can illustrate, but everyone can shoot a photograph. Stylistic application can clearly express a point of view, create a varied range of emotions and appeals such as exaggeration, attitude, desperation, expressiveness and personality traits, as well as project a laid-back or upbeat approach, to name just a few. Dial back stylization and illustrations can depict a simple graph or chart. Conceptually, not only are illustrations and graphics used less often than photography, but they are also a more expressive design option.

Illustrations are less expensive to use than photographs and can be much easier to use in diverse types of media. Bleed is still a critical consideration during the design process. As with photographers, the illustrator will need to know if bleed needs to be added to the overall finished size.

If using multiple smaller visuals like those inserted into copy blocks, illustrations and line art often reproduce better than any type of photograph because small details can be highlighted or beefed up during the development process, ensuring quality.

Visual options continue to evolve. The newest commercial option is *photo illustration* that combine photographs and illustrations to create a single, more graphic, and interpretive image.

Budget-Oriented Clip or Stock Art

If the budget is tight, consider using either clip or stock art. **Clip art**, often free, is an existing line-art drawing. *Stock art* typically must be purchased, and refers to existing photographs. Both options offer a diverse selection of images that can be used without the worries of copyright infringement. The only problem with using these types of images is they are not original imagery, or art created especially for advertising your brand. So there is a small chance stock or clip art may have been used in the ad of another brand. It is still possible for the art director to ensure a unique appearance by combining one or more photographs together and/or removing or cropping out unwanted areas.

The Visual Voice of Graphics

A *graphic* uses a combination of visuals and/or shapes and type to colorfully, symbolically, and uniquely represent an idea or concept.

Representational graphics, or logos, can solve a visual problem using abstract or realistic images that are often accompanied by text. Bright colors, often chosen for their symbolic meaning are combined with geometric and organic shapes to create modern and bold designs. These shapes, when used in a design, are often separate, disjointed images, and they are used to create a more whimsical or simplistic view of the brand and/or its use. If set off by a lot of white space, or placed in an unexpected location, this design style is not only interesting but often screams off the page, especially if surrounded by advertising using traditional photography. Graphic images have been used to represent some of advertising's most iconic brand images, such as tech-giant Apple's Apple, McDonald's Golden Arches, Nike's swoosh, and the Breast Cancer Campaign's Pink Ribbon, to name just a few.

When designed especially for a brand, text is another type of expressive graphic image, as is the overall alignment, spacing, size, and color treatment used to create the company or brand's verbal personality.

Simple But Powerful Graphic Elements

If the goal is to clean up, align, divide, or announce, then the addition of simple graphic elements can help without dominating the overall design. These quiet, often unremarkable graphic elements might include lines, shapes, bars, and boxes that all add additional dimension and/or organization to an ad.

An emotionally charged line, as we have learned, can be straight, curved, thick, thin, wavy, or dashed. A simple single line can be used to divide the page or separate content, or used to control how the viewer's eyes move within the ad.

Very diverse in appearance and meaning, shapes can be either geometric or organic. They can hold an image, text, or color, and be stacked on top of, or overlap, other images. Functional shapes such as arrows can be used to show direction, and snipes and bursts can be used as bold announcement devices.

Graphic bars can be of any thickness and color. They can be used as an announcement device where type can be reversed out of the dark-colored bar to white, or some other lighter color to highlight important information. Graphic bars also help to break up the monotony of a grey copy-heavy page or screen with bold contrasts of color.

Typically, graphic images are very bold, since they often employ flat colors rather than tonal qualities. Color or the absence of color can create or fill any shape, reflect a mood, a use, or a brand's personality. Designers choose colors that are vibrant and that often have symbolic meaning. Whether boldly applied through multiple colors or more subtly through just one, color is iconic and memorable.

Outline with a Border or Frame

Use a border if you want to frame or confine your design. Borders or frames are not a required design element, for most mediums, but they can help in calling attention to your ad on the page or screen. Borders are often used as a graphic or decorative device, tying an ad together and setting it off from surrounding copy or other ads. These simple unobtrusive devices can also be added inside the ad around photographs, illustrations, or bulleted callout boxes, creating a defined focal point as well as allowing the art director to crop any image tightly and pull the reader's eye towards the center of the action. An additional option might be to add a drop shadow that appears around the bottom and one side of these boxes, giving it a three-dimensional feel, emphasizing it further.

Borders, in certain mediums, can also be used to define the dimensions or edges of an ad, or be inset in any medium. An *inset graphic border* is a half-inch smaller on all four sides than the printable or viewable size of an ad. They can either confine all images and type inside, creating a ring of white space around the ad, or allow the background colors to bleed off one or more sides.

Diverse in appearance, they can be fat, thin, double, or decorative, to name just a few. Borders also do not need to be consistent in size. For example, you may want to make both the top and bottom borders of the ad, slightly thicker than the sides; like an inset border, this visually shifts the weight away from the center of the ad, creating the illusion of additional white space and making the ad appear larger.

In the end, choice should reflect the overall design of the ad. Since they are a decorative device, borders should never interfere with the sales message or other images. So avoid overtly graphic or detailed illustrative borders. Using too many of these unnecessary images interferes with the visual/verbal message and clutters up the ad and eliminates large amounts of white space. Remember, less is always more. If white space is an issue, create more by eliminating the border. Good judgment should be used when deciding to border or not to border. Readability, legibility, and design esthetics should always dictate.

A Very Few Border Rules

There is nothing tacky about using graphic borders, unless they are used indiscriminately or incorrectly. Consider the following rule of thumb: For high-end stores and merchandise, use a thin or elegant-looking border, and for discount establishments, a heavier border might be required. Beyond these basic rules, look to your typeface for guidance. By matching the thickness of the border to the overall weight of your typeface you can create structure between components.

The take-away here is that visuals speak to the viewer or reader. Some are simple, others more complex, but each must be able to tell its own visual story. Choice will depend on the budget, the target, and the overall concept and medium in which the ad will be placed. There are few rules dictating which work better at solving the client's advertising problem and reaching the target. Because of this, it is up to the creative team to ensure its voice is strong, colorful, bold, and meaningful.

Bibliography

Hecker, Sidney and David W. Stewart. 1988. "Nonverbal Communication: Advertising's Forgotten Elements," in *Nonverbal Communication in Advertising*. Lexington, MA: Lexington.

Stribley, Mary. "30 Advertisement Design Tips That Turn Heads: Brilliant Case Studies." Retrieved from: www.canva.com/learn/advertisement-design-tips/.

Touchette, Amy. 2017. "Color vs. Black-and-White Photography: How Palette Affect What We See—and Feel." Retrieved from: https://photography.tutsplus.com/.../color-vs-black-and-white-photography-how-palette-affect-what-we-see-and-feel.

CHAPTER 5

Type as a Design Element

Chapter 5 Objectives

1. The reader will learn the vocabulary that defines type style and use.
2. The reader will understand types role in design.
3. The reader will understand type's diverse role in both print and digital advertising.

Type Choice Reflects Brand Image

Psychologically, the typeface used in logo, ad, and package design visually has as much to say as the message itself. Understanding the visual message of type is critical to executing your concept and building or maintaining a brand's image.

Type is more than functional; it should be thought of as a type of graphic voice for the brand. The typeface selected is not an impulsive or temporary choice, it will repetitively represent the brand in the same way as color, headline, layout style, or a spokesperson might do for years or even decades. Type is an art form of shapes, curves, circles, lines, and thicknesses. Using these diverse shapes to project both the brand's image and personality is an extension of the conceptual process. Type has a big job to do. No matter its appearance, it is important that it be both easy to read and understand at a glance, tell the brand's story, reflect the personality of the brand and the target audience, and reflect use.

Type seen on a printed page is very different from type seen on a digital screen. Sizing, spacing, and line lengths will differ, depending not only on where the ad will be seen but also in what size it will be viewed. In future chapters, we will deal with how type needs to be adjusted per medium. In this chapter, we will concentrate specifically on design aesthetics.

Of all the design elements we have discussed thus far, type design is arguably one of the most interpretive aspects of advertising design. However, there are rules, specifically dealing with both design, and readability and legibility issues. Once you know them, you can more easily adapt your choice to fit the variety of media vehicles any one ad may be seen in.

Type Is Both a Visual and Verbal Tool

The typeface used in an ad should reflect both its image and the key consumer benefit the concept is designed around. There are hundreds of different typefaces available to the creative team, each having its own voice and personality. As a way to further personalize a typeface for a brand, many art directors will alter a typeface's overall appearance by changing its weight, or the thickness or thinness of its lines and curves, tightening the space between letterforms and lines of text, or by lengthening or shortening parts of the letterform. The only hard and fast rule of type design is to ensure readability and legibility. *Readability* is achieved when the target can read an ad quickly, meaning that it is not too small, too tightly kerned or leaded, too decorative, set in an unfamiliar format, or has lost some of its clarity during printing. *Legibility* refers to whether, in that short look, the target could read and understand the entire message. The search for the most appropriate and personable typeface should begin with the creative brief and initial brainstorming sessions to strategically ensure the brand's key consumer benefit is accurately represented.

The Vocabulary of Type Design

Thanks to the diverse array of typefaces, finding the right one to represent the brand conceptually will take some work. Start by determining the style you want to use. There are five distinct varieties of *type styles*: Serif, sans serif, script, display or decorative, and modern. Use depends on your concept, the target

DOI: 10.4324/9781003255123-6

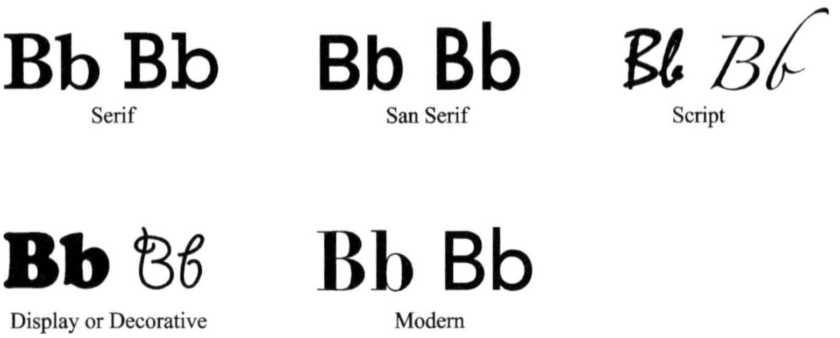

Bb Bb
Serif

Bb Bb
San Serif

Bb Bb
Script

Bb Bb
Display or Decorative

Bb Bb
Modern

Figure 5.1 Examples of the different styles of type.

audience to be reached, media choice, type size, and brand image. Let's take a look at each one. See Figure 5.1 for examples.

Type Styles

Serif

A *serif* typeface has delicate lines that are attached to the end of a larger, thicker stroke or line that protrudes from the edges of the letters. These thinner lines can appear at either the top and/or bottom of a letterform. This elegant style has a traditional, sophisticated and stable appearing personality, with many having a more feminine appearance. Brands employing this type style can project both respectability and long-standing reputations, or can appear stoic and uptight.

Serif typefaces are often used in print for smaller, lengthier text blocks because it is easier to read. More introverted in appearance when used at smaller sizes, this diverse set of type styles does not concern itself with doing anything more than creatively delivering the brand's message. Popular typefaces include Baskerville, Garamond, Georgia and Times Roman.

Sans serif

Sans serif typefaces have no thin lines attached. This simple and straightforward style has a more masculine, modern, clean, and geometric feel. The type you are currently reading is an example of a sans serif typeface. Having few adornments, sans serif styles place greater emphasis on the message and less on type design elements. This style is often used for larger copy blocks in digital media. Popular typefaces include Futura, Gill Sans, Helvetica and Verdana.

Script

Script type styles replicate handwriting giving them a more personal appeal. Very feminine in appearance script styles project elegance, friendship and intimacy. It works best when used in small amounts such as in logo designs because it can be difficult to read. Popular typefaces include Landone, Mistral, Punchello, Snell Roundhand, Swoon, Trinket and Zapfino.

Display

Display or decorative type styles have a loud voice and often an unusual or irregular appearance meant to attract attention. Because of this, they need to be large in size to be more easily read. They can have serif or sans serif characteristics and may tend to be more interesting to look at than practical to use. Because of their unique appearances, they are best used in small amounts such as in logos and headlines and subheads, due to readability and legibility issues.

Display or decorative typefaces are not meant to be used for large blocks of copy. This style can scream out your key consumer benefit or brand name with personality and impact. Don't get caught up in their voice. When incorrectly or overused, they can make your design look tacky and amateurish and often completely unreadable. Popular typefaces include Cooper Black, Giddy Up, Spaceage Round, and Valencia.

Modern

A *modern* type style can project a corporate, forward-thinking, trendy, and futuristic personality. Younger audiences in particular find modern styles to be more progressive and stylish. They can run the gamut from simple and utilitarian to new-age elegance. Many styles are better suited for use in logo design than ad design due to not only readability and legibility issues but also the fact many come in only all caps or overly expanded or condensed styles. Popular typefaces include Bodoni, Didot and Elephant.

Typefaces

Each set of styles is categorized by its *typeface* or name, such as Futura or Times, that identifies its unique set of letters, numbers, and punctuation. All typefaces are a larger part of a type family, which includes all the sizes, styles, and weights associated with that particular typeface. A *font* consists of all upper- and lowercase letters, numbers, and punctuation for a specific typeface. More simply, you buy a font package and use a specific typeface in your ad or graphic design.

The majority of available typefaces come in diverse weights. *Weight* refers to the thickness or thinness of the typeface's body. Very diverse in appearance, a typeface's weights come in a graduated range of thicknesses, such as ultra light, light, book, medium, demi bold, bold, ultra bold, and ultra black, to name just a few. Many will have stylized versions such as narrow, condensed, extended, italic, or all caps.

Alternating weights is a great way to attract attention, create eye flow, and add contrast to the page. But, as with all design elements, don't go overboard; too many combinations can compromise the design. Weight can also be used to give a typeface a more masculine or feminine appeal. For example, Futura is a clean but robust sans serif typeface, featuring shapely lines, triangles, squares, and circles that can go from elegant to authoritative. It is a good representative of form over function, since it lacks any decorative appendices. Diverse Futura comes in an assorted range of weights including light, medium, and bold oblique options, book, medium, demi, heavy, extra bold, bold, and varied weights of condensed options. You might also consider looking at your brand for help with type choice. Its overall appearance may help you decide whether choice should be thick, round, short and squat, or tall, thin, and wiry. See Figure 5.2 for examples.

Gill Sans

Gill Sans

Gill Sans

Gill Sans

Gill Sans

Gill Sans

Gill Sans

Gill Sans

Gill Sans

(Top to bottom): Gill Sans Light, Light Italic, Regular, Italic, SemiBold, SemiBold Italic, Bold, Bold Italic, and UltraBold.

Figure 5.2 Example of the different weights for a single typeface.

Type Size and the Up and Down of Letterforms

A typeface's overall size or height affects what you want the reader to see first, second, and so on, and can be used to create contrast on the page or screen. Like the choice of typeface and style, a typeface's size can directly affect readability.

The height of a letterform's body is measured in points. *Points* are very small measurement devices; to help you out, there are 72 points to an inch. This can be deceiving since not all typefaces are sized equally. Size deals more with the physical space the letterform occupies than its actual measurable size. Most typefaces are available in multiple sizes. Any design software can set any face at any size.

To ensure readability, what size you use will depend on the job your type has to do. For example, attract attention with largest boldest text, inform further with medium-sized text, tell the brand's story with the smaller text, and tell them what they need to know about how to buy and/or how to contact customer service with the smallest text. If the design uses any banners or body copy subheads, they should be noticeably smaller than any headline or main subheads. Your ad might look something like this:

Headline:	42 points, with
Leading of	39 points
Main Subhead:	22 points, with
Leading of	20 points
Secondary Subhead:	16 points, with
Leading of	14 points
Banner:	18 points
Body Copy:	11 points, with
Leading of	12 points
Detail Copy:	8 points, with
Leading of	9 points

As you work—and become more familiar—with the various typefaces available to you, sizing will become less complicated.

Finally, not all targeted groups view text in the same way. For example, a younger demographic will be attracted to less formal layouts and will have no trouble reading or viewing lighter, smaller-sized text (10-to-12 point), whereas older consumers typically prefer cleaner, more structured layouts that use larger (12-to-14 point) type sizes and somewhat bulkier typefaces.

Size is also affected by *x-height* or the height of a typeface's lowercase letters, and the length and height of the face's ascenders and descenders. *Ascenders* are the part of the letterform that extends upward from the main body of a letter, as with the letters "b," "k," "h," "d" and sometimes "i" depending on the height of the dot. *Descenders* are the part of the letterform that extends downward below the *baseline*, or the invisible line that type sits on, as with the letters "g," "p," and "j." Ascenders and descenders play an important role in how close or open the spacing between lines of text will appear and ultimately a typeface's overall graphic appeal. See Figure 5.3.

The Manipulation of White Space Between Lines of Text and Letterforms

Beyond style, and weight a typeface can also be manipulated and personalized by altering the space between lines of text and letterforms.

Leading and Line Spacing

The terms "line spacing" and "leading" are both used to describe the amount of white space between lines of text. The difference depends on where you are in the development process. *Line spacing* is used to describe line spacing in design. *Leading* is a computer and printing term that assigns a specific numerical point value to the amount of white space appearing between lines of text. See Figure 5.4.

How much white space to show between lines of text is a designer and media choice. The tighter you make your line spacing, the

more elements will need to be manipulated. For example, if you like tight spacing, that shows less white space between lines of text, then ascenders and descenders can often get in the way and must be designed around. This means the art director gets to manipulate or slightly redesign the typeface. A few options include connecting an ascender from one line to the descender on another, or you might just want to remove small sections and shorten each ascender and descender evenly. No matter whether you prefer open and airy or closed and compact, there are some basic rules of thumb to keep in mind. Copy set in larger point sizes such as headlines or subheads will often have the least amount of white space between lines, giving them more bulk from other components on the page or screen. When working with leading, each line will need to be manually manipulated. The goal is for all lines, whether they were manipulated or not, to *appear* equally spaced.

Alternatively, type set in a smaller point size like body or detail copy needs additional white space inserted between lines of text, to make it easier to read. For example, in print, body copy set at 10 point, with 11 points of leading between lines of text. This means the white space between lines of text, will be slightly more than the height of a 10-point capital letter. Leading is measured from baseline to baseline or from one line of text to another, and in this example it is the height or depth of an 11-point capital letter. Size will ultimately depend on the typeface chosen. Readability is enhanced if body copy is set at least 10 on 11, or

ascender
x-height
baseline
descender

Figure 5.3 Example showing ascenders, descenders, x-height, and baseline.

Copy Is Fun Any Way You Wink At It

Headline: 36-point Times Roman with 33-points of leading. Letters and words have been kerned.

Copy Is Fun Any Way You Wink At It

Headline: 36-point Times Roman with 36-points of leading. No word or letter kerning.

Figure 5.4 Example of no leading or kerning.

Copy is funny any way you wink at it yet it allows you to ramble on no matter the date or time of day.
    When the tiger reads he purrs with delight until the hyena nips him in the bud and attempts to steal his reading material. That would be okay but the tiger has a family to educate on top of everything else.
    Kicky copy raises the hair on the back of the porcupines' neck. He prefers a good mystery about the Savanna any day of the week. The plots are much more interesting and he may have met one or two of the characters.

Copy is funny any way you wink at it yet it allows you to ramble on no matter the date or time of day.
    When the tiger reads he purrs with delight until the hyena nips him in the bud and attempts to steal his reading material. That would be okay but the tiger has a family to educate on top of everything else.
    Kicky copy raises the hair on the back of the porcupines' neck. He prefers a good mystery about the Savanna any day of the week. The plots are much more interesting and he may have met one or two of the characters.

Copy set 10 pt. with 10 pts. of leading and a 1/4" indent.

Copy set 10 pt. with 11 pts. of leading and a 1/4" indent.

Figure 5.5 Examples of body copy showing leading.

Copywriting

Example With No Kerning

Copywriting

Example With Kerning

Figure 5.6 Examples of kerning.

11 on 12. If space is at a premium, small text could be set on itself; in this case, the leading is the same size as the type size, for example, 10 on 10, or 11 on 11, also known as set solid. See Figure 5.5.

Why is leading so important? Your eye uses the space between lines of text to travel back from the right margin to the left, to the next line of text. By increasing the amount of space between lines of text, you not only eliminate the chance of your target rereading the same line of text twice, but also make reading smaller text easier.

Kerning and Letterspacing

Letterspacing, a design term, and *kerning*, a computer term, refer to the removal or addition of white space between letterforms. Kerning is a term, used in both printing and digital design, where a number represented in points, most often a negative one, is assigned to the space between letterforms.

Kerning allows the designer to manually adjust the space between letterforms for a more tailored and personalized appearance. Tightening the letterspacing and line spacing and sometimes even the word spacing allows you to enlarge your headline, creating even more emphasis to draw in your reader or viewer. As a rule, because of their size, headlines need the most kerning, with

subheads following close behind. Because it would drastically affect readability and legibility, small text such as body or detail copy is rarely if ever kerned in any medium. See Figure 5.6 for examples.

Depending on the letter combinations, and the difference between typefaces and designer preferences, how much kerning you do will vary. Certain letter combinations appearing together can be problematic, for example, those with strong slants such as V, A, W, and Y, or those with wide arms and legs such as a T or L, will often need additional kerning or manipulation. Words set in all caps, such as ENTRANCE, will almost always have inconsistent spacing issues. If you squint at the letterforms, with this narrow view, you will see the inconsistent spacing between the letters RA as compared to the other letterforms. By kerning, or closing up the space between these letters, the designer can alleviate inconsistent spacing that can oftentimes make one word look like two. Sans serif faces can look blocky if over-kerned, so watch spacing. Serif typefaces on the other hand, allow you to overlap serifs to get an even tighter look without affecting readability or legibility. Like line spacing, the amount of the kerning between individual letters is up to the art directors. Consistency is key; kerning or leading adjustments should not be noticeable to the target. See Figure 5.7.

How do you know if you've kerned or leaded too tightly or inconsistently? Some designers suggest a great way to ensure the consistency of both your kerning and leading is to look at it upside down. By upending your text, the eye will focus more on letter and line pairings rather than on reading what is said. Another option as previously mentioned, is to print out a copy and give it the old squint test. If you see an equal amount of visual, not mathematical, white space between each letterform or line of text, it's not only consistent in appearance but both readable and legible. This freeform type of measurement is known as *eyeballing,* because the letterforms have not been systematically or equally spaced. The goal is to ensure any manual manipulation of letterforms *appear* to be equally spaced. How much manipulation will be done, will depend on the designer, the typeface, size, line breaks, and the media the ad apppears in. You do not want one line or combination of letters to appear tighter than the others. They must match visually, not

ENTRANCE
ENTRANCE

Large serif text especially if set in all caps often needs kerning between letterforms. Do no be afraid to touch or overlap serifs.

ENTRANCE
ENTRANCE

Large sans serif type whether set in all caps or not often needs less kerning between letterforms. Be careful you don't kern to tightly. Avoid over tightening letterforms when possible to ensure maximum readability and legibility.

Figure 5.7 Example of the kerning needed when using all caps.

mathematically. Be careful, there are extremes to both kerning and leading, for example, type that has been kerned or leaded too tightly can become an unreadable blob, not a design element. Type that is too open, on the other hand, can become a white hole, breaking up the design. The take-away: Don't over-design your type, manipulate where needed, and let the rest go.

In the end, design-driven leading and kerning should be not be thought of as an occasional need, but as a type of signature that will become a part of the brand's distinctive identity.

Type Alignment: Setting Type on the Page or Screen

Type alignment refers to the way type is aligned on the page or screen, and is driven by the layout style employed. The ease with which type is read can also be affected by how it's visually placed on the page. There are five ways that type can be represented in an ad: 1) Center on center, 2) flush left, ragged right, 3) flush right, ragged left, 4) justified left and right, and 5) wrapped. See Figure 5.8 for examples.

Text that is set center on center or has one line centered over another is a balanced way to emphasize your headline or subhead. Best used with headlines featuring multiple lines of copy, this alignment can create white space and improve both readability and legibility when multiple line-breaks alternate between short-long-short or long-short-long pattern. It is best to avoid setting body copy center on center; not only is it difficult to read, but the text often looks more like a greeting card or poem rather than informative copy.

Body copy is most easily read when set flush left, ragged right. This alignment look begins each line of text along the same set-left margin. The end of each line is of varying lengths. Depending on the layout style employed, it is not uncommon to see headlines and subheads set in this alignment. Type can also be set flush right, rag left. This alignment is typically used when the design uses two columns of copy that wrap around a visual placed between the two blocks of copy.

A justified left and right alignment style aligns both left and right sides of the text to set margins, creating lines of equal lengths on both sides of the text block. Most commonly seen in newspapers, direct mail, or brochures, this alignment style often features multiple hyphens, which should be avoided at all costs, no matter the alignment, to avoid unsightly gaps between words, and one or more words that are stretched out across the column. Because of its inconsistent look, it is not used often in ad design. When it *is* used, these inconsistencies must be designed out, or written to fit the space. Not only is this time-consuming and thus expensive, it often ends up as a large gray blob of text, if not broken-up by multiple subheads. Using a justified alignment for headlines and subheads should also be avoided, unless your goal is to create an impenetrable-looking wall of text.

Another popular alignment is called a text wrap. A *text wrap* is used when type is designed to specifically wrap around a visual. To ensure the visual/verbal components operate as one thought, it is crucial the wrap follow the shape of the image as closely as possible, to avoid a disjointed look or irregular holes of white space appearing at the end of lines. For larger canvasses, it is important for the text to have at least one-quarter inch of white space between columns of text or around any visual. This gutter, or white space, keeps the eye from getting lost in the visual, or from jumping from column to column. Smaller canvasses will typically use one-eighth of white space. The amount of body copy, the layout style chosen, and the media will all play a role in which alignment style you employ, as well as how many columns of copy you will use. See Figure 5.9 for an example.

Columns

The length of typed lines of smaller text also can affect readability and legibility. Body copy, or the small storytelling text, can be set in either one column or in two or more columns. Body copy, just like the rest of the page, needs to be designed, so there are a few things to consider. Depending on the size of the ad, the length for a single column of text should be no longer than 6 inches, or 50–70 characters for a Web ad; anything longer makes eye movement back to the left margin more difficult for readers. See Figure 5.10 for a two-column example.

Copy is funny any way you wink at it yet it allows you to ramble on no matter the date or time of day.

When the tiger reads he purrs with delight until the hyena nips him in the bud and attempts to steal his reading material. That would be okay but the tiger has a family to educate on top of everything else.

Kicky copy raises the hair on the back of the porcupines' neck. He prefers a good mystery about the Savanna any day of the week. The plots are much more interesting and he may have met one or two of the characters.

Great for headlines and subheads, body copy set **center on center** has a greeting card appearance making it hard to read. This text shows a hypen and an orphan, both should be avoided.

Copy is funny any way you wink at it yet it allows you to ramble on no matter the date or time of day.

When the tiger reads he purrs with delight until the hyena nips him in the bud and attempts to steal his reading material. That would be okay but the tiger has a family to educate on top of everything else.

Kicky copy raises the hair on the back of the porcupines' neck. He prefers a good mystery about the Savanna any day of the week. The plots are much more interesting and he may have met one or two of the characters.

Great for headlines, subheads, and body copy **flush left, rag right** text is clean and easy to read. By indenting each paragraph you increase the amount of viewable white space.

Copy is funny any way you wink at it yet it allows you to ramble on no matter the date or time of day.

When the tiger reads he purrs with delight until the hyena nips him in the bud and attempts to steal his reading material. That would be okay but the tiger has a family to educate on top of everything else.

Kicky copy raises the hair on the back of the porcupines' neck. He prefers a good mystery about the Savanna any day of the week. The plots are much more interesting and he may have met one or two of the characters.

Flush right, rag left alignment is a great choice when setting type in two coloumns that wrap around a central image.

Copy is funny any way you wink at it yet it allows you to ramble on no matter the date or time of day.

When the tiger reads he purrs with delight until the hyena nips him in the bud and attempts to steal his reading material. That would be okay but the tiger has a family to educate on top of everything else.

Kicky copy raises the hair on the back of the porcupines' neck. He prefers a good mystery about the Savanna any day of the week. The plots are much more interesting and he may have met one or two of the characters.

Justified alignment inserts unwanted hyphens and condenses and pulls type into unattracctive lines that are often very difficult to read.

Figure 5.8 Examples of the different types of alignments.

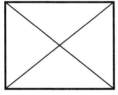

Copy is funny any way you wink at it yet it allows you to ramble on no matter the date or time of day.

When the tiger reads he purrs with delight until the hyena nips him in the bud and attempts to steal his reading material. That would be okay but the tiger has a family to educate on top of everything else.

Kicky copy raises the hair on the back of the porcupines' neck. He prefers a good mystery about the Savanna any day of the week. The plots are much more interesting and he may have previously met one or two of the more interesting characters.

Figure 5.9 Example of a simple text wrap.

Text set in multiple columns will measure anywhere from 3 to 4¼ inches wide. For balance, make sure all columns are of equal width and depth. The last column can be shorter if balanced with the logo wrapped into the column. Using quarter-inch *gutters*, or white space, between columns is fairly standard across mediums. Anything more and the eye has to jump too far. Anything closer and the reader could mistakenly read across the gutter rather than down the column. See Figure 5.11 for a text-wrap example.

For digital projects, because of their diverse sizes, unlike print, line length is not always a fixed size. Length will depend on the viewer's platform (that is, Mac or PC), browser and version, the resolution of the screen, set preferences, and how the text is coded. What is consistent across all media is the overall design aesthetics and need for all copy to be readable and legible.

Finally, it is also important when designing with one or more columns of copy to watch out for widows and orphans and

Copy is funny any way you wink at it yet it allows you to ramble on no matter the date or time of day.

When the tiger reads he purrs with delight until the hyena nips him in the bud and attempts to steal his reading material. That would be okay but the tiger has a family to educate on top of everything else.

Kicky copy raises the hair on the back of the porcupines' neck. He prefers a good mystery about the Savanna any day of the week. The plots are much more interesting and he may have met one or two of the characters.

Termites love to read at breakfast, it tastes the same to them no matter the genre. Color offers an especially tasty treat, better than eating a cactus or carcass in the a.m. It's also a family affair to be shared on a warm summer night with the kids, grandma and the neighboring mounds.

Copy is funny any way you wink at it yet it allows you to ramble on no matter the date or time of day.

When the tiger reads he purrs with delight until the hyena nips him in the bud and attempts to steal his reading material. That would be okay but the tiger has a family to educate on top of everything else.

Kicky copy raises the hair on the back of the porcupines' neck. He prefers a good mystery about the Savanna any day of the week. The plots are much more interesting and he may have met one or two of the characters.

Termites love to read at breakfast, it tastes the same to them no matter the genre. Color offers an especially tasty treat, better than eating a cactus or carcass in the a.m. It's also a family affair to be shared on a warm summer night with the kids, grandma and the neighboring mounds.

Figure 5.10 Example showing two columns of equal width and depth with a gutter of a quarter-inch.

Copy is funny any way you wink at it yet it allows you to ramble on no matter the date or time of day.

When the tiger reads he purrs with delight until the hyena nips him in the bud and attempts to steal his reading material. That would be okay but the tiger has a family to educate on top of everything else.

Kicky copy raises the hair on the back of the porcupines' neck. He prefers a good mystery about the Savanna any day of the week. The plots are much more interesting and he may have met one or two of the characters.

Termites love to read at breakfast, it tastes the same to them no matter the genre. Color offers an especially tasty treat, better than eating a cactus or carcass in the a.m. It's also a family affair to be shared on a warm summer night with the kids, grandma and the neighboring mounds.

Copy is funny any way you wink at it yet it allows you to ramble on no matter the date or time of day.

When the tiger reads he purrs with delight until the hyena nips him in the bud and attempts to steal his reading material. That would be okay but the tiger has a family to educate on top of everything else.

Kicky copy raises the hair on the back of the porcupines' neck. He prefers a good mystery about the Savanna any day of the week. The plots are much more interesting and he may have met one or two of the characters.

Termites love to read at breakfast, it tastes the same to them no matter the genre. Color offers an especially tasty treat, better than eating a cactus or carcass in the a.m. It is also a wee family affair to be shared at night.

LOGO

Figure 5.11 Example shows two columns of copy set equal width and depth with a logo wrap.

Copy is funny any way you wink at it yet it allows you to ramble on no matter the date or time of day.

When the tiger reads he purrs with delight until the hyena nips him in the bud and attempts to steal his reading material. That would be okay but the tiger has a family to educate on top of everything else.

Kicky copy raises the hair on the back of the porcupines' neck. He prefers a good mystery about the Savanna any day of the week. The plots are much more interesting and he may have met one or two of the characters.

Termites love to read at breakfast, it tastes the same to them no matter the genre. Color offers an especially tasty treat, better than eating a cactus or carcass in the a.m. It's also a family affair to be shared on a warm summer night with the kids, grandma and the neighboring

mounds.

Copy is funny any way you wink at it yet it allows you to ramble on no matter the date or time of day.

When the tiger reads he purrs with delight until the hyena nips him in the bud and attempts to steal his reading material. That would be okay but the tiger has a family to educate on top of everything else.

Kicky copy raises the hair on the back of the porcu-pines' neck. He prefers a good mystery about the Savanna any day of the week. The plots are much more interesting and he may have met one or two of the characters.

Termites love to read at breakfast, it tastes the same to them no matter the genre. Color offers an especially tasty treat, better than eating a cactus or carcass in the a.m. It's also a family affair to be shared on a warm summer night with the kids, grandma and neighboring mounds.

Figure 5.12 Column 1 shows an example of a widow at the end of Paragraph 3. Column 2 shows an orphan at the top of the column, and an offensive hyphen in Paragraph 4.

eliminate them when they do appear. Although these two terms are often used interchangeably, the important thing to know is never use either one. A *orphan* occurs when one word, or the last line of a paragraph of copy appears at the top of the second column of type. A *widow* on the other hand, is a single word or first line of a paragraph at the end of a paragraph. These unwanted stragglers create a visual interruption not only to readability but also to the design. And for the first time, the resulting extra and unwanted white space from either offense, can cause the ad to look both messy and unbalanced. See Figure 5.12 for an example.

Indents

Using paragraph indents, typically a quarter-inch for body copy, is a quick and easy way to increase white space. It also makes the body copy appear shorter and less blocky and thus more readable. Another way to accomplish this is to insert multiple subheads into large blocks of text to break up the copy into smaller, more digestible, chunks.

Over-Designing: Common Type Faux Pas

Type is a design element, and art directors love manipulating it. However, over-designing can negatively affect readability and legibility. The need to "design" with type can often result in solutions that have neither rhyme nor reason and as a result, junk up the design. Remember the old adage: "Just because you can do it, doesn't mean you should." Let's take a look at a few of the most common design faux pas. See Figure 5.13.

All Caps

This unexpected type presentation is hard to read and should be avoided. It is best used when a headline is no more than one to three words long or the design uses little to no body copy. Since we are used to seeing a caps/lowercase look in almost all text-heavy materials, an all-caps format will make reading slower and tedious. The use of all caps also requires a great deal more manipulation to both letter and line spacing.

ABCDEFGHIJKLMN OPQRSTUVWXYZ

All Caps

ABCDEFGHIJKLMN OPQRSTUVWXYZ

Reverse

ABCDEFGHIJKLMN OPQRSTUVWXYZ

All italicized Caps

Decorative faces are great for logo design but should be avoided due to readability issues on advertising pieces.

Figure 5.13 Decorative faces are great for logo design, but should be avoided due to readability issues on most advertising designs.

Reverse Copy

Text that is considered reversed is set with white or light-colored text on a black or dark-colored background. The use of reversed text for large blocks of copy should be avoided. Readability is difficult because small reverse text is not only hard on the eyes but, depending on the paper stock or screen resolution, the background color can bleed into the copy, causing it to fill-in or drop out. Reverse text works best for larger point sizes such as headlines, subheads, and banner announcements, like those announcing grand openings or a new location.

Italics

Italics, due to the same readability issues discussed earlier, should also be avoided. Italics imply importance or emphasis, such as to highlight a single word or phrase, or a quotation, so use them sparingly.

Display or Decorative Faces

The more fancy or froufrou typefaces falling under this category have limited uses in advertising design. Those that boast

elaborate flourishes and decorative appearances specifically, make readability and legibility almost impossible in any media. However, these extroverted and personable typefaces can often be used successfully in logo design.

The Rules of Type Design Are Malleable

After vocabulary, it is important young designers understand the fundamental rules or the principles behind type design. All rules can be broken or at the very least manipulated, but you must know the rules before you can do either. Provided that readability and legibility are not compromised, you can avoid playing by the rules so long as any type alterations are used consistently and repetitively throughout the design.

The more effective ways to emphasize and combine varied typefaces and styles usually rely on a few basic typographic principles. Let's take a look at a few of the most common rules that directly affect design.

Control the number of typefaces used in an ad. Copy has an important job to do, ensure readability and legibility. No ad should use more than two typefaces per layout. Consider choosing an extroverted typeface for large text such as headlines, subheads, announcement devices, and prices, and an introverted or more neutral-feeling face for body and detail copy. Before adding an additional typeface, ask yourself, can I accomplish what I want to do by varying the weight or size of the existing face(s)?

It is important to point out that logo designs are not a part of this count. Although covered in more depth in Chapter 10, logos are considered a graphic element and as such are not considered a separate typeface or subject to the same readability and legibility standards.

There are no rules on the number of different weights or point sizes that can be used within a design, but for an ad to look both unified and structured, the number should be controlled. Too few variations and there is not enough contrast on the page or screen; too many, and eye flow is disrupted, resulting in an ad that can appear messy and disorganized, both of which affect readability and legibility.

There have never been any set rules governing the mixing of serif and sans serif styles in a design but there are a few things to initially consider. Typically, they can be mixed together without incident thanks to the diversity in sizing, weights, spacing, and color options, making these pairings an expressive way to design with type. When combining varied type styles go for contrast, but watch out for conflict. Different isn't always harmonious. Generally speaking, no matter how diverse in appearance, typefaces that pair well together will share or have similar qualities such as overall proportion, geometric or organic shaping, or even comparative x-heights. You might also look for a single typeface that comes in both a serif and sans serif versions. Newer faces known as *super-families* are specifically designed to complement each other making pairing easier such as with Museo and Museo Sans. But be careful, these are safe and may be overused by too many brands.

Mixing type styles is not a requirement nor is it considered taboo, but when carefully considered, it is a viable design option. The key to such use is to be sure both typefaces, no matter the style, complement each other without clashing or mimicking the other too closely. Figuring out what works and what doesn't will take a bit of experimentation and basic trial and error.

One of the safer design options is to pair typefaces from the same type family. Your best bet will be to choose from families that have a range of weights, styles, and upper- and lower-case options. By using a single style throughout, you can achieve a unified look thanks to the built-in compatibility. Be sure to increase contrast by varying type size and weight. See Figure 5.14 for some examples.

The choice to use a single font family is almost foolproof and thus a safe one for young designers. The perfect combination is built in, so the need for a time-consuming search to find that great "pairing" is greatly reduced, if not eliminated altogether.

Another consideration is ensuring the typeface is historically accurate for the brand. New-age technology should not speak through a traditional-looking typeface.

Beyond shape and form, eye flow, readability, and legibility can also be controlled with color. Black type is not the only color option available to the designer. Use of other dark colors such as navy, dark green, or brown, are easily readable, can be used to portray an emotion, create contrasts, and say more psychologically than standard black type. However, small text is always easier to read when reproduced in black. Type set in light or pastel colors should be avoided, especially when set in a small point size. The lack of contrast between the type and the stark white of the printed page or digital screen, makes the type difficult to see and again slows the reader down, making them reread in order to understand the message.

Finally, and on a more cautious note, smaller amounts of type do not have to be set horizontally. Other options include placing headlines or announcement devices vertically down

Powerful
Practical
Imaginative

Elegant
Graceful
Delicate

Authority
Diplomatic
Casual

Figure 5.14 Fonts from the same type family pair well together and can have distinctly different personalities. The families used here include Arial Black, Arial Narrow, Arial Rounded MT Bold, Baskerville Bold, Baskerville SemiBold Italic, Baskerville Regular, Rockwell Extra Bold, Rockwell Bold Italic, and Rockwell Regular.

the side of the page or screen. This is a great idea if you are considering designing in an asymmetrical format. Type set on an angle or on a curve should be used sparingly. Not only can readability and legibility be adversely affected by any alternative direction, but the overall look of your design can also suffer, creating a cluttered, unruly look that often lacks eye flow. If you are compelled to set type on a curve or an angle, to avoid a disjointed look or unsightly white hole be sure to repeat the pattern somewhere else in the ad or run it around a visual, matching the shapes to create a more organized appearance.

Using type as a design element is an art. It is important for young designers to understand that type does more than speak for the brand; it also visually and verbally represents the emotions of the words, as well as the reflects the brand's image and the target's self-image, in its unadorned lines, peaks, and valleys, or colorful rounded curves. The more you know about the basic rules of type design, the better you will get at developing and defining its visual and verbal role of pairing the art of design with the goal of business.

Print: The Breakdown of the Typeface Generation

Type quality is affected by the diverse steps leading up to printing. When you are working on your ad design in Photoshop, InDesign, and Illustrator, the images you see are first generation or their teen years. The file is then packaged up and sent to the printer where they will utilize a computer-to-plate system that reproduces the ad directly onto aluminum plates; this is generation two, or the middle-age years. The plates reproduce the ad onto paper, creating generation number three, or the retirement years. Although printing processes have improved drastically over the decades, unless your ad is seen online where it can keep its relatively youthful glow, or is printed on a digital printer (used for small press runs), it has to go through at least two or more generations before being viewed by your target. With each generation, if care is not taken to understand and pretest how your typefaces and their varied sizes will print on the chosen paper stock, you could have type that begins to fall apart causing both appearance and readability issues.

Type quality can also be adversely affected when placing certain serif typefaces or those with exceptionally thin lines, on a dark or heavily screened background. The thinner areas of smaller text in particular, can "fall out" or even "fill in" during printing on uncoated paper stocks. Once parts of your typeface disappear, not only is the integrity of the design affected but readability and legibility are as well. See Figure 5.15 for some examples.

So if you're choosing a serif face for packaging or direct mail for example, be sure it's at the slightly bulkier end of the spectrum. Most sans serif typefaces work great on uncoated paper stocks; they are sturdy enough, and often fat enough, to withstand multiple generations of printing on lower-quality paper.

Figure 5.15 These typefaces would be difficult to read in any medium. In print, specifically, thick-to-thin faces can lose clarity when pieces "drop out" during printing, affecting readability. Be sure to select a face that will hold up on coarse or textured paper stocks.

The Differences Between Type for Page Design and Digital

Digital media has special requirements distinctly different from print. The most important aspect of moving from print to digital is to make sure the same typeface is employed across both print and digital pieces. Unfortunately, this is not always possible. But today it is very easy to choose a face that matches almost exactly. Small changes are typically not noticed by consumers. In digital design, it is important you use a typeface that is web-safe—that is, one that displays correctly not only on a website but across different browsers and devices. Digital typefaces have often been modified to enhance readability. Alterations might include 1) a taller x-height, 2) shortened ascenders and descenders, 3) wider letterforms, 4) more white space inserted between letterforms, 5) thin type lines and serifs made heavier, reducing the contrast between thick to thin lines, and 6) modified curves and angles. The only thing that should never change is the brand's logo, which is primarily imported as an image.

Typically, the typeface used on digital devices should be sans serif, especially for small text like body copy. This type style not only displays better than most serif style faces on varied digital platforms but is also easier to read. However, as screen resolutions increase, serif typefaces have become much easier to read and thus more prevalent on digital pieces. Because of its legibility issues, it is best to avoid script or decorative typefaces on digital pieces. Like print, type size depends on the device but as a general rule the minimum size is 14–16 point for body copy; for larger text like headlines, can typically range from 18–48 point. Line lengths also need to be controlled and will differ depending on where the content will be viewed. Typically, the ideal line length is anywhere from 50–75 characters including spaces and punctuation.

Thanks to the larger typefaces used on digital material, the type needs more white space than print material. Digital leading is referred to as *line height* due to how the back-end code works. When front-end designers are working on digital pieces, the general rule of thumb is that the leading should be 120 percent of the useable typeface at a minimum. For example, if the type size of the body copy is 16 point, then the leading would be around 19 to 20 point. Kerning is something that should be avoided when possible on digital pieces. Like leading, the more white space the easier it is to read and understand what is being said. Because of this, it is best to keep your kerning at the default or pre-set settings. Typefaces that are naturally tightly kerned should be avoided when possible, or you will need to open up the kerning to improve readability.

Type Design for Multiple Media Vehicles

There is no formula or set of rules for choosing a typeface that will speak for your brand across multiple media vehicles, just a lot of old-fashioned trial and error. Before deciding on any representative typeface, go back and reread the creative brief. Make sure you understand what you are being asked to do and whether your type needs to tell a detailed story, set a mood, take a subservient role to the main visual, or speak on the visual's behalf. Remember, type choice does more than tell the brand's story, it is also a powerful design element. When choosing a typeface for your brand, consider the following: 1) Know what typeface or faces competitors are using, 2) review your brainstorming sessions to help determine what face, style, and weight, will best represent the brand's image and conceptual direction, 3) know what media vehicles will be used, 4) know your intended target, and 5) know the brand's current life-cycle stage. The more you know, the better chance you will have to create a unique and coordinated visual/verbal look or message.

In the end, type choices require no small amount of research. Never settle on a typeface because you like it. Choice instead must match both the brand's and target's self-image, and use. Conceptually, type must visually and verbally speak for the brand, and must be readable and legible across all media vehicles employed, whether used on the web, in print, as mobile text, in a catalog, a brochure, or on out-of-home media (billboards, posters, etc.). If it cannot, keep looking.

As a design element, it is also important to know where and how the typeface will be used. Will it be used in headlines, body copy, or both? Will it be placed on top of a colored or screened background? Used in any reverses? Will it be set in a color or only in black? What type of paper stock will it be printed on? What size of screen will it be viewed on? How will that affect your choice? Knowledge of the media vehicles to be used will help determine choice and type design options.

Beyond speaking for the brand, the typeface chosen, if appropriate, should also reflect the ambience of the service or store in which it can be purchased. The openness or tightness of line and letterspacing can promote this look and feel further, creating a signature look for both the brand and store. Work with type; learn how to break or manipulate the rules; make it the client's, and in time, the brand's.

The Many Visual and Verbal Voices of Color

Chapter 6 Objectives

1. The reader will understand the theory and psychology behind the choice of colors used in an ad.
2. The reader will develop a strong understanding of color theory terms.
3. The reader will understand how color tells a brand's visual/verbal story locally and globally.

The Theory of Color

Just thinking about a certain color sends a visual message to our brain, which in turn elicits some kind of interpretive emotion. The meaning we assign colors are rooted in our cultural beliefs and the world in which we live. Because of this, we tend to react to a color on a subconscious level; we may be drawn to, or repulsed by, a color's brilliance, dullness, or neutrality.

Color, like the choice of visual and verbal message, has a very distinct, emotional, and psychological voice. To harness its evocative and associative nature, we must understand the theory behind its various hues. Very basically, color theory can be defined as a set of principles used to create harmonious color combinations. Artist Mark Chagall defined it more simply saying "all colors are the friends of their neighbors and the lovers of their opposites." To ensure you correctly harness the complexity of friendly and harmonious color, you need a color wheel. A *color wheel* helps the art director to understand how the target will perceive and react to a color and how colors mix, match, or clash. See Figure 6.1 for an example of a color wheel.

Color theory tells us that harmonious color combinations are created by using any two colors opposite each other on the color wheel (complementary colors), any three colors next to each other (analogous colors), or any three colors equally spaced around the wheel creating a triangle (triadic colors), or two pairs opposite each other, think rectangle (tetradic colors). These "harmonious" color combinations are known as *color schemes* or *color palettes* and are considered in harmony regardless of the wheels rotation angle.

Color attracts attention and ignites an emotional response. Over time, colors have become more definable as to how the target will react to certain colors, and less abstract or emotional. It is important to point out however, that depending on age, gender, experience, and country of origin, color can affect how your target both sees and interprets color. For example, bright colors attract a younger target, while an older target will prefer quieter, more subtle color combinations. Internationally, the color yellow, for example, may mean happiness in one culture and be considered vulgar in another.

Color is a mood enhancer and image definer. The more positive the relationship, between brand image, use, and the target, the better the chance of brand adoption. Not all purchases are entirely rationally based, some will be emotionally driven. Niche brand Harley Davidson, for example, sell more than motorcycles; they also sell a lifestyle and each purchaser sees that "color" differently. Because of this, there is no ideal color or combination of colors. The creative team has to understand the meaning behind colors to enhance and correctly project the visual and verbal message.

By understanding color theory, you can set a mood, show use, attract attention, develop a memorable brand identity, and enhance or create brand image. Color choice allows the brand to move through a range of emotions within varied environments.

Emotionally, color can take both your brand and your target, from a relaxed state of mind to one of excitement, affectively creating both a mental and physical reaction. So what do we need to know about color to build a strong brand identity, reflect brand image, and suggest a mood, use, and concept? First, you must

DOI: 10.4324/9781003255123-7

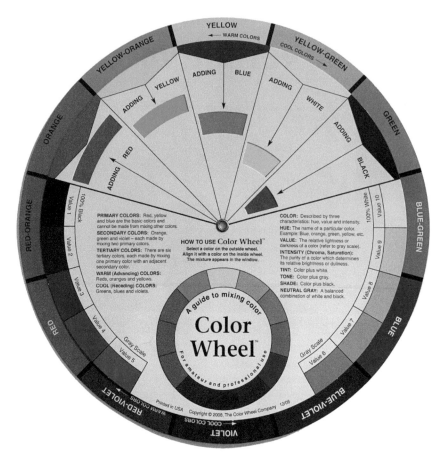

Figure 6.1 Example of a color wheel. Image courtesy of Robyn Blakeman, University of Tennessee.

understand how important color is to brand recognition. Color alone can increase a brand's identity by up to 80 percent. Think about the last time you walked down the detergent isle at the grocery store. Shelf after shelf of seemingly unending options appear on first glance to hide your favorite Tide Pods. But once you get your bearings, you zero in on the familiar orange container or even perhaps the colorful orange, blue, and yellow logo. After that it is a quick grab and drop into your basket and you move on. Color is powerful. A lot of research has been done on the physiological and psychological effects of color on both the brand and consumers. Consumers, for example, decide whether or not they prefer one product to another within 90 seconds or less. Ninety percent of that decision is based when applicable, exclusively on color. Studies have also shown that purchasing intent is affected by color based on whether or not choice is perceived as appropriate to not only the brand category but also the brand itself. Finally, and the most uncontrollable factor, 66 percent won't buy if the brand does not come in their preferred color. Brands, especially ones with little or no differences between competitors, can affectively use color as an eye-catching brand identifier.

In order to better tap into this visual aspect of advertising, you must understand the basics of color theory. It is important that color choice have a point, it should not be a random or un-researched decision. Choice should project the concept, and complement the key consumer benefit and the use, attitude, and/ or emotion it reflects. But before we tackle color options, let's look at a few definitions that affect color choice.

Contrasting Colors

Basically, *contrast* is how one color stands out from another. It is important to make text and images or graphics stand out from any background colors such as grey, silver, creamy yellows, pinks, light blues or beige, to name just a few. The best way to test whether your colors have enough contrast and to ensure readability and legibility is to convert them to grayscale on the computer. If they stand in *high contrast* to each other, such as the way yellow and dark blue are clearly distinguishable from each other, keep them. If they are *low contrast* or it's hard to distinguish one color from another, such as with yellow and pink, keep adjusting the contrast of your color scheme until a clear differentiation is reached.

Low-contrast or tone-on-tone colors are great for backgrounds but should be avoided when choosing type colors—because of their subtlety, they can be difficult to read.

As a rule, high-contrast colors are the best choice for attracting attention. You don't want everything to jump off the page or screen, however. Remember, your key consumer benefit and the need for only one dominant image on the page or screen will help you determine not only color combinations but also the level and amount of contrast needed.

Degrees of Color: Tints, Shades, and Tones

The overall reactions the target will have toward a color will depend not only on the color itself but also on its overall intensity. Every color has a diverse range of tints, shades, and tones. Adding white, black, and gray can further alter every color on the color wheel. These colors or *hues* can lighten, darken, or mute a color. When white is added to a color to create a lighter hue, it is known as a *tint*. Think adding red and white together to get pink. A *shade* is created by mixing in black. For example,

a mix of red and black will create a wine or burgundy color. A *tone* is created by mixing in both black and white, resulting in a grayer color. Tones create a darker, subtler, and less intense hue. White, black, gray, and sometimes brown and beige, are considered neutral colors because they don't compete with other colors for attention. Neutral colors, although lacking in excitement, are important to creating balance and focus, and accent colors that help to enhance your message. With that said, color theory does not recognize tints, shades, and tones—only the relationship between pure colors. See Figure 6.2 for color wheel examples of tints, shades, and tones.

The Color Wheel

The color wheel has been around since the seventeenth century when Sir Isaac Newton first developed it. Although it has changed quite a bit over the centuries, its job as an advertising tool is to help the creative team understand both color combinations and best-use practices. The colors that make up the modern-day color wheel help ensure that any color combinations you choose will work well together.

Figure 6.2 Example of a color wheel, showing tints, tones, and shades. Image courtesy of Robyn Blakeman, University of Tennessee.

A modern color wheel consists of twelve colors that can be grouped into three distinct categories: Primary, secondary, and tertiary or intermediate colors. The basic *primary colors* are red, yellow, and blue. *Secondary colors* include green, orange, and violet, and are created by mixing two primary colors together. A mixture of red and yellow, for example, creates orange; a mix of blue and yellow creates green, and a mix of red and blue creates violet. *Tertiary* or *intermediate colors* include red-violet, and blue-violet, red-orange, yellow-orange, yellow-green and blue-green, and are created by mixing a primary and a secondary color together. See Figure 6.3 for an example of primary, secondary, and tertiary positions on the color wheel.

Warm and Cool Colors

If you draw a line through the center of the color wheel, you can segregate the *warm* or active colors (reds, oranges, and yellows) from the *cool* or passive colors (blues, greens, and violets). Warm colors are vivid and energetic and tend to appear larger and to advance on the page or screen. Cool colors, on the other hand, are more calming and tend to appear small and recede on the page or screen. Understanding the temperament and moods a color can project can help you determine how color choice can maximize your brand's identity.

The Harmony Between Colors

There are five basic color schemes on the color wheel we will look at: Complementary, split complementary, analogous, triadic, and tetradic.

Primary

Secondary

Intermediate/
Tertiary

Figure 6.3 Example showing primary, secondary, and intermediate/tertiary color options. Drawing courtesy of Robyn Blakeman, University of Tennessee.

Complementary Colors

Complementary colors, such as red and green, blue and orange, and yellow and violet, are opposite each other on the color wheel. Because complementary colors are high in contrast, they create a kind of visual tension, so a little goes a long way. They are great at differentiating images or sections or as attention getters, such as drawing the eye to the logo or packaging. Be careful, large amounts of bright contrasting colors can overwhelm the message, so consider separating them with a tint, shade or tone. Additionally, because they have a tendency to radiate or appear to move, using them for large amounts of small text, like body or detail copy, should be avoided.

The best advice when using complementary colors is to use one as the main or dominate color and the other as an accent. A complementary scheme looks best when a warm and a cool color are paired together, such as red with blue or green.

Split Complementary Colors

A variation of a complementary color scheme, *split complementary* colors are a combination of three colors. One is the base or dominant color, and the two adjacent colors such as blue, yellow-orange, and red-orange are used as accents. Although split complementary colors have a strong amount of contrast, there is typically less tension, making it a good choice for beginner designers. See Figure 6.4 for an example of complementary and split complementary positions on the color wheel.

Analogous Colors

Analogous colors are three colors that sit next to one another on the color wheel such as red, orange, and yellow. Because of their close association they typically reflect a calm and harmonious feel. Analogous color schemes typically use one color to dominate, the second for support, and the third, along with black, white, or

Complimentary

Split
Complementary

Figure 6.4 Example of complementary and split complementary color options. Drawing courtesy of Robyn Blakeman, University of Tennessee.

Analogous

Figure 6.5 Example showing analogous colors. Drawing courtesy of Robyn Blakeman, University of Tennessee.

gray, will be used as an accent color. Watch placement to be sure you have enough contrast between components. See Figure 6.5 for an example of analogous positions on the color wheel.

Triadic Color

Triadic color schemes use three colors that are evenly spaced around the color wheel—think triangle. The use of a triadic color scheme creates visual contrast with bright, vibrant, and dynamic color combinations. To ensure a harmoniously balanced color scheme, be sure one color clearly dominates while the other two play supportive roles as accents.

Tetradic Colors

Tetradic color schemes, also known as double-complementary colors, uses four colors arranged into a rectangle, or two complementary opposing pairs on the color wheel, such as blue and orange paired with yellow and violet. This richly diverse group of colors, like the others we have looked at, is best used when one color dominates the page or screen to ensure the design looks balanced.

It is best to avoid using equal amounts of pure color. Consider adding tones or shades and/or a balance between warm and cool colors to control eye flow.

How to Choose a Color Scheme

From a pure design standpoint, and setting aside readability, legibility, budget, medium and cost for the moment, the creative team will typically work with color schemes using one, two, or three colors in order to elicit the desired response from the target audience.

For example, a monotone or *monochromatic* color scheme (usually black and white) uses a single color and its various tints, shades, and tones. If you are looking for a stark and minimalistic look, the use of a single color palette will garner the best results. But be careful, it is easy for simple to become monotonous and dull. Although not limited exclusively to black and white, a

monochromatic color scheme can use any single color plus its various levels of tints and shades.

A *monotone achromatic* color scheme employs all the tints and shades falling between black on one end of the spectrum and white on the other. What differentiates it from a monochromatic color theme is the addition of a "spot" of color. As we have already learned, this is a great way to attract attention and focus the eye on a specific area.

Many print materials will use a two-color scheme of complementary colors. Color psychology has shown that the most appealing color schemes are on the opposite sides of the color wheel such as red/green, yellow/purple, and orange/blue.

Modern digital design tends to use a triple color scheme to create a louder more unique aesthetic. In order to create a more harmonious effect, the three colors should be equally spaced on the color wheel, such as blue/red/yellow, and orange/purple/green. Now that we understand the language of color, let's take a look at its colorful and symbolic voice.

The Mood And Meaning Behind the Color

Like layout styles, color choice is a design element. The lightness, darkness, or intensity of a color or combination of colors evokes emotional responses. Because of this, color can be used to set a mood, attract the eye, or give meaning to a brand beyond a specific use. Because color is memorable, in the unfortunate event of the target forgetting the brand's name, often the use of unique color or combinations on packaging or in the logo can help with recall when the target is considering purchase.

When properly matched to a brand and its use, color can tell its story, help build brand identity and thus brand equity, and even help determine the brand's visual and verbal voice. Its constant background chatter quietly sets a mood and tells us without words which feeling to tap into. The elegance, reassurance, or casualness of a color comes from life's experience; we see life in color and use it to describe events, emotions, the passage of time, or a journey. Emotionally diverse, color can make your target feel warm and fuzzy, cold and desolate, stressed or excited, restless or relaxed, pumped up or lethargic. It can draw attention to a specific product feature or give meaning to a graphic image. As part of our vocabulary, we often use color references to express our emotions, such as "having the blues," or being "so angry I saw red." It speaks volumes about clean clothes, luxury cars, sinus congestion, and beer. When used correctly, color becomes part of the advertised message.

The Psychology of Color in Advertising

Color psychology is an inexact science that determines how color influences both behavior and decision making. Determining which colors to employ in an ad, however, is an art, because we all interpret colors differently. Purple, for example, may look closer to black to some and more reddish to others. Some may find it makes their mouth water, while others cannot tolerate it as a food color. So the key rests with the proper combination of colors. With that said, no color scheme has been successfully assigned to a particular brand category. Instead, we need to understand the meaning behind colors so that they can tell your brand's story in the way the creative team intends it to be told. When carefully considered, a colorful story can affect the target's purchasing behavior both effectively and efficiently.

The colorful visual and verbal voice a brand presents to the world is not based on arbitrary decisions. Typically, every logo, every package design, every layout, is carefully analyzed, tested, developed, and colorized. Color choice is one of the most scrutinized and lasting decisions for any brand because it will become the brand's identity, or visual and verbal voice, and represents use and quality, or if improperly chosen, the lack thereof. Many brands find it so important they have trademarked their color choices. Both Target and Coke have claimed ownership of both their distinctive red colors. UPS owns its earthy brown, Home Depot its bright orange, and Post-it has dibs on yellow. Having a distinctive color(s) is important to brands because color leaves a lasting impression on consumers and speaks loudly for the brand's identity. So how exactly do you choose meaningful colors? Here's a breakdown of some of the more common color options.

Color Tells a Brand's Conceptual Story

Colors that catch our eye or repel us are often hard-wired by our gender, age, education, the culture we grew up with, societal beliefs, childhood associations, and overall life experiences.

The following discussion explores how color can enhance a brand's visual and verbal voice in the marketplace. It is important to mention that these are just rules of thumb since all colors have been found to have both negative and positive traits. With that said, all rules and preconceived ideas can be successfully broken if your concept is both strong and informational.

Red

Red is a dynamic, assertive and dangerous color with great strength. It can signify valor, passion, lust, and heat as well as blood, fire, and revolution. Whether reflecting positive or negative emotions, it is full of action and reaction. Red is an appetite stimulant, and is often used in restaurants. It is great for men's products or any product requiring a warning label. It also works well for impulse products, such as candies, and is often used to advertise toys, pizza, and meat entrees. Because of its intensity, red brings text or an image forward on the page or screen. It is a great choice if you need to create a sense of urgency and grab the target's attention; this is why many sales and clearance pieces use red. Just remember this bold color should be used in moderation since it can appear pushy, tacky, and aggressive.

Red comes in many diverse hues, such as maroon, a dark bluish red that represents controlled or thoughtful actions. Burgundy is darker and has more purple in it, giving this rich color a more sophisticated and serious feel. Crimson has hints of blue and projects a more sensual than sexy feel, and scarlet needs a bit of orange to give it an enthusiastic and defiant feel. Best-known brands that use red include Coke, Target, Tesla, Marvel, ESPN, Lego, Kellogg's, Nestlé, Red Bull, and Honda.

Red to Your Target
The psychographic breakdown of a target member attracted to red might include courageous lovers of life who are action oriented and positive. Because they are often quick to judge and base their opinions on initial impressions, they tend to act emotionally rather than rationally.

Yellow

Yellow is welcoming, open, vivacious, and cautious color. It is a light, warm, comforting, upbeat color suggesting laughter, or on the flip side, anxiety and impatience. It taps into the logical, more practical, left side of the brain to stimulate memory and perception, and inspire inquisitiveness. It is a decisive, mentally challenging, yet unemotional, highly visible color. It can be used to represent deceit or cowardice, represented by the phrase "He has a yellow streak down his back." Most brand types can successfully use yellow or yellow highlights, but some of the obvious include vegetables, fruits, sun products, hair products, or paper products. Yellow takes on more weight and stands out when combined with a dark color. This bright, energetic color is a great choice when used to create a friendly, open brand image.

Yellow's many diverse hues have a clear story to tell. For example, light yellow improves alertness. Lemon yellow, a bright color with a touch less white, denotes order and self-reliance. However, it can tend to disappear on a white page or screen, so consider paring it with a dark color to make it standout. Citrine, a bit browner, is considered a superficial, fickle, and deceitful color. Golden yellow has a bit of blue and red, and suggests a loner, and curiosity and sensitivity. Creamy yellows, more white than yellow, is an idea generator on one hand, and suggests a lack of confidence on the other. It is important to note that lighter shades of yellow are visually unappealing because they tend to become dull and lifeless. Darker shades of yellow can reflect depression, melancholy, low self-esteem, and cynicism. Considered an unstable and spontaneous color, you should avoid using yellow if you want to suggest stability and safety. Advertisers look to yellow if advertising toys, dairy products, health foods, and desserts. Best-known brands that use yellow include Caterpillar trucks, Nikon, McDonald's, Stanley, Post-it, Hertz, Bayer, and Peanut M&Ms.

Yellow to Your Target

Yellow tends to be favored by a more intelligent demographic. Those within your target that will be attracted to yellow tend to be high-minded and controlled, and seek the admiration of others. A true friend, they tend to outwardly reject flattery, but inwardly love recognition for their efforts or style.

Blue

This solid typically masculine color can be relied upon to take control of the page or screen, particularly if depicting difficult times. Blue is an earthy color, signifying water, the sky, ice, trust, stability, and justice. Blue, depending on its hue, can be used to project a reserved, quiet, or depressing mood. Blue is a relaxing, reliable, responsible, and refreshing youthful color that projects an inner security and confidence. It is an idealistic, self-expressive, safe, and non-threatening color, making it one of the most universally liked colors by all demographic groups. It can also be perceived as being too rigid, self-righteous, unstable, conservative, predictable, and aloof. Although projecting a calm and compassionate exterior, it can often seem unemotional and pessimistic. With that said, it is also considered a color that reflects power and integrity. Due to its universal popularity, it is a great choice if you are trying to promote trust and simplicity.

Blue in any shade has a diverse emotional appeal. Light blue, for example, requiring the addition of white, is representative of creativity. Sky blue has many shades all created with varying degrees of white and purples, and speaks of calm, love, and fidelity. It is a non-threatening, nature-based way to overcome physical and mental obstacles. Azure blue also comes in varying hues, is slightly more green and purple, and typically represents contentment, determination, and ambition. Dark blues have varying degrees of black added, and denote conservatism and

responsibility. When combined with warm colors like red, orange, or yellow, blue can project a vibrant personality.

Because it is considered stable, blue is often used on expensive items, where a decision has a lot riding on it such as the purchase of a car; this is why so many financial institutions use blue. Blue can represent such products as cold beverages, frozen-food products, cleaning supplies, airlines, and travel options. Additionally, it is often seen promoting toys, health foods, dairy foods, and desserts. Use blue when your sales depend on projecting an image of reliability and confidence. Best-known brands to use blue include Tiffany's, Facebook, Twitter, USPS, Oreos, Pepsi, Oral-B, Ford, and Bud Lite.

Blue to Your Target

Lovers of the color blue tend to be more conservative and dignified. Sensitive to others, they are possessed of a solid character and have a rational mind. Good listeners, they never monopolize a conversation. They like to have a good time but when they've overdone it, they tend to feel guilty and look to find a way to justify their actions.

Green

Green is a relaxing color. It is the color of nature, cleanliness, good health, balance, harmony, rebirth, renewal, and money. Mixed from a combination of yellow and blue, it can absorb the characteristics of those colors, such as the optimism of yellow, and the calm and insight associated with blue. Having a strong sense of right and wrong, green suggests good judgment on one hand and can be considered judgmental or overly cautious on the other. It is stable and enduring, persistent, and champions overcoming adversity. It represents prosperity, abundance, and safety. As a negative color, it is often associated with the phrase "green with envy or jealousy."

Visually and verbally, it can speak in many languages due to its many variations in color. Light green, for example, created with varying amounts of white, represents youth or new growth, immaturity, and inexperience. It offers up a new perspective such as a fresh start. Emerald green sits between green and blue-green on the color wheel and is created with a little blue, yellow, and black; it is inspirational and suggests abundance and wealth. Jade, a dark rich green with a bit of yellow and black says trust, confidentiality, tact, and diplomacy, and can create a feeling of anticipation. Lime green requires a bit more yellow and blue, and is considered youthful, naïve, and playful, a color well received by a younger target. Dark greens need a bit of black, and are the shades of resentment, greed, and selfishness. Turquoise, a light greenish blue, is considered calming, protective, and suggests healing. Olive green, more yellowish in color, is typically associated with peace, "offering an olive branch," or overcoming adversity. Adversely, it can also strongly suggest deceit and treachery. Yellow-green, a color to be avoided in most cases, represents cowardice, conflict, and fear. Kelly or grass green, a bright deep green requiring a bit of yellow, black, and blue, screams money, self-confidence, security, and health.

This strong, powerful color is a great choice for brands that want to project reliability. Because it is the color for go, green makes sense for more emotional purchases like computers, where the target feels little need to get permission before making an expensive purchase. Consider green if promoting vegetable entrees, garden equipment, tobacco products, pickles, pasta, drugs or medical equipment, health foods, environmentally safe or "green" products, toys, and financial services. Best-known brands that use green include John Deere, Starbucks, Heineken, Land Rover, Android, Double Mint Gum, and Sprite.

Green to Your Target

A target member attracted to green is most likely an outdoorsy type who is ecologically driven. They are interested in world affairs and tend to view most topics in a more liberal way. They are agreeable, well-read, great budgeters without being miserly, and are always looking for ways to improve their standard of living. Worldly, they have many friends, love to travel, tend to spend on sensible forms of luxury goods, and love a juicy piece of gossip.

Orange

Orange reflects the autumn harvest, fire, and the heat of the sun. It is a weighty color, suggesting depth and volume. It evokes intense feelings, is energetic, inspirational, friendly, stimulating, and denotes good health. The mix of red and yellow gives it the energy associated with red and the cheery feel associated with yellow. It talks emotional strength, gut instinct, optimism, and rejuvenation. It can be perceived as being enthusiastic, spontaneous, positive, motivational, risk-taking, competitive, and independent. This is a movement color that is extroverted, uninhibited, and showy while at the same time being warm, inviting, and mentally and physically stimulating. Under-utilized, orange is a color a younger target will respond to thanks to its impulsive nature.

A color that encourages idea generation, self-respect, and the need to respect others, it can speak with a bold or mild voice. Some possible options include subtle shades of peach, each requiring the addition of varying degrees of red and white, which is best used to encourage communication and conservation while putting people at ease. Its soft voice does not scream anywhere as loud as pure

orange, giving it a more genteel and cautious voice. Yellow-orange is vital and self-controlled. Amber, more yellowish-brown in color, is located midway between yellow and orange on the color wheel and inspires confidence and self-esteem, but can also be a bit arrogant. Dark oranges need the addition of varying amounts of black, feels overconfident, and appear to try to hard for attention, and are often associated with the opportunist. A great appetite stimulant, products that work well with orange include pasta, precooked entrees, and insect repellants. Best-known brands that use orange include Home Depot, Dollar Shave Club, Hermes, WNBA, Harley-Davidson, Orange Crush, Reese's, and Tide.

Orange to Your Target

Psychographically, target members attracted to orange tend to be very social and have a hearty love of life. They hate being alone so they typically surround themselves with fun friends, both sinners and saints, and good food.

Purple or Violet

Regal, imaginative, spiritual, sophisticated, wealthy, opulent, peaceful, mysterious, and spiritual—this introspective color promotes thoughtfulness and energy. A mix of red and blue, purple can project the strength associated with red, and the integrity and peace of blue. An un-earthly color, it suggests the balance between the physical and spiritual world, or body and soul. It is imaginative, meditational, calming, and grounding. It can speak sensitivity, compassion, and selfless love. If you need to show uniqueness, extravagance, humanitarianism, respectfulness, ambition, individuality, or independence, think purple. When overused, it can become aggravating, or even depressing, so be sure to use it sparingly. Because of its air of glamour and preference by women in particular, this color is a great choice for any type of beauty product. If you don't want your purple to read feminine, go with a deeply saturated or deep shade of purple, and consider pairing it with blue.

Optional colors choices include lavender; its light hue gives it a fragile, sensitive, and vulnerable appeal. Lilac boasts a more pinkish tint and is considered immature, superficial, youthful, extroverted, and enthusiastic. Its soft tone gives it an inspirational, glamorous, romantic, and vain feel. Mauve, a pale purple with a gray tint, promotes good choices and decisions, and screams out for justice. It can also represent a level of commonality or reflect those who are social climbers or want to fit in. Amethyst, ranging from a light to dark purple, is considered a mystical and intuitive color that is associated with humanitarianism and is protective of the vulnerable and downtrodden. Plum is a deep reddish purple color. It is considered an honorable, traditional, preachy color that harkens back to another era. Finally, deep purple can be either more red or blue in color, depending on the emotion you are trying to achieve; it is thought to be a power color that not only suggests arrogance and ruthlessness but also spiritual enlightenment. Best-known brands that use purple include Cadbury, Curves, Suja, Wayfair, Hallmark, Fed Ex, Yahoo!, and Taco Bell.

Purple to Your Target

Two different types of people are drawn to purple: Those who are very profound, and those who wish to appear understanding. This dignified color tends to attract people who are artistic and who see themselves as respectable and mysterious. Great achievers, they are easily satisfied with their own personal actions, giving them an air of superiority and conceit. With that said, they can appear to others as lazy. They are typically easy to live with, since their personality traits do not scream out like the color red, nor are they anywhere as subtle as the color blue.

Pink

This soft, non-threatening pastel color is representational of unconditional love, compassion, health, youth, and femininity. A mix of red and white, this color derives passion and power from red, and wholesomeness and purity from white. The deeper the intensity of the color, the more passion and energy it projects. It is an intuitive, insightful, tender, kind, hopeful, and positive form of warm fuzzies. It is a calming, nurturing color that reassures, erasing feelings of anger, aggression or resentment. Pink can be representative of good health, as the phrase "in the pink" signifies. It feels sweet, innocent, naïve, inexperienced, and childlike. On the negative side, it can suggest weakness, a lack of willpower, self-reliant tendencies; it can reflect a lack of self-worth, and feel cautious. If using this color, consider adding a darker color such as blue or green to counter the weaknesses associated with pink.

Although having fewer variations than other colors we have talked about, pink still has a lot to say, for example, rosy pink, a mature and intuitive color that projects love and unity. Salmon boosts a bit of sassy orange, giving it a flirty feel. Orchid, a purple and pink mix, is associated with the unconventional or non-conformist. Fuchsia is a deep blue-pink color considered inspirational and mature. Hot pink, a very bright almost fluorescent color, is a passionate, playful, warm lover of life. Thanks to its soft non-threatening feminine appeal, pink is often used to sell cosmetic and beauty products as well as children's toys. Best-known brands that use pink include T-Mobile, Dunkin Donuts, Avon, Baskin Robbins, Victoria's Secret, Breast Cancer Foundation, Lyft.

Pink to Your Target

Pink lovers tend to be optimistic, shy, kind, and generous people who are sensitive to needs of others. They are friendly, approachable, and nurturing individuals who have a tendency to put the needs of others ahead of their own. They see the world through a romantic lens and are very sensitive and sensual. Methodical and organized, they can be unapologetic to those who are not.

Brown

This nature-related color projects security, material wealth, eccentricity, neutrality, wholesomeness, simplicity, friendliness, dependability, and health, and is also a good appetite stimulant. A serious color, it denotes a sense of family obligation, hard work, industriousness, physical comfort, and simplicity. Brown represents friendliness, dependability, honesty, and sincerity, with a practical dose of common sense thrown in. A frugal color, it is not at all superficial or wasteful. It does represent materialistic tendencies, but it values quality and everything in moderation. Full of confidence and reassurance, strength and maturity, this color is not out to make a bold statement on the page; it leaves that to the colors that surround it. However, its few negative connotations are powerful, and include cheapness and drabness.

Alternatives to solid brown include tan; a light brown with a yellow undertone, it is considered a friendly, ageless, approachable, straightforward, and genuine color. Dark brown is considered strong, sad, materialistic, and wise. Ivory is almost white, so it projects a sense of calm and a reserved and sophisticated continence. Beige is brown with orange undertones, and is considered practical, reliable, conservative, and loyal. Best-known brands that use brown include UPS, Hershey's Snickers and Plain M&Ms.

Brown to Your Target

Target members attracted to brown tend to be honest, salt-of-the-earth types that are reliable, hardworking, and confident. They are both friendly and sincere and have an acute sense of duty and responsibility. A homebody, family and security is important to this dedicated personality, as is physical comfort, simplicity, and quality. A loyal and trustworthy friend, they are sensitive to the needs of others and tend to be offended when personally confronted with criticism by others. They feel a strong need to be in control and often see life as a struggle, believing that day-to-day living is not meant to be easy. Moderation and frugality is their mantra, when they do make a purchase, it is based more on quality and less on frivolities.

Silver

Considered a feminine color, it is emotional, sensitive, and mysterious as well as calming, soothing, and pure. It typically represents personal reflection and life changes, and intuitiveness, and is seen as being able to deflect negative energy. It represents prestige and wealth, is considered glamorous, sophisticated, modern, and high-tech. A versatile color, typically used as an accent, it is elegant, respectable, courteous, dignified, responsible, unbiased, patient, determined, and organized. Its diversity and illuminating quality makes it an excellent and energizing fit with most colors. Unlike the calm, low-key qualities of gray, silver has a tendency to be more upbeat and optimistic. However, it can also be considered indecisive and lacking a sense of commitment, as well as appearing dull, lifeless, neutral, and insincere.

There are no other color options for silver, to find variations you would need to go to gray, white, or black. Silver is often called upon to represent dairy foods, and more expensive items like jewelry. The best-known brand to use silver is Diet Coke.

Silver to Your Target
Silver attracts the intuitive and insightful individual with a heightened sense of spirituality. They tend to be imaginative, creative, and introspective, often living in their own little world where they constantly search for the meaning of life. They often possess an understated air of sophistication, graciousness, and passivity. Modern and loving yet moody and sometimes snobbish, they do not let matters of the heart rule their life or decision-making process. They have strong creative imaginations, making their view of the world somewhat rosy and fantastical.

Gold

Gold is the international color of wealth, success, achievement, luxury, prosperity, sophistication, and extravagance. Considered a masculine color, it exudes the energy and power of the sun, whereas feminine silver emanates with the energy and sensitivity of the moon. This optimistic color adds richness and reflects a sense of wisdom, understanding, and enlightenment. It suggests knowledge, spirituality, compassion, and leadership. Most often used as an accent color, the confidence of gold makes it an eye-catching color that can be shiny and exciting, or dull, muted, and traditional.

Like silver, there are no additional color options for gold; to find variations, you would need to look at browns or yellows or even oranges. Gold is an excellent choice for any high-end product. Best-known brands that use gold include Halo Top, Twix, Caffeine Free Diet Coke, Godiva, Ferrero Rocher Chocolate.

Gold to Your Target
Gold attracts individuals who like nice things and have an inflated sense of self-worth. They tend to be intelligent, first-to-own types who value comfort and are willing to pay for any brand that can prove its worth.

Black

Black symbolizes sadness, isolation, and death, or the need to set something apart or end something. It can also be sexy, mysterious, protective, and conservative, as well as denote elegance, confidence, honor, and dignity. Black is the absence of light and the absorption of all color. Black recedes and white advances on the page or screen. This dramatic, powerful, authoritative, introspective color can be intimidating, unfriendly, and unapproachable thanks to the strength it projects. Sophistication is implied when we refer to the "little black dress," or the "black tie affair." Ads with too much black can be difficult to read and can be heavy and depressing in appearance. An ad with only the power of black and the purity of white, for example, feels controversial and argumentative. Soften the argument by stepping in between with a pop of a bright color. Black contrasts extremely well when surrounded by bright jewel tones. It is often used for expensive products such as jewelry, cars, perfumes, or liquors. Black can also be used as an accent color to pop lighter, more vibrant colors off the page. Best-known brands that use black include L'OREAL, which uses black and gold on their ELVIVE shampoo and conditioning bottles, and also Guinness beer.

Black to Your Target
In the lover of black, you will find someone who finds both power and prestige important. They can be independent, driven, dignified, and always seeking to be in control of any situation. Stuffy, conservative, and conventional, they can appear intimidating even to close friends and family members. Their air of authority can be a front to cover feelings of insecurity. An introspective personality, they tend to keep people at a distance and love projecting an air of mystery and intrigue. They have a tendency to be very methodical in all things and expect any purchase to be constructed and presented in much the same way.

White

This ethereal color denotes purity, wholesomeness, cleanliness, simplicity, elegance, and innocence. White is considered the color of perfection, signifying a blank page, or new beginnings. Containing an equal balance of all colors within the spectrum, it represents equality, fairness, and impartiality. It is clean, protective, full of encouragement, peaceful, and calm. Its job in advertising is to instill a sense of elegance and order to a design on either the page or screen. Alternately, it can be considered cold, isolating, sterile, detached, and empty. Too much white or an ineffective use of white, on the other hand, can cause feelings of isolation and emptiness; it can be too perfect, leaving little room for error. Many products that want to portray cleanliness, value, efficiency, or simplicity use white as their main color. Best-known brands to use white include Apple, Pepperidge Farm, Head & Shoulders, Crest, Chobani.

White to Your Target

Rarely is this a favored color early in life. White tends to grow on people when they are going through some type of transitional period. Favored by those who require a tidy appearance in all things, they expect those around them to also adhere to their high and immaculate standards. They are long-term planners with a confident, self-assured, positive, and optimistic outlook, who believe in the value of discretion in both themselves and others. Practical and careful with money, they tend to exert a great deal of self-control when it comes to making purchasing decisions. Very self-sufficient, they can often be considered loners; they work to hide their flaws from others, and are often sexually prudish thanks to their excessive need for perfection. Although they often appear shy, they have very strong opinions and love the chance to share them with others.

Gray

This neutral yet diverse color denotes coldness, detachment, indecision, compromise, distinctiveness, stability, conservativeness, moodiness, formality, and sophistication, depending on the depth of color. Thanks to its subdued hue, it can feel quiet, reserved, boring, and depressing. It is considered a conventional, reliable, and practical color. It's never used to stimulate, energize, rejuvenate, or excite on its own. Stable, it softens other colors on the page or screen, helping to tone down stronger, more effervescent colors while offering depth to lighter colors. A simple color, we would typically think of gray as a mixture of black and white; however, it often is accompanied by additional colors such as blue, pink, green and yellow to give it more depth. Too much gray on the page or screen and you can depress your target, so consider adding a bright color to pop off the page. Gray is often used for expensive, high-tech products.

Although created with multiple colors, it has few additional color variations to choose from. The short list includes light gray, considered soothing and enlightening. Dark gray on the other hand, is conventional, serious, solemn, inflexible, and strict. The best-known brand to use gray is Lexus.

Gray to Your Target

Gray is usually used as an accent color, making it acceptable to both men and women. Target traits tend to align more with the accent colors used with them.

The Symbolism of International Color

You can't talk color without talking about how color is viewed and perceived internationally. We live in a global society, so it would not be unusual for you to be advertising your brand in very diverse cultures. Because of this, it is important to be aware of the symbolic meanings associated with specific colors when conceptualizing the visual/verbal message. Symbolically, color is uniquely embedded within all cultures; its rich and diverse hues have varied meanings and elicit a variety of emotional responses. As in domestic advertising, color's visual symbolism can wordlessly tell a brand's story, help overcome literacy issues, build brand image, and can establish the brand's tone of voice as well as assist with positioning. Because of its unique associations, when used incorrectly, color can easily offend, confuse, and affect the perception of quality.

Color choice is rarely universally standardized, even within a single culture. Many brands will work with local agencies to help avoid any colorful mistakes or miscues. Knowledge of cultural differences can help the creative team understand that red, for example, represents luck and good fortune in many Eastern cultures and parts of Africa, whereas many Indian cultures see it as a symbol of purity. Alternatively, in parts of Europe, the United States, Australia and New Zealand, it suggests aggression or danger, and Germanic and Slavic cultures see fear, anger, and jealousy. Considered unlucky in Chad, red is considered a lucky color in Nigeria, China, Denmark, and Argentina. Dark red colors depict mourning in Ivory Coast regions and death in Turkey. The United Kingdom sees red as garish and tacky, but as always affordably priced.

To the Chinese, yellow represents happiness, luck, purity, and royalty, to the Japanese envy, anger, and jealousy, and to Koreans happiness, adventure, and good taste. To certain South African tribes, yellow is associated with birth. Germanic and Russian cultures see yellow as the color of envy and jealousy, while many Latin American cultures believe it to be a color representative of envy and infidelity. Although considered a youthful, feminine, warm, happy color in the United States, and representative of strength and reliability in Saudi Arabia, in France yellow signifies infidelity; and mourning in Mexico.

The calming color blue symbolizes immortality in Iran. In many Western and Eastern cultures, blue signifies quality and trustworthiness. Malaysia and Sweden perceive it as evil and cold, whereas India sees purity.

Green is associated with environmentally safe products in the United States; with love, happiness, good taste, adventure, and high-tech in Japan; luck in the Middle East; death and danger in tropical regions, and is forbidden in Indonesia. To many South African tribes, green is seen as a fertility color. Many Eastern cultures see green as pure and reliable, trustworthy and dependable, while in Malaysia it is the color of danger, and in Belgium, signifies disease and envy.

Internationally, orange is considered sacred for Hindus and Buddhist monks and is not even recognized by some Zambians.

Slavic cultures see purple as representing anger, envy, and jealousy. To many Eastern cultures, it is a symbol of love, and to the Japanese, it represents sin and fear. All three cultures believe purple is the color of expensive products. In Mexico, purple speaks of anger and envy, and in Brazil represents mourning, and wealth in certain Asian cultures.

In Russia, Poland, Mexico, the United States, and many Germanic and Latin cultures, black represents fear, anger, and grief as well as elegance, whereas in China it stands for trust and quality. Asian cultures and the United States see it representing expensive and powerful brands; they also see it as dependable, trustworthy, and being of high quality. In India, black is representative of dullness and stupidity.

In Western cultures like the United States we see white as innocent and wholesome. In many Eastern cultures, it is associated with mourning and death, but in Australia and New Zealand, it represents purity and happiness. Both China and the United States see white as a wedding color but is considered a masculine color in France. Representative of ambition and peace in India, in the United Kingdom white is representative of low-quality products.

The United States views pink as weak, while the United Kingdom sees pink as young and hip and affordably priced.

Brown, almost universally, is seen as an earth color. However, lighter shades in the United Kingdom, for example, are considered as elderly, that says expensive, boring, and dull.

The above is certainly not a comprehensive list. Cultural color associations both positive and negative are often centuries old and engrained in tradition. However, thanks to the growth of global markets, specifically via the Internet, varied cultures are becoming more tolerant to these inherent feelings on color. With that said, never fully abandon cultural associations all together. When in doubt, to neutralize any possible negative connotations consider mixing varied color combinations to soften or even alleviate one color or color scheme from dominating the page, package, or screen.

Before making your final color choice ask yourself the following:

- What does the brand stand for?
- Who is the targeted consumer audience?
- What makes the target buy in terms of color associations? What do they feel?

- What color palette matches use? Does the brand scream elegance, and uniqueness? Is it for the conservative buyer, or is it a purely emotional purchase? Does it promote good health, or solve a problem?
- Can a unique color be developed for the brand, one that is unique to the category? Or can another color be combined with the brand's existing color to make it bolder or refresh its image?
- What are the hot color palettes of the day? Fashion and/or decorating have a tendency to decide current trends or fads.
- Understand cultural preferences. If working with an international audience, is the current color choice(s) appropriate or do changes need to be made? Do your research—colors often have very different meanings to different cultural groups.
- Know about competing brands. What colors, graphics, and so on are competitors using in their advertising, on their packaging and in their logo design?
- Make versatile media choices. Be sure color(s) can successfully transfer from a digital screen to print, packaging, television, and so on. Different media environments do affect how colors are perceived.
- Test color choices. Test your color choices in a focus group if working with a new or reinvented brand.

Before choosing a representative color or combination of colors, the creative team must intimately know their brand, the brand category, and competing brands. Once your research is complete, start by playing it safe with one strong color and build out from there.

The Visual/Verbal Message of Color in Advertising

So far we have talked only about color as a design element, but from a business perspective the use of color is expensive. Depending on the client's budget, a designer may be able to apply multiple colors, through visuals for example, or may be forced to work with a single monochromatic color. When color cannot speak for the message, designers have to find other ways to bring attention to the ad. Single-color ads, typically black-and-white, don't have to be boring. They can be enhanced with high-contrast visuals, and depending on the medium, use colored paper stocks, or by adding a simple reverse or screen tint.

As we have already learned, a *reverse* places light colored text onto a dark colored background. Strong focal points, they are best used as an announcement devices, to highlight headlines, or for subheads to break up blocks of long text.

If you are going to place text on a colored background, be sure the contrast between the background color and the text is severe, to assure readability. Reverses are great at drawing the target's eye and drawing them in, but use them sparingly; too many bold contrasts can overwhelm the rest of the ad's message. Serif type in small point sizes can break up and should not be placed on a solid colored background anywhere. Reverses are the most easily read when type is large, bold, and has strong lines. Any dark-colored background can be used, so long as it creates enough contrast to highlight the text. Reversed text need not be white, but any light color.

Screen tints also known as *shades* are an inexpensive way to offer tonal depth to any one single color. A screen tint can add a diverse range of gray shades to a simple black-and-white ad. For example, solid black is 100 percent of saturation, or a solid color. A 10-percent screen of black would give you a very light-gray tint, a 50-percent screen of black would give you a mid-range gray, and so on. The computer allows the designer to lighten any solid color into varying shades of that color, creating depth and thus giving each new shade the appearance of a new color.

If you are still confused think about it like this: If you're holding a black-colored pencil and you color lightly, putting little pressure on the pencil tip, you get a light-gray tone. The harder you push down on the tip, the darker and more varied the tones become. The addition of these varied tones gives a black-and-white ad specifically a deeper, more interesting appearance, creating distinct foregrounds, middle grounds, and backgrounds.

Screen tints are a great option for callout boxes, drop shadows, banners, backgrounds, snipes, and line-art accents. Screen tints or their cousins, drop shadows, should not be added to type, because they would drastically reduce overall readability and legibility.

For ads with multiple colors, it is important that color works as a compliment to what is being said and shown. In my book *Advertising Campaign Design*, I talk about how "color should not compete with what is being said. Headlines, not color blocks, need to capture the reader's attention." Readability and legibility of the brand's message are also affected by how color and type are used conjunctively in design. I continue:

> *When placing type on top of a colored background, [like a reverse] make sure the depth or intensity of color does not overpower the type. A background should be subtle and calm, not heavy and distracting. As a rule, warm colors like red, brown, orange, and yellow are appealing when placed on lighter, warm backgrounds. Similarly, cool colors such as blue, green, grey, and pink work best when paired with contrasting cool colors. Body copy or other small text can lose detail if placed on a background that is too busy or too dark. (p. 97)*

To ensure memorability, color can be used as a unifying element across multiple diverse mediums when developing a campaign of multiple ads.

Finally, the choice of color used within a brick-and-mortar store can also send a message. Soft colors such as pink can be soothing, bright colors can suggest a youthful energy and darker, more subdued colors suggest elegance and luxury. Warm colors are great at not only attracting consumers into a store but for store windows, entrances and point-of-purchase displays. Alternatively, they are considered disruptive when it comes to making a quick purchasing decision. Cool colors on the other hand, tone down displays and are a great choice if the target is going to have a difficult purchasing decision to make, due to cost.

Even Color Is Seen Differently When Printed versus When Seen Digitally

As we have learned, the mixture of colors on the color wheel lead to a diverse array of additional color choices. The concept of mixing colors is also used in modern-day digital display and printing. All digital colors and images are recreated by mixing (R)ed, (G)reen and (B)lue, known as *RGB*. In printing, mixed colors are known as *four-color process,* or more commonly as *CMYK.* (C)yan, (M)agenta, (Y)ellow, and (K)black are the four colors that, when used together, make up every color that appears in a printed photograph, illustration, or graphic.

The Pantone of All Color Choices

If the creative team is searching for a specific color, they will define it by giving it a *Pantone Matching System* (PMS) number. Very similar to the color swatches you would find in a paint store, Pantone numbers need to be specially mixed during printing to ensure the color is the same every time it is used. This adds an additional cost to any print job. There are two types of Pantone options to match paper options: Coated and uncoated. To distinguish between the two options, colors mixed especially for coated or shiny paper stocks are designated with a "C" after the number, such as Pantone 102C a bright Yellow. Those printed on uncoated paper stocks such as newsprint or certain types of packaging, for example, would have a "U" designation such as 102U.

Interestingly enough, these would not print exactly the same color on the two different types of paper stocks, since, for example, the ink appearing on coated stocks will be brighter because it will not soak into the paper, as it does with uncoated stocks, making the color(s) appear darker. There is no proven way to match color exactly—it is a little hit and miss. The best place to start is with a Pantone swatch or chip book that will help you see just how the color will look on either coated or uncoated stock. As a rule of thumb, when using a PMS color on an uncoated stock, the creative team should start by going two shades or numbers lighter to get a more exact match for use on coated stocks.

As a visual and verbal voice, colors are effective for many reasons; some encourage a quick purchase, while others reassure and excite. Still others are calming and relaxing and project a feeling of confidence. So which should you use? The answer lies in being able to align and successfully define your brand's identity. If your brand is about improved lifestyle, luxury, or safety, then there are colors that can clearly represent that essence. As a

rule, it is unwise to go against the image of your brand or your target. Getting anyone to reevaluate how he or she feels about a particular color or shade would be not only time-consuming and expensive, but also unadvisable.

Bibliography

Blakeman, Robyn. 2011. *Advertising Campaign Design: Just the Essentials*. Armonk, NY: Sharp.

Marc Chagall Quotes. (n.d.). BrainyQuote.com. Retrieved from: www.brainyquote.com/quotes/marc_chagall_158969.

CHAPTER 7

The Stages of Advertising Design

Chapter 7 Objectives

1. The reader will understand the role each of the stages of design has in developing and showcasing the visual/verbal message.
2. The reader will understand the role of the visual/verbal cues in design.
3. The reader will understand how to show a quick idea if creatively challenged.

The Stages of Design: Developing, Solidifying, and Constructing the Idea

Once the creative team has read and thoroughly dissected the creative brief, it's time to move the brand through the varied *stages of design*. Referring to the creative process—or the idea, design, and construction phases—the five developmental stages of design include concept, thumbnails, roughs, super comprehensives, and camera-or production-ready art. Let's take a look at each one.

Conceptual Development

As we have already learned in Chapter 2, the first stage in the design process is brainstorming or concept development. *Concept* refers to your thoughts and ideas on how you can creatively solve the client's advertising problem. Brainstorming sessions shape the boring business of advertising into creative artistic solutions. Any one brainstorming session can produce dozens and dozens of acceptable and not-so-acceptable ideas. Most will be forgettable, others will be worth pursuing further; all will be exposed, analyzed, and reworked or discarded at some point along the conceptual highway. Whatever the level of creative brilliance, all are worth sharing. The key is to never feel self-conscious. Every idea should be fearlessly expressed to the creative team,

other professionals, or your classmates. However, you can rest assured all openly expressed bad ideas will often carry feelings of regret. No matter how off-strategy or off-target, or what level of stupidity, you will need to accept that 1) you are not alone, 2) you will probably be teased, 3) you will never be allowed to forget it, but 4) you will never be criticized. Each good and bad idea expressed out loud will help other team members imagine a new direction. Eventually, there will be one idea that grows and blossoms; that is when art direction gets exciting. Before moving on to the next stage of design, let's take a look at a few of the visual and verbal cues that can further assist in highlighting a great idea.

Visual and Verbal Relationship Cues

Holistically, brainstorming is all about constructing a visual and verbal relationship that tells a cohesive story. To do this effectively, it's important that every visual element seamlessly reflects what is being said in the ad. If it does, the target is more likely to not only interact with the message but act upon it, by either calling a toll-free number, stopping by a brick-and-mortar store, or visiting a social media or website for more information or making a purchase.

It doesn't matter if an ad is loaded down with informative copy or speaks more simply through the visual and logo; both techniques must strategically scream out the key consumer benefit or concept. It is also important to consider the brand's current life-cycle stage when musing over visual/verbal options. Is it a new brand launch, a current brand leader, or a struggling newcomer? Is it a mature or old favorite, or does it need to be repositioned to show updates or correct an existing reputation?

Whatever the problem to be solved, the more creative solutions you work through, the better the chance you'll have of reaching the target with a message that will interest them.

DOI: 10.4324/9781003255123-8

The Role of Visual and Verbal Cues

Visual and verbal components must do more than just tell a story. They must also construct a visual and verbal highway that ensures the reader or viewer will move through the ad in the proper sequence. This requires the creative team to know what types of visual or verbal cues will not only capture the target's attention and strategically push the key consumer benefit, but also help determine how the target's eye should move through the ad.

The construction of informative visual cues is all about finding varied ways to show or focus attention on the key consumer benefit. Let's take a look at some possible visual cues:

- Framing. A frame can be more than a simple graphic box. Any type of horizontal or vertical image, such as a doorway or window, can also highlight content and draw the eye inside the ad. Line work around the frame need not be straight, it just needs to enclose or *frame* the image.
- Placement. Placement as used in this text refers to the brand's distance from the camera and deals with where the product is in relationship to the camera. Is a close-up required to highlight specific details or a distance shot to show size and scope? How should models be posed? Will a profile, a head and shoulders, or a full body shot, better show and tell the target what you want them to know? Placement defines how much the target needs to see in order to understand what is being said and shown.
- Arrangement. Arrangement refers to composition, or where the brand is placed in relationship to other components or people within the ad. All images have a foreground, middle ground, and background. Making use of these diverse, yet distinct, areas can help place the brand in an appropriate setting and visually and physically tie the image(s) to the verbal components, creating the appropriate emotions. The goal is to deliver a believable visual and verbal environment that helps reflect brand image, a feeling, or overall use.
- Lighting. Light helps set a scene. Sunlight is happy, sunsets are peaceful, and low lighting can be either relaxing or isolating. Light that streams through a window or pools on a surface creates natural eye flow and it's a great way to draw the eye to some important point, like the copy, brand, or logo.
- Color. Color as we have already learned, is a great way to express diverse emotions.

Color that is strategically placed is another great way for drawing the eye to a spot such as the logo, packaging, or brand. The lack of color can also draw the eye, such as with a high-contrast black-and-white photo placed in a medium that predominately uses full-color images.

Now that we have broken down the visual cues, let's discuss how they can be tied to the verbal message.

- Logo. The best-known verbal option is also a very visual brand identifier. A logo is the symbol (visual) that represents a brand or company name (verbal).
- Slogans or taglines. Logos can also have an accompanying slogan or tagline (verbal) that represents the company's philosophy or mission statement (slogan), or the campaign's key consumer benefit (tagline).
- Headline. What the headline explains or announces, the visual needs to show. The largest piece of copy on the page needs to stop attention by featuring the key consumer benefit. It should tie the feature and benefit to the target's lifestyle and/or needs and wants, as well as project the strategy in the appropriate tone.
- Body copy. The body copy will expound on the story begun in the headline and explains in more detail what the visual shows. Body copy is where the actual sell is made, so it needs to tell a good story to keep the reader or viewer moving through the ad. To do that, it needs to grab attention, inform, and educate.

In the end, the visual and verbal combination employed should successfully answer the target's question "what's in it for me?" or what the brand offers them personally. If it doesn't, the ad will ultimately fail.

Remember, to ensure success, both the visual and verbal options should radiate the concept and brand personality. It is also important to use visuals that interest the target. For help, look to the psychographic and demographic profiles to find ones that will both grab their attention and support the headline. Verbally, the headline's visual punch should relate the message in its entirety, with the details left to any copy. Keeping the needs, wants, and interests of the target audience in mind will help keep the visual/verbal message on-target and on-strategy.

Conceptually, the choice of visual and verbal cues must reflect not only the brand's image, but be written and designed specifically for the targeted audience to be reached in a visually stimulating and verbally informative language the target can relate to, solve a problem they have, and appear in a medium they are sure to see and use.

Thumbnails: Small Ways to Visually and Verbally Brainstorm

Thumbnails, or *thumbs*, are the second stage in the design process. It is here where the best ideas from the brainstorming or conceptual development session will begin to take shape. These internal, often hastily hand-rendered, layouts are used by the creative team exclusively.

Thumbnails are small, hand-drawn, *proportionate* sketches or doodles, large enough to easily see and understand each component's role in expressing the overall concept direction. Depending on the medium and overall concept, thumbnails can have any number or combination of components, including a readable headline, one or more readable subheads, a recognizable visual or visuals, lines to indicate any body copy placement, a readable tagline or slogan, and a logo. Simpler ads may have nothing more than a visual and a logo. Drawn on paper, each thumb should be enclosed in a proportionally sized box, symbolizing the final size and shape of the ad and should be, as a student, tightly drawn and consistent in size. Each should show a different concept direction—no two should be alike. Try to use a different layout style, visual(s), headline, and subhead for each concept. Don't hold on to any one idea or direction at this point, to ensure further development continues to inspire alternative concept approaches.

Thumbs are typically done using a black marker. Color should be added and color tested when working within a color medium. Always work with markers. Avoid pencils.

Markers allow you to concentrate on multiple ideas rather than one over-erased idea. Mistakes are a part of the process, so are ideas that just don't go anywhere. Hate it, no problem, just cross it out and move on—that's erasing, designer style.

Thumbs are not works of art, but they should be rendered tight enough for the other team members to be able to understand the concept direction. The thumbnail should be large enough that the headline, subhead(s), slogan or tagline, and logo can be written out cleanly and placed in position on the thumb. Visuals should be quickly sketched or traced, if hand skills need support, into position. Any body copy should be indicated with parallel lines. These lines represent the number of columns used, placement, and show the approximate amount of width and depth the copy might take up. As a side note, it is important for students interested in pursuing a career in creative to produce good, clean, well-designed thumbs that can go directly into a thumbnail book for presentation in your portfolio.

Depending on the assignment, you may create anywhere from 10 to 100 thumbs in any one session. Don't settle, flex those creative impulses until you have exhausted all possible and not-so-probable options. The more solutions imagined, the more creative and diverse the possible solutions. But no matter how many you end up with, you will rarely have a single thumb that

makes the brilliant cut. More than likely, two or more will need to be combined together to create the overall look of the final idea.

The goal behind the development of multiple thumbnails is to yield a variety of visual solutions that showcase a diverse array of placements, colors, headlines and subheads, and layout styles. The goal is to produce as many different ideas as possible exhausting as many idea directions as possible. It is important to understand there is never one way to visually and verbally depict an idea. Each thumbnail rendering will depict a multitude of varied options for promoting the key consumer benefit. The point is to have multiple options for the creative team to discuss. This will also allow you to change your mind or introduce new ideas into the design mix.

Finally, because thumbnails can be drawn on any surface, the creative team can work anywhere. No one, not even working art directors, do their best work on demand a few hours before a deadline. Ideally, when given enough time to "mull over" an assignment or job, solutions will come easier and faster. Being able to sketch out ideas as they materialize, wipes out the pressure associated with a blank page. Getting away from the confines of a computer and to the free-thinking sketches can make idea generation feel less like a chore and more like actual creative thought. See Figure 7.1 for a thumbnail example.

Figure 7.1 Example of a color magazine thumbnail. Image courtesy of Brian Starmer, University of Tennessee.

Roughs Still Have a Life to Live

Roughs or *layouts* are the third stage in the design process, and they emerge from your best thumbnail ideas. Roughs are often quickly drawn ideas, used to simulate how the final ad will look. Professionals often use roughs as their idea-generation stage, skipping thumbnails all together. Hand drawn, they are faster than creating super comps on the computer, and can be used to present initial ideas to the client, especially an established client, the account team, or creative director for design approval. Roughs are done in the size of the final piece, and in color if relevant.

If you are presenting preliminary concept directions to a new client who has no representative typeface or wants to reinvent their brand's image, roughs present an opportunity to show alternative typeface choices on each completed rough. Anytime you can *show* a direction is always better than *talking about* what it looks like. It is also a chance to see the visual relationship between the chosen typeface and visual and verbal personality. Remember, the image or personality each typeface projects for the company, service, or brand plays an important visual role in the development of an identity or brand image. If a signature type style already exists for your client, continue to use that typeface on all roughs.

Each rough should include a key consumer benefit-driven headline, have a supporting main subhead if required and visual(s), and showcase a diverse range of layout styles if presenting multiple concepts. If creating a campaign series, each ad in the series should use the same typeface, layout and headline styles, as well as differing visuals that highlight a visual theme, such as using all domestic animals, versus repeating the same species repetitively unless a visual representative, and a logo, slogan, or tagline.

Any roughs used as a quick substitute for a super comp that will be seen by the client should be tightly rendered, clean, and accurate. Never present any creative to the client before checking it against the creative brief to ensure they are on-target and on-strategy.

Because the client will see roughs whether in their final form or not, a clean professional look is always a priority. If hand skills are a bit shaky, use a ruler to draw the frame, any graphic boxes, and body copy lines. All large type such as headlines, subheads, taglines, or slogans, should be tightly drawn in the appropriate typeface and placed in the correct position within the ad. As a student, if you don't feel comfortable with free-handing the type, set it on the computer and then trace it into position on the rough. Body copy, although usually written by this stage, is like

the thumb, represented using lines to show width, length, depth, and placement, or whether copy will be placed in one, two, or three columns. An actual completed copy sheet will accompany the rough to the client. Logo placement is present, as are any coupons, order forms, and so on, that might be a part of the final design.

If you need a little help with your drawing skills, consider taking a few drawing classes to enhance or tighten skills. To be an art director, you do need to have strong conceptual skills, but not expert hand skills. A New York City creative director sums it up this way, "drawing and computer skills are important skills obviously, but being able to imaginatively conceptualize for any brand is really what's important."

Visuals need to also be rendered tightly enough for the client to understand what they are looking at, its relationship with what is being said, and the typeface used within the ad. See Figure 7.2 for an example of a rough.

Once the roughs are complete, the account manager will present the client with three to five different visual/verbal versions of the creative solutions developed from the business parameters introduced in the creative brief, to review. Any changes big or small to the copy or layout, will need to be made by the creative team immediately. Deadlines never change no matter the level or amount of revisions required. Final client-approved ads will be reproduced on the computer.

Technology Finishes the Design

The fourth stage in the design process includes the creation of the *super comprehensive*, or *super comp*. A super comp is the finished design executed on a computer. Most ads will skip the rough stage and go directly to the computer to finalize an idea. Like the roughs, the headline and subheads are readable and appear in their final typeface. All text has been kerned, leaded and sized, and placed in their final position on the page. For the first time, all body, detail, and/or promotional copy has been written and appears in the proper position within the ad. If for some reason body copy has not yet been completed, greeking may be used. *Greeking*, also known as placeholder text, is illegible copy consisting of a haphazard arrangement of letters, numbers, punctuation, and paragraph breaks that is used to temporarily represent blocks of body copy. This allows the client to see how text will look on the page.

On a super comp, the layout style is clearly evident, and any and all color is present. If the photo shoot is complete, all

Figure 7.2 Example of a color magazine rough. Image courtesy of Brian Starmer, University of Tennessee.

images will have been sized, cropped, and placed in their final position(s) within the ad before presentation to the client. If, for some reason, the final images are temporarily unavailable, stock imagery that closely resembles the final image(s) will be placed temporarily in the ad and clearly marked with "for position only" (FPO), meaning the image seen is not the final image but a placeholder image that will be replaced before printing or uploading. See Figure 7.3 for an example of a super comp.

Ideally, the super comp will mimic the look of the final ad as closely as possible; however, this is your final opportunity to make any final adjustments to the design before it is seen by the client for approval.

For students interested in pursuing a career in creative, the super comp will be an integral part of your portfolio to show off your varied talents. Not only do you get to flesh out your

concept skills in your thumbnails and/or in your body copy, but you can also showcase your layout and conceptual skills as well as your knowledge of the computer/software and production skills.

Camera-Ready Art

The fifth and final step in the idea, design, and construction process is the production stage. *Camera-ready art* is the rough or super comp's preparation for final printing. This is the only stage in the design process that is often not done by the art or creative director. Instead it is handed off to the production department, where it is prepared by breaking it down into its individual parts and colors.

Figure 7.3 Example of a color magazine super comp. Image courtesy of Brian Starmer, University of Tennessee.

Camera-ready art must be scrupulously assembled and should be considered pieces of artwork in their own right. If every detail is not addressed during construction, a once-great idea on paper can look disastrous in print. "The creative team," according to an art director from Atlanta,

> is responsible for the project from concept to approval of concept. In order to get client approval the work ultimately needs to be in a 'close to final' stage. Creative then hands it off to production. Production is responsible for "prepping" the final concept/design across multiple vehicles while maintaining the integrity of what was approved. Production also is responsible for implementing hi-resolution print/digital quality art, and pre-flighting to ensure successful production (print or digital).

This is the point where exact colors are defined to ensure color consistency across mediums, and imagery is placed into the proper format for print or digital use. All details big and small are meticulously checked for any errors. An art director from Chicago explained the need to know more than design this way:

> When I started out, I had no knowledge of anything besides the ideal resolution for print projects (300 dpi) and web projects (72 dpi). I learned more as I worked with the in-house production teams. It is their area of expertise, and they can be the best education. However, when working for a smaller agency/design firms, it is great to know how to prep files for a printer (packaging files, bleed, print resolution, and types of photo resolution, etc.).

The take-away here is know a little bit about what happens to your design once it leaves your hands. It is also important to understand that any errors that occur here are both time-consuming and expensive to fix. Worst of all, if missed entirely, mistakes will show up in the final printed or digital piece, so a critical and detailed eye is required at this last crucial stage.

Note: Unattributed quotes in this chapter are from working art directors, whom I interviewed for research purposes in 2017.

CHAPTER 8
Layout Options and What They Say

Chapter 8 Objectives

1. The reader will learn the role of varied layout options to showcase components within an ad.
2. The reader will understand how price does not destroy an ad's overall look but is a positive driving force in retail advertising.
3. The reader will learn how layout styles can be combined to better showcase an ads visual/verbal components.

Diverse Layout Styles Speak Both Visually and Verbally

A brand's use, personality, and overall quality, can be expressed through its *layout style*, or how its components are arranged within the ad.

What do you want the concept direction to represent? Will you be using lots of white space to project luxury and/or elegance? Will your dominant component be the headline, or a single image, or group of images? Will there be a need to demonstrate some aspect of the brand with copy and images? Will the ad boast graphics and show a lot of color? Do you want to section off the ad, to show the viewer multiple benefits?

Think of layout styles as the concept's personality. Is it colorful, simplistic, modern, sophisticated, or busy? Does it educate through copy, or show and tell with visuals? It is critical when choosing the look of the layout to decide what you want the design to express visually to the target as well as what and how it verbally delivers the conceptual message. In this chapter, we will look at 15 of the most commonly used layout styles including big type, circus, grid pattern, copy heavy, frame, Mondrian, multipanel, picture window, rebus, silhouette, symmetrical, asymmetrical, repetition, anomaly, and concentration.

Big Type

Big type places the focus squarely on the headline. If the brand can boast a unique key consumer benefit, the ad should say it as large and as loud as possible. Any images employed play a secondary role in this layout style. The ad's personality and image are represented by the choice of typeface and what it says. Typically, the size and weight of the typeface will vary, but should create a distinct and orderly pattern. The informative beauty of this layout style is very direct and clean. Type works as a graphic, creating mood and projecting image. If images are used, they play a subservient role to the headline, not competing or interfering with what is being said. If you are attracted to the shape, texture, and expressiveness of type, the chance to use it as a graphic verbal component is the strength of this layout style. Big type is best employed in mediums boasting a lot of space, such as web pages, magazines, billboards, and direct mail to name just a few. See Figure 8.1 for an example.

Grid Pattern

The *grid pattern* layout style uses a grid to organize individual visuals into a box where they can stand alone from the other components or visuals on the page. Each visual will usually have an accompanying headline, a small amount of descriptive body copy and price point(s). Usually appearing in the bottom quarter or third of the page, the grid itself is usually outlined in black or another dark color. The top portion of the ad may be filled with a large visual or headline and often a bit of body copy. Although the smaller size of the visuals used should be taken into consideration, this layout style is great for use in most print and digital mediums. See Figure 8.2 for an example.

Circus

The *circus* layout style is always a hodge-podge of every visual/verbal component in a designer's toolbox. It is not surprising to see multiple type sizes and faces, multiple images without accompanying type, assorted *snipes*—black triangular shapes used as announcement devices, usually placed in the a top corner of an

DOI: 10.4324/9781003255123-9

Figure 8.1 Example of a big type layout style. Image courtesy of Katie Truppo, University of Tennessee.

ad—and *bursts*—a star-shaped announcement device that pushes grand openings and sale dates in bold reversed text. The resulting layout has no eye flow, structure, harmony, or balance, only chaos. There is always too much randomly being said and shown. Unfortunately, many clients will have a lot they want to say and show, so it is imperative to control that chaos. For example, consider combining multiple visuals and accompanying copy in some type of pattern or grouping compatible images based on size, use, or color, to place emphasis on a single dominant area. Whatever choices employed, the goal is to try and create as much white space as possible. By creating a strong structure, you can create much-needed eye flow, and the target can more easily move between components or between geometric blocks of visual and verbal information without missing anything. Structure also eliminates that chaotic look and grounds the design. Try to avoid

using this layout style anywhere, but it is usually seen in one form or another in bill stuffers and direct mail.

Copy Heavy

Both headlines and visuals play secondary roles in a *copy heavy* layout style. All the focus is placed squarely on the body copy. Visuals are small and often wrapped into the body copy to show use. Visuals may also be used to show the brand alone, packaging, and/or the logo. Because it has a lot to say, this type of layout style is used most often to introduce or reintroduce a brand in mediums where the target is sure to spend some time reading the copy, such as magazines or web pages. This layout style is an excellent choice for young copywriters, who want to promote their writing skills.

Figure 8.2 Example of a newspaper ad, using a grid pattern layout style. Image courtesy of Robby Cockrell, University of Tennessee.

Frame

Frame layouts are a great choice when you want to draw the target into the ad or isolate your ad from surrounding text. Frames or borders can be of any weight or design, and they often define ad size. Frames can be simple unobtrusive lines, pin-striped, detailed, created via colored backgrounds, or illustrative or graphic in nature. The examples on the next page show varied weights for simple frame borders. See Figure 8.3 for sample frame options.

Frames, whether simple or created with more complex, often gaudy, or ornate images, are considered graphic additions. Be careful if adding images to a border, although decorative, they can be distracting, especially if the page or screen on which they will be viewed already has a lot going on. If a boring box or screaming graphics just won't work, consider adding decorative corners.

Except in rare situations, simple will always be the best design option. This layout style can be successfully employed in most print and digital mediums. See Figure 8.3 for sample of frame with decorative corners.

Mondrian

This layout style uses the same graphic principles as Dutch painter Piet Mondrian's art. The *Mondrian* layout style boasts multiple, brightly colored sections. Bold graphic shapes, blocks of text, diverse color pallets, and/or screen tints are used to segregate the ad into multiple parts that are used to lead the target through the ad. Each geometric or organically shaped section placed focus on a component used within the ad, such as headlines, subheads, body copy and/or visuals that creatively shows and tells the brand's story. By isolating individual elements, the layout ensures that each component is viewed independently.

The choice to use solid geometric shapes such as circles, squares, rectangles, triangles, and lines are a colorful and graphic way to isolate specific areas within an ad giving them a whimsical and at times three-dimensional feel when strategically placed near large areas of white space. When isolating bold colors within a shape, or reversing large text out of a colored background, you have a great opportunity to draw the target's eye, so be sure to take advantage and say or show something important.

Although best when used in a medium with color, this layout style can also be seen in black-and-white with each section represented with a different screen tint or shade. Overuse of shades can grey down the page, so be sure to incorporate strong blacks and whites and if possible, add a spot of color to this softer, more recessive, look so it will "pop." See Figure 8.4 for an example.

Multipanel

The *multipanel* layout style uses pictures with captions to tell a story, or to feature multiple products set up in equal-sized boxes. This layout style uses alignment to create an orderly pattern by placing boxes in a line(s). They can butt up against each other or have a small, equal amount of white space between shapes. Another alternative is to place smaller inset, or over-printing images, on top of one larger image to highlight details. Although traditionally placed body copy can exist, it is usually replaced by copy captions that are placed either inside the boxes or underneath. This layout style is a great choice when showing your key consumer benefit is more important than telling a lengthy story, when you want to make some kind of comparison, or are bringing the sight, sound, and motion of a television or video spot to the static printed or digital stage. See Figure 8.5 for an example.

FIGURE 8.3

8 pt.

6 pt.

4 pt.

2 pt.

1 pt.

FIGURE 8.3

Figure 8.3 Example of some of the types of borders that can be used in a frame layout style.

Picture Window

The *picture window* layout style features one large photograph, often with the headline overprinting the photograph. The type used in this show-and-tell layout style can be a solid color, or reversed out of the background. This is a great choice when you want to pull the target into the action showcased in the visual. For example, your visual might picture a grill with steaks and vegetables. The headline might say: "The Sizzle is the First Step to Mouth Watering Taste."

Any time you place type over any image, keep readability top of mind. Never place the headline over a busy portion of the headline, such as the grill, and trees or patio furniture, seen in the background. Choose a quiet portion such as a fence, pool, sky, or even patio decking or patios. To ensure readability, you may need to try a few different type sizes and/or weights. What makes this layout style work, is that you have to create a strong visual/verbal relationship between elements. This visually heavy layout style is best used in larger formats such as magazine, newspaper, alternative media, and most digital options. See Figure 8.6 for an example.

Rebus

If you need to show multiple smaller visuals, consider using a *rebus* layout style. To tell a strong visual/verbal story, visuals are often wrapped into the body copy. Images can also be used to replace words in the headline. This is a clean, elegant layout style

The Art of Wine and Food Mastered
Come Taste Time and Craftsmanship in Every Bite and Sip

Calling wine lovers and wine skeptics alike: The Winery at Seven Springs Farms has delicious wines and local food that will delight your pallet like never before. Separately, the wine and food is delicious and expertly crafted; but when paired together, expect to taste new and exciting flavors unlike any other. With every wine created on site, come enjoy a unique experience provided by local flavors and accompanied by a scenic view.

Everyone has a preference for their favorite types of wine, which is why each wine is specially crafted to be different but delectable. While our wines are unique, so are our other products; such as wine slushees or our grape juices which are made from the same delicious grapes as our wine. With a scenic view, tasting experience, and the combination of local food and wine, you will enjoy a fun and flavorful experience that you won't soon forget.

@thewineryatsevenspringsfarm
@winerytn

THE WINERY
AT SEVEN SPRINGS FARM

1474 Highway 61 East,
Mayndarville, TN 37807
www.winerysevenspringsfarm.com
865-745-2902

Figure 8.4 Example of a magazine ad with a moderate amount of body copy, using the Mondrian layout style. Image courtesy of Katie Truppo, University of Tennessee.

that works well with instructional copy, where an image can be used to explain copy points. Images can be consistent in size or alternate from small to large helping to create focal points and assist with eye flow. Since the visuals are often small, this layout style is best used in mediums with good production quality like magazines or digital screens. See Figure 8.7 for an example.

Silhouette

The *silhouette* layout style relies on the grouping of images within an ad to create one dominant visual element. To increase importance further, be sure a large amount of white space surrounds the grouped items. This layout style is a great option when you have multiple products of equal importance that have to be showcased. Consider grouping components first before

isolating them in a straight line floating across the page, with copy to support them. The grouping of like items and/or uses such picnic supplies encourages multiple rather than single purchases. Finally, when images are grouped in irregular shapes, you create additional interest as well as eye flow. See Figure 8.8 for an example.

Callouts

If the design calls for type to accompany each visual, consider using *callouts*, which are most commonly used with the silhouette layout style. Callouts include a couple of lines of descriptive text that appear near each image in the group and are connected by a small line. Text might point out sizes, colors, shapes, etc. Additionally, each callout will have a short informative headline

Figure 8.5 This example of a multipanel magazine ad shows the use of two columns of body copy to balance the design. Image courtesy of Carly Reed, University of Tennessee.

Figure 8.6 This picture window newspaper example shows the use of type wrapping around smaller visuals. Image courtesy of Natalie Rowan, University of Tennessee.

and feature one or more large bold price point(s). Be sure to balance the callouts evenly around the visual. This layout style is a great option if you want your visual grouping to break up the headline or copy, or when the image slightly overlaps the headline or subhead, creating an even stronger visual/verbal tie. White space is at a premium when items are grouped. When images are similar in shape or size, the silhouette layout style can be a little too static or flat looking. To alter its overly symmetrical or balanced appearance, consider allowing items to randomly touch the edges of the ad in opposing areas. Dramatic and eye-catching, this layout style works great in most all print and digital formats.

Symmetrical

An ad using a *symmetrical* layout style is considered balanced when components on either side of an implied centerline are not only perfectly centered or balanced on the page, but identical in weight, number, and size. This commonly used layout style is great for comparing various qualities, or presenting "both sides" of a brand. Simple and direct, this layout style works great in almost all print and digital formats. See Figure 8.9 for an example.

Asymmetrical

Broken into two unequal parts, an *asymmetrical* layout style lacks symmetry because it varies in size and shows different visual and verbal images. The unbalanced sides can be divided by either a drawn or implied line. Objects within the ad appear to be disproportionately placed on either side of this line. Usually the components of an ad are not of equal weight, size, or number. To counter the unbalanced look and to create an overall balanced appearance, the ad's components must be arranged, grouped and/or sized so that both sides appear to be balanced or of equal weight. This type of layout is generally more visually stimulating than one that is perfectly symmetrical. An attention getter, this layout style will work great in most all print and digital formats. See Figure 8.10 for an example.

Figure 8.7 This newspaper rebus layout example shows the use of two different but balanced use of margins and a coupon. Image courtesy of Lindsay Frankenfield, University of Tennessee.

Repetition

As the name implies, a *repetition* layout style creates organization—a pattern, or movement. Some aspect of the design is repeated throughout the ad. Same-shape elements are arranged to show a relationship. Movement can be created by slightly overlapping same-shape elements that grow in size or move from light to dark. This works great for showing growth or change. Repetition is also a form of consistency, such as using the same typeface throughout an ad or campaign, or the same size visuals, colors, logo, or ruled lines. Repetition can also be found in type size. For example, be sure all subheads are the same size and body copy is sized consistently from page to page, or ad to ad whenever possible. In the case of a campaign, the repetition of visual and/or verbal elements throughout an ad or campaign unifies the design with a consistent look. Because

visuals are sometimes small, this layout style is best used in mediums with quality paper stocks or a digital screen. See Figure 8.11 for an example.

Anomaly

An *anomaly* layout style focuses attention on the misfit within an orderly pattern. When you want your product to stand out from the crowd of similar products, consider creating a pattern of like products. Your product is placed within the pattern, showing its uniqueness among competing brands. Do not place your product in the center; use an asymmetrical placement to draw the eye to your brand, making it easier for viewers to remember its uniqueness among competitors. As to how many items it takes to create a pattern, this is hard to define; it will depend on the size of both the ad and the images employed. But for your target to get the idea of a repeated pattern, think somewhere in the range of 10–20 and go up or down from there. Like the repetition layout style, an anomaly has smaller visuals so it is best used in mediums using quality paper, and printing techniques and in larger digital formats. See Figure 8.12 for an example.

Concentration

The *concentration* layout style is all about movement and eye flow, or the distribution of an image. For example, if you were to spill a can of paint or dump over a box of cereal, the contents would be highly concentrated near the spill and then spread out across the page at random. The eye will follow the flow, spill, or even a beam of light to a predetermined point such as the body copy, product, packaging, or logo. This layout style works great in nearly all print and digital formats. See Figure 8.13 for an example.

Finally, it's important to point out that although diverse in visual scope, do not be afraid to combine one or more layout styles together. For example, going all out with a show-and-tell concept by using a combination picture window and rebus styled layout. Varied layout styles go in and out of fashion, so not all of these styles may be currently relevant to what is happening in design today. However, the more knowledge of the options you have will keep your design cutting edge, as you create diverse looks and personalities for your brands. Because of this, there are no hard and fast rules per se as to which layout style(s) are best suited to a specific medium. However, as a guide to deciding which style or combination of styles to use, look first to your key consumer benefit, and then consider how that visual/verbal message will be delivered and perceived. Readability and legibility issues, along with those concerning the principles of design, will play the same crucial role in your choice of layout style as it does in the choice of typeface, or visual.

Every eccentric style needs a dash of unique taste.

Experience Morton Sea Salt with all the benefits of organic health.

Harvested from the Mediterranean.

Add unique flavor to your next dinner party!

Naturally Original.

Figure 8.8 Example of a silhouette layout style. Image courtesy of Ally Callahan, University of Tennessee.

Most Ads Will Have a Lot to Say and Show

Typically, most ads will have multiple components, many of which on first glance may appear as being equal in importance. Although clients often see it this way, it's the art director's job to organize those elements into a cohesive package that lead the target on a predetermined journey through the ad. Components as we have learned in Chapter 3, might include a screaming headline, subhead(s), body copy, announcement devices, and one or more visuals, links, video, descriptive copy, and/or price points, depending on the media and life-cycle stage. You may also need to add a slogan or tagline and certainly a logo that will not get lost along the clutter highway. Traditionally, the number of components will help you determine the most appropriate layout style to employ.

Ads with too many components are the most common problem found in design. So before beginning the layout process, always look first to your key consumer benefit, then the relationship between components, and finally the medium in which the ad will be viewed. Your key consumer benefit and the number of components that need to appear in the ad will determine how you arrange each component on the page, as well as whether you need to educate by explaining, or showing

Figure 8.9 Example of a symmetrical layout style, with the headline set on a curve to match the visual. Image courtesy of Madison Duncan, University of Tennessee.

exactly what the brand is, how it works or is used, when and where it will be available, and who is selling it. If you just can't eliminate an element from an already cluttered-looking ad, remember, a discriminating dose of white space and use of one dominant visual or verbal image will clean up the look. Your job is to decide what that one dominant element should be. A large headline assists in announcing an event; placing the key consumer benefit in the headline personalizes the brand; showing the product alone allows the target to imagine themselves using or interacting the brand. Any additional visuals can be smaller and placed lower in the ad or within the body copy. Once the ad has the target's attention, it needs to entice him or her into the body copy, or, if well known, to the logo.

Price as a Design Element

Whether print or digital, almost all mediums have to sell something and I would be remiss to not talk about prices and layout styles in the same breath. Many of the layout styles we have looked at can be used to showcase price points. They are ugly and usually distracting, but are a must in all but a few mediums. A good-looking ad that the target can relate to is important, but just as important to all consumers is price. We are as attracted to price as we are to any visual. Show it boldly when you can by making it an integral part of the layout.

Image-based advertising like that found in magazine design or any number of alternative and promotional pieces encourages

Figure 8.10 This asymmetrical layout shows the headline overlapping the visual and the use of colored type. Image courtesy of Kristen Eddleman, University of Tennessee.

Figure 8.11 Shows an example of the repetition layout style. Image courtesy of Paul Domingo, University of Tennessee.

your visual(s) to take center stage and dominate the page; this type of advertising often forgoes showing price to focus attention on showing the product alone or in use. A large photograph or illustration attracts the eye—as does a group of several items, causing a large mass of tones, lines, sizes, color, and black-and-white contrasts. As tacky as they are, even image advertising has to give a price(s) somewhere, whether it is delivered through a link to a webpage, in a brochure, through a mailed catalogue or direct mail piece, or via promotional pieces found in brick-and-mortar stores, to name just a few.

Using Margins to Organize the Ad

No matter the layout style employed, margins play a big role in the layout process. Margins help to not only ease readability and legibility issues but also ensure an organized and consistent look throughout the design.

All layout styles need margins, or the white of the page *inside* the ad where only visuals and graphics are allowed to invade. Text must never go beyond the set margins, created for example in

Find a new guilty pleasure.

Halo Top's extra creamy ice cream is high in flavor and low in guilt.

Low calorie ice cream isn't a new concept, but creamy low calorie ice cream is. We are the world's first all-natural light ice cream. You can enjoy an entire pint of Halo Top for 360 calories or less. And Halo Top ice cream isn't just low in calories, it's protein rich and sugar poor. We've sweetened the deal with stevia, a natural plant-based sweetener that has

been used for hundreds of years all over the world. We pack the protein from nothing but the milk and cream we use to craft this ultra-creamy dessert. That's way less than traditional ice cream, and the desserts that inspire our flavors. With 17 flavors to choose from, you'll never have to be deprived of the decadent ice cream you crave.

low-calorie *high-protein*
Get the scoop on healthy.

Figure 8.12 A magazine example of an anomaly layout style. Image courtesy of Jordan Vandergriff, University of Tennessee.

InDesign, to safeguard the verbal message by ensuring text is not accidentally cut off during printing or runs off a digital page.

Although not drawn on the page, these implied lines are clearly visible to the reader or viewer. Very simply, their job is to align elements and corral chaos on the page. For example, if you have a headline that is flush right, rag left you would want any subheads or body copy beneath it to align along that same implied flush right margin. On the opposite side of the ad, a visual that does not bleed beyond the margin will set the implied margin for anything under it. If the visual does bleed, the left side will follow the same margin setting as on the right.

The amount of white space employed will depend on the size of the ad and the overall design. A poster, for example, may have

three inches of white space showing on all four sides. Whereas a magazine ad may have one-quarter inch of white space while a mobile ad may have one-eighth inch. Margins do not have to be equal but they do need consistency. For example, the top and bottom of the ad could have a half-inch margin, while the left and right sides have a quarter inch. This consistency in placement is one of the ways chaos is controlled and eye flow is employed.

Beyond an organizational tool, the judicious use of white space, as previously discussed, can isolate a visual or verbal design component, drawing the reader or viewer into the ad. Remember, the more white space available, the sleeker and more elegant the ad will appear. Ads that lack or have an inconsistent amount of white space appear more cluttered, projecting a negative message to the target about quality, no matter how much it is discussed in the copy

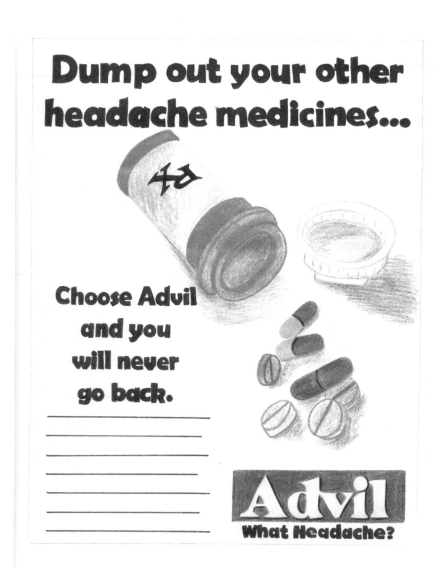

Figure 8.13 A magazine example of a concentration layout style. Image courtesy of Carly Reed, University of Tennessee.

or shown in the visual(s). If the ad looks chaotic and is lacking a strategic use of white space and is crowded, it reflects poorly on the message and by association the brand. Always keep in mind that perception can out outweigh a million words and a dozen visuals.

Just as distracting is placing disproportionate amounts of white space between or around items. Use the white of the page to frame components and lead the reader from one visual/verbal component to the next. A form of eye flow, the controlled use of white space allows the art director to determine when and how each essential visual/verbal design component will be seen by uniformly and informatively moving the target through the ad.

The lack of consistent white space between components such as type, visuals, graphics, lines, boxes, and bars, not only affects visual relationships, but readability and legibility as well as the look of the layout style, causing it to look clustered in certain areas, open in others, and cluttered overall. How much white space should be placed between components varies. As a rule of thumb only, start with a quarter inch and go up or down from there as dictated by your concept, the medium and overall size of the ad.

In the end, the layout style employed is not an afterthought and should be given careful consideration. Always try out different styles during the brainstorming and thumbnail stages of design to see your brand in different settings. If it does not strategically represent the brand or target's image, its use, price point(s), life-cycle stage, or if it doesn't reproduce well within the medium in which it will be seen, it should not be used.

Spokespersons and Character Representatives as Part of the Concept

Chapter 9 Objectives

1. The reader will learn the difference between spokespersons and character representatives.
2. The reader will learn the varied types of spokespersons.
3. The reader will understand how brand representatives of any kind speak for the brand across multiple mediums.

Spokespersons and Character Representatives: The Real and Animated Brand Voice

When you have something you want to visually project with personality, consider using a brand representative, also known as a spokesperson or animated character representative.

A *spokesperson* is represented by a real person that is an unknown or known personality, and a *character representative*, is an imagined or animated figure. Both are enduring brand symbols, and their job today is the same as brand representatives of the past: Personify the brand's image. The advertising industry has a long and successful history of using both forms of brand representatives. Both can visually and/or verbally speak for any type of brand in any type of media. They are particularly well suited to television and varied digital mediums, where sight, sound, and motion can bring their unique personas to life, and where relationships between the brand and target audience can be further developed and nurtured. As a message delivery device, these very individualized images can be uniquely tied to a brand by look, feel, sound, tone of voice, and overall message. The more creative solutions can single-handedly build equity for brands that have few or no discernible differences from competing brands. The

more likeable and distinctive they are the more likely they are to be remembered and motivate the target to repeatedly tune in, log in, and/or follow them to see what they are up to next.

Today, a brand is more than just a name, or a logo; it's an icon for an image and a lifestyle. When developing a brand's visual and verbal voice, the creative team must think memorable, relatable, and long-lasting. For a brand to capture the target's attention, it should strategically, tirelessly, seamlessly, and creatively be able to tie its importance to the target's overall life, health, and happiness. One of the more compelling ways to accomplish this is to assign a face and personality to the brand the target can relate to by employing the use of a spokesperson or character representative.

The Role of the Spokesperson or Character Representative

In a marketing world where all brand categories are crowded, it's the brand's perceived demeanor that sets it off from the competition and makes it memorable, especially if there are no major differences between brands in the same category. Creatively, the use of a spokesperson or character representative can 1) create brand awareness and build brand image, 2) build trust and help to create brand loyalty, 3) give brands a repetitive visual identity making it easier to remember, 4) easily show consumers how to use the brand, and 5) project both the brand's image and the target's self-image. The correct "personality" can become more recognizable than a brand's logo and sometimes the brand itself. Popular spokespersons like Flo from Progressive Insurance ads for example, actually have more social media followers than the company itself.

DOI: 10.4324/9781003255123-10

Once recognition is achieved, it is important to keep your brand representative, whether real or imagined, growing and changing to remain a brand asset and not become stale or appear old-fashioned. Modern advertising no longer simply sells something; it must also entertain. No one tunes in or logs on to view advertising. Your target must be engaged with the message to ensure they do not fast-forward or click out of the message. Today, to ensure interaction, it is important that the advertised message be as entertaining as the programming it is associated with. One proven way to accomplish this is to introduce a brand representative that has a soap opera-style story to tell.

One of the best and most successful examples of entertaining storytelling and continual change is the Allstate Mayhem guy. Mayhem, played by actor Dean Winters, is part of everyone's life and Allstate successfully tapped into this shared experience by showing potential disasters in an unusual way. Each ad, diversely and comically represents situations we have all had, or will possibly run into. Initially looking for a unique way to compete against GEICO'S Gecko and Progressive's Flo, Allstate introduced Mayhem in 2010 where he first appeared in the guise of a falling tree branch. Over the next several years, he has stoically played the role of a teenage girl, a raccoon, a puppy, fog, snow, a pigeon, and a ringing phone, to name just a few. His purpose is to get consumers asking themselves, "Does my insurance cover that?" Thanks to his changing personas and constant and diverse reminders that annoying and destructive things happen, he keeps the campaign fresh, and builds awareness and thus brand image.

The Conceptual Evolution of a Brand Representative

Product categories that lack sex appeal, such as insurance, appliances, banking, or cereal, to name just a few, need a unique creative approach to set the brand apart not by features but by status, image, relatablity, or personality. When you decide to use a spokesperson or character representative, you not only give your brand a personality, but a face. To endure, and stand out among competing brands, it is critical to not only deliver a message the target can relate to, but when possible, deliver the message in a unique way. For example, the iconic E-Trade talking baby was the result of a strategy that wanted their target to understand that E-Trade could deliver easy-to-use financial tools that simplified the buying and selling of stocks and bonds. How easy are the tools to use? So easy "a baby could do it." Creative not only because of the talking, slightly sarcastic baby, but because a tough intellectual topic was reduced down to a simple message, and strategically delivered by a cute and memorable spokesperson.

When properly targeted, developed, and delivered, consumers will buy into a created and creative image over the status quo; it just needs to fit their image and their needs. Inspirationally, the choice to use a brand representative will begin with the creative brief and further developed during the brainstorming stage.

Conceptually, the decision to employ a brand representative is only the first stage in a multi-step evolutionary development process. The creative team must begin by asking themselves: What are we strategically being asked to do? Do we have the budget for a brand representative? Will the client consider a spokesperson or character representative a viable creative option? What kind of tone do we want to set? What kind of personality can best deliver that tone and personality? Will a spokesperson or character representative strategically accomplish the objectives? If the answer to these questions is yes, the next step is to decide if the personality chosen will be a real or imagined one.

The best place to start when determining who will speak for a brand is with the key consumer benefit. Unless the brand is new or completely reinventing itself, review its current image, then define possible scenarios for use, and branch out from there. By highlighting characteristics that may be taken for granted, you can exploit them by giving them a bit more star quality. Next dissect your target audience. Will the target buy into a spokesperson or character representative speaking for this brand? What psychographic traits can you tap into? What visual, social, and cultural initiatives is the target interested in? What does the target currently think about the brand, the competitors? How do they, or would they, use the brand? Answers to these questions will help the creative team determine how the designated brand representative should look, act, and speak.

Once the choice between using a living, breathing spokesperson or an animated personality is made, the next step is to determine their visual and verbal voice. What will they look like? What clothing, accessories, and colors will they wear? Will they be male or female? Young or old? Cranky, quirky, or sexy? Tall, short, stout, or wiry? Will they have a deep voice, or a high scratchy one? Will they have an accent of some kind? Each decision is as important to determining how your target will view the brand, as the choice of layout style, visuals, colors, and typefaces. The next step is to brainstorm how the message will be delivered.

Finally, to ensure the brand representative resonates with the target, each step should be thoroughly researched, debated, and tested. If the wrong personality is chosen to represent the brand, it can be a costly blunder and can adversely affect not only how the target views the brand but effectively erode brand image. To increase the odds of success, be sure when developing a character representative or hiring a spokesperson, that each of the following traits are designed into the persona:

- Relatable appearance
- Likeable personality
- Trustworthy demeanor
- Expertise
- Credibility.

No matter what their appearance, the ultimate goal of any brand representative is to convince the target that your brand is the perfect accessory to their lifestyle; if they can do that, you will successfully create brand awareness and build the personality that defines your brand's image.

A Spokesperson as the Brand's Visual and Verbal Voice

The choice of spokesperson should be based on their relationship with, or resemblance to the target, their overall style, or some aspect of their personal lives, interests, or professional accomplishments. Spokespersons can be broken down into four basic types: Celebrities, Specialists and CEOs, Common Man and Social Influencers, and Politicians. Let's take a quick look at each one.

The Star Power of Celebrities

Celebrities, such as actors, athletes, musicians, and singers, are chosen for their popularity, especially with younger targets, the tenor of their voice, their sex appeal, their success, or their political or charitable affiliations. Most brands choose to use celebrities as their spokesperson in order to project their credibility, acceptance, and personal image onto the brand. The choice is not an arbitrary one. It is important that the celebrity's professional image match the brand and the message. For example, no one wants to see a young movie star or fashion icon selling bladder-leakage products.

Some of the most popular brand categories that typically employ varied types of celebrities include fashion, hotels, liquors, food, and cars. The problem with using a celebrity spokesperson is their current popularity or level of fame is often fleeting. If they are no longer playing, acting, or performing the job title that prompted their notoriety, they can make the brand seem passé. Additionally, and perhaps most importantly, celebrities are not perfect people. Any character flaws or indiscretions that might arise over time can and will reflect negatively upon the brand. Finally, there is

what is known as the "Vampire Effect," which refers to a brand representative that effectively becomes so recognizable as the face and voice of a brand that they drain the lifeblood from the brand to the point that consumers cannot recall the brand name.

Celebrity endorsements can be broken down into four different areas:

Unpaid Onscreen Spokesperson. Charities supported by a celebrity are the most common types of unpaid onscreen spokesperson. Thanks to their popularity, they can continually talk about their charitable interests beyond advertising efforts, when doing promotional interviews for their latest movie or upcoming TV show.

Paid Onscreen Spokesperson. Paid onscreen spokespersons are the most often used types of spokespersons. Celebrities are paid to tie their image to a brand and appear in a preset number and types of advertising. Jennifer Aniston is the spokesperson for Aveeno, Matthew McConaughey is the on-screen persona for Lincoln and Wild Turkey, and Jeff Goldblum pushes Apartments.com, to name just a few.

Celebrity Voice Over. This type of spokesperson is used for radio, television and many types of digital ads. Because the celebrity is not seen in any advertising efforts it is less expensive to use their distinct voice. Oscar winning actor J.K. Simmons for example, is the well-known voice of the goofy yellow M&M. Jon Hamm of "Mad Men" fame is the voice of Mercedes-Benz, and both Robert Downey Jr. and Bill Hader have given Mr. Peanut a voice. Celebrity voice-overs are not a great choice for use in a campaign, since a voice alone cannot be used on all media vehicles.

Dead-Person Endorsement. A dead person may not be able to speak, but their image certainly can. Use of old interviews, movie clips, or headshots can associate personality traits, political activism, and even nostalgia with a brand. The use of this type of spokesperson can feel contrived and is often controversial and often considered tacky. Recent resurrections include Jimmy Dean for Jimmy Dean Sausage and Harland Sanders the original KFC colonel.

Specialists and CEOs Know Their Stuff

I've heard that David Ogilvy once said in an interview, "You had to be desperate to use your CEO as a spokesperson." I couldn't find the quote anywhere but it sounds like something he would say, basically because CEOs can often lack personality. However, for technical, new, or reinvented brands, you may want to consider using CEOs, company presidents, or specialists such as scientists, engineers, or doctors, to give a brand credibility. Steve Jobs became the visual and verbal voice for all things Apple. Since the early '90s, Jay Bush, the great-grandson of BUSH's founder

A.J. Bush, and his loyal dog Duke have been selling baked beans, but no secret recipes for years. But just like celebrities, personal images and thus brand images can be easily tarnished. Papa John's Pizza founder John Schnatter resigned after admitting he used racial slurs. Martha Stewart resigned her position as director and chief creative officer at Martha Stewart Living after her conspiracy conviction. Working damage control, Uber relied on its new CEO Dara Khosrowshahi to clean up the brand's image after a sexual harassment scandal brought damaging publicity to the young company.

The Believability of the Common Man or Social Media Influencer

To avoid any preconceived personality characteristics, the use of unknown talent offers the creative team a more moldable and diverse way to develop the brand's face and personality. Since the creative team will be searching through a larger pool of available actors, it will often be easier for them to find models that more appropriately represent the brand's image, and the target's self-image, demeanor, and style. See Figure 9.1.

Figure 9.1 Progressive's very popular spokesperson Flo. Photograph courtesy of Robyn Blakeman, University of Tennessee.

Another option is to use testimonials, where actual users talk about their experiences with the brand. Alternatively, these testimonials can be delivered by an actor who is paid to represent the Common Man, based on feedback from real consumers. Actors are used as an accepted replacement option because they can deliver the message with more expression, conviction and, ultimately, believability. However, any time an actor is substituted for an actual brand user, it must be stated or shown in the ad.

Professionals are great, but today's consumer prefers seeing and hearing a Common Man talk about his/her personal experiences. Today's consumers tend to believe unpaid spokespersons over big-paycheck celebrity endorsers, no matter their level of fame or believability. It is thought that celebrities, with all their power and faults, have saturated the market and are becoming less believable. They also limit the length of time a campaign can run. Star power rarely lasts as long as a brand's does.

Social influencers as spokespersons for a brand offer consumers the opportunity to actually interact with someone knowledgeable about a brand, who is more like themselves than millionaire celebrities or athletes. Today, it is often more popular to use multiple influencers or users of the brand, to help build a relationship between the brand, the target, and use.

Politicians Represent Authority

Relatively new to the spokesperson category are politicians. The endorsement of a brand by a former local, state, or national politician, can be very persuasive. This diverse group can be risky, but are typically a great choice to represent varied types of charitable organizations. Former Presidents George H.W. Bush, Jimmy Carter, Bill Clinton, George W. Bush, and Barack Obama teamed up with OneAmericaAppeal.org to raise money for recovery efforts after Hurricane Harvey.

Designing and Developing Character Representatives

When a live actor who fits the client's or the creative team's conceived personality for the brand cannot be found, one will need to be created. Character representatives like Mr. Peanut or Chester Cheetah are created on the page or screen to represent the voice and face of the brand. Although more expensive initially to create, animated character representatives are a lot cheaper to maintain over the long haul and a lot more reliable than real people. They are created specifically for the brand and are controllable; they will not be arrested or seen advertising another product. They *are* the brand. Character representatives also have a longer lifespan than any spokesperson. Their popularity does not rely on a single game, show, concert, or movie. Their only job is to speak for the brand, in the persona developed for them. Mr. Clean, the Pillsbury Doughboy, and the Keebler Elves have survived for decades because they are lovable, reliable, and have never taken a political stand or been involved in a scandal. See Figure 9.2.

Just as successful at attracting attention as spokespersons, character representatives can 1) more easily be developed into likeable and memorable personas, 2) be easily adapted to changing trends, 3) age gracefully with a brand for decades, 4) build stronger connections with the community by employing locally recognized mascots, such as those representing a local university or theme park, 5) successfully be used across all media and at varying sizes, and 6) be merchandised and sold or given away at promotional events.

When you start image development from scratch, it is easier to match the character representative's look and demeanor to that of the target and the brand, since they are created in the animator's imagination. Thanks to their graphic nature, animated figures are not limited to realistic forms, or traditional sounds or colors. Every aspect of the brand, from its shape, sound, name, color, and possible uses will be used as inspiration for character development. For example, shape was the creative foundation for iconic character representative Bartholomew Richard Fitzgerald-Smythe, better known as Mr. Peanut. His initially less-than-stellar appearance was personified once outfitted with a monocle, gloves, spats, and a top hat and cane, giving the dapper little legume a touch of class. Word association can also spark inspiration, such as with the American insurance company Aflac's duck quack. Creative associations can be tied to use, such as Energizer batteries use of a Pink Bunny toy that "keeps on going and going." In a metaphorical nod to packaging, Progressive uses a talking box known ironically as "The Box," that represents their multitude of packaged insurance options. Other associations might

be tied to folklore, historical characters or events, an existing or resurrected trend, or even come from one of the creative teams past experiences—the options are limitless.

One advantage to using a character representative over a spokesperson is how adaptable and changeable they are, making it relatively easy to update them without retiring them. Not all character representatives live forever with a single look. Images can be updated or adapted to reflect a new direction in the advertising, sagging sales, or current cultural trends. For example, the Kool-Aid character representative has gone through several incarnations before becoming the Kool-Aid Man seen today. McDonald's updated Ronald McDonald with hipper-looking duds and a more coiffed look. Kellogg's has refurbished Tony the Tiger's appearance regularly over the last 60 years. He now boasts a younger character representative's muscles and proudly stands at 6 ft. 2 in.tall. But perhaps one of the most creative updates over the decades has come from M&Ms. Developed on a relatively small budget, the recognizable and iconic characters we see today were created to revitalize the brand. This successful reinvention took the colorful candy-coated chocolate candies and gave them individualized personalities based on color. Red's demeanor is sarcastic, yellow is a little on the simple side, blue radiates cool, green seduces, orange oozes paranoia, and brown is intellectual. Not only does each color uniquely speak for the brand, but there is also a color, depending on the day's events, that will speak to the target's colorful personality. See Figure 9.3.

Thanks to their longevity, it is not unusual for aging reps to get a facelift from time to time, but big changes to a beloved character can be tricky and should be done slowly but deliberately. Any changes should make sense for the brand and the rep, so as not to damage the brand's existing image.

Figure 9.2 Geico's gecko, one of the longest lasting character representatives, is just one of many diverse voices used in their advertising. Photograph courtesy of Robyn Blakeman, University of Tennessee.

Figure 9.3 Shows one of the ever-popular M&Ms "spokescandies." Photograph courtesy of Robyn Blakeman, University of Tennessee.

Here are a few additional character representatives you may recognize:

- The GEICO Gecko
- The Travelocity Gnome
- The Burger King, King
- The Coke Polar Bears
- Mr. Clean
- The Pillsbury Doughboy
- Chick-fil-A Cows
- The Dow Scrubbing Bubbles
- The Michelin Man
- Jack in the Box

Character representatives are easy to work with; they have no contract demands, are never late, and never grow old; they can change with the target, are exempt from the ever-changing trends in the marketplace, and will never have to retract a

tweet. Their images can and often do last longer than a live spokesperson.

Brand representatives can both visually and verbally represent a brand successfully across multiple mediums. They are not a temporary choice, often lasting decades, so they can hinder creative options if not possessing a unique personality. Those that do can often outshine the logo and the brand itself. Conceptually, the goal of all brand representatives is to create a relatable association between the brand and what consumers will get from using the brand.

Finding a visual and verbal voice your target will relate to is critical if you are planning to use either a real or imagined brand representative. What they look like and what they have to say is critical to building a relationship, and capturing and holding your target's attention. No matter what life-cycle stage your brand has reached, a spokesperson or character representative can successfully and entertainingly tell your brand's story.

CHAPTER 10
Graphic Design, Logo, and Package Development

Chapter 10 Objectives

1. The reader will understand the role graphic design plays in advertising.
2. The reader will understand the rules of logo design and its role in the brand's visual/verbal voice.
3. The reader will understand the complexities to package design.

Graphic Design Decoded

Graphic design can very simply be defined as the art of combining imagery with text to solve a conceptual problem. So you might ask what is the difference between graphic design and advertising design? It's perceptual actually. Advertising design focuses on strategy, idea generation, conceptual development, and campaign management across multiple mediums. Graphic design focuses on how to execute the concept. Art directors and copywriters conceptualize from market research. Graphic designers design aesthetically, using human perception and experience to creatively show more than sell.

The foundation for all graphic design begins with a thorough knowledge of the principle and elements of design, imagery, color, and text, and how to use them in a creative way to tell a relatable story about the brand or corporation.

The photographs and/or illustrations used in the graphic images seen in advertising and promotional pieces tend to be more imaginative rather than realistic. Images can be simple and straightforward, or striking and provocative, and often reflect trends in pop culture, religion, art, or politics. The odds of finding these types of images in real life is small to none, so a lot of work is done to create imagery in Photoshop and Illustrator.

When the focus is on thought-provoking graphic design imagery, the visual must convey the entire message, without the need for large amounts of copy. Whether seen in black-and-white, large or small, in print, or on a digital screen, the image must radiate the key consumer benefit, and resonate with the target.

When the design does call for type to be the visually dominant element, graphic designers will typically design it when possible, rather than work with what comes out of the computer. Although the science of readable and legible type design is never abandoned, new and/or existing typefaces will often get a liberal dose of artistic manipulation to ensure the face will visually and uniquely speak for the brand or corporation. See Figure 10.1 for an example of a logo development pictogram.

Versatile, graphic design can encompass all forms of visual and verbal imagery, come in varying shapes and colors, and be seen everywhere from common highway signs to CD covers, magazines, posters, greeting cards, direct response, and alternative media pieces, and on digital devices, to name just a few. However, the most recognized and commonly seen forms of graphic design are logos.

The Logo Visually and Verbally Speaks for the Brand

Before a brand can achieve equity, develop or maintain loyalty, or distinguish itself from competing brands, it must first have a consistent and recognizable brand identity. This consistent identity begins with the development of a logo design that appears in all communication efforts and on all packaging. A *logo* symbolically and/or typographically represents a company, brand, or service's name, image, or use. It will practically or abstractly represent the brand's image, use, personality, or reputation, as well as its successes and/or its failures. A brand's *visual/verbal identity* should both define its personality and image. It should also represent a viable solution to the target's problem. To ensure a brand will stand out amongst competing brands, it must have a distinctive look.

DOI: 10.4324/9781003255123-11

Figure 10.1 Example of a pictogram showing how a realistic image can be altered and then simplified down into a simple logo design. Image courtesy of Samantha Jones, University of Tennessee.

Research and Brainstorming Are the Best Places to Start

Logo design is not about moving a couple of typefaces and images around and showing them in different colors. It has a big job to do and it must do it in the loudest voice possible. It will take time. As with any design project, the best place to start is with a list of brand features and their corresponding benefits. Then take a look at the brand's corporate philosophy or mission statement, and then to the intangibles, like current image, use, and the target's thoughts on the brand. Once you have a firm understanding of what the logo needs to project, you can begin brainstorming and ultimately working with varied imagery, colors, and typefaces. Ten or twenty ideas will not cut it. Before you finalize what ideas the client will see, you might have done a hundred or more versions. Keep analyzing your designs—once you've narrowed down which options to move forward with, go back and look over what the brand needs to say and/or show. What would happen if you altered the typeface or changed the size, style, or color? What if your symbol was softened just a bit, or made larger, or placed in another color? Simple changes can make big differences; if you think your imagery, shape, or typeface feels too masculine for example, consider softening it with a lighter or more feminine color.

The Visual and Verbal Message Behind Logo Design

Logos speak for a brand often for decades, so its overall design is important. It must be both visually interesting and memorable. Unlike an ad, a logo does not need to tell a complicated story, but it must representationally speak for the brand and/or the corporation. To do this effectively, there are eight different types of visual and verbal logo design options to explore: Lettermarks, wordmarks, symbolic marks, abstract marks, mascots, combination marks, emblematic marks and subliminal marks.

Lettermarks

The *lettermark* logo style, also known as *monograms*, is a type-only design that takes a long complicated name and shortens it

amazon.com

Figure 10.2 Amazon's logo is a great example of a wordmark.

into an acronym to be more memorable. For example, it is much easier to remember UNICEF than United Nations International Children's Emergency Fund. Other notable lettermarks include NASA, FIAT, CVS, ESPN, GEICO, and M&Ms, to name just a few.

This very clean and unadorned look offers fewer options to personalize a logo design than any of the others we will look at. Because of this, it is important that the color(s) used and the typeface(s) chosen, whether existing or created from scratch, reflect the brand's image and use, such as sturdy, reliable, classy, playful, and so on. If working with a new brand it is not a bad idea to initially include the brand's full name anywhere the logo is used to assist with name recognition.

Wordmarks

Wordmarks, similar to lettermarks, are often used interchangeably. However, it is different because it focuses specifically on a brand or corporate name, such as Coca-Cola, Ray Ban, Disney, or Facebook. This logo style is particularly suited if the brand name is unusual sounding, distinctive, or easy to remember. For example, Amazon was named after the river to show scale, and when first created, website listings were alphabetical. See Figure 10.2 for an example of Amazon's logo design.

Disney's script-style logo, on the other hand, is representative of fantastical and imaginative thoughts and Walt Disney's signature. The bright red, blue, yellow, and green colors that make up the eBay logo project joy, enthusiasm, creativity, and energy. The diverse color choices and tight kerning are meant to represent the connectedness and diversity of the eBay community. SIEMENS, an industrial manufacturing company, is named after its company founder. The color turquoise was chosen because it represents serenity, freshness, nature, energy, and environmental production of the company.

Symbolic Marks

Symbolic marks, also known as *pictorial* or *brand marks*, are probably the most recognizable type of logo design. This style uses a literal or recognizable image to represent the brand, such as the iconic once-bitten Apple logo or the Target bull's-eye. These types of logos personify how a picture is worth not a thousand words, but just one. However, to stand alone, they are only successful after extensive advertising. One downside to the symbolic mark is that if the image is to literal, it can make future brand expansion into other areas difficult without change. A good example of this is Domino's rebrand in 2012. Going beyond just selling pizza, they minimized the look by moving away from the larger diamond-shaped graphic to a smaller more linear one, and dropped the word "pizza" from its new logo design.

Abstract Marks

An *abstract mark* is an ambiguous symbol, given meaning by its association with a brand or corporation. Abstract logo marks are very conceptual and tend to represent an idea or philosophy over a more literal approach. Typically, these types of marks use an abstract geometric or organic image over a realistic one. These very graphic and equivocal marks work best for large corporations with a diverse range of brands. Because the imagery is unique—think the Nike Swoosh, or Pepsi's red, white, and blue ball— corporations can drop or add to its product line without the need to change or update the design over time. Both abstract and symbolic marks can work great for both domestic and global brands, especially if a company name is hard to pronounce or does not translate well internationally.

Mascots

Mascots, also known as character representatives as discussed earlier in Chapter 9, are animated figures that represent the brand. Mascots are a great choice for brands that want to project family values or target younger audiences. One of the greatest advantages to using a mascot in the logo design is the opportunity to create interactive opportunities with the brand. See Figure 10.3 an example of mascot development.

Combination Marks

A *combination mark* or a logo containing both a visual and verbal component probably comprises the largest share of logo designs. As the name implies, it is the combination of a symbolic or abstract mark, or a representative mascot, with a word or lettermark. The design can feature the image and text laid out side-by-side, stacked on top of each other, or combined together to create a single visual/verbal image.

Toyota uses a symbol centered over a wordmark. Microsoft placed its symbol to the left of the wordmark, and IBM is symbolically created with lines. Burger King placed its name inside what looks like a hamburger bun, surrounded by a blue whirl. Tech giant LG combines two options in its logo. The first is an abstract version showing its inventive side in a colorful circle with the LG manipulated to create a face. Beside it to the right is a strong sans serif LG representing reliability. Red Bull uses both a wordmark and a symbolic mark. The name appears in red and the symbol places two charging bulls atop a gold circle. Nike's brand name comes from the Greek goddess of victory, an appropriate name for an athletic shoe. The "swoosh," or checkmark, stands for speed and movement.

A combination mark is best used when the brand can successfully tie an image with its name. The use of both helps your target associate the brand name with the symbolic image, allowing future logo updates to alleviate the need for letter or wordmarks and to rely solely on the image.

Emblematic Marks

The *emblematic* logo design places the brand name inside a symbol of some kind. Recognizable examples include Harley-Davidson, BMW, and Starbucks. This type of logo design never separates the brand name from the image. Because so many logos are used as apps, this often detail-heavy logo design can be difficult to read in reduced-size versions.

Subliminal Logos

Some logos are so intricately designed they incorporate hidden imagery within the design. For example, the sturdy FedEx logo

Figure 10.3 Logo design can take many forms before being broken down into a simple black-and-white image. Image courtesy of Sarah Fadule, University of Tennessee.

uses the negative space between the E and the X to create an arrow, meant to subtly show the company's forward-thinking delivery methods. See Figure 10.4.

The famous NBC peacock uses the multiple and diversely colored feathers to represent their varied entertainment divisions, and as a frame for the peacock's body, whose head is facing right to represent their forward thinking. See Figure 10.5.

The Pittsburgh Zoo's very unique logo makes great use of the negative space around the tree. If you look closely, the simple tree shape is actually the frame for the faces of a gorilla, a lion, and even a few fish. See Figure 10.6.

Logos with seemingly hidden images are memorable as the eye slowly picks out the not-so-hidden images.

Figure 10.4 The FedEx logo is a great example of a subliminal logo. Photograph courtesy of Robyn Blakeman, University of Tennessee.

Figure 10.5 The NBC peacock is another example of a subliminal logo. Photograph courtesy of Robyn Blakeman, University of Tennessee.

Figure 10.6 You have to look very closely at the Pittsburgh Zoo's logo to find the hidden images that make up this very creative logo design. Photograph courtesy of Robyn Blakeman, University of Tennessee.

When choosing to use any of these logo design options, it is important to ensure it is both readable and legible in any medium and at any size; it should have enough contrast to print in either color or black-and-white if needed.

Symbols and Images Replace a Thousand Words

More and more focus is being placed on the use of symbols over lengthy and detailed brand names and designs. Nike was one of the first brands to go textless. They have all but eliminated the use of their name and "Just Do It" tagline emphasizing instead its symbolic swoosh. Apple, MasterCard, and McDonald's are a few more examples of brands that have adopted a textless format after transitioning from a logo and tagline format. This simplified approach to logo design is a direct result of modern use on computer screens and apps. It also allows corporations greater flexibility to branch out into more diversified industries without needing to continually redesign their logos. According to an online article by Kalle Oskari Mattila in *The Atlantic* entitled "The Age of the Wordless Logo," this simplification by big brands is known as

> *debranding or decorporatizing—a strategy based on paring down that can only be deployed by the most identifiable of brands. Some marketers believe that debranding can make global brands appear 'less corporate' and more personal to consumers. Nameless logos can evoke more personal and immediate reactions—which is important in a media environment with plenty of possible distractions and diversions. Researchers have demonstrated that the use of visual imagery (vs. verbal imagery) in advertising increases consumers' attention and challenges them to interpret and understand the ad's message in a more active manner than words do."*

We live in a world of symbols, and it is extremely important to understand something about the power of symbols to wordlessly speak for a brand. A creative workhorse, a symbol can seamlessly 1) represent the brand's quality and use, 2) reach an often culturally diverse, targeted audience, 3) represent the brand and its overall use, and 4) tap into the target's overall beliefs, attitudes, opinions, and lifestyle. How well the brand is interpreted and remembered will depend on how well it matches what the brand is intended to offer the target and its ultimate use.

The symbols employed in logo design can take abstract concepts, ideas, uses, and values and translate them into tangible attributes that can be touched, seen, heard, tasted, or smelled. It gives a brand relatable characteristics. Logo design uses two basic types of symbols: Shape or imagery, and color.

Shape

Every shape—circles, ovals, ellipses, squares, rectangles, triangles, and lines—has a personality and a voice. Consumers will respond to these varying shapes in different ways. Since every shape (geometric or organic) can imply a different meaning, choice is important.

Circles, ovals, and ellipses are positive images that suggest femininity, community, friendship, stability, and endurance. Circular, elliptical, oval, and soft organic shapes are less intimidating than, say, triangles. They are uniting, calming, family friendly, and youthful. Organically shaped images that do not fit snugly into a geometric circle mold are interpretive. Typically, these shapes are found in nature, so they appear safer and less threatening or energetic, making them a great choice for natural or organic brands. Rare to logo design are spirals. Spirals are infinite, they are great at creating eye flow and, depending on the simplicity or complexity of the spiral, can represent creative or technology-based brands.

Squares and rectangles are considered stable and practical. These powerful shapes, thanks to their angles, are great at projecting intelligence, technology, sleekness, and stability. These strong attributes can be downplayed with color or typefaces that are on the thinner or rounder side. Because of their sharp angles, they are great for brands with an edgier, less traditional feel.

Triangles tend to appear more masculine, and project powerful, precise, and dependable personalities. Thanks to their directionally strong points, triangles lead the viewer somewhere, making them great symbols for religion, science, and the law. If using this strong shape to indicate direction or motion, be sure that it points up or to the right. Downward-pointing arrows or those pointing left reflect a negative or backward-looking philosophy.

Simple lines also have a lot to say. Straight lines, depending on their color, can appear weak, but when shown in bright colors can project professionalism and efficiency. It is believed that subconsciously we view vertical lines as masculine, powerful, and stable, while horizontal lines are perceived as more grounded, balanced, and tranquil; both can be used to represent speed and movement. Diagonal lines are dynamic, directional, and a bit dangerous. All line types are frequently combined with other shapes to sharpen or clarify their emotional effect.

Finally, there are also cultural symbols that can be tapped such as crosses, X's, hearts, or ribbons, to name just a few.

Whatever shape or combination of shapes is used in a logo's design, its overall appearance can say a lot about a brand. It can wordlessly project a powerful, scientific, artistic, modern, or traditional image. The meaning behind these shapes can be further manipulated through the choice of accompanying color and typeface combinations.

Color

Review the discussion on color psychology from Chapter 6. The choice of color(s) can bring multiple layers of meaning to your overall logo design. It is important that a color relationship be strategically drawn between your target, the brand, and the company philosophy. It is always best to begin your logo design in black-and-white. Fall in love with the idea first, before the color choices. Make sure your brand's color scheme distinguishes itself from competing brands, and can be used in varied mediums. Color will most likely be the first thing your target notices about the logo. Color choice will depend on what the brand wants to communicate. So know what the brand is about, before choosing the color(s) that will help you communicate that to the target.

Typeface

Typefaces used in logo design have far fewer restrictions than those used in ad or package design. Although readability, legibility, and media options are still an issue, more decorative, modern, and script faces can be used. Also logo design is a great place to design a typeface that is uniquely owned by your brand.

A simple place to start your search for the most appropriate typeface, symbol, and/or color is with a list of your brand's features, benefits, possible uses, and personality traits. Pair each word with one or more different typefaces or symbols. Change up the kerning and colors. Keep up this process until you can see and hear your brand in the design.

The Gestalt Principles

To extend your use of design psychology beyond shapes, color, and type, familiarize yourself with the Gestalt Principles. *Gestalt* translates to "unified whole" and is a set of theories that deal with visual perception. Developed by German psychologists in the 1920s, they determined the human brain tends to organize visual imagery into groups or unified shapes when certain principles are applied. Gestalt theorists believed that the whole is greater than its individual parts, meaning that a complete logo for example, carries a different meaning than its individual components (color, type, shapes).

Figure 10.7 The WWF logo is a great example of using the Gestalt principle of closure. Photograph courtesy of Robyn Blakeman, University of Tennessee.

There are five principles that relate to logo design: Similarity, continuation, closure, figure and ground, and proximity. *Similarity* occurs when shapes have a similar appearance. We tend to look for similarities in groups of shapes in order to develop a definable image. Throwing an anomaly into the pattern can create emphasis. *Continuation* refers to eye flow, where the viewer's eye can easily move between design elements. *Closure* refers to the brain's ability to complete or close an incomplete but recognizable shape. In other words, if enough of the shape is present, the brain will correctly interpret it by filling in the missing parts, giving closure to the design. See Figure 10.7.

Figure and ground refers to the eye's ability to differentiate any type of image or figure, from the surrounding ground or background. Finally, *proximity* occurs when multiple shapes are placed close together in a perceived grouping. Separate shapes, when placed close together, become unified and their close proximity forms a perceived shape.

Reasons for Redesign

There are two types of logo redesigns: Rebranding and repositioning. *Rebranding* takes place when the brand's look needs to be modernized. There might be a small to moderate change to the brand name, typeface, graphic, and/or color(s). These changes, primarily superficial, are meant to subtly alter the target's attitude about the brand. This "makeover" focuses on creating a more vibrant and timely look. Brands with equity will typically need only minor tweaks overtime. *Repositioning* is the result of major corporate changes, such as when brands have expanded their product offerings, there is a need to alter negative publicity, they have introduced a new or a major update to existing product offerings, the overall goals and values of the corporation have changed, or they want to be able to more easily pave the way for future product expansions. More simply, rebranding deals with the

outward appearance of a brand's image, and repositioning deals with both internal corporate and brand changes.

Corporations that have undergone some type of name change or merger will see some of the biggest changes. When this happens, you might see some type of combined logo design through the wordmark, color(s), or image to help maintain brand loyalty between the two target groups. However, if one brand has a better brand image than the other, the more successful brand will take top billing in both the name and design.

Where Can It Go Wrong?

Pretty much anywhere. When the client or creative team does not do market research to evaluate how the target will respond to the overall design, it can result in a lucky break or a very expensive design disaster. Clothing company Gap found out what happens when you up and change the logo without warning or target input. Their goal was to simply modernize their look, but the uproar on social media was so negative, they immediately reverted back to their traditional design to further avoid offending brand-loyal shoppers and ultimately affecting brand equity. Brands that want to update their image, especially if there are no major changes to the brand or corporation, in order to drum up publicity for an aging brand for example, should not begin with a logo redesign, but with advertising and promotion.

A logo's design is the end result of dozens and dozens of stops and starts, miscues, possibles, better and best designs. They are not an afterthought or something to be done at the last minute; they are the most enduring visual and verbal voice for the brand and will require a great amount of designing, redesigning, and debate before the final design is chosen. To alleviate a few of the most common faux pas, avoid:

* Using trendy colors and typefaces; they do not age gracefully over time.
* Incorporating religious or political images into the design that could alienate a portion of your target audience.
* Using irrelevant images that communicate nothing about the brand.
* Using visual and verbal imagery that sends an inconsistent message and that lacks cohesiveness or appears inharmonious.
* Using clip art; it will never be original.
* Designing with colors and with typefaces you love, ignoring what is best for the client and their brand.
* Working with designs that are overly complex. A simple logo design can be more consistently used in multiple mediums and at varying sizes.

- Relying on color alone to speak for the logo design. Every design at some point will need to be printed in one color.
- Choosing a typeface that does not match the symbol or graphic images used.
- Using too many typefaces. Keep choice to no more than two.
- Designs that too closely match an existing logo for another brand. Do your research.

The goal of every logo design is simple: Speak openly and easily for the brand and be original, memorable, and representational.

Logo Use in Design

The design of a company or brand's logo does not need to match any other advertising component. The logo is a separate visual and/or verbal design voice from any other advertised message it is associated with.

When used in advertising print design, it is still a good idea that it be the last thing the reader or viewer sees in an ad to help with memorability. Since in the Western world we read from left to right and from top to bottom, the logo should appear in either the lower right-hand corner or centered at the bottom of the ad, making it the last visual and/or verbal message the viewer sees. You can place the logo on the left side of the page only when your design is void of any type, and the eye flow, thanks to the visual, is moving or facing to the left.

For web pages, the logo can appear in the upper left, middle, or right. However, during the dawn of the Internet, logos were customarily placed in the upper left corner and traditionally that is where they are still found. In television commercials, the logo or the logo and the packaging will typically close every commercial. On packaging, placement near the top or centered on the package tends to work best.

If using a tagline or slogan, placement of these one-line phrases or statements can appear either above or below the logo. There is no right or wrong placement; it just depends on how you want it to read. Whatever choice is made, be sure the arrangement remains constant and does not change from ad to ad, to avoid confusion and to ensure consistency.

Uniformity can also be maintained through size and placement. In a campaign, when possible be sure the logo is always seen at the same size. When this is not possible, be sure it is in the same proportion, or it matches the appearance and size to other ads. Finally, if you place the logo in the bottom center of one ad, make sure it appears in the same position on all advertising and promotional pieces. Most brands will have very specific rules surrounding how the logo can be used in varied mediums, so be sure you are acquainted with them before beginning any design project.

Package Up the Brand

Like your logo, packaging can give your brand personality as well as set it off from competing brands on the shelf. Two simple ways to do this is through color and shape.

The psychology behind color choice is the same in packaging as it is in ad and logo design. However, building color combinations gives additional meaning by giving your brand a chance to say something at the point of purchase that other brands are not saying. A brand's shelf appeal is arguably the most tangible and memorable statement a brand can make.

Since all *consumer packaged goods* (CPG), or products that are frequently used and then replaced, will be surrounded by an assortment of competing brands, it is important the choice of color(s) for your brand's packaging be carefully considered. Remember, research tells us 80 percent of brand recognition is driven by color and that 85 percent of consumers buy a particular brand based on color. Why? Because the psychology of color is both highly personal and conditional. Color, as we already know, is suggestive, and can trigger varied feelings and thoughts, both positive and negative. Color affects all of the senses and our feelings. Just seeing a particular color can change our mood or perception.

With that said, color theory tends to bind brands to traditional "category"-based colors as a way to clearly relay information and incite an emotional response. For example, many natural and organic products tend to be packaged in brown, or sporting earthy green colors, while luxury or high-tech brands will often be seen in black, gold, and silver. This safety color net is helpful, but has a tendency to create packaging that is not only unremarkable, but fails to significantly differentiate one brand from another. The key is to determine what you can do differently. For example, just because all brands of peas come in green cans and feature a photograph of peas, doesn't mean your brand of peas couldn't employ a bright colorful vegetable-based illustration or graphic on a green can. If you're really feeling bold, how about placing the image on a deep purple can. No one will believe your peas are purple, but they will know your peas are fresh.

The choice to use an uncharacteristic color(s) can send a message of individualism and exclusiveness. If you are already working with a brand that has a color-based brand identity, don't be afraid to combine it with another color to not only stand out but differentiate it from other brand options. Coke used this color strategy for its diverse range of soda options, placing original Coke in its signature red packaging, with Coke Zero using black, Caffeine-free Diet Coke using gold, and Diet Coke using silver, to name just a few.

Beyond color, a brand's packaging should be a very engaging and tangible brand experience. Your target can touch it, smell it, feel its weight, and read or scan the label for more information. To ensure they get this far, you first have to attract their attention. Ask yourself: What will persuade my target to walk towards my brand in a crowded competitive environment? What is it about the packaging that can pique my target's interest? Is it the unusual package design? Loud and colorful graphics? Trendy imagery? A distinctive brand identity? Maybe, but chances are the color or combination of colors will be what first attracts their attention.

An individualized and unique color scheme and creative imagery will work synergistically to create a brand's initial and hopefully iconic identity. Many brands are known by the colors they use on their packaging; the Cracker Barrel cheese wrapper is brown, Bayer aspirin is yellow, and IBM is blue. When a brand "owns" a self-expressive color, it is imperative it be seen on not only its packaging but should become the blow-horn it uses on the shelf to attract the target's attention.

Although knowledge of color psychology is important, when it comes to package design it is typically more important for a brand's color(s) to support the brand's image or personality and overall message, than arbitrarily adapt to certain color stereotypes.

Because of this, it is best when determining a package's overall color palette to never start with a vast number of colors. Think one color at a time and work up from there; if you want "pop," think unusually shaped packaging instead.

The Shape of How Things Are Packaged

The psychology behind package design doesn't stop with color, it also includes shape. Packaging needs to connect emotionally with the target through color, shape, type, and graphics. Eye-catching designs help to set the brand out and away from its competitors

on the shelf. Consumers will typically care more about packaging that is easy to use, open, carry, and store, than one that is irregularly shaped and difficult to manage. Added values include packaging that is obviously tamper-proof, is recyclable or in some way ecologically friendly, and that has all nutritional or warning information clearly stated.

It is important to understand that the reason you don't see more unusually shaped packaging is because it is very expensive to produce and often difficult to use. It would be great to place your toilet bowl cleaner in a toilet-shaped package that shoots out cleanser when a button is pushed; however, although cool and original, it would be cost-prohibitive and probably more difficult to store.

But shape is important. Symbolically, shape, as we have learned, can say a lot. For example, masculine products are often packaged in angular-shaped containers, while feminine products' packaging have a tendency to be more curved. Prestige can also be projected through size. Smaller packages tend to be seen as higher quality, especially if designed with prestige colors and graphics. Larger, bulkier designs tend to scream bulk purchase and can often be heavy and difficult to store. Of course not all good things come in small packages, so be sure to keep the brand's intended use in mind.

Another form of packaging is shopping bags. Those with unique designs and colors not only attract attention but are sure to be saved and used over again, giving the store name a second, third, or fourth round of attention. The most intricately designed bags will typically be found in smaller niche stores. Since these often locally owned boutiques do less advertising, the expense to print them is often offset by their original and eye-catching designs, that tell anyone seeing the bag what the store is all about.

Never be afraid to let your packaging speak beyond your advertising. This is especially important to brands that are purchased online. Since the package will arrive much later than when it was first viewed, unique packaging can remind the buyer why they purchased that particular brand in the first place.

Getting Down to the Business of Design

The best place to start when designing the brand's packaging is to start by checking out 1) the colors used within the brand category, 2) the brand's logo, 3) the image your target already has of the brand, or that you want them to have, and 4) your key consumer benefit and corporate philosophy. Once you understand what needs to be accomplished, you can begin experimenting with color combinations, placement, and packaging shapes and materials.

The number of colors used on any package design should be given a great deal of thought. The more colors employed, the less credible and more low-end your brand will appear. So it is important to reflect on your brand category. If you are advertising health-related products or expensive jewelry for example, think no more than two colors as a rule of thumb. Brands in the technology, athletic, or even some food categories can boast a few more colors. It is important to note, if using a color other than white for your background or package color, it will affect any colors placed on top, so be sure to double-check your colors to ensure a correct color match.

What the Packaging Has to Say and Show

The typeface used on packaging can play an important role in how a brand is perceived. Keep it simple, be sure the size and type style chosen is readable and legible. Packages covered in type set in a large point size are often perceived as cheap, since pricier brands tend to use a smaller, more minimalistic, typeface(s). Larger faces are permissable, just don't over use them. Limit them to headings or secondary information in the same way you would in an ad design. Try to stick with a single typeface that has a diverse range of weights to project continuity with other advertising materials. Avoid scripts or overly decorative faces— they are great for logos but greatly reduce readability when used anywhere else.

To ensure optimum readability, avoid placing light-colored type on a dark background, or placing a delicate serif face on uncoated paper stock. Go for strong contrasts between the background color and the typeface, be sure to avoid over-stylization of letterforms, and don't forget about applying the appropriate amount of kerning and leading.

The imagery used should be useful. At its simplest, it should show the brand, ingredients, and/or use. At its most creative, it could incorporate all of these visuals into a single graphic image. For example, the visual imagery used on Tropicana's juice cartons, is a fresh orange impaled by a straw; not only does it show the brand, ingredients and use, it's a great visual example of a mnemonic device. Other options might include using a spokesperson or character representative, or designing some type of interactive options into the package design.

Interactive and intelligent packaging can be defined as packaging that has properties beyond encompassing and protecting the brand. It is an engaging, informative, and entertaining way to get your target interacting with your brand beyond initial purchase and use. Products that used to just sit on the shelf can now talk, interact, inform, educate, and entertain consumers, by delivering sensory experiences and added advantages that enhance consumer engagement. Whether they are edible, savable, or reusable, interactive packaging is growing.

The type of packaging selected will also make a visual statement. Coated packaging's bright colors and slick and shiny appearance feels more modern and expensive compared to the duller-finished, color-absorbing, aged and rugged appearance of an uncoated package. Clear plastics give the viewer a peek inside, while solid surfaces have a bit more mystique. Glass packaging says safety and preservation and offers up a lot of label-design options.

Always think unique not just utilitarian when coming up with your package designs. Those that use unique colors, imagery, or icons, or that are engaging in some meaningful way, have diverse package size and/or shape, use an individualized typeface and style, and have a creative logo design, will help to create a one-of-a-kind image within the brand category.

In the end, if the brand's overall logo design and packaging does not express the brand's image and use, and reflect the target's needs and self-image, it will not stand out from competing brands, attract attention, or create any level of brand loyalty, or build brand equity.

Bibliography

Mattila, Kalle O. 2016. "The Age of the Wordless Logo." The Atlantic.com (September 8). Retrieved from: www.theatlantic.com/business/archive/2016/09/the-ag-e-of-the-wordless-logo.

Writing Copy That Strategically Promotes the Brand and Talks to the Target

Chapter 11 Objectives

1. The reader will understand the role copy plays in advertising.
2. The reader will learn about the roles of each of the varied verbal components.
3. The reader will understand how to ensure copy and imagery work together to tell the brand's story.

Is Copy Still Important in Today's Visual Environment?

Thanks to social media and the Internet, images and video often define how a large portion of advertising messages are delivered and digested today. Although eye-catching, these often caption-only ads can curb a brand's ability to tell an informative story. Visual-only formats are interpretive, meaning every viewer will see something different and assign it a personalized meaning, whether right or wrong. As we have learned, a picture *is* worth a thousand words, which is why they should be carefully chosen by the creative team. The wrong interpretations can lead the target to believe the brand is promising to (or can) do something, it cannot. It's the copy that correctly defines and explains for the reader or viewer what they are seeing and its connection to them.

To ensure the target knows what the visual is saying requires an informative and creative form of visual and verbal storytelling that can hold the interest of even the most copy-avoidant target member, no matter its length.

Because modern-day consumers want to connect with brands on a more personal level, they need to know what the brand is about. Visuals alone cannot build or maintain a lasting relationship between the target and the brand. Visuals can show corporate philosophy but without copy, the target doesn't know why it's important or how it will affect their lives. Victor Schwab in the book *How to Write a Good Ad*, tells us, "The longer your copy can hold the interest of the greatest number of readers, the likelier you are to induce more of them to act" (p. 66), and the more likely you are to ingratiate your brand into their lives.

Lengthy copy, when vividly and usefully written, can help personalize the relationship between the target and the brand. But the copy must have a purpose; it must say something tangible and interesting to the target or why read it? Copy must firmly anchor the key consumer benefit and maximize its importance to the target. To do this, it must both show and tell. Showing a box of decongestant and a red nose could be made visually interesting, but it doesn't enlighten about ingredients, differentiate it from competitors' brands, or most importantly tell how your brand works to un-stuff a nose faster, without copy. If the target has allergies, or is a long-time user of a competing brand, a visual alone cannot tempt them to switch brands; only concrete information can help accomplish that. Because the art of informed persuasion will always be in fashion, advertising copy still has a critical role to play in many mediums in our visual world. To stay relevant, it must tell a relatable story of the target's interaction with the brand.

Copywriting: The Verbal Side of Concept Development

Once the digestion of the creative brief is complete and the conceptual direction has been solidified, it's time to start thinking about copy. Although the copywriter and art director are working

DOI: 10.4324/9781003255123-12

at the same time on the same job, they are no longer working together. Because of this, it is imperative that the copywriter and the art director are working towards the same solution visually and verbally.

The copywriter will develop the copy's verbal voice based on the direction decided upon during the brainstorming session(s). The goal beyond meeting the parameters set up in the creative brief is to ensure the copy relates to, and ultimately complements, the visual message, speaks clearly and creatively to the target about a problem they have and how the brand can solve that problem, and motivates them to act on what they have read.

Every sentence, statement, or block of copy, no matter its length or the medium it appears in, needs to capture and hold the target's attention in the first three seconds of viewing to ensure they do not click out, turn the page, or change the channel. This grab-them-or-lose-them mentality used to be reserved solely for radio and television advertising, but today there is so much advertising noise competing for customers with zero attention spans, that all messages must quickly get to the point, or get missed. Memorable advertising that captures attention and motivates is a mixture of a little luck and some good old-fashioned writing skills, that can successfully infiltrate an often apathetic, distracted target's imagination.

A Copywriter's Role

John W. Crawford, quoted in the book, *The Design of Advertising*, by Roy P. Nelson, saw a copywriter's job as composed of "two coequal and commingling parts." The first is comprised of "a never ending search for ideas," and the second is "a never-ending search for new and different ways to express those ideas" (p. 161). Once found, each strategically chosen word must conceptually deliver the right message to the right target audience, no matter the media vehicle employed.

To ensure this, copywriters will write and rewrite until the right words are found to verbally state the visual direction. Like art directors, they will never be content with the first round of drafts. The secret to great copy is never initially settling on a single way to deliver the key consumer benefit. Writing is a start-and-stop process. Once copywriters get their copy ideas on paper, they will repeatedly move words and paragraphs around, change up the tone or language, and edit down. These rewrites will spell doom for more than one version of not so brilliantly written prose, as they are deleted and/or recycled as crumpled paper balls tossed towards the trash basket.

The best copywriters not only understand the visual direction, but are well versed in all types of writing, since an idea may take a diverse array of forms such as a story, an editorial, a poem, or even a play, to name just a few. Advertising copy is that perfect mix of visual word play, either written or spoken, that will compel the target to take a certain action after being exposed to it.

What makes good copy? In a 2014 online article entitled, "19 Timeless Quotes That Will Make You A Better Copywriter," Steve Maurer focuses on how some of the best in the business looked at their craft. For copywriter Shirley Polykoff, it's all about telling it like it is: "Copy is a direct conversation with the consumer." For William Bernbach, it was quality: "Let us prove to the world that good taste, good art, and good writing can be good selling." For Leo Burnett, it was all about capturing and holding the target's attention: "Keeping it simple. Make it Memorable. Make it inviting to look at. Make it fun to read." For Henry David Thoreau, from the book *Quotationary*, by Leonard Roy Frank, it was all about imaginative writing: "Sentences which suggest far more than they say, which have an atmosphere about them, which do not merely report an old, but make a new, impression ... to frame these, that is the art of writing" (p. 957).

What makes a great copywriter? Well, you have to write well. Beyond that, you have to be inquisitive and a voracious researcher, be constantly in search of an answer to a stated problem. You have to be passionate about your craft, be a good grammar tactician, know the rules—so you know how to break them, be self-motivated, creative beyond borrowed clichés and the been-there-done-that copy of days gone by, even if you just saw it yesterday, be able to create something new from something old, be open-minded, and don't mind multiple rewrites and creative editing by the client and criticism.

The Skeletal Structure of Copy

A discussion of copywriting is a good time to reevaluate the importance of an informative and insightful creative brief. Like their designer teammate, a copywriter has to write within the parameters of the brief. Copy must further define the key consumer benefit and strategically tie its benefits to the target's lifestyle and needs. Most creative teams would agree with poet T.S. Eliot about the virtues of working within a framework of rules. Alan Joseph's online article entitled, "Give Me the Freedom of a Tight Brief—The Copywriter's Mantra," highlights this stance, telling us "When forced to work within a strict framework, the imagination is taxed to its utmost and will produce its richest ideas. Given total freedom, the work is likely to sprawl." Not an advertising man himself, you might think that is easy for him to say; however, a copywriter from Nashville, Tennessee is in agreement, saying: "I like to know what the limits are. The worst brief ever is account [service] telling you to do what you want or something like that. To do what you want, it is too wide, you don't have anything to bump up against" (Blakeman and Taylor, "Team Creative Brief," p. 44). All creatives hate boundaries, but they know if there is no direction, both copy and layout will come back for redesign or rewrite, both of which can be time-consuming and frustrating.

The copy's voice, like the concept direction, is the direct result of the creative brief. Once a creative direction or concept has been decided upon, the copywriter must determine what needs to be said, how much copy it will take to say it, the tone and style appropriate to project the concept, and how to adapt that copy to multiple media vehicles.

Diverse in its roles, copy can be broken down into six main areas: Headlines, subheads, body copy, detail copy, slogans and taglines, and promotions. The headline, subhead, and body copy all need to work together to build and explain a single message. Let's take a look at the role each plays in creatively delivering the key consumer benefit.

The Verbal Elements That Bring the Creative Idea to Life: The Different Parts of Copy

Once the key consumer benefit has been determined, copywriters give it both entertainment and informational value. Headlines promote it, subheads defend it, body copy develops and highlights its many virtues, and detail copy tells you where and how to get something. Copy is the brand's tone of voice. If a copywriter can't write copy that visually and verbally tells the brand's story, then they can't solve the target's problem and meaningfully separate their client's brand from competing brands.

Headlines Creatively Highlight the Key Consumer Benefit

While every element on the page plays a role in the success or failure of any type of ad, it is the headline that carries all the weight of engaging the reader in the copy. If it does not capture the target's attention, they will either miss or ignore it, never

getting down to the body copy where the actual sale is made. A headline seen anywhere has only a few seconds to 1) attract the readers or viewer's attention, 2) connect with the target in a relatable and memorable way, 3) lure the intended target into the body copy, 4) summarize the key consumer benefit, 5) identify the brand, 6) offer a tangible benefit, and 7) create a strong visual and verbal relationship. To accomplish this, the headline needs to draw out the *inherent drama* from your key consumer benefit. What is its essence? Its value? What aspects are interesting or unusual? How can it benefit your target audience? How is it different from competing brands? The inherent drama must be developed from the target's point of view to be eye-catching and beneficial.

Many headlines are ineffectual because they 1) ask a question that has nothing to do with the brand being advertised, 2) lack a relevant consumer benefit, 3) try to go for clever, rather than informative, and 4), insult, condescend, or patronize one or more groups in an effort to be creative.

We see headlines in all forms of advertising, for example, in the subject line of emails on homepage banners, near imagery and text seen on Facebook ads and Twitter posts, in click-to-skip ads seen on YouTube, on podcasts, on paid search ads, on direct response television, and on billboards and print ads. Without a great headline, advertising has no chance of making an informative first impression.

A *headline* must always be the first and boldest piece of copy seen in any medium, whether it appears above or below a visual. It is the largest and most dominant copy on the page or screen and because of that will likely be the first piece of copy the target will notice. It does not matter if it is a one-line statement or comprised of multiple sentences, a headline must scream out the key consumer benefit as well as answer how this particular feature and resulting benefit will solve the target's problem. When an ad promotes a feature that offers a highly targeted benefit, the consumer can view themselves using and benefiting in some tangible way from their interaction with the brand. It is also an excellent way to differentiate the brand from competing brands, for creating or elevating brand awareness and defining a brand's identity for the target.

Headlines Have a Big Job to Do

Every headline needs a bit of verbal intrigue in order to tempt the target into the ad. It should ignite enough interest to seduce the target into staying with the message instead of clicking out or turning the page. No one opens a magazine or boots up a computer to read ads, but their interest can be captured and held because the headline screams out the key consumer benefit in a creative, informative, thought-provoking, or even suggestive way.

Its job is to tell the target how the brand can benefit them and/or solve a problem they are having.

With that said, most consumers don't get past the headline. It is arguably the most important first impression your brand will make. If it fails to attract the consumer's attention, they will look to competing brands to meet their needs. The three-second attention span of the modern consumer puts a lot of pressure on the headline to do its job. Those that do it well can start not only a meaningful conversation with the target, but possibly turn that prospective customer into a sale.

Headlines as a Visual and Verbal Design Element

Headlines should have a presence on the page, not only because of what they say but also because of how they look and sound. Depending on their size and typeface used, most headlines will be set in a bold weight, and require a fair amount of kerning and leading to increase their dominance on the page. Placement will depend on the layout style employed. Just be sure the headline is not being swamped by too much white space. If it is too small, consider enlarging it or changing the line breaks to equalize space.

Headlines should not be blocky; for the sake of readability and legibility, it is best not to have lines of equal length. To avoid a weighted appearance and to increase white space, consider breaking multiple lines into short-long-short, or long-short-long, breaks. According to Roy Paul Nelson, every headline should have a "sense of rhythm associated with the line breaks." Nelson goes on to explain that "a headline should sound as though the copywriter tapped their foot while writing it" (p. 129). The best line breaks often simulate a conversational pause, or act like a period ending a sentence. No matter how you break it, be sure to never ignore grammatical rules, and be mindful not to hyphenate a word to make it fit the space, or break a proper noun.

There are times when headlines are not the best choice for promoting the key consumer benefit. Sometimes it is easier to show the key consumer benefit in action, placing the headline in a supporting role. No matter how the key consumer benefit is verbalized, it is important that it relate to the visual. There is no visual/verbal relationship if the headline and the visual deliver separate messages. W. Keith Hafer and Gordon E. White put it best in their book *Advertising Writing*: "The visual and headline are indivisible." Many headlines are so closely tied to the visual they would not make sense if seen alone. For example, if you see a headline that says, "Kills bugs fast," what do you think of? Bug spray? If we add the visual of a bright red Porsche appearing to race down the highway we see, understand, and feel, very differently about that headline.

To ensure the headline and visual are working together ask yourself: Does it at a glance convey the spirit behind the key consumer benefit you want to deliver to the target? Does it both show and tell? Does the visual and verbal imagery together tell a strong and unique story? If it does, you have created a strong visual and verbal relationship that is indivisible.

Getting Your Thoughts Down on the Page

Before setting down to write, the copywriter must review the creative brief and brainstorming sessions, conduct or run down any additional research that will be needed, and review the key consumer benefit and the media options.

Once you have your head around the problem, it's time to write a few things down. Start out by recording your initial first impressions of the brand and relevant competing brands, the target, brand uses, and any additional information you believe is pertinent to solving the client's problem. Finally, clearly define your interpretation of the feature/benefit combination that makes up your key consumer benefit. It is important to point out that brand features are interesting and relevant, and are usually the first thing young writers focus on, but alone they will not sell anything. Benefits, or the "What's in it for me?" mantra, is what ultimately captures attention and finalizes the sell. The more focus placed on the benefit in the headline, the better. As previously discussed in Chapter 1, features are easy to copy, competing brands either already have them or soon will. Benefits, although also shared between brands, can be made unique to a brand through advertising.

The next step is to start writing. In these early stages, it is not important to be creative or even grammatically correct, just on-target and on-strategy. By giving yourself permission to edit later, you worry less about perfection and more about multiple solutions. Start out by writing as many ways as you can think of to interpret the key consumer benefit. When you start to slow down, rely on your initial notes for some possible key words or phrases that might lead you in a new direction. If inspiration still hasn't struck, try creating a "word list" to help you exhaust every conceivable angle.

Read each headline out loud, to test the line breaks, the grammar, the language. Keep pushing yourself to continually rework what you have, to ensure the key consumer benefit is clear and diversely stated, speaks directly to your target, and is strategically written in just the right style and tone. Cut, paste, scribble, combine options, delete, start over. Your best idea will never be your first or even fifteenth idea, but it could be a combination of the two. You will know you are getting close when you are no longer inspired about what to do, but with what you have. Try not to get too excited about a single idea's direction right away. Run a few by your art director teammate to get their thoughts before finalizing your direction.

The process of writing and rewriting helps eliminate all the clichés and the "been-there-done-that" ideas to ensure your idea is original, cutting edge, and informative. All this rewriting and copyediting will result in a lot of ideas being banished to your real or digital trash can. Stop before you empty the trash, many of your rejections might be reimagined as slogans or taglines, subheads, or used as opening sentences in the body copy.

Pick Your Words Wisely

Believe it or not, word choice can be as important as what is actually said. Studies have shown that certain words do have the power to attract attention and draw the reader or viewer into the ad. Some are simple while others are more descriptive or thought-provoking; all are effective at grabbing attention. Although certainly not exhaustive, the list shown in Table 11.1 spotlights a few known "eye-stoppers," that will create interest in both print and digital mediums.

Once you know what the headline needs to say, the next step is corralling the appropriate tone of voice and style the headline will use to express the key consumer benefit.

Determining the Headline's Verbal Style

The tone of the copy's voice is the creative expression of the message. Style refers to how the headline delivers the message. The following list of headline styles is not absolute and presented only as a place to start. Many headlines may use a combination of styles. The brand's overall persona, image, concept, and message direction should assist with the choice of headline style, helping

Table 11.1 Showcases a few eye-stopping words that will help to grab your target's attention.

Free	New	Love	Product
Offer	Exclusive	Secret	Just Arrived
Sale	Breakthrough	People	Video
Proven	Your	Now	Announcing
Save	Shocking	How-to	Discover
Safety	Why	Numbers	This
Easy	You	Bargain	Last Chance
Facts	Quick	Results	Why
Introducing	Health	Amazing	Guarantee

to alleviate a repetitive or cookie-cutter voice. Take a look at the following list of headline styles as another way to brainstorm ideas and project the key consumer benefit.

- *Direct*. A direct headline delivers the key consumer benefit with little or no creative bells and whistles. It works best when you have a strong offer for a known brand: "Cashmere Sweaters You Can Wash, 30% Off."
- *Indirect or Curiosity*. Indirect or curiosity headlines create interest in a brand that is not yet on the market. They can talk about the brand without showing it, by teasing or dropping hints. One great way to do this is to ask questions, test existing knowledge, or use very visual wording. This style works best when the message can be "leaked out" in small chunks across multiple mediums at different times: "What is White and Read All Over? Hint: It's Not a Newspaper."
- *Major Benefit Promise*. This headline style is best used, when the key consumer benefit is a unique selling proposition (USP), or something unique to only your brand: "56 Color Choices That Last One Hundred Years."
- *Play on Words*. Always risky but both visually and verbally interesting, it is important there be a point to using this style. A play on words uniquely shapes words, often giving them special meaning in order to match the campaign's conceptual direction. If you want to attract attention and give the copy personality, consider using this often-quirky headline style. Wordplay can be fun, but just be sure it informs and pushes the key consumer benefit. A recruitment ad for Gap used a popular holiday song as a foundation for their play on words closing with "Working is a winter wooly land."
- *Question*. A question headline style asks the target a pointed question, requiring the audience to think and thus participate in the ad. The key is to ensure the question is both thought-provoking and cannot be answered with a simple yes or no, so the more open-ended the question, the more the target has to think. Questions can help tie the headline to the target's problem, interests, or needs and wants, by talking about and showing the solution: "Are You Afraid of Your Wife's Purse?"
- *Metaphors, Similes, and Analogies*. These visual styles compare the client's product to something else. A *metaphor* looks at two dissimilar items or traits to make a point of comparison, and tends to pair the intangible with the literal, for example, "I am so hungry I could eat a horse." A *simile*, is a figure of speech, and uses the word "like" or "as" to make a comparison: "They fought like cats and dogs," or "your explanation is as clear as mud." Similes and metaphors help construct an analogy. An *analogy* compares two characteristics that can creatively be seen as similar, for example, a headache compared to a hammer or drum.
- *News, or Announcement*. A news or announcement headline tells the target something newsworthy about the brand. Maybe

it has received an award, or is new and improved in some measurable way, or perhaps a new use has been discovered. Perhaps the client or the brand has won an award for quality or service. Being first at anything is not only newsworthy but a great sales device: "Arm & Hammer Baking Soda is No Longer Just For Cooking."

- *The Reason Why*. The reason-why headline style gives the target a good reason or list of reasons to use the brand: "If You Want to Lose Weight and Feel Better, Eat Better."

- *How-To*. How-to headlines tell the target how to do or find out something, or explains how the brand can solve a problem. These work well when tied to psychographical information, for example, how to save money or lose weight. Command Strips simplifies decorating with: "Peel. Stick. Press."

- *Product Name*. Headlines that feature the product name can appear repetitive and often lack a creative voice, so use only for brands with hard-to-pronounce names, new product launches, or reinvented brands. This headline style often lacks a meaningful brand benefit so not only is it harder to capture the target's attention, but will rarely build or reinforce the brand's image without visual support: "Leinenkugel: A beer drinker's favorite tongue-twister."

- *Testimonial*. This one's easy—if a member of the target audience has had a great experience with a brand, then let them do the talking. Their interactions with the brand are more believable than any advertised message. Be sure to place quotation marks around a headline to clearly indicate it is an actual quote.

- *Humor*. Humorous headlines look at the brand and/or the target in an unusual or outrageous way. No matter the situation, the brand solves the problem. Humor is tough, since each of us views "funny" differently. Charmin uses, "We know where to go for a little inspiration."

- *Command*. If you want to firmly tell the reader what to do, a command headline style can succinctly help you make your point. It should encourage action based on the benefit the brand offers. The best command headlines lead off with an action verb: "Stop feeding your dog like he's a wild animal. Feed him health instead."

- *Practical Advice*. The practical advice headline spells out how the target can solve a problem, such as how to alleviate cold symptoms, use a tool, or cook something. Everyone is open to tips: "If It's Cold, Close the Window. From Another State."

- *Sexual Images and Innuendos*. Sex is a proven way to attract the target's attention. No matter what you say or show, even today's sophisticated consumer can still be shocked by the often-controversial use of sex in advertising. To be used successfully, it must have a point, or it's just tacky and/or inappropriate. Jeep used this headline to stop attention for its open-top model: "Admit it. You've always been crazy about topless models."

- *Problem/Solution*. Sell the solution, not the problem. Don't waste words pushing the problem, the target already knows the problem; a solution is the attention-getter: "Has your back got that achy, breaky, feeling? We've got the heat to get you moving without pain."

- *Reminder*. The reminder tone keeps well-known products such as table salt or seasonal products in the mind of the consumer. "Reminder: Wrinkled Clothes are a Refection of You. Time to Reorder Scruffy."

- *Flag*. Flag headlines are great signposts for small but exclusive audiences. This headline style calls out and talks directly to a specific group, for example, new mothers or people with bad backs: "If Your Back Cries Out In Pain, Stomp Can Silence It For Good"

- *Scarcity*. If it's produced in limited quantities or is hard to find, it will attract certain types of consumers. Scarcity headlines encourage action, and increase the need for, or the value of, a brand. The need to be first or one of the few to own something creates status. Ikea used this holiday headline: "Holiday savings you won't want to miss!"

- *Slice of Life*. Slice-of-life headlines take a bite out of the target's life and either demonstrates or dramatizes it. There are four stages to a slice-of-life concept: Problem, introduction, trial, and solution. American Express tapped into the problem and solution with "Our Thing Is Helping You Do Your Thing."

- *Fantasy*. The make-believe aura in a fantasy headline should take your target and your brand on an adventure. It takes the reality out of an otherwise predictable product/solution and makes it both fun and usually memorable. DeBeers got their target thinking with "If You're A Frog, Turn Yourself Into a Prince"

- *Warning, or Fear*. This red-flag style warns the target there is something they need to watch out for or avoid. There are no rules about how much negativity the consumer will tolerate before being annoyed, so common sense in relationship to brand benefits or problem/solution should be taken into consideration: "Warning: if you don't invest now, how will you live when you retire?"

- *Talking Head*. A character, spokesperson, or consumer tells the brand's story or their personal experiences with the brand. HPV uses talking heads to highlight awareness with "Mom, Dad, Did You Know?

- *Personal Benefits*. A personal-benefits headline offers the target something they care about such as beauty, health, quality, adventure, prestige, and so on, either explicitly or subtly. A magazine ad for Porsche asks: "Honestly now, did you spend your youth dreaming about someday owning a Nissan or a Mitsubishi?"

- *Authoritative*. Use an expert such as a doctor, scientist, dentist, or engineer to point out product attributes. Other official devices that might be employed to back up claims include scientific studies or survey results. Apple shows authority in a short headline that very simply says, "Genius Bar."

- *Product Feature, or Product as a Star*. A feature-based headline concentrates on the feature associated with the brand's key consumer benefit. Because no benefit is pushed, it is best used for mature brands that have more to show than tell. If the feature is unique to your brand, terrific—anything can be made unique if the competition is not pushing it in their advertising, and the concept is believable and memorable. Product-as-a-Star headlines place the brand as the hero that solves the target's problem. The feature headline for The Health Education Council is "No." you have to get into the subhead to find out more.
- *Inherent Drama*. Inherent drama differentiates a product or service from the competition by creating interest or drama around the key consumer benefit. This works well for brands that have few, if any, unique characteristics. An ad promoting cat adoption from Heart of the Valley Animal Shelter shows a cat collar with the headline, "If you like it, put a ring on it"
- *Lifestyle, or Narrative*. Focus is placed on the target and the role the brand plays in their lifestyle rather than on the brand itself. ACE focused on lifestyle with "Back In The Day, Handy Man Wasn't a Trade. It Was A Husband."
- *Price Point*. This type of headline features the price boldly. It might be so bold it's actually twice the size of the headline's point size. Fiat's Mini knows you get a lot for a little: "Get Change Back From Twenty. Starting at $19,950."

The choice of headline style will set the tone for the visual and any and all copy that follows.

Headline Length Depends on Its Job Description

The headline's length, size, and even color will be dictated by what needs to be said, the brand's life-cycle stage, visuals, the media vehicles employed, and the ad's overall tone of voice. As a loose rule, headline length starts from a five- to seven-word statement to two complete sentences. New brands and reinvented brands require a longer headline in order to introduce the key consumer benefit and establish or reestablish a brand's image. Mainstream brands that already have an established brand identity tend to be more visual and are less copy heavy. This type of reminder advertising focuses on building or maintaining the existing brand image or campaign theme by focusing on varied uses or the social benefits of using the brand.

Ads that are not blessed with large amounts of usable space, such as outdoor boards, posters, or transit, to name just a few, will be verbally confined to using only the key consumer benefit and nothing more. Writing headlines for digital mediums follows similar rules. Mobile, search, and social media for example, use headlines that are typically only 20–30 characters long. To ensure the target stops and clicks on an ad, digital headlines must be descriptive, feature relevant key words, use a conversational approach, relatable discussions, and, most importantly, engage the target.

A Subhead's Job Is to Support the Headline

Headlines often cannot deliver everything you need them to say. In order to extend the message, you can use a subhead. These optional copy pieces are a great addition if working with a complicated key consumer benefit. They allow the copywriter to expand on the statement made in the headline and further encourage reader interest.

The *subhead* is the second largest and boldest piece of copy on the page and can be used as an announcement device, as a support for the headline, or to break up long blocks of copy. There are three basic types of subheads: Overline, underline, and copy breaks.

An *overline* or announcement subhead is typically one sentence that is placed above the headline and is used as an attention getter or teaser. If the headline rambles or appears too long, requiring it to be set at a smaller size to accommodate length, or if you need to announce a new webcast, sale, address change, hours, etc., and don't want to clog up your body copy, consider using an overline subhead.

An *underline* or main subhead appears below the headline and explains in greater detail what the headline is saying, offers up additional supporting information, or answers the question posed in the headline. Be careful not to use the subhead to introduce a completely new idea or direction, or repeat information already stated in the headline.

Since main subheads deliver additional information, you should avoid using a statement, opting instead for one or two complete sentences.

Copy-heavy ads will use subheads or *copy breaks* to break-up long blocks of copy that tend to gray down any page, with a strong black or pop of color. Copy breaks help divide the copy into smaller, more digestible discussion points, helps to cut down on eye fatigue, especially online, and adds visual interest. These types of subheads work like chapter heads, informing the reader about the subject matter in the subsequent paragraphs. Because they are used as announcements or informative devices, they are usually statements running anywhere from three to seven words in length. Placement within the copy is not arbitrary; each copy break should mark a new benefit, use, or highlight a major change in the copies direction.

All subhead types are optional on print pieces, but on websites, copy breaks in particular are a great way to incorporate *search engine optimization* (SEO), or the inclusion of relevant links to other sites to increase engagement in the copy.

The Visual Look of Subheads

The main subhead should not compete with the headline for attention, although a unified appearance is important. It should be set in the same typeface, typestyle, color and weight as the headline. Size is somewhat more subjective and depends on the medium and size of the ad. A good rule of thumb is to start by making it 50 percent smaller than the size of the headline and going up or down from there. Due to its larger point size, it will need some kerning and leading, albeit less than the headline, to tighten up its look.

Alignment will usually match that of the headline but is also governed by the layout style chosen. Just remember consistency between elements is critical. If your subhead has two or more lines, like the headline, be sure to stagger the line lengths to optimize white space and increase readability and legibility.

Finally, because the headline and the underline subhead work as a team, no other copy should appear between them. It is only acceptable to break up the pairing with a visual if it strengthens the bond between the two and further promotes the message.

Copy breaks will be anywhere from two to six points larger than the body copy and will match the typeface and typestyle used for the copy. Kerning and leading at these smaller sizes will be dictated by the typeface used, and the designer's preference. These subheads tend to be set in bold, centered above the copy block and can match the color of the headline and underline subhead.

If the subhead does its job well, it will not only hold the reader or viewer's attention while dispensing additional information, it will lure them into the body copy to find out more.

Copy Isn't Dead It Just Needs to Be More Creative

Body copy or the smaller paragraphs of text seen in both print and online ads have to fight to gain reader or viewer attention. If

it's true fewer consumers are reading copy, then we as advertisers have to improve our storytelling skills. With that said, I find it hard to believe anyone buys a car, television, computer, security system, or other high-investment product without first doing a little reading. Copy helps us determine what we can afford, defines multiple features and benefits, and helps differentiate one brand from another. If the copy taps into something your target is interested in, and meaningfully ties it into their lifestyle, no matter the length, or tone of voice, you will ignite interest and most importantly hold their attention.

Body Copy Sells the Sizzle

Body copy is the nitty-gritty heart and essence of the key consumer benefit or concept. Copy is about the brand and its relationship with the target. Two stories merged into a single relationship is your brand's story. The old adage of "sell the sizzle not the steak" translates into "sell the brand's benefits, not its features."

Relatable copy will concentrate on a brand's benefits rather than its features. Benefits can be uniquely owned by the brand and made unique by tying them to the target's needs, wants, and lifestyle. It is important to remember that most competitive brands will already have, as we have learned, either the same or similar features so alone, they are not overtly special or unique. However, if a distinctive use can be established, copy can introduce a unique niche the brand can build on, setting it firmly apart from competing brands.

Benefit-driven storytelling must entice the reader through each verbal and visual element to ensure they land on the body copy, where the actual sale is made. The goal is to vividly bring the brand experience alive with writing that combines their interests or needs with appeals so well crafted the target can actually experience how the brand works, tastes, or feels, when being used. The body copy uses the same style as the headline to unite the verbal elements together and back up any claims made. If the headline asks a question, the body copy will answer it in detail; if the headline focus is on practical advice, then the copy will focus on offering up helpful tips. Copy's job is to continue the key consumer benefit's unique story by educating the target on uses, and any supportive features and benefits such as sizes, colors, uses, and any relevant studies or testimonials that confirm or simplify claims.

To get a firm grasp on what you need to say, how you need to say it, and ensure it's interesting enough to make your target stop, look, and listen, think of it as a novel. Perhaps, it's about how bourbon is made, or the safeguards behind a self-driving car. Whatever it is, it must be visually written, be rich in detail, and have a distinctively structured beginning, middle, and an end.

The first or initial paragraph(s) elaborate on the statement introduced in the headline and further developed in the subhead. Your story begins by breaking the brand and the key consumer benefit down into who, what, when, where, why, and how to help frame or flesh out your copy direction. The interior or middle paragraphs is where the actual sale will be made. Here is where brand features and benefits are tied to target needs as body copy specifically lays out how the brand will solve the target's problem, or improve their lives. The closing paragraph is a call to action. It needs to tell the target what they should do next, such as go to a website, call for more information, or come on down to a brick-and-mortar store. Advertising is all about selling something. Sometimes closing that sale takes several steps, so don't be hesitant to tell consumers what they need to do. To encourage them to act now, or even within the next 30 days, gives the target an incentive such as reduced pricing or free shipping.

Heavy body copy, using seemingly meaningless facts, can easily bore the target. If your target can't see the brand in their life, either enhancing it in some meaningful way or solving a problem they have, they will not read it. To help ensure you keep them engaged, consider adding some type of relevant interactive component, such as sending them on a scavenger hunt for upgrades, asking for their opinion on possible new products, or encouraging them to use their phone to reveal some type of hidden feature or coupon. Interactive ads not only stop and hold attention but also are memorable and sharable. No matter the content, each brand's storyline needs to include a strong plot (key consumer benefit), which is advanced and colored by events that affect the brand (features and benefits). These event(s) must somehow affect the characters (target), moving them to some kind of climax (call to action).

Each paragraph needs to collectively build upon each point made. It should never offend, use slang, or be politically charged. Every sentence should feel like a one-on-one conversation between the target and the brand. To ensure this feeling of intimacy, be sure to personalize your copy by writing to a single targeted individual using "you" instead of "them," "they," or "we," to allow the reader or viewer to create a meaningful connection between the brand and their own lives. Do not say things like "people, or "the target," or "they will," but rather "you will." Use short sentences, simple but expressive words, and multiple short paragraphs of no more than three or four sentences, to make both reading and comprehension faster and easier. Be sure copy uses a personalized and conversational style that talks to the target in a language they will understand about events that are important to them.

Here are a few additional tips to keep in mind when you sit down to write your copy:

- Write concisely. Creative and cleaver copy is great but if it is confusing, rambles on, or does not strategically focus on the key consumer benefit you may lose your targeted reader. Short sentences are always better than long, overly explanatory and complicated ones with a lot of run-on commas. It is *occasionally* okay to use sentence fragments, just not too many. Always reread your copy to be sure there are no *double entendre*, or words or images with a double meaning. For example, a very high-end department store gave the appearance of promoting date rape when their ad pictured a visual of a women looking off to the left. The man standing next to her was looking at her. Between them the headline reads, "Spike Your Best Friend's Eggnog When They're Not Looking" Did they mean to imply date rape? Of course not, but it's a short step from overly creative, to overtly offensive. All ideas really must pass the devils advocate and sarcasm test.
- Appeal to both the target's need to know with facts (rational), and the resulting benefits (emotional). In other words, present the information factually, and tie those facts to how they will make the target feel, change their life, or solve a problem.
- Always write in an active voice. It will make the copy more immediate.
- Work to ensure you create easy transitions from one sentence to the next and from one paragraph to the next. Abrupt changes in direction can be confusing and disrupt the flow of the copy. You can transition easily between one thought or idea at the beginning of the sentence, which is more obvious, or the content of the sentence itself can be the transition. If you're really stuck, insert a copy break subhead.
- Consider comparing your brand to something uniquely different. Figures of speech can not only help dramatize what you're trying to say, but clarify it. If your brand can *be* like something else, it then can be *perceived* as something else. Build a new personality.
- Keep it real, and stay on target. Even the most creatively delivered body copy will not produce a sale or convert a competitor brand's loyal user, if it is off-target or off-strategy, or minimizes the key consumer benefit.
- Avoid the following three things: 1) Using abbreviations and technical jargon, unless writing copy for a particular profession, 2) using "etc." anywhere in the copy, and 3) using hyphens, unless used to link compound words or words that have a combined meaning, such as *good-hearted*.
- Avoid using exclamation points anywhere. If you have to use them to make your point, you obviously didn't make your point.
- Avoid using exaggerated claims, nobody believes them anyway. Bragging is rarely successful, even if it can be backed up with facts.
- Write to the educational level of your target. No one likes to be talked down to, or be confused by big words. Know the

demographic and psychographic backgrounds of your target before putting fingers to the keys or pen to paper.

- Avoid bastardizing a word and any grammar faux pas when possible. Many words come with different spellings that mean different things such as night, knight, and the oft-seen nite. Creative teams have long used these differences to their creative advantage, but they are technically misleading. Roy Paul Nelson points out: "Copywriters, like most writers, often fail to write with precision. 'We couldn't care less' becomes 'We could care less,' which in reality means the opposite. Instead of allowing something to 'center on' a copywriter might have it 'center around,' an impossibility. 'All right' becomes 'alright,' a non-word [or considered substandard] in most dictionaries [but not Word], and 'a lot' becomes 'alot,' another non-word or wrong spelling for 'allot'" (p. 161).
- Dangling construction or those ... before and after a sentence should be avoided ... They tend to be confusing. Say what you mean to say, and show what you mean to show.
- To make a word or phrase stand out, consider indenting and/or italicizing it instead.
- As a design component, always be sure to place only one space after a period to avoid creating a hole in the copy. When writing for anything other than video or broadcast, avoid using contractions. They make sense when someone is talking, but they have a tendency to be just a bit tacky when seen in printed copy.

Advertising copy has many verbal roles to play depending on where it will be seen. Some copy will be lengthy, such as in a brochure, direct mail, or website, while others will be short, such as in magazine, newspaper, mobile, or social media. Because of this, it is important the meaning be just as clear within a headline as it is in multiple paragraphs of copy. Copy should not only be creatively written, but informative, informal, conversational not preachy, and when appropriate, intimate.

Copy Length Depends on What Needs to Be Said

How long should body copy be? The answer is simple: Long enough to inform and spur the intended target into the desired action. The length of body copy depends on how familiar the target is with the brand and whether the advertising or promotional efforts are meant to remind, alter, or maintain the brand's image or use. The copy's overall length can also be influenced by:

- The target audience. The older and better educated the target, the more likely they are to read longer blocks of copy in order to find out more about a brand. Younger readers are less likely to invest their time reading through long copy, but do respond well to large, colorful visuals with informative copy captions and video options.

- The brand. Rationally based purchases or things we need to survive, that can get us from place to place, or that help us in our jobs, will need more information to explain the key consumer benefit and significantly stand out from competing brands. Emotionally charged brands or things we just can't live without, have few, if any, distinctive features from those of competing brands that will need to be explained in detail. So items such as shoes, clothing, jewelry, perfumes, beauty products, liquor, snacks, or soft drinks, will typically use minimal or no copy at all.

These types of ads will rely more on the visual to tell the story.

Longer copy may also be used for:

- Reinventing or repositioning a brand's image
- Expensive product purchases
- New product introductions
- Technical copy.

Shorter copy is a great choice for:

- Reminder advertising
- Mainstream products
- Emotional products
- Inexpensive product purchases.

Lengthy copy can be intimidating to invest time in. Design around it. To entice your target into the copy, consider inserting multiple copy-break subheads and/or relevant visuals that work to demonstrate both features and benefits, and help to break it up into smaller, more readable, less intimidating chunks. On the flip side, too little copy may not set the brand apart from the competition, clearly deliver the key consumer benefit, or strengthen or build the brand's image.

Say It with a Tone That Has Style

In our headline discussion, we learned every ad has an individual tone or style that not only defines the message but the brand's personality or image. How it is expressed depends on the tone of voice employed to deliver the key consumer benefit. It is important the copywriter thoroughly understand what kind of image the brand should project. Can that image be created and expressed with a factual, fantasy, or humor-based tone? Is it newsworthy, or should a specific feature or perhaps multiple benefits be highlighted? Should the target be reminded or will building curiosity work better? Perhaps a demonstration or instructional tone will more strongly deliver the key consumer benefit? An ad's tone of voice has a big, multifaceted job to do. First and foremost, it needs to successfully push the key consumer benefit, and build both brand image and brand loyalty.

Formats for Expressing a Message's Tone of Voice

The body copy's tone was initially determined in the creative brief. Tone is the body copy's voice or how it will sound. To ensure a cohesive verbal style is used throughout the ad, copy should follow the verbal tone used in the headline. For tonal options, see the section on headline styles.

These tones or styles are just a starting place for conceptual development. They are not meant as a template but as a jumping-off point. Consider combining any two rational or emotional tones or one or more emotional or rational tones together, or envision an entirely new and different way to say something about the brand.

Detail Copy Tells the Target What to Do Next

One of the most forgettable pieces of copy on the page or screen is detail copy. This small, detail-laden information section includes one or more of the following: Store address or addresses, hours, web address, phone number(s), credit cards accepted, and any pertinent social media apps. Not all may be applicable for all ads or mediums.

Detail copy makes finding the brand, purchasing, and/or getting questions answered easier. To ensure it is seen, or found, it is important it be placed in one convenient location. In print, placement is pretty stagnant. It can either appear above or below the logo, and placed in a single line with bullets or small dots separating each copy point. If you need a map, or need to show multiple locations, consider stacking the detail copy in a small individual block, either under or on either side of the logo. Be careful when using this last option; be sure each individual block of copy is equalized in spacing and depth to avoid creating an unbalanced appearance, or a white hole.

Online, it might appear in the top left or right corner of the page or be hidden under a "Contact Us" or "About Us" tab, or appear as a clickable link at the bottom of the screen.

The smallest copy on the page, detail copy should be set in the same typeface as the body copy and in print be no smaller than 8 or 9 points and digitally no smaller than 12 or 13 points to ensure readability.

Slogans and Taglines Define Image in a Few Words

To help communicate and solidify a brand's use, image, personality, and differentiating characteristics from other brands, consider adding a tagline or slogan to the logo. The typeface used on these catchy little phrases or statements will typically not match any used on the logo. It is important, however, to ensure it complements, not clashes, with the appearance of the logo design. For example, if the logo is thin and elegant, choose a slightly bulkier face, to ground the design. A modern-looking logo design should be coupled with a slogan or tagline that is set in an equally modern typeface.

There is a lack of agreement currently in the industry whether the use of a slogan or tagline brings any relevant benefits to the brand, since so many are considered, well, pretty worthless. On the other hand, why not work at creating a useful statement that reinforces the brand message and helps connect your key consumer benefit with your target.

Slogans

Memorable slogans encapsulate the corporation's overall strategy, philosophy, or mission statement, giving them longevity. The slogan must aid in positioning the brand. It must simply express what the target needs to know about the company or brand. Good slogans have longevity and can not only enhance a brand's image, but build brand equity. Slogans tend to run anywhere from three to seven words and can be placed above or below the logo. According to a July, 6, 2016, AdAge article by Al Reis entitled "Sound advice for creating a slogan," "good ones [slogans] employ one or more of the following memory-enhancing techniques: Rhyme, alliteration, repetition, reversal and double-entendre, pun."

Slogans are meant to last a long time, but there are few that have lasted longer than the Maxwell House coffee slogan "Good to the last drop." The Coca-Cola Company first used it in 1908, and its origin can be traced back to a statement made by Theodore Roosevelt to a party guest to describe the coffee he was drinking.

Taglines

The major differences between a tagline and a slogan is that taglines have a shorter lifespan, and they tend to be a bit more superficial or irrelevant. Their job is to quickly tell the target what the brand is all about. These catchy lines of text are typically anywhere from three to seven words long and can be a complete sentence or a statement. They can appear above or below the logo, and are typically tied to the current campaign concept.

Changes big or small typically appear when new campaigns are introduced. Taglines associated with brands having a strong brand identity can last a little longer, such as Nike's "Just Do It" tag, when tied to life-cycle stages. Try to avoid superlatives such as "the best," especially if you're not, as well as imperatives or delivering a command. Go with your key consumer benefit—it's succinct and tells the target why you are the best option quickly. Good taglines will 1) deliver a clear and concise message about who and what your brand is all about, 2) give your brand a separate identity from other competitors, for example, 7Up originally positioned themselves as "The Uncola," 3) create an emotional bond with the brand's use and/or personality, 4) speak for individual brands offered by corporations with a diverse assortment of products and services, 5) push the key consumer benefit over values when appropriate, and 6) grab attention, especially if they are grammatically rough around the edges, causing your target to reread them.

Today, taglines and slogans no longer hold a position of prominence in advertising, basically because today's ads have less copy, thanks to shorter attention spans. The rise of digital media, especially mobile, has made the screen smaller and most messages are confined to 140 characters or 6–15 seconds of video. Shortened messaging needs to place more emphasis on the logo and overall message, and less on a catchy slogan or tagline. Additionally, thanks to the rise of *niche marketing* or the fracturing of target groups into smaller, more specialized segments, multiple messages may be needed to reach each audience.

With all that said, they are still a great way to deliver a message for a new or reinvented brand. You might consider using a tagline if 1) you want to showcase the values of the brand, corporation and employees, 2) you need to reposition or reinvent the brand or corporation, or introduce a new brand offerings, and 3) you want to build or reinforce brand loyalty between the brand and consumer. Neither a tagline or a slogan needs to last indefinitely; either can be retired once the brand's image is secured.

A reminder: Since creative teams are often working on more than one job, often for multiple clients, don't forget to put the logo on the copy sheet. It is particularly helpful, if using a tagline or slogan to see placement.

Writing and Designing for Promotional Devices and Order Forms

Many digital and print ads have some kind of promotional device, such as coupons, or have an order form that needs to be completed in order to make a purchase. It is the copywriter's job to write any and all promotional copy.

Coupons

To encourage purchase, brands often reduce the price or offer an additional incentive to make it more desirable. Promotional devices like coupons are a way to offer the target something in return for their loyalty or as an inducement to try a new brand. Coupons are effective, temporary sales devices. They should boldly and clearly state the offer, be easy to remove from the ad, load onto a loyalty card, or be scanned from a mobile device.

Coupons are a great way to nudge your target into making a purchase decision within a set period of time, but as a sales-inducing device, they have little to say. Most simply state the promotion, display the coupon's expiration date, the logo and any tagline or slogan, and perhaps a marketing code.

When multiple coupons appear in a single design, the goal is consistency to ensure balance, symmetry, and structure. Each promotional offer or "headline" should be set in bold and be the same size in each coupon, as do any percentages or cents-off claims. Size will also be maintained, even if offers are of different lengths. For example, in an ad with three coupons, aligned across the bottom of the ad, two may have promotions that are broken into three lines while the third is only two lines long. Placement order will help balance the coupons. Consider placing the shortest coupon in between the two longer ones. Be sure all lines are set along the same baseline in the same point size using the same amount of leading. The shorter promotion will have more white space, but in this instance is not considered a white hole because of the two balanced coupons on either side. This balanced attack will maintain both continuity and structure. Consider placing a dashed line around the coupon to visually encourage the target to cut, tear, or print them out.

Since coupons are removed from the ad, it is important that the logo and any slogan or tagline appear on the ad and all coupons to ease brand identification. Because they need to be easy to remove and they tend to junk up the look of an ad in print, multiple coupons are typically found balanced at the very bottom of an ad and occasionally running vertically up one side. In digital ads, they're often hidden under a tab or link.

There are several copy and design issues to consider when adding one or more coupons to an ad:

- Size can vary, but will typically depend on the number of coupons used and overall size. Just be sure they are big enough that all copy can be easily read.

- The coupon headline should clearly state the promotional offer: "Buy One Dinner Entrée And Get A Free Dessert."
- The promotional offer should be set in the same bold typeface as the headline and subhead when possible.
- If the offer is a simple cents-off or percentage-off promotion, use a larger and bolder point size to better stand out. If it's too small, it looks like the offer is not a great deal.
- If the offer can only be used at a grocery store, a small amount of body copy is needed to tell the grocer how to redeem the used coupons.
- Grocery and some retail store coupons also need to have a *Universal Product Code* (UPC), those recognizable vertical black bar codes that are scanned during checkout.
- Be sure the logo appears on every coupon. Once the target removes the coupon from the ad, or clicks or transfers it to their phone, it works as an important reminder device as to what brand is hosting the promotion and where to redeem it.
- All coupons have an expiration date. Do not hide it or make it so small it's hard to find or see. Display it prominently at the top of the coupon above the promotion. To give it even more emphasis, consider enclosing it in a box, using a bold and/or italicized typeface.
- If the brand comes in multiple varieties of any kind that could be misidentified by the target, consider adding a picture of the brand to make it easier for them to find the correct item.
- Coupons, particularly those for fast foods, may also include a marketing code, usually a letter and a numbers, that tells the retailer what media the coupon originated from.

Freestanding Inserts

Freestanding inserts (or FSIs) are single-page, full-color ads full of coupons that are inserted into a newspaper or found in your mailbox. They are often double-sided and usually feature coupons on one side that can be redeemed at different times within the next 30 days, and a full-page color image, headline, and logo on the other, that typically announces a special sale or promotion. Sizes range, but are typically 8½ x 11 inches. These nationally distributed inserts are also known as *supplemental advertising*. Many of these colorful inserts will have perforations, or small cuts, around each coupon to make them easier to tear out and use. Whether to include perforations or not will depend on the budget.

Order Forms

Order forms have become a lot easier to fill out, thanks to computer or mobile auto-fills. You've probably never given them a second thought, but they do need to be both written and designed. Because an order form requires the target to do something like place an order, express an opinion, take a survey, or request a free sample or additional information, it must be easy to use.

Order forms are commonly seen in both print and digital media. They are often attached to, or found in magazines, direct mail pieces, or on web pages, to name just a few. No matter where the target comes in contact with them, they must be well written, with a clean design, and be easy to find, understand, and use.

For purchases, the order form closes the sale. No matter how creatively the key consumer benefit was delivered in the advertising, if the order form doesn't work, or confuses or frustrates your target, they will not take the time to struggle through filling it out. It should not only be a way to place an order, but be a concise sales device. As the final step in the sale process, it needs to act as a call to action, the last interaction between the target and the brand. Print and digital forms differ in both appearance and the amount of information that will appear.

A print order form should include the following:

- A headline that clearly calls attention to the offer.
- Easy step-by-step instructions on the order process.
- Ordering options such as toll-free and fax numbers, relevant social media hashtags, and website addresses.
- A short paragraph of copy, no more than one to three sentences long, that reminds the target of the offer. Even if the offer was mentioned in the body copy, repeat it here to ensure clarity and briefly tell the target what he or she needs to do.
- Catalog purchases particularly still enclose a self-addressed envelop so separate copy needs to be written for it (usually after the order form copy on the copy sheet), and labeled appropriately. If not including one, be sure to include the address the target will need to mail in the form.

Both print and digital forms require:

- Digital forms will offer a link or tab to click on that takes the target directly to the order form.
- Blanks for name, address, apartment number, city, state, ZIP, day and evening phone numbers, e-mail, and perhaps a date of birth. The type of site or print piece you are ordering from will determine what needs to be included.
- A box for appropriate titles such as Mr., Mrs., Miss., Ms., and instructions for what to do next (Click or Circle One).
- If the brand requires the target to pick a specific color or size, for example, provide boxes they can check off or click on. For online orders, be sure to show the order alongside the form, so any last-minute changes are easy to make.
- If the target is asking for more information, additional questions are needed to ensure appropriate materials are sent out. For example, a form for more information about life insurance might include questions about current coverage and

dependants.

- Any return policies or guarantee or warranty information. Tell how the product can be returned, any steps that need to be taken or applicable conditions, and how long it will take for a refund to arrive.
- Clearly and boldly state the prices.
- Payment options, such as credit cards accepted. A list of shipping options, and how long it will take for the purchase to arrive.
- A box to check or click to receive additional promotional devices either through snail mail or e-mail.
- Be sure to show the logo and slogan or tagline.

Online orders need to immediately send a confirmation e-mail that includes an order number and summary, along with shipping information. Once the order does ship, a follow-up e-mail or link to the shipping company to track their order will be sent. Once the order arrives, a final e-mail or text should be sent to confirm its delivery and to offer an opportunity to rate both the brand and their overall experience.

Photo Captions

Photo captions are one or two sentences, typically set in a smaller typeface than the body copy that are placed below a photograph, succinctly, not creatively, describing what the reader or viewer is seeing.

Prices Are Ugly but Important

There are a lot of print and all digital mediums that have to tell how much something costs. It should *never* be placed in the body copy or be hard to find. If you really have a great brand and a great deal, don't be afraid to highlight its cost. Price can be featured in the headline, the subhead, or as a callout near one or more images. Headlines are a great place to go big if your price point is really good. Subheads, because they can be a little longer, are a great choice when you have a range of prices to talk about. Callouts accompany an image and are the best choice if you are showing an array of products on a website or to highlight individual prices in a silhouette layout style.

The only time in print when prices are not prominently featured is when promoting exclusive or high-priced brands that focus on image. These ads rarely highlight price; instead focus is placed on exclusivity of ownership. Some may allude to special sales and

financing packages available only if you visit the website or a brick-and-mortar store.

The Critical Relationship Between Visuals and the Verbal Copy

For an ad to tell a cohesive story, the copy and visual images must work together. Because of this, it is important that copywriters understand and keep the visual direction in mind when writing copy. It is just as important that the copy create a visual image for the art director. These images might have been worked out during brainstorming sessions, or may need some tweaking when the team gets back together to go over the copy and layout before presenting it to the account manager and/or client.

Creative ideas that are not visually and verbally tied together create confusion. If the headline is talking about the luxury driving experience associated with this brand of car, and the visual shows a tricycle and scooter, the point is difficult to grasp without the body copy filling in the details. The target will not understand what these three things have in common unless the connection is made both visually and verbally. But if the concept is luxury, then the ad should show and tell potential luxury car owners they have come a long way from basic wheels that everyone owned, to extraordinary wheels, which only a few can own. For your target to understand the analogy, the visual and verbal message need to work together.

The layout style used also plays a role in copy. For example, a picture-window layout style requires a headline that draws the reader into the photograph, a rebus works great for copy that tells a story or gives the reader directions, and a Mondrian layout has a youthful feel and works well with copy that is upbeat or energizing.

Copy is every bit as complicated as design. The team needs to ensure the visual and verbal elements creatively focus on the key consumer benefit or what needs to be accomplished, and clearly demonstrate how the brand can solve a problem by offering a solution. Additionally, it needs to accomplish the objectives, and push the creative strategy and tone laid out in the creative brief. Beyond that small task, copy needs to accomplish the following: 1) Attract attention, with the headline and/or explain the visual, 2) engage the reader or viewer, through the subheads and opening copy paragraphs, 3) make the sell in the interior paragraphs of copy, and 4) induce action in the closing paragraphs. If copy entertains, and is relatable and informative, it can still define the brand's image and create a unique identity within the brand category.

Writing for Global Brands

Like color used on global branding, copy will also need to be adapted to effectively address cultural differences and ensure the original meaning does not get lost in translation.

Translating ad copy from any medium means ensuring the visual/verbal message correctly references the culture. To ensure this, the adoption of advertising copy into different languages requires more than just a literal translation; it needs to be transcreated. In her online October 27, 2017 article entitled "Translating Advertising Copy," Sophie Howe tells us that transcreation "translates advertising copy creatively." It is not unusual for ads that use idioms, humor, slang and/or culturally based references to have difficulty translating into multiple languages. Transcreations role then is to 1) preserve the original brand positioning and image, 2) continue to strongly and clearly push the key consumer benefit, 3) use the same tone and strategy, and 4) optimize cultural relevancy.

In short, its job is to preserve the original visual/verbal message, not repeatedly reinvent the creative wheel. Howe goes on to say, "Although the translated text may be quite different to the source text after transcreation, the creative ideas behind it and the emotions that engage and influence consumer behavior are kept."

Any visual/verbal components seen within an ad can all be adapted to ensure that the readers and/or viewers experience the ad in the same way. A July 13, 2020 online article entitled "Marketing Translation" offers up a transcreation example for "Intel's slogan, 'Sponsors of tomorrow,' when translated into Brazilian Portuguese, the slogan implied that Intel would not deliver on its promises immediately. As a solution, Intel decided to use 'Apaixonados pelo futuro,' which translates to 'In love with the future.'"

The Nuances Associated with Translation

Advertising copy can rarely be translated verbatim. It requires an in-depth knowledge of diverse cultural nuances, word meanings or interpretation, and the proper use of cultural references in both copy and images. Advertising copy often uses slang and references from pop culture; because of this, the translation needs to take into consideration the subtleties within the original message and how that can be conveyed in diverse languages. Many puns or metaphors, for example, may work well for an audience in one area of the world but might not make sense, cause confusion, or even offend in another. All copy whether seen in print or digital formats needs to be localized to successfully sell the brand and reflect its personality and use. Adding an additional layer of complexity is that the translation of English into almost any other language will require additional space, ultimately affecting an ad's overall copy depth and even character count. For example, Tara Johnson in a February 21, 2018 online article entitled "How Global Brands Translate International Ad Copy and Creative," points out that many German words can be very long, effectively shortening social media posts.

The Changeable Length of Transcribed Copy

Copy for any ad is written to fit within the allotted space and relate to the imagery used. However, when writing for multiple languages, it is important to understand that not all languages will use the same number of words to say the same thing. Additionally, the length or spelling of a single word can be very different among varying languages and even within English-speaking countries such as with localise vs. localize, or color vs. colour, to name just a few. Other differences to watch out for are currency symbols and units of measurements.

Although the goal of a lot of advertising copy these days is shorter is better, often the problem with translated advertising copy, is it tends to increase in length. According to Johnson, "if you translate an English phrase into German," for example, "it could grow the length of the copy by 35 percent." Because of this, a good deal of editing and even rewriting will be required.

The reimagining of slogans and taglines can also be very time-consuming and difficult to translate into multiple languages, requiring anything from subtle tweaks to significant alterations to deliver the intended message. Because of this, global slogans are rare, the most notable being McDonald's 'I'm lovin' it.'"

Finally, it is also important to point out that a translation from the original language can often render many key search words useless, so care needs to be taken when rewriting.

Dialogue Also Is Affected by Translation

Digital ads such as radio, television and social media, will also need to be adapted in the same way as print ads, but with a few additional issues that will require attention. For example, will you need subtitles or will any visual elements need to be changed out or even reshot to correctly address any cultural nuances? Subtitling is when a translation of the spoken word is seen on the screen. Will you dub, or use a voice-over, or someone who speaks over the original copy? If so, you will need to determine whether the length of the translated copy will match that of the original. If not, frames may need to be slowed down to allow more time for the audio. Dubbing requires translating the script and hiring a local cast of actors to deliver the content in the target's language.

Be Careful Not to Offend

This may sound obvious but if not closely monitored by a native speaker, the message can accidentally offend, making it imperative that all ad components be scrutinized by native-speaking creative teams. This is also the best way to ensure the ad does not lose its intended meaning as copy, colors, and imagery are adapted.

Ultimately, when a poor translation causes the meaning of an ad to change, it can easily offend, and cost the brand equity and adversely affect brand image. A good example of this according to Tara Johnson, is when KFC fell a little short when translating their copy for a Chinese audience: "In English 'finger lickin' good' fried chicken sounds delicious, but the literal translation of this phrase in Chinese is, 'We'll eat your fingers off.'" Not great for building a tasty brand image.

The choice to market a brand globally requires in-depth research, knowledgeable translation help, and knowing what cultural references, images, or colors will resonate with the target audience. Writing copy for diverse languages involves more than simple translation. It requires the creative team to creatively see the ad in varying visual and verbal ways, in varying types of mediums. To creatively adapt to these language nuances, it is important to keep in mind that at its core, advertising copy is about communicating ideas that inspire and that address the target's needs, wants, and lifestyle.

Copy Sheets Record the Ads Story

Finally, all copywriters will organize and submit completed copy on a copy sheet. No matter how simple or complex, every word for every ad will appear on a copy sheet. More complex ads might have a headline, multiple subheads and/or blocks of body copy, callouts, a slogan or tagline, a logo, detail copy, and any coupons, order forms, guarantees or warranties, and even any legal jargon. If it does not appear on the copy sheet, it will not be seen anywhere. A good copy sheet is clearly labeled with each verbal component placed in the order in which it will be seen on the ad. The client, account manager, art director, and production artist will use the copy sheet as both a visual and verbal guide. See Template 11.1, for a sample copy sheet taken from *Integrated Marketing Communication From Idea to Implementation*.

Template 11.1 Copy sheet

Headline:	The headline should appear here.
Main Subhead:	The main subhead should appear here if using one.
Callouts or Photo Captions:	Place any callouts or photo caption information here if using. Delete this section if not needed.
Body Copy A:	Tell the brand's story here.
Subhead:	Multiple subheads are great when making a transition or breaking up a copy-heavy page.
Body Copy B:	Continue the copy here.
Subhead:	You need not use multiple subheads if the copy is short.
Body Copy C:	Continue the copy here.
Tagline or Slogan:	If using a tagline or slogan (label appropriately), place them here or below the logo. Match positioning to the Creative Brief.
Logo:	Type the brand name here.
Detail Copy D:	Consider placing detail copy (address, phone, hours, website, social media, etc.) here. Detail copy can also be placed above the logo. Placement will depend on the medium, and the designer's preference.
Promotional Copy:	If you have coupons(s) and/or an order form, or any other type of promotional device, place them here. Write out any and all copy for the promotion, including the logo and tagline or slogan if using—*nothing* is assumed. Delete if not needed. See example below.
Coupon 1:	If more than one coupon, place copy for the first coupon here. Delete if not needed.
Coupon 2:	Place the copy for the second coupon here and so on.
Order Form:	Place all copy for an order form here. Delete if not needed
NOTE:	HOW MANY SECTIONS OF BODY COPY AND SUBHEADS YOU HAVE WILL DEPEND ON THE MEDIUM, THE COPY COUNT, AND YOUR ASSIGNMENT. THIS IS JUST AN EXAMPLE OF OPTIONS.

There is of course no standard format for any type (print or digital) of copy sheet. Each agency or in-house creative department will have their own formula and format. The example shown here is only one of many possible options.

In this example, the copy is double-spaced and set up in two columns, with all labels placed in the left column and all copy confined to the right column. Slogans, taglines, and detail copy can be rearranged depending on whether they appear above or below the logo.

Bibliography

Blakeman, Robyn. 2018. *Integrated Marketing Communication: Creative Strategy from Idea to Implementation*. 3rd ed. Lanham, MD: Rowman and Littlefield Publishing.

Blakeman, Robyn and Maureen Taylor (2018), "Team Creative Brief: Creative and Account Teams Speak Out on Best Practices." Journal of Advertising Education, 23(1), 39–52.

Frank, Lenard R. 2001. *Quotationary*. New York: Random House.

Hafer, Keith W., and Gordon E. White. 1982 *Advertising Writing*. 2nd ed. St. Paul, MN: West.

Howe, Sophie. (2017). "Translating Advertising Copy." Retrieved from: www.comtectranslations.co.uk. October 27.

Johnson, Tara. (2018). "How Global Brands Translate International Ad Copy and Creative." Retrieved from: https://tinuiti. blog/ecommerce/translate-international-ads/. February 21.

Joseph, Alan. 2010. "Give Me the Freedom of a Tight Brief: The Copywriter's Mantra" (August 23). Retrieved from: https:// abranddayout.wordpress.com/2010/08/23/give-me-the-free dom-of-a-tight-brief-the-copywriters-mantra/.

Joseph, Alan. (2020). Marketing Translation. Retrieved from: www. web-translations.com. July 13.

Maurer, Steve. 2014. "19 Timeless Quotes That Will Make You a Better Copywriter." (April 21). Retrieved from: http://hub. uberflip.com/blog/copywriting-quotes.

Nelson, Roy P. 1989. *The Design of Advertising*, pg. 8, 168. 6th ed. Dubuque, IA: Wm. C. Brown Company.

Reis, Al. 2016. "Sound Advice for Creating a Slogan." (July 6). Retrieved from: https://adage.com.

Schwab, Victor O. (2014). *How to Write a Good Ad*. Robert C. Worstell. Midwest Journal Press, p. 66. https://books.google. com/books?id=ICPrCgAAQBAJ.

Concepts That Incorporate the Visual and Verbal Voice of Individual Media Vehicles

Chapter 12 Objectives

1. The reader will understand the relevance of both newspaper and magazine advertising in today's digitally driven marketplace.
2. The reader will learn what visuals work best in print.
3. The reader will understand the difference between retail and image-based advertising.

The Visual and Verbal Design of Newspaper and Magazine: Is Traditional Print Dead?

There is a rumbling in many businesses and almost every advertising course that print is dead. With the introduction of each new digital media vehicle, another virtual nail appears to be hammered into print's (newspaper and magazine) coffin. I think the talk about the demise of print is not only premature but unimaginative. Traditional media including newspaper, magazine, radio, television and out-of-home, are still viable options for imaginative-thinking brands, especially if paired with newer digital options such as quick response codes (QR), or ad-specific URLs, to name just a few. It is also a great place for presenting explosive imagery and informative copy that encourages viral or social sharing on sites like Twitter or Facebook, giving marketers additional platforms to reach their intended target.

It is true that print circulations have certainly declined over the last decade, but the upside is that only the most engaged and dedicated reader remains, which makes targeting and message delivery in these mature vehicles not only more desirable, but

turns a mass-media vehicle into more of a niche, or smaller, more specialized media option.

Although print vehicles can seem dated and are often more expensive and time-consuming to produce than many digital options, they do have their advantages such as 1) instilling a greater sense of trust than digital advertising, thanks to their age and reputation, 2) remaining excellent outlets for delivering complex visual and verbal storytelling, 3) building brand identity, awareness, and loyalty, and 4) ensuring enhanced levels of engagement and memorability. Additionally, and most importantly, what continues to make print ads both a valuable and viable media option is the nearly undivided attention that readers give to magazine and newspaper content and, as a result, the advertising. Loyal readers are more focused and less likely to multitask than when consuming digital content.

The Tortoise and the Hare of Print and Digital Advertising

If you want to get your message out quickly, print cannot match digital for speed. Print takes longer and is more expensive, thanks to the additional steps needed to produce and print the vehicle. Because of this, the brand's ultimate *return on investment* (ROI), or how much money was spent on advertising versus how much money was made, will take considerably more time to determine than with digital options. On the plus side, print is more permanent, making it a better option for delivering a lasting and thus more memorable message than a temporary digital banner, flashing ad, or pop-up, for example. Digital ads are often fleeting, making it difficult for the target to recall and remember the message, both necessary components to making a sale. Print

 DOI: 10.4324/9781003255123-13

aficionados often pick up a vehicle specifically for the advertising, often lingering over ads for a longer period of time whereas digital ads are often considered intrusive and rarely a place one wants to linger or take the time necessary to explore further.

Digital advertising is a lot more flexible, offering up multiple platforms and options, but it does have its limitations. Print ads have fewer formats but offer up more visual and verbal options to help highlight the message. Because print advertising can appear in diverse sizes and include some kind of simple interactive devise such as folds, or more complex options like *augmented reality* (AR), to name just two, they can be both engaging and interactive, and thus more memorable than a simple link offers. Print is also a better medium for telling a lengthier and more captivating visual and verbal story, something many digital ads cannot match.

The Versatility of Print

Because newspaper can be targeted by section and magazines by content, they can be easily personalized to larger niche or segmented audiences rather than by individual consumers. "The principles of digital marketing," according to an online June 2018 article by E.M. Developer, entitled "Print Advertising Isn't Dead: Here's Why It Matters" which points out that a "minimum investment for massive reach, used to be the principles of print advertising. Now print marketing is about forming relationships and speaking effectively to marketing segments about their problems and personalities. Print marketing campaigns are integrated with digital marketing to gain accessibility and reach, to target the right audiences in a way that feels personal."

Finally, before dismissing any media vehicle as dated, it is important to understand that trends change, regularly. What appears as an unstoppable decline today, will eventually see interest in these specialized vehicles resurrected. With that said, I am not sure traditional advertising is down for the count so much as in a state of evolution.

Newspaper's Role in Modern Advertising: When to Use Newspaper

The majority of newspaper advertising, is *retail advertising*. It must accomplish two things: 1) Sell a brand or promote a service, and 2) entice the target to act quickly. This is a tough job. The target has to see the forest through the trees of written information (news), in both print and digital forms, before noticing an ad amid a very busy page that defines the look of a typical newspaper page.

The ads seen in newspaper are known as *display ads*, or ads that feature both visual and verbal elements. Each ad has approximately three seconds to catch the eye of your target, so having a simply stated, powerful visual and verbal message working together that is both easily readable and legible is critical.

As we have already learned in previous chapters, advertising is basically a relationship between words and imagery. The creative team's job is to create a match between what is said and what is shown. Many print ads can have a lot going on, and knowing the job of each visual/verbal component is the key to creating structure and ensuring eye flow. The key elements of print are divided between copy and imagery. As previously discussed, the copy or verbal elements include headlines, subheads, body and detail copy, slogans/taglines, and promotional options. Imagery or visual elements include black-and-white or color illustrations, photography, graphic designs, charts/graphs, and logos, as well as type and layout styles. Some ads will have all of these visual/verbal components.

Encouraging the target to buy takes a strong memorable sale that informs and engages. Creative teams need to ask what attracts the target's attention? What is most important to the target before, during, and after the sale? How will they use the brand? Where can purchase take place? The answers can be found through knowledge about how retail advertising works, why the target uses this particular medium, and the appropriate layout techniques to reach the target and reflect the brand's message and image.

Newspaper Is All about Finding the Best Price

Beyond news, both print and digital versions of newspapers are where the target goes for sales by local businesses. Everybody loves a bargain. There are a lot of them in retail, and they push predictable action-oriented themes such as "Buy Now," "70% Off," or "Limited Quantities" to capture the target's attention. Brands with physical storefronts can run sales and offer coupon promotions that can be used daily, weekly, or monthly. The goal for all retail sales is, or should be, how the client's sales can break through the target's apathy with a routine sale, such as bringing in a downloaded coupon that requires a code, only found in the ad, and so on. Good sales don't have to be easy, only better than the competitors.

Find a way to cut out the routine. Give the client's sale a personality that reflects merchandise sold or image. The ultimate goal of a sale is to move merchandise, but if you can increase foot traffic into a brick-and-mortar or online store, you can ring up additional sales. Most sales are predictably tied to holidays or special events that attract a lot of attention. But what about a private image-building sale on a Sunday evening for the most loyal customers that really does boast the lowest prices ever. Once word gets out (and it always does), more people will want to be a part of this exclusive club. Newspapers' favorite sales devices are coupons and freestanding inserts (FSIs), which were covered in greater detail in Chapter 11.

A Sale Is Only as Good as Its Lowest Priced Item

Retail advertising is all about price. Scream out prices largely and boldly—no one buys or considers buying without more information and a price for comparison pricing. Prices are not a tacky subject, when displayed as a part of the design. You do not want the price hidden or squeezed into the ad, giving the impression it is not that good, or is an afterthought or add-on. Most consumer package goods, for example, need to be promoted through price points to assist with comparison shopping and ultimately purchase, whereas service categories such as banking and investing, to name just two, often focus more on customer service issues.

The creative team has multiple options when deciding how to promote a brand's price. The boldest option is to place it in the headlines, which are a great choice if you have a single price point you are pushing. For example, if you have "If Hawaii Is On Your Mind, For Rest And Relaxation," imagine getting there from anywhere for $99. Setting the price in the same size type as the headline will look utilitarian. But a phenomenal price needs a big presence to be noticed and flagged as important. So consider setting the price twice as large as the headline. See Figure 12.1.

If you have a range of prices to promote, consider highlighting them in the main subhead. See Figure 12.2.

If a range of prices need accompanying descriptions use callouts. See Figure 12.3.

Never hide prices in the body copy. Small, or hidden prices suggest they are non-competitive with other brands in the category. If they must go small for whatever reason, consider placing them in a box, perhaps with a drop shadow, along with accompanying bullet points. See Figure 12.1 for an example.

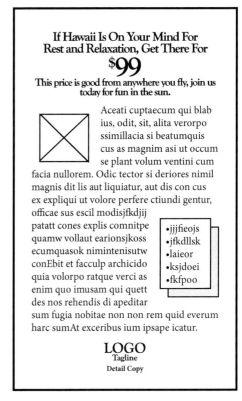

Figure 12.1 This example shows a large single headline price, a test wrap, and a drop shadow box with bullet points. Sample layout courtesy of Robyn Blakeman, University of Tennessee

The Effect of Newsprint on Design

Before we look at the varied visual and verbal options for newspaper advertising, we need to talk about the quality of the surface on which your ads will be been seen. The paper your ad is printed on directly affects the readability and legibility of type and the fine details within visuals. Newspapers are printed on a low-grade paper stock known as *newsprint*. Newsprint is a poor printing surface. The coarse, uncoated, highly bleedable stock affects overall quality and can adversely affect both black-and-white and color reproduction, if used incorrectly. Colors do not "pop" on newsprint; photographs can look flat, and can appear to recede into the page. Illustrations and typefaces with delicate line work can easily "dropout" or completely disappear when printed. Additionally, type and imagery can also fill in, creating blobs of thick or concentrated color, effectively disrupting both readability and legibility. Good design choices can help to alleviate these problems. Make sure the chosen typeface has a single line width and open shapes, as well as large chunky typefaces and rectangular blocks of eye-catching black on the page. Headlines and subheads that are small and set in a delicate face, even when set bold, create an excess of white space. Either option

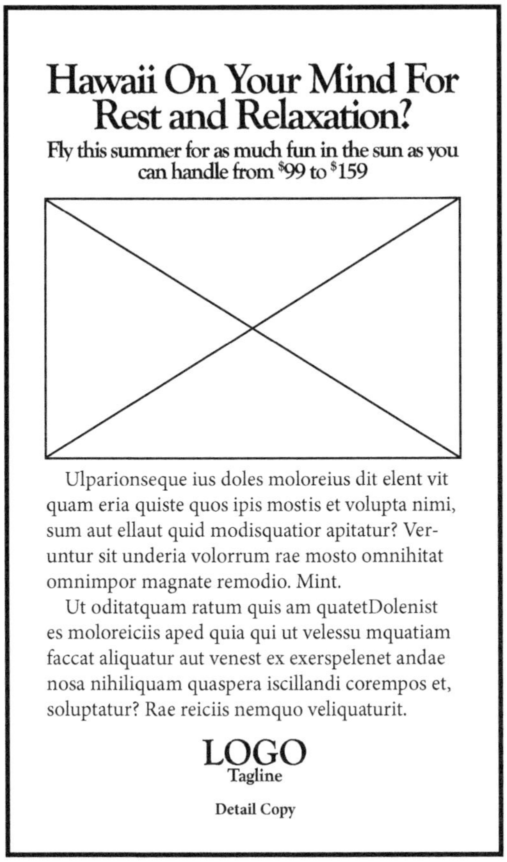

Figure 12.2 This example of a symmetrical layout style shows a range of prices placed in the subhead. Sample layout courtesy of Robyn Blakeman, University of Tennessee.

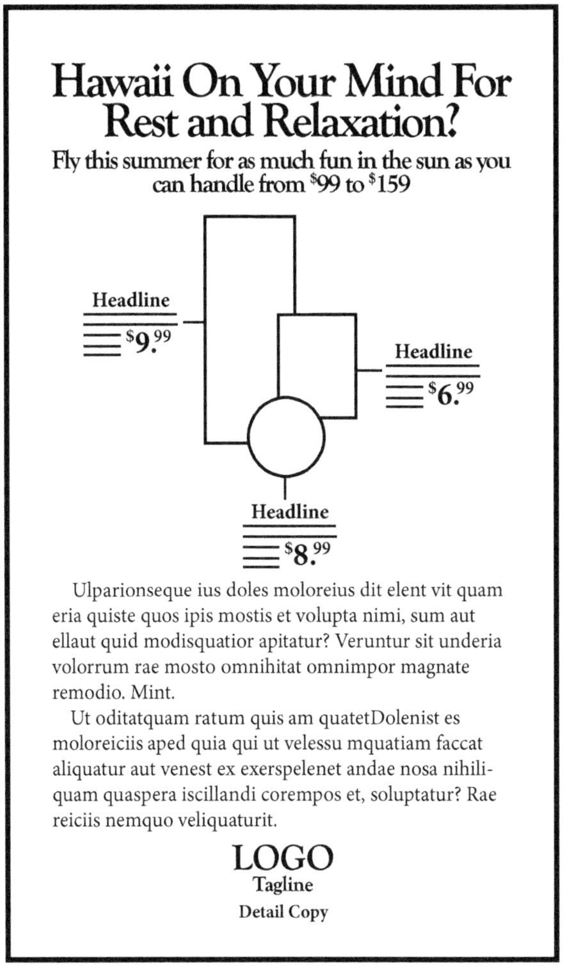

Figure 12.3 This silhouette layout style shows the use of callouts. Sample layout courtesy of Robyn Blakeman, University of Tennessee.

can produce positive results as long as the typeface chosen has weight or thickness to it. It is also important to not reverse out body copy or place it on top of screen tints, or visuals to avoid affecting readability.

Sizing Up Newspaper Columns

Ad sizes are diverse. Newspaper space is measured in column inches, or the width of a column of typeset copy plus the gutter, the white space seen between columns. Column width is measured in increments, starting from 2^1/16 inches up to 13 inches. The depth, or length of an ad, is measured in quarter-inch increments up to 21 inches, or a full newspaper page. Design decisions must fit into one of the preset column widths, but ad depth is determined by the creative team and of course the budget. Table 12.1 shows choices for column widths.

The typical newspaper ad doesn't need to hit the target over the head with a complicated design but does require good organizational skills. It is important each ad has a strong visual

Table 12.1 Sizes for newspaper ads.

1 column	2 ^{1}/16 inches
2 column	4 ¼ inches
3 column	6 ^{7}/16 inches
4 column	8 ^{5}/8 inches
5 column	10 ^{13}/16 inches
6 column	13 inches

and verbal presence on the page. Headlines need to boldly inform the target about the key consumer benefit, and visuals need to feature the brand and/or its use; either can be used to promote price when relevant to the brand. Every ad needs to have strong black-and-white contrasts between elements, feature a single dominant visual or verbal element, and use white space effectively. Type should be easy to read and be brand-image specific. The ad should flow easily down the page from element to element, closing with the logo, slogan, or tagline, and detail copy to make shopping easier and faster. Let's take a look at the visual, verbal, and interactive options associated with newspaper design.

Chaos Is a Result of Unstructured Clutter

Far too many retail ads have way too many elements. But the clutter and chaos are only one layout decision away. Seasoned art directors know the role each visual/verbal element plays in an ad. Because of this, they organize each element in the exact order it needs to be seen or read. Remember, if you start out thinking of the varied components as being geometric shapes, order will ultimately reduce chaos, as you size, stack, arrange, and rearrange each component across the page. To suggest elegance and order, and to highlight quality over price, large amounts of white space should be used "around" components, rather than "between" them. Orderly structure is always appreciated over busy movement that visually says too much.

A Look at What Newspaper Design Has to Say and Show

We talked a lot about general copy elements in Chapter 11. Let's take a brief look at how they are used in newspaper design. In newspaper design, headlines play a more dominate role than body copy and often, visuals.

Headlines

A headline in newspaper design has a big job to do. As the largest type on the page, it needs to push the key consumer benefit and more often than not, a price in a quick and informative way. As a rule, try to keep your headlines to no more than a single sentence and around five to seven words. Short, simple, and to the point gives you room to go big and bold. Due to their size, they will often require a liberal dose of both kerning and leading. Tighter spacing, both horizontally and vertically, allows you to enlarge the headline to give it a bolder appearance and to more easily capture the reader's attention.

Subheads

Not all newspaper ads need a subhead, but it is a great option if you want to focus on the range of prices associated with your brand. The second largest piece of copy on the page—that is, the subhead's job—is to elaborate on what the headline is saying and help advance the headline style; for example, if your headline asks a question your subhead will answer it in a complete sentence.

Body Copy

Body copy should be kept to a minimum if used at all. Highlight only what the target needs to do, and include enough about the brand to seduce the reader into action. An ad that has only a headline, a visual, and a logo is missing an opportunity to engage and educate the target. Unless you are a mature brand, like Coke or Reese's Peanut Butter Cups, your brand has a story to tell, and the best way to inform is through body copy. Be sure your copy is written in a conversational tone, and speaks to your target's educational level. You will not have a lot of room, so make every word count. Every word and sentence should explain why the brand can solve the target's problem. It is rare to see body copy in newspaper ads today. But if you want to stand out and ignore current trends, consider using copy that ranges anywhere from 50 to 250 words. Consumers read newspaper advertising for deals, not long-winded storylines. Minimal copy leaves more room for bigger headlines and any visuals you need to effectively show and tell the brand's story.

Finally, be sure the final paragraph has a strong call to action: What do you want your target to do next? Do you want them to visit your brick-and-mortar store, or call or log on for more information, such as a free evaluation, a discount, or free trial— to name just a few.

Detail Copy

Don't forget detail copy. Don't just list your website or throw in some social media icons. Put in every contact option you have. You want to give every member of your target group every possible option to get in touch with you. Don't assume just because you like to surf the Web that everyone has time to do that. Some may want to call to get specific questions answered, while others may want to visit a brick-and-mortar store to interact with the brand and the sales personnel.

Announcement Devices

If you want to scream out important sale, or other promotional information, consider using snipes, bursts, or banners. A *burst* looks like a cog in a wheel, while a *snipe* is a simple black triangular shape, visually confined in one of the ad's top corners. Black bars, or *banners*, like bursts and snipes, are typically placed at the top of an ad, to keep from breaking it in two. The type placed inside these typically solid black devices is reversed out to white or another light color, and should be set in a larger, bolder typeface—usually 18- to 24- point type—to ensure readability and legibility. Announcement devices like bursts and snipes should not be considered for magazines, for newspaper ads with a more elegant or upscale image, or for higher-end sales; they can make an ad appear cluttered and under almost all circumstances have a tacky and low-budget feel.

The Show-and-Tell of Type

The choice of typeface should reflect a brand or company's personality. Type is not a whimsical or temporary choice. Once a typeface is chosen, it should appear in every ad—no matter what the media vehicle. The typeface should become a representative device for that brand. Remember to limit the number of typefaces to no more than two per ad. To create variety, consider using multiple weights or even italics for emphasis. An ad's layout style, as well as type choice, should also reflect the target audience. Bigger type and less formal layouts work well when attracting younger consumers, whereas cleaner, more structured layouts work best for older targets.

To attract attention, consider setting your headlines, subheads, and prices in bold to project a stronger voice. Any bulky serif or sans serif typeface will hold up on newsprint and stand out on the page. Finer, lighter serif or sans serif typefaces on the other hand, will recede and can break up. Body copy can be set in either a serif or sans serif face. Look to your design and brand to determine the most appropriate styles.

Choosing a Layout Style

We talked in-depth about the varied layout styles in Chapter 8. But to ensure you make the best choice for the design, the brand, and the target, it is important to know which style works best in what medium. The styles best suited to newspaper include Big Type, Circus (only if you must), Frame, Multipanel, Picture Window, Rebus; if placing larger images in the headline or using simple illustrations over photographs in the body copy, then Silhouette, Symmetrical, Asymmetrical, Repetition, Concentration, and Anomaly. For diversity, any layout style can be combined with one or more styles, depending on whether you are placing emphasis on the visual or verbal elements.

Visual Imagery Shows the Brand's Story

Visuals tell the brand's, and thus the target's, story in pictures. A dominant visual can draw attention in the same way a dominate headline would. Visual options include featuring the brand with or without a background, in use, placed in a setting, or all alone on the page. A dominant visual can easily be enlarged to stand out, based on size, or created by grouping multiply related, but diversely shaped and sized images, and grouping them together, such as with a silhouette layout style. The resulting imagery is bigger, stronger, and louder on the page.

When you have a lot of related visuals to show, consider using a large visual to showcase use or placement within a setting. Then consider isolating each product in a drawn grid with corresponding callouts and prices to control the chaos and educate at the same time.

The visual you choose to place in your newspaper ad is important. You should take into consideration the paper stock used, as well as the brand advertised. The visuals your target will eventually see is a representation of the client's brand. The creative team, and overall budget, decide the type of imagery used. Options include photography, illustrations, line art, or graphics. If budget is an issue, simple line drawings bring stark black-and-white contrast to the page. Whatever the type of image style and/or its subject matter, be sure it pushes the key consumer benefit in the headline, is representative of the brand's image, and will reproduce well on newsprint. Always go with visuals that have strong black-and-white contrasts to avoid graying down and flattening the imagery. If using color, try to bump up the highlights and shadows to create a greater range of color contrasts.

Framing a Print Ad

A common addition to newspaper ads are *frames* or borders. Frames are used to tie an ad's elements together and set it off from surrounding copy or other ads on the page.

Frames define the overall size of a newspaper ad. They can be fat, thin, double-ruled, or defined by graphic images. Remember, because of the bleedable nature of newsprint, don't let the lines get too thin, or use double lines placed too close together, as they can fill in and delicate lines can break up or disappear entirely.

For a more expensive or exclusive look, consider using a 1–2 point frame for a more subtle-looking border. Discount establishments often showcase multiple items creating a more cluttered appearance, so a heavier border of 2–3 points is required to stand out. For guidance, it is a good rule of thumb for line thickness of any frame to closely match the weight of the typeface used. Another option is altering the weight of the frame. To draw the eye inside, consider making the top and bottom lines slightly thicker. Keep the additional thickness to around ⅛-inch, anything more weighs the ad down, anything less will look like a mistake. This simple addition, helps disperse the weight away from the center of the ad, creating the illusion of additional white space and making the ad appear larger.

To ensure the frame does not interfere with either the visual or verbal images used in the ad, be sure to include at least ¼-inch margins around the inside of the ad. Borders can be used as simple graphic elements inside the ad, such as inset borders, that are smaller than the size of the ad, placed around photographs or callout boxes, to emphasize an image or any copy points that require special notice.

Remembering the Importance of White Space, Eye Flow, and Dominant Elements

The amount of white space can say as much about the quality of your brand as words can. An excess of white space says elegance and quality, while a lack of it says just the opposite. A good ad exploits the white of the page, so use it judiciously, and keep clutter to a minimum. Newspaper often has little to say and a lot to show. Be sure only one visual or verbal element dominates the page and use the size and placement of elements to control eye flow down the page.

Although there are no set rules as to whether the visual or verbal image should dominate the design, it will ultimately depend on what the ad needs to accomplish. The goal of both is to promote the key consumer benefit. Dominant headlines are a great choice when you have something simple and straightforward to say. Visuals work better for more complicated key consumer benefits, where showing will be faster and easier than talking about it. As a rule, headlines have a greater presence on a newspaper page, while visuals have greater presence on a magazine page.

Interactive Options of Newspaper

Newspapers are fighting to stay relevant as younger generations turn to the Internet, social, and 24-hour news channels for news of the day. Finding ways to engage the target and offering something they cannot find anywhere else is crucial to sustainability. Although ads appearing in digital subscriptions have a color advantage, they still have to fight to be noticed in the same way as their print cousins. But they have one very distinct advantage print ads lack: They are interactive. These engaging little sales tools have the ability to transport the target to a web page for additional information, or to deliver one or more coupons. Once the link is clicked on, the visual/verbal message no longer competes to be noticed amongst the clutter of the page.

The very act of saving, tearing out, or printing a coupon is both interactive and engaging. The choice to include a coupon opens up numerous promotional opportunities, such as "try me" offers, and giveaways, such as water bottles, T-shirts, or toy characters, to name just a few, that can be given out in local fast food restaurants when the target presents a code, or gives the correct answer to a trivia question found, for example, only in the newspaper ad.

Ads that feature a link can easily whisk the target away to a website, perhaps to request an information packet, talk to a customer service representative, or even to make an immediate purchase.

Including a QR code is another way to transport readers to a different location or provide more information. They are a great way to create interaction and increase the time spent with the ad. By including information on social media outlets, you give the target a chance to post or discuss their brand experiences with other loyal users, seek out additional promotional offers such as entering a contest or sweepstakes, or even to sign up to receive a free product sample, to name just a few.

Another option is a co-op promotion. The *New York Post* found a way to engage a younger target by using a promotional *cover wrap* or an ad that takes over the front page above the fold, that featured the cult streetwear brand Supreme, known for its creative limited-edition promotions. The simple wraparound ad was blank except for the *New York Post* header and the red Supreme logo. Interest was so high in what many considered a collectable edition, the paper was sold out before 10 a.m.

Magazine Design: The Visual and Verbal Style of Magazine Advertising

Magazine advertising concentrates on developing an image or creating a mood by developing strong visual and verbal relationships. In order to capture the reader's attention and hold it, magazine advertising needs to create a conceptual environment that the target can both relate to and experience through the words and visuals. The show(first)-and-tell(second) nature of magazine advertising allows a brand to show a problem and creatively and colorfully demonstrate solutions. Brands advertising in magazines are diverse in type, ranging from exclusive or unique and expensive to own, to everyday items whose features may be indiscernible from those of competing brands.

Like newspapers, magazines are more frequently consumed by wealthier, educated, audiences. Thanks to their highly targetable content based on interests, values, and hobbies, advertising is often considered less intrusive. In fact, it is not unusual for readers to purchase a magazine as much for the advertising as the content. This built-in interest allows the advertising to talk directly to the individual most likely to purchase the product, or use the service. It also helps expand the viewing life of magazine advertising. Because of the highly targetable content, consumers tend to keep magazines longer, often trading with other enthusiasts or friends. This gives advertising a new set of eyes to educate and inspire as well as help expand the targeted audience.

Depending on the type of publication—whether consumer, special interest, or business—advertising will typically match the editorial style of the magazine in which it appears, for example, home decor magazines will have advertising for paint, furniture, flooring, and lighting and plumbing fixtures. Creative teams can take advantage of a diverse assortment of design options both visually and verbally, such as using varied sizes and types of imagery in black-and-white or color, employing varying types of layout styles, including interactive components, and using copy that tells a lengthy, visually motivating story, or one that says very little or nothing. Concepts that tap into lifestyle will by default address image. Colorful imagery and dynamic copy work together to inform and educate the target, helping them not only to imagine having the product in their life, but also encouraging them to seek out additional information.

Unlike retail newspaper advertising where the focus is on sell, sell, sell, image-based advertising places focus on the benefits of owning or using the brand and interweaving the brand's image with the target's self-image, eliminating any hard-sell tactics or the mention of price.

For brands with little or no meaningful differences between them and their competitors, the advertising must sell image by projecting an aura of affluence, beauty, and even intellect. These types of ads tend to minimize copy and let the visuals, that often take up over 60–65 percent of the page, speak for the brand. The visuals job is to develop a personality and create a visual image for the brand, as well as allow readers to be able to experience the benefits associated with the product or service mainly through the visual message. The optimal coated surface that magazines are printed on allows for visual discussions through photographs, illustrations, and/or graphics that can show a product in use, and assist with image development, as well as create an illusion of exclusivity or fun.

Copy that defines image or is used as an educational device for new product launches or mature brand reinventions for example, can use longer, more fact-based copy that relegates the visual to a supporting role in the design. Longer copy that is creatively written can hold the target's interest long enough to educate, demonstrate, build curiosity, or simply and quickly inform.

Whether visually or verbally heavy, both types of ads need to focus on highlighting the benefits associated with owning the brand or using the service by visually and/or verbally showcasing how the brand can successfully solve the target's problem, as well as encourage them to call, engage a mobile app, log onto a web or social media site, or visit their nearest retailer for more information or purchase. To do this successfully, the more the creative team knows about the target's interests, lifestyles, and general demographics, the stronger and more engaging the visual/ verbal message will be.

Designing for Magazine

Magazine advertising should provide a visually stimulating experience and/or verbally entice the target. Visual images should help explain brand's benefits as well as develop an identity and create a visual personality for the brand. The job of these colorful, informative, and sometimes provocative visuals is to record daily life, capture lifestyle, and immortalize trends. Copy should take the target on a journey, with the brand as the star. Visuals should work to tie the brand and target's self-image together.

Everything about designing for magazines is more creative and visually exciting than designing for almost any other medium, except perhaps alternative media. Elite products, color, and varied visual options allow the designer's fantasy world to come alive.

The choice to use the visually stimulating pages of a magazine to bring prestige to a brand and reflect the target's interests, self-image, and lifestyle is a design journey into the study of human nature. Magazine advertising can be anything the creative team wants; it can be elegant, engaging, and/or interactive, colorful, fun and imaginative. It is a great choice for introducing a new brand and developing an image, maintaining the allure of an established image, or assist with repositioning or repairing the image of an old brand. Let's take a look at the printing surface, and the diverse visual and verbal elements, and interactive options available in magazine.

The Paper the Design Is Printed On

Magazines are printed on a smooth, high-quality clay-coated paper stock. This means the ink will not bleed or move on the page. Shiny, coated paper stocks are far superior to dull, uncoated stocks. Coated stocks reproduce crisper and more detailed imagery, and boast brighter, more saturated colors. Coated stocks are thicker than newsprint and require less ink when printing, because the stock does not absorb the ink into the fibers. However, the coating on many papers makes writing on them difficult, so don't choose it for forms that need to be filled out—use an uncoated stock instead.

Sizing Up Magazines and Layout Options

Magazines have fewer size options than newspapers; however, they are not as standardized as they are in newspaper. Publication sizes differ, and so do ad sizes, so it is best to check with the publication before sitting down to design.

The size of a typical full-page magazine ad is 8.5 x11 inches; other sizes include one-eighth, one-fourth, one-half, and two-thirds page. Beyond single-page ads, options include two-page ads, double-page spreads, and the big three-page foldouts.

Whether an ad will be placed on a left or right page needs to be considered during the conceptual stage and then again during the photo shoot. Any imagery containing people, animals, or anything that can gaze in one direction or another, should gaze towards the inside of the magazine. This hold interest inside the ad, not off the page. With that said, this is no longer a hard and fast rule, but it is a good place to start. Almost all design rules can be broken as long as you have a point or a justifiable reason for changing the rules, as long as it does not affect eye flow, balance, or structure.

Single ads placed on multiple pages, also known as two-page ads, allow the key consumer benefit to tell an ongoing story. Placement, whether on succeeding pages or separated by several pages, will depend on what you are trying to say and show. These ads might also feature a foldout, where additional information is hidden under a fold.

Double-page spreads can tell a longer visual/verbal story. Everything can be enlarged and more detailed. The biggest problem is that designing horizontally creates new design challenges, often making it a difficult layout option. It is important to use page space wisely by avoiding gaps and any unnecessary white holes.

Additionally, a spread has a *gutter* that must be designed around. It is very basically the part of the center or inner margins of the magazine that is pulled into the binding when printed. It is important no visual and/or verbal information falls into this dead area. Be sure to use page space wisely, by avoiding overly vertical images, gaps, and white holes. To avoid any issues, be sure to leave at least a quarter- to a half-inch of space on either side of the gutter for text. Visuals can be pulled into the gutter, just be sure you don't let faces or anything that pushes the key consumer benefit or supports the headline to be pulled in, resulting in un-viewable details. As a beginning designer, I would suggest you show the gutter parameters when working in InDesign so that you do not forget about them and can easily design around it.

Magazine Images Visually and Verbally Speak for the Brand

Whether large and dominant or small in stature, the compelling imagery used in magazine ad design needs to tell the brand's story in a creative and informative way. It is up to the creative team to decide whether full-color, black-and-white, or spot color

photographs, illustrations, or graphics can best promote the key consumer benefit, work within the media, and fit the overall budget.

Photographs, the most common imagery employed, bring an exclusive viewing opportunity to the page. Thanks to the high-quality paper stock and printing capabilities used by magazines, the target can clearly see the brand's details and how it is used, or the benefits it brings. Photographs bring the brand alive in the target's imagination. Textures and patterns are magnified, colors are highly saturated and pop off the page, quality is enhanced, emotions are highlighted, and taste buds awakened.

This diverse visual variety offers designers the option to work with one or more images, include background, or isolate the product or image by eliminating background clutter. How visuals are displayed in all ads is important. There are eight distinct ways to visualize your brand in both print and most digital mediums.

1. Show the product alone. This very clean and brand-focused option, shows no background or relevant settings. Focus is placed entirely on the brand.
2. Show the product in a relevant or irrelevant setting. Emphasis is placed on the brand in a location where it is most likely to be seen or used. If using a fantasy or humorous tone for example, an irrelevant placement, say within a rabbit hole, attracts attention.
3. Show the product in use. This is a great choice if you want to demonstrate how the brand is traditionally used or if promoting a new use.
4. Dramatize. Typically, visuals focus on showing ways the brand can make life easier, better, or more interesting.
5. Explain brand uses. As the style suggests, visuals show and tell different ways to use the brand.
6. Show specific brand features. Visuals focus on the benefits associated with each feature.
7. Make comparisons. If you plan to compare your brand to one or more competing brands, showing a comparison between brands, or before-and-after results is very effective.
8. Visual and verbal ties. A great choice if your visual can show exactly what your headline is saying.

Beyond full-color photographs, additional design options include using black-and-white photographs, or ones with spot color accents. Spot color is a great way to control eye flow, as the reader is drawn directly to the spot of color.

Ultimately, the number, type, and size of imagery used will depend on what needs to be shown and the layout style employed. Almost all layout styles work when designing for magazine except for the cluttered Circus style layout. The choice to use one or more layout styles will, like your choice of imagery, ultimately depend on your concept, the budget, and overall brand image.

Designing within the Live, Trim, and Bleed

The layout of magazine ads is fairly regimented to ensure nothing gets cut off when the magazine is trimmed to size during printing. There are three areas that make up a magazine layout: Live, trim, and bleed.

Live. The *live area* is centered inside the trim. For an ad measuring 8.5 x 11 inches the live area would be around 7 x 10 inches. All type must be confined within this safe zone. Only visuals and graphics can extend beyond the live area. Its job is to protect components from being accidentally cut off when the magazine is trimmed down to its final size.

Trim. The *trim* size is 8.5 x 11 inches for most full-size ads. Trim size refers to both ad size and the magazine size, and is where the magazine will be trimmed or cut during printing.

Bleed. The *bleed* area extends beyond and around the trim. Any photograph, illustration, graphic, or background color that is designed to come up to the edge of the trim size must bleed at least an eighth- to a quarter-inch beyond the trim size. Since the trimming of a magazine is not an exact science, bleed photographs not extending beyond the trim can leave small, unsightly slivers of white space, showing around the edges of the ad after trimming. Although bleed ads are a great visual choice, they are also more expensive. Before choosing to design with one, it is important to determine whether your client can afford adding one or more bleed photographs. If the budget is there, then the photographer must be made aware of all bleed shots during the photo shoot to ensure they don't come in too close during shooting. If they do, there will not be enough of the photograph left to accommodate bleed later during the design, production, and printing, stages. See Figure 12.4 for an example of live, trim, and bleed.

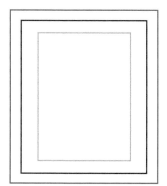

Figure 12.4 This illustration shows the layout of live, trim, and bleed as used in a magazine.

Finally, whether to use bleed or focus more on the white of the page is a designer's choice. An abundance of white space will always make body copy easier to read and images will pop off the page.

The Unique Voice of Illustrations and Graphics

A more unique, whimsical, dramatic, or practical option is to use illustrations or graphics. Graphic designs and/or colorful illustrations draw the target's attention by highlighting interesting and creative imagery, often with brilliant color variations. Illustrations create an image of youth and vibrancy, as well as a clean way to display charted information. The colorful interpretations of the brand in use or in a setting can reveal a brand's personality. The graphic or illustrative style chosen, along with suggestive color choices, can re-create time periods, give the imagery energy or stability, and suggest liberal or conservative views. Imagery that does not exist can be created around the brands and thus the target's image.

Cool Images versus Informative Copy

Although visuals dominate the pages of magazines, don't get caught up in the showing and forget about telling through informative copy. Visuals help an ad get noticed, but it's good, cohesive visual and verbal ideas that will resonate with your target longer and help make your ads more memorable.

When writing for magazine, you need to captivate and inform both visually and verbally. The copy and imagery need to work together to creatively show and tell the same story. Not all magazine ads will have equal amounts of both visual and verbal components. The choice to use a single headline, one or more subhead(s), or short or long body copy will depend on your key consumer benefit and the life-cycle stage of your brand. Ads for mature brands for example, typically have nothing more than a visual and a logo. Others might add a headline and those with more to say, such as a new product launch or reinvented brand, although rare today, will add a subhead and body copy to flesh out the necessary details. Let's take a quick look at the use of each one.

Headlines

The headline will be the first thing your target reads in an ad. Those highlighting strong key consumer benefits draw in the target by relating brand benefits to image and lifestyle. Unlike those seen in newspaper ads headlines, unless graphic, the magazine headline should not overpower the ad but should be designed into the brand's personality or around the ambience created within the design. Headlines, no matter their size, should seamlessly blend with the imagery rather than simply dominate the page. Sizes for headlines vary in magazine ads, but typically they should take up no more than 10–20 percent of the page. As a rule, they should never be so loud or bold, decrease or interfere with the brand's image, or insult the educational or social level of the target. Loud is always out; structure and informative class are always in.

The color of your type also reflects brand image and your concept. Typically, color is added only to the headline and subheads. Although not a hard and fast rule, body copy is the easiest to read in black. To determine your type's colorful voice beyond what is being said, study color psychology and/or look to your visual, to help determine direction.

Finally, thanks to the built-in relationship the target has with the magazine, their attention can be held longer, so the headline can be longer and more educational.

Subheads

Like newspaper, not all magazine ads will need a subhead. If using a main subhead, be sure it does not overpower the headline or the visual. If the design calls for the use of lengthy body copy, it can often dull or gray down even a magazine page. To counter this, consider adding bold or colorful multiple copy break subheads between paragraphs to break up the copy into more digestible and contrasting blocks of information.

Body Copy

Focus on the benefits the brand brings to the target. Except in rare instances, keep it short, simple, and to the point. I recently read an article that claimed research has proven that humans actually have a shorter attention span than goldfish: Humans hang in there for eight seconds and goldfish for nine. True, I don't know for sure. But what I do know is to capture and hold the attention of a distracted target, your ad needs to get to the point quickly, and be concise and easy to understand at a glance. Finally, when possible use multiple paragraphs and keep both your paragraphs and sentences short.

All copy needs to be written from your target's point of view. On first glance, the target probably is not interested in buying or even trying your brand. But they will hopefully want to buy your solution to their problem if they can be enticed into the body copy and educated.

Body copy can be lengthier since readers selectively spend more time with a magazine than they do with a newspaper, or it can be virtually nonexistent, short, medium, or long, depending on the type of magazine and the message being explained or introduced. Today, the average consumer magazine ad often has only a few lines of copy, just enough to remind or place focus on the key consumer benefit. Special-interest magazines on the other hand, often

showcase copy of medium length, where a more in-depth dissection of the key consumer benefit can be discussed along with any additional yet relevant attributes. Longer copy allows storylines or plots to focus on promoting uses, scientific studies, demonstrations, purchase options, and trends, to name just a few. Copy should take the target on an informative journey of experiences with the brand. Be as descriptive as possible, bringing the experiences alive by tapping into the target's senses and emotions. There is no immediacy in magazine advertising as peddled in newspaper advertising. Magazine advertising is not impersonal; its job is to make the target experience the brand in their life. Remember, the job of informative body copy is to build a storyline that shows how the brand can be incorporated into the target's lifestyle.

Type That Speaks Design

Depending on the overall concept, magazine design allows you to get a little bolder with your choice of headline type. It can be larger, longer, more colorful, graphic, and just downright cool. When type is used as a graphic image, it will dominate the page at any size, so be sure any other images appearing in the ad are either smaller or bleed, so they do not compete with each other for attention.

Keeping readability and legibility in mind, headline styles might include modern, decorative or display, and script. Use a critical eye—anything too decorative edges toward tacky and garish, not to mention that it will always be difficult to read. Magazine ads may successfully hold the target's attention longer, but no one is going to invest time into understanding illegible headline text. If using a decorative face, set it in either caps/lower case, or initial caps/lower case, never in all caps, and be sure it matches both the tone of the ad, and the visual(s).

If you want to strengthen your visual/verbal tie, consider letting your main visual(s) slightly overlap the headline type. When type overlaps a photo, or vice versa, it needs to do more than simply touch the image, which looks like a mistake; it should in fact overlap. However, too much overlap can affect readability. Consider starting at an overlap of one-eighth of an inch. See Figure 12.5 for an example of type overlaying a visual.

How much overlap is acceptable will often depend on the typeface and its weight. Headline type that is too small or dainty can be overwhelmed by a photograph that is too close. Other considerations include looking at what the headline is actually saying. If the headline automatically creates a visual/verbal relationship, for example "If It Hurts We Have A Solution" and the visual shows a man stooped over holding his lower back, then a strong tie has been made between what is being said to what is being shown.

Illustration of the Imagination

Do you hate when your pens bleed through the other side of the paper? The new Sharpie Pen writes like a fine tip marker but does not bleed.Its smooth writing is perfect for taking notes or sketching. The Sharpie Pen allows you to doodle your ideas on both sides of the paper. Once you use the Sharpie Pen, it will become your everyday writing necessity. Visit our website and tell us how you use your Sharpie Pen

LITERALLY SHARPIE

Available at fine retail stores. For more information, visit www.sharpie.com

Sharpie

Figure 12.5 Example of type overlaying visual. Image courtesy of Alex Crutchfield, University of Tennessee.

Body copy for both newspaper and magazine will typically be 10–11 point with 1 extra point of leading. This is a great place to start and by adding additional leading makes it easier to read. To ensure both readability and legibility, consider using a common typeface such as Times or Times Roman.

Lengthy copy will require the type size to be smaller. As a rule, never go any smaller than 9-point type with 10-point leading. If all the copy still won't fit, consider reducing the headline or one or more visuals, or ask your copywriter for a tighter edit. Detail copy should be no smaller than 7–8 point and social media icons no larger than a ¼ inch.

A Few Additional Design and Type Rules for Print

Design for any medium is multifaceted. There are many principles that need to be applied and rules to be followed. Some are easy to remember, based more on common sense than design knowledge, while other smaller more aesthetic design rules can be more easily missed or forgotten. Here are a few to keep in mind when laying out your design:

1. Your reader will notice the image first, no matter where it is placed on the page. Optimally, a good rule of thumb is to place your image in the "optical center" of the page, or centered one-third of the way down the page.
2. The best designs will always be the simplest ones. An ad that appears busy, cluttered, or lacks eye flow, will be dismissed by your target.
3. Be sure your choice of typeface(s) is easy to read, and your type and imagery work together. Simplicity or minimalism is the goal. A single image or group of images will deliver your message more succinctly than having multiple images scattered across the page. Employ only those that push your concept and get rid of the rest.
4. Do not be afraid to use the white of the page as a design element. Do not feel compelled to cover the entire page with type or a bleed visual or screened background. Remember white space speaks elegance, expensive, and simplicity.
5. White space also needs to be balanced within the ad. Don't shove everything to one side or center some components and push others to the side. Aesthetically, a balanced ad is visually more appealing and easier to read and understand than one full of white holes.
6. Placement of components will depend on the overall design and art director's preference, but a good place to start is to ensure all type is placed at least ¼ inch away from other elements on the page, such as visuals, graphic lines or boxes, and any graphic inset frames, to avoid appearing cluttered or sandwiched-in, and to ensure readability and legibility. Remember, consistency is key.
7. Do not forget to emphasize your logo, tagline, or slogan and include any detail copy necessary to make purchasing or getting additional information simple and easy.
8. Make sure the visual and verbal message work together. If they don't, start the brainstorming process over again until they do.
9. If your concept is a little on the abstract side, great, just be sure your target can figure out what you're trying to say and show quickly. A creatively obscure idea may seem brilliant to you, but nonsensical to your target. They will not spend more than a couple of seconds trying to figure you and your design out.
10. Be sure to think contrast when choosing your typeface and type sizes. Contrast is achieved through typeface(s) selection and the use of varied point sizes. Contrast also refers to the placement of your type on a specific background. For example, dark gray or navy type on a black background is low in contrast and virtually unreadable. Dark type on a light-colored background is high in contrast and both readable and legible.

11. Screened backgrounds, when possible, should not appear under the body copy. If the background is too dark, it can drastically affect contrast on the page as well as readability and legibility. Delicate serif faces can often break up, even on coated paper stock. If you do design with a full-page bleed screen, be sure it is no darker than 10–15 percent.

12. When possible, eliminate large blocks of copy. Choose instead to use smaller, more succinct copy. If you must use a large amount of copy, consider breaking it up with bullet points or multiple copy break subheads to create additional white space and appear less intimidating and more readable.

13. The choice to use a serif or sans serif typeface is a designer's choice. Just be sure to follow the design, style, and personality suggestions discussed in Chapter 11.

14. Remember to use no more than two typefaces per ad. Set the large text such as headlines and any subheads in one face, and the smaller text like body and detail copy in the other. Go with multiple weights to increase contrast between elements.

15. The main thing to avoid in both newspaper and magazine design is clutter. To ensure a cohesive whole, choose what single component, type, or image will dominate the page, use large doses of white space, and use each component to lead the reader's eye toward the logo. The overall result should be the seamless blending of type, imagery, and white space to create an informative and/or elegant, classy, playful, or imaginative appearance.

Finally, if you need to inform with lengthy copy or grab attention with color, magazines are a good choice. They are also a strong medium to help promote trying a new brand, develop a brand's identity, or tie brand image to the target's self-image. Magazines bring elegance, prestige, and social acceptance to the brand. New, old, and reinvented brands with messages based on image or innovation are ideal for magazine use.

Interactive Magazine Design

As previously discussed, interactivity begins by asking the target to do something: Call, log on, sign up for a contest or sweepstakes, visit a social media site, come into the showroom, call for an appointment, or take a test drive. Readers viewing ads on tablets or mobile devices might be asked to shake or turn the device, download a game, view Instagram images, or a video. Other options might include encouraging trial, perhaps by including a small product sample or a scratch-and-sniff card. More creative alternative options might include 3-D pop-ups, interactive mobile phone demonstrations, QR codes, or even the ability to fold and use the ad to complete a specific task, such as open a

bottle. The multitude of possible interactive options designed into a magazine ad can be both engaging and memorable.

Increase Engagement with a Fold or Two

Another great interactive device common to magazine advertising is a fold. The type of fold typically used is called a *gatefold*. A gatefold can consist of one or more folds that fold inward toward the ad's center when the magazine is closed, and can fold out to view in its entirety.

These simple interactive folds can vary in size, but the most commonly used is an often full-size third panel cut back, one-sixteenth- to one-eighth-inch smaller than the overall page size. This allows the magazine to close without creasing the ad. Another common option is a quarter-page fold, which can vary in size but is typically around 2.5–3 inches wide and 8.5 inches deep.

The job of the gatefold is to extend the ad, offer a quick and easy interactive activity, and pique curiosity. By just extending the photograph a few inches, the target is encouraged to open and inspect the panel, inviting them further into the ad with a hidden message that holds their attention for a bit longer. Hidden copy might hold a coupon, announce a contest or sweepstakes, or even offer a small sample. These smaller gatefolds typically overlay the bottom photograph making it critical that registration or alignment of the two images be exact when printed, bound, and folded. Any type of additional fold is expensive, so it must have relevance and fit within the client's budget.

Newspapers, Magazines, and Cooperative Advertising Opportunities

It is not unusual to see brands advertised in newspapers and magazines participate in co-op opportunities. Co-op, or *cooperative advertising*, means that two or more separate but compatible brands have joined together to encourage their target to use the brands together. These common and successful relationships might pair a wine with a particular brand of cheese. Other partnership ventures might include a free Uber ride to get your Covid vaccination.

There are two types of cooperative advertising: Vertical and horizontal. *Vertical cooperatives* feature one dominant advertiser that pays more, and has a larger visual/verbal voice in all advertising efforts. *Horizontal cooperatives* have equal budgets and equal visual/verbal exposure.

The benefit of co-op advertising to the target is the ability to combine two viable brands into a package savings deal. Repetitive brand pairing, when done consistently and over a relatively long period of time, gets the target into the habit of thinking a specific package rather than random pairing when repurchasing.

Summary: Print Is Alive and Well

Print isn't going anywhere; it is not dying, nor is it already dead. Print advertising drives consumer behavior. For example, according to an online article in *Media Space Solutions* by Jenna Bruce, neuroscience research points out "that print ads make a better impression than digital ones." She goes on to say that studies by Kantar Millward Brown have shown that "people process print content with greater engagement and focus, than they do content viewed on a screen." Very simply, as consumers we tend to scan digital content quickly, as opposed to print, where we tend to read more slowly increasing the rate of overall comprehension.

When print is combined with social media, augmented reality, and quick response codes to name just a few, it is a great way to not only create brand awareness and increase recall, but present a creative and interactive platform that increases the target's engagement time with the ad.

Bibliography

Bruce, Jenna. 2017. "Will Print Advertising Still Work in 2018?" Retrieved from: www.mediaspacesolutions.com/blog/will-print-advertising-still-work-in-2018/, par. 2.

Developer, E.M. 2018. "Print Advertising Isn't Dead: Here's Why It Matters." Retrieved from: http://gearycompany.com/print-advertising-isnt-dead-heres-why-it-matters/, para. 15. (June 14).

The Visual and Verbal Design Behind Broadcast

Chapter 13 Objectives

1. The reader will understand the role of television to deliver a brand's message.
2. The reader will be able to define radio's role in today's advertising.
3. The reader will be able to create both a radio and television script, as well as an advanced television storyboard.

Why Traditional Broadcast Is Relevant

If you're wondering if traditional broadcast (radio and television) media are still viable advertising mediums, the short answer is yes. Numerous research studies have shown that both radio and television are still the best and most used channels for discovering new brands. It's true consumers of all ages are spending more time using digital outlets. However, when it comes to trust in message content and overall message recall, traditional media is still the most respected and believed. Beyond that, today's consumers are looking for more from their broadcast mediums than generic messages. The rise of digital media options like Pandora, Spotify, Netflix, and Hulu is driven by convenience, anytime-anywhere content accessibility, and the personalization and diversity of content. It is up to the creative team to make sure advertising content is relevant and meaningful to both new and existing audiences. Let's take a look at how radio and television advertising is developed.

Radio: The Imagination Medium

As a spoken-only medium, radio is often today considered old-fashioned and a second-rate medium when compared to other media vehicles. Limited by its need for active listening by the target, radio must work hard to successfully deliver both the visual and verbal message. It must be written with the target's lifestyle in mind, so that they can "imagine" the message based on their personal experience, and interaction with the brand. Radio must tap into the target's imagination—not easy when they are typically not actively listening.

Radio ads must create a visual experience for the target. Radio advertising must tie the target's experiences, or needs and wants, with copy that quickly and clearly lays out the key consumer benefit. To encourage the target to imagine the visual copy, the verbal message must be "picture perfect" in how the brand will meet and accomplish their expectations, in order for it to make a lasting impression. This is a great medium for building awareness, for local, inexpensive brands, or as a support vehicle, for larger regional and national brands.

Targetable, Inexpensive, and Timely

Radio's specialty is its ability to deliver short, inexpensive messages to smaller niche audiences. Any brand that needs to get a message out quickly will find ads can be written, produced, and aired, in only a few days. Very adaptable to changing market conditions, radio makes any message updates affordable.

Thanks to the popularity of local radio personalities, a very personalized medium makes building relationships between the target and the brand easier, especially if the spot is read by the DJ. Their appearance of endorsement gives the brand an aura of credibility.

The overall length of the ad or spot: 15, 30, or 60 seconds, determines cost, as does the time of day the ad will air. Ads that run during "drive times," or mornings from six to ten and afternoons from three to seven, are the most popular and expensive slots. Midday and evening hours are less expensive, as the audience number drops off after listeners begin or end their workday. Additionally, costs will include production and creative

DOI: 10.4324/9781003255123-14

expenses such as the hiring of talent, or who will read the copy and what sound effects (SFX) or music will be needed, and the frequency with which the ad airs.

Brand image is verbally created in radio, so copy needs to be imaginative and colorful. Copy can be visually stimulating if it supports and builds the target's self-image. If the target can imagine personally using the brand, their perceived interaction will be stronger and more realistic than one created by advertising efforts. Local or *spot* radio is where most advertising is placed. This relatively inexpensive medium offers small local business owners and national advertisers the same opportunity to tailor their message to a specific demographic based on a station's format, psychographically based on lifestyle, and geographically based on location.

Find a Way to Involve the Listener in the Message

The creative team has three seconds to get the listener to stop and "tune in" to the message. Ads have a better chance to accomplish this if the spot is interactive in some way. The most memorable ads will give the target an activity. The better the activity sticks in their mind, such as singing a catchy jingle they can clap or hum to, whether the ad is airing or not, helps with recall. Other promotional opportunities include call-in trivia games, and other types of contests and sweepstakes, or giveaways. Broadcasts from a remote location or outside the station encourages meet-and-greets with DJs and hopefully some kind of interaction with the brand, such as free fries with a burger purchase, or a test drive. The brand can also give out freebies, such as water bottles, hats, or T-shirts.

Another option would be to bring back old-time radio storytelling, sponsored by one or more brands, and creating a daily Game of Thrones or The Walking Dead-type of storyline, for example. If aired during drive times, interest would be higher, and storylines could expand their scope with humor, fantasy, intrigue, or some other imaginative or interactive direction, such as building a scavenger hunt into the plot where the target can win prizes, once the found item is returned to a sponsoring brand location. A compelling, well-written story, will always capture attention. Like television, radio can parcel out episodes to encourage the target to repeatedly tune in.

Any type of story can be told in radio if visually written with compelling dialogue. Messages that can capture and hold the target's attention while confined to their cars in traffic will be memorable. Ads with a sense of urgency can move products if creative. Finally, radio is a great choice if you want to give a voice to a character representative or spokesperson from print. However, radio is not a good choice for any message that has to

inform through lengthy copy in order to educate or that needs to be demonstrated.

Ways to Deliver the Message

There are a number of creative options you can use to deliver a radio message. Let's take a quick look at each one:

- Music and Jingles
- Narrative Drama
- Straight Announcement
- Celebrity Delivery
- Live Donut
- Single Voice
- Dialogue
- Multivoice
- Sound Effects
- Vignette
- Interview
- Humor
- Sponsorships

Music and Jingles. Music and catchy jingles are memorable. Places and emotions are tied to music, whether it be new age, hip hop, or a golden oldie. Music, especially an oldie for any generation, attracts attention by reigniting memories. These imaginative musings will enhance and enrich the current message. Music can also be used to set a scene or mood in the same way it might in a movie or television show. For example, if the advertised brand lacks spark, for example banks or grocery stores, it's up to the creative team to create sparks through music familiar to the target. The memories attached to music help the target to remember the client's brand.

Jingles are sticky. They get in our head and stay there—we find ourselves humming or singing them in the shower, during a meeting, or while at the dentist. A jingle's sticky attribute makes them both interactive and memorable, and an excellent way to extend a brand's message.

Narrative Drama. The use of a narrative approach is a great way to tell the brand's story with dramatic flair. Narrative dramas take a brand-related bite out of the target's life and delivers it as dialogue between characters.

Straight Announcement. A straight announcement uses an on-air personality to simply and concisely deliver the brand's message. This type of ad does not have a visual/verbal storyline. Copy focuses on the feature/benefit associated with the key consumer benefit and closes by asking the target to do something like visit a website or brick-and-mortar store.

Celebrity Delivery. If the brand uses a character representative or spokesperson, he or she should be the one to deliver the advertised message on air. Brands without a real or imaged spokesperson may want to use a recognizable celebrity voice. It is important the choice of celebrity matches the brand's image. An authoritative or expert spokesperson will attract attention and bring credibility to any brand.

Live Donut. Copy that needs to be routinely updated might benefit from using a "live donut." Here, an advertiser prerecords a musical opening and closing. Often the music will fade under or be reduced in volume, creating a musical bridge that ties the opening and closing together. The center or "donut hole" between the opening and closing is then filled in with scripted copy that is read live by an on-air personality. This keeps the message moving and does not allow room for the DJ to ad lib. The music is the constant that ties the ads together as copy is regularly changed out.

Single Voice. One recognizable voice is used repetitively on all spots.

Dialogue. Written discussions between two or more characters is a good way to push brand characteristics and uses. Characters will appear more credible if an announcer is added to make the sale.

Multivoice. In a multivoice approach, several characters deliver the message directly to the target rather than through scripted copy between the characters.

Sound Effects. Ads that have sounds, other than the spoken word, such as a chirping bird or crying baby, help bring visual images to the verbal message. Sounds bring reality to a spot. They can also help make a situation relatable, such as the feeling associated with a growling stomach and acid indigestion.

Vignette. A vignette is an ongoing storyline. Plots are linked together by characters, music, a jingle, a slogan or tagline, or a spokesperson, that is repeated in every ad. The first vignette introduces the target to the key consumer benefit; subsequent ads will either build upon the storyline or be used as reminder spots.

Interview. This approach allows the target to speak about the brand through testimonials. Typically, a brand spokesperson or DJ will solicit and/or deliver the interviews. Testimonials by current users bring credibility, and those delivered from an on-site location bring immediacy.

Humor. Be sure the commercial is funny to the target, or avoid it like the plague. Humor can do more harm than good if not done well or is offensive to listeners. When done well, the listener looks forward to the commercial rather than switching the station until it's over.

Sponsorships. If the brand sponsors the news or traffic report, its name will automatically pop into a listener's mind before paid advertising airs.

The creative team can use a single or a combination of these techniques to get their messages across on the radio. The most appropriate approach to use is the one that is most likely to reach or "talk to" the target.

Things to Remember When Designing for Radio

To grab a distracted listener, radio advertising must accomplish the following:

- The message must attract attention, quickly.
- Deliver the brand name and key consumer benefit within the first three seconds.
- Brands with names that are hard to pronounce should be repeated often to help the target remember it. To help accomplish this, consider using word association or a rhyming scheme.
- Copy needs to reflect how the target speaks. Grammatical accuracy is great in print but does not transfer well to radio. Keep conversations short to make features and benefits easier to remember.
- If there is a way to cement and control the visual copy in the target's mind, do it. For example, if the brand's packaging is unique in shape or use of color, inform the target.
- Repetition is great in radio. Repeat the brand name and key consumer benefit often. It will not get annoying as long as the repeated aspects are delivered diversely and engagingly.
- Make the message timely.
- Don't bore with facts. You do not want to drive the target to change the channel. Detailed messages do not work well in radio. Use it to build awareness, but if you need to build brand image or reposition a brand, there are media vehicles better suited for that task.
- Repetitive messaging binds all ads within a campaign together. Options that transfer well to radio include slogans or taglines, character representatives or spokespersons, headline themes, copy tone of voice, SFX, music and/or jingles.
- Be careful with sound effects. These stimulating attention-getters are great but they can be overdone, to the point where they stop moving the storyline along and begin to annoy. Think about the noises volume and where it will be heard. Too loud and realistic can distract and/or scare a driver. Finally, it is critical that all noises are relevant to the storyline and easily recognizable to the target.

Choosing Who Will Speak Your Copy

The individual(s) chosen to deliver the dialogue heard in the radio spot needs to represent the brand's image and target demographics. It is also important to be sure every word is spoken clearly so that the message can be understood.

Every radio spot should use conversational dialogue. No preaching, no doom and gloom. Keep the tone upbeat, laid back, fun, or friendly. Once the tone is set, be sure it is carried throughout the spot to avoid a choppy or disjointed feel.

To decide whether to use talent or an announcer to deliver the copy, look to the creative brief for direction and the proper tone of voice required. If using an announcer, be sure they can speak with authority about the brand's characteristics.

Letting an On-Air Personality Speak for the Brand

The majority of radio spots arrive at the radio station in a prerecorded digital format that is ready to be aired. But another, less expensive option exists, such as sending a script or fact sheet to an appropriate radio personality, that can be read live and/or be prerecorded.

The target will tune into a station based on the genre of music played and the local radio personality. These trusted individuals can give an additional boost of credibility to a brand. *Fact sheets* are nothing more than a comprehensive list of the brand's features and benefits the DJ will use to talk about the brand and perhaps their experience with the brand, in their own words, for 30–60 seconds.

Fact sheets give the on-air personality the chance to talk without a script about the brand. If the personality has had a chance to use the brand before the spot airs, he or she can add those personal experiences to the discussion. To ensure the key consumer benefit plays a prominent role in the discussion, the fact sheet will list the brand's features and benefits in the order of importance to the target. Often, the more familiarity the DJ has with the brand, the better chance it will get more than the purchased 30–60 seconds of airtime. On the flip side, personalities can go too far, and talk about the brand in a cynical or sarcastic way as a result of their attempt at humor. Although a great option, using an on-air personality should be employed only when that person is reliable. Scripts that are read live are not a good choice if more than one person will be speaking, or SFX are required to help make a point.

The safest, most controlled and professional option is to prerecord the commercial. If the script uses any SFX, music, or requires multiple speakers in any combination, a prerecorded spot will ensure that the structure and timing are precise.

What Was That? Sound Effects

Sound effects (SFX) are very simply the noises we hear in ads. Every discernible sound needs to grab attention and move the storyline forward. Sounds should not be used as senseless noise

makers; they need to have a point. A SFX job should help the target imagine what is being said.

A good copywriter uses verbal imagery to deliver a message, and uses sound to invoke a sense of excitement, a dose of reality, or to attract attention. No matter how well copy is written or how engaging the talent, it may still not be enough to hold the target's attention. SFX are an excellent way to enhance copy. There are all kinds of SFX the creative team can tap into to help deliver the message. How do you know how many is too many? Simple, if the sound doesn't help the copy deliver an imaginative point, leave it out. If there is any doubt the sound could be misinterpreted, tell listeners what they are hearing.

The Timing of a Radio Script

Radio advertising uses a copy sheet known as a *script*. For the copywriter, a script is their verbal canvas; informative words and visually constructed sentences use the target's ear to imaginatively paint a picture in the consumer's mind about the brand, its benefits, and uses. For the picture to be clearly imagined and understood, it must be the right length.

The most common radio spots are 30- or 60-second spots. The copywriter needs to know how many words can be spoken in the allotted time to ensure the copy does not sound rushed when being read, or drags to fill the time. Word count is not static, the number allowed will depend on the talent reading the script, their delivery speed, and whether the copy contains any difficult word pairings or technical terms. Multiple speakers will also use up more time. The following list shows the approximate word count for spots of varying lengths:

* 10 seconds: 20–25 words
* 15 seconds: 30–35 words
* 20 seconds: 40–45 words
* 30 seconds: 60–70 words
* 60 seconds: 150–180 words

The key to any script, no matter the word count, is to ensure the copy has a fluid conversational manner, and is detailed enough that the talent reading the script has enough copy cues to quickly understand what direction beyond copy, such as music or SFX, is coming up. In the next section, we will break down the steps to using a script and what type of cues make reading the script easier.

Setting Up the Formatting for the Script

Scripts are typed on 8.5 x 11 paper and are double-spaced. Scripts that are double-spaced add an additional dose of white space to the page, making it easier tor the copy to be read. The following formatting options are very detailed and are only one possible way to present a script. Set up the script using one-inch margins.

A script is broken into two columns. Place one inch of space between columns. Column 1 or the left side of the script is where all labels and any audio, such as SFX, MUSIC, ANNOUNCER, TALENT, and so on, are placed. Each should be set in all caps, to help make production instructions clearly stand out from the readable copy for the talent.

Column 2 or the right column should align with the corresponding label in Column 1. The right-hand column is where the dialogue, music, and SFX are placed. If the creative team wants any specific instructions, such as the need for the talent to clear their throat for example, or suggestions for where certain words or phrases need emphasis, it will appear here and be indicated in (ALL CAPS AND PLACED IN PARENTHESES). All dialogue will be placed in Column 2, and needs to be enclosed in quotes and typed using caps/lower case.

Any SFX used needs to be typed in all caps and placed in Column 2. A *dashed line* will appear directly underneath. This dashed line works as an additional visual cue to the talent reading the dialogue that a sound will be added. More importantly, it tells the production crew responsible for inserting the SFX where they appear within the dialogue.

Any music-related instructions will also placed in Column 2, and also appear in all caps. A *solid line* will appear directly underneath, and is another visual cue for production to know where to insert preselected music or a jingle.

If the creative team has decided to use a recurring character introduced in another medium, give them a name to create a small amount of intimacy between the brand and target. If no recurring character will be used, the label ANNOUNCER can designate the speaker.

We do not live in a quiet world, so be sure to use appropriate SFX or music to set a mood. Sound helps hold the listener's attention.

Finally, it is important that every spot close with the brand name, any slogan or tagline employed, and a clear call to action. Let the target know where the brand can be purchased, location(s), social media options, especially if a coupon can be found there. When writing copy for radio, be sure to mention the key consumer benefit, and brand name at least twice in a 30-second spot. Although this may seem repetitive, you need to be sure it is woven into the copy in diverse ways and not just repeated, a sure

way to both bore and annoy, Be sure to close the spot with the brand name, slogan or tagline, and a call to action. Here is an example of how a radio script should appear:

Advertiser:	Target:
Run Date:	Strategy:
Length:	Key Consumer Benefit:
SFX:	THE SWOOSH OF A DOOR OPENING. PEOPLE TALKING AND A SMALL DOG BARKS.
	SOUND EFFECTS ARE TYPED IN ALL CAPS AND SHOULD BE UNDERLINED WITH A DASHED LINE.
	- -
SALES PERSON:	"Welcome to PETHOUSE. I see you've brought a furry family member with you today. Can I help you find anything?"
	(Straight dialogue should be typed in caps/ lower-case and should include quotation marks. If you are not using a recurring character, label the speaker as ANNOUNCER or give them a title or label.)
DOG MOM:	"Yes. Mr. Barks (BARK) is allergic to everything known to man. We are always itching and scratching aren't we Mr. Barks (BARK). I need to find him some kind of food that will not aggravate his allergies further."
	(Any special instructions or suggestions for emphasis should be shown in (ALL CAPS AND PLACED IN PARENTHESES) If you are introducing a recurring character, then give him or her a name or title.)
MUSIC:	PITY MUSIC PLAYS IN THE BACKGROUND.
	(MUSIC IS TYPED IN ALL CAPS AND UNDERLINED WITH A SOLID LINE. Why the different line work? Remember, this is being read aloud. The lines easily show the reader or talent what is coming up or going to happen.)
SALES PERSON:	"This is an easy one. Allergies Gone will fix Mr. Barks (BARK), oh my (CHUCKLES), will fix him right up."
DOG MOM:	"Allergies Gone? Never heard of it. Is it safe?"
SALES PERSON:	" 10 out of 10 vets recommend it. Can't do much better than that."
DOG MOM:	" I'm sold. Where can I find it?"

SALES PERSON:	"Right this way."
SFX:	SERIES OF RAPID-FIRE BARKS. **(Do not be afraid to intersperse the spot with ear-catching sound effects. It will help to hold the listener's attention.)**
ANNOUNCER:	"No matter your pets needs, at PETHOUSE they will always get VIP treatment. Stop by and see us at 0000 Dog Patch Lane, behind McDonald's Mondays through Saturdays, 10 a.m. till 8 p.m. and Sundays 12 till 6, or visit us at www.pethouse.com. We'll have treats waiting." **(Be sure to close with the product name and, if applicable, the tagline, the location where the product can be found, including landmarks, and/or a phone number or website address if it is easy to remember.)**

Why Is Television Such a Big Deal?

What we wear, drive, use in our home, and aspire to own has its influential origins in television advertising. It is an excellent vehicle to influence style, introduce a fad or new trend, demonstrate, set a mood, or create a memory, thanks to its show-and-tell format. Television is the best mass-media vehicle to reach the target audience, build awareness, and develop or reinforce an image, despite its expensive, and cluttered advertising environment.

Through the use of sight, sound, and motion, television ads can inform, show use, entertain, and attract and retain the target's attention. Although a mass medium, it is a highly targetable vehicle, thanks to specialized programming options that allow the brand's story to be woven into the target's lifestyle, and address their interests and needs.

When used as a primary medium, television is a great option, if you want to launch a new brand, remind the target about a mainstream or mature brand, or reposition an old brand. However, it is too expensive for small brands to use, or any brands with nothing unique to say and show, or does not possess any type of inherent drama that sight, sound, and motion can exploit.

How We View Television Is Changing: Traditional Advertising versus Interactive Advertising

In its current form, television advertising is a very passive medium. For it to grow and survive, it must have more interactive properties. One of the best options for interactivity is known as *direct-response*, or *interactive*, television.

Direct response ties the target and their lifestyle to the message by asking them to do something. *Interactive television* offers the target the chance to click on a link, via keyboard or remote, or take a picture of a QR code seen on their television screen. These small steps can engage, inform, and give the target a chance to make an immediate purchase.

Interactive options require both action and meaningful contact, so each ad should show a toll-free number, website, or hashtag, constantly throughout the duration of the commercial. This lets the target know where they can go to quickly find additional information about any technical assistance, or help to place an order. Once the target sees the message, and decides to purchase, they can get a direct response from the advertised brand by clicking their mouse or making a few key strokes. Because the target makes a conscious decision to view the advertised spot, advertising clutter plays less of a role.

On the flip side, it can take weeks or even months for traditional advertising to build brand awareness and motivate a distracted target to react to an uninvited advertising message. Direct-response advertising happens in real time, allowing the target to purchase often before the ad even finishes airing. If the target does purchase immediately, or is one of the first hundred callers, there is always an attractive incentive offered. An attentive target can significantly shorten the time needed to build awareness, as the target does all the work seeking out additional information on their own.

It certainly doesn't hurt that most direct-response commercials have little to no competition, making remembering the brand easier for the target. Direct-response copy is relatively straightforward: Attract attention within the first three to five seconds, deliver the offer as clearly as possible, offer multiple ways to order, use expert presenters when possible, highlight testimonials or relevant studies to validate claims, demonstrate how to use the brand, show various sizes, colors, and so on, and of course repeat the key consumer benefit in multiple ways, as often as possible. This no-frills form of writing may appear straightforward, but unlike traditional televised advertising it takes a bit longer to say it all, using up to 90–120 seconds. This additional time allows the target to hear and/or see the brand in use or in a setting. Direct-response ads are basically a shorter version of the infomercial.

Infomercials: Long-Form Commercials

The majority of direct-response advertising can be found on cable stations that have more specialized programming and are less expensive than network rates. Infomercials are the most common form of direct-response advertising.

An *infomercial* is basically a long commercial, that last about 30–60 minutes. These long-form commercials will incorporate demonstrations, testimonials from users, one or more professional endorsements from nutritionists, doctors, engineers, or scientists, and of course, payment and ordering options. The goal of these extended commercials is no different than their shorter 15–30-second cousins,that is, to attract attention, inform, and entertain the target while encouraging purchase. Infomercials are popular and effective because they are informative and offer multiple ways to purchase, returns are easy, merchandise comes with a guarantee, and reviews can easily be seen online.

Sight, Sound, and Motion Brings the Brand Alive

Television engages the target through sight, sound, and motion. Sight and sound both set and reflect the tone, and motion allows the target to see how the brand works or see how it looks in a setting. Used in combination, sight, sound, and motion can successfully place the brand in the target's life. A very expensive media vehicle, it is crucial the target is actually watching. Thanks to specialized programming on both network and cable television, advertising can reach the target with a message they care about in a medium that research shows they are using.

When used in a campaign, as in any other ad, it is important to push and/or reinforce the key consumer benefit, project the strategy, and visually and verbally reflect the appropriate tone, no matter the vehicle used. Other copy and images used in other advertising vehicles will help determine the appropriate visual/verbal direction used in television. Additional considerations include color(s), spokespersons or character representatives, and headline style to blend multiple ads together.

By including an interactive component, television can draw the target to a web or social media site, or to customer-service representatives. These additional message resources can assist with building relationships between the brand and the target and lay the groundwork required to build brand image, loyalty, and eventually equity.

Tying television to a brand can create additional interaction. This media marriage is more about stealthily integrating a brand into television programming, known as *product placement*, rather than interrupting programming to blatantly sell the brand. When television and social media are used together, it's known as *social TV*. Social TV, unlike direct response, is not about a hard sell. The goal is to create a positive user experience, or enhance the value of the brand in the target's life.

Today's television viewers are using multiple devices to virally share insights and ideas not only about programming but also the advertising running while they are watching. This interaction offers valuable opportunities for the brand to engage, and extend the message's lifespan.

Messages Need to Cover All the Relevant Bases

Writing for television is difficult. Copywriters must balance copy to the video portion of the ad, and art directors need to keep the action moving and relevant. What is the best way to believably tell the brand's story in only 15–30 seconds? In that short time, what will make the key consumer benefit stand out strategically? Consider the following options:

*   Open with the key consumer benefit. Make sure it is screamed out so it cannot be missed.
*   Make the key consumer benefit relevant to the target and their lifestyle and/or show how it can solve a problem, in every frame.
*   Always talk to the target in words and about situations they can relate to.
*   Be sure the commercial uses the same or similar visual/verbal aspects, and tone of voice, as used in the other pieces within the campaign.
*   To capture attention with a more powerful message, you may have to do more showing than telling.
*   Both audio and video must work cohesively together.
*   To ensure the target remembers the brand's name, be sure to mention it often and show the packaging repeatedly.
*   The goal is to always involve the target in the commercial. Show the target how the brand works, how it will keep the lawn manicured, or cushion their feet. Be sure to deliver the benefits in a believable, relatable way. To hold interest longer, give the target a chance to do something, such as download a mobile app, call customer service, or visit the website, in order to gather more information or make a purchase.
*   Time out the commercial. Every piece of audio and video should not appear rushed. Make sure every second is spent talking about the brand and the benefits to the target.
*   To assist with recall, especially for a new or repositioned brand, be sure to close the ad with the logo, and any slogan or tagline. In lieu of showing the logo alone in the last frame, you can if relevant show the logo and the storefront, or just the packaging.

It is easy to get caught up in the excitement of creating a television commercial and forget the key consumer benefit needs to be pushed in every frame. It cannot be shown just once, or alluded to. Inattentive audiences, and television's short lifespan and fleeting message, demand the key consumer benefit to be front and center in every frame no matter the commercial's length.

Setting the Scene for the Television Shoot

Nothing about television is random; every sight seen, every sound heard, and motion made, is meticulously planned out. It is all about deciding: What setting will the brand be placed in? Who will best deliver the message? What kind of lighting will be needed to set the appropriate scene? What props or costumes will be used and seen? And what type of music will best set the mood? Finally, the pace or delivery of the visual/verbal message must match the overall look and tone of the message.

A television commercial requires the development of a storyboard and a script. There are two parts to a storyboard: The visual (video) and verbal (audio) aspects, known as frames, and the script, that shows all copy, sounds and camera angles. It takes a lot of people to produce a television commercial or spot. The scripts are much more detailed than a radio spot. The storyboard and accompanying script must educate not only the client, but also directors, talent, light and sound people, camera operators, producers, editors, food stylists, computer animators, and composers, to name just a few possible users of the script and storyboard.

Planning and Producing a Television Shoot

It is a complicated and lengthy process to design, plan, and shoot a television commercial. A shoot can take anywhere from a few days to several months to complete. Once the storyboard and script is completed, the creative team and then the director, will go over every aspect of the shoot, anticipating problems, and any changes that may arise. Next, they must hold auditions, check out possible locations, and gather together props and costumes. The production crew will advise on technical issues that need to be considered while shooting, such as, but certainly not limited to, lighting and sound, and camera positions, all before any actual footage is shot.

The team will also need to look at the budget and media placement to decide whether the commercial should be produced on film, on videotape, or digitally. Most decisions will be made during the preproduction, production, and postproduction phases. *Preproduction*, or the first step, covers development of the script and storyboard, and the hiring of talent, a director, and a production crew. The *production* stage covers the shoot, and *postproduction* covers the editing process.

Location Says a Lot about the Conceptual Direction

Where a commercial is filmed depends on the brand, the budget, and the concept. Television shoots do not need to have huge budgets. Those made locally, where the brand and/or the agency are located, can be shot and produced relatively inexpensively.

Local shoots are simple and straightforward and often let the client speak for the brand. These shoots tend to get the message out as fast and efficiently as possible.

Commercials that are shot nationally (or internationally)—that is, not necessarily in the brand's and/or agency's hometown, state, or even country— on the other hand, tend to pull out all the stops, using all the pomp necessary to creatively attract the target. With big budgets, these commercials are often produced and shot in major advertising markets and then delivered to the major affiliates or cable television stations. These "on location" shoots can take place in a local alley, or on some exotic beach. These types of shoots lend a hefty dose of reality to the message, allowing the target to actually see the brand in a setting and possibly in use.

It is not unusual for some types of national spots to stay in the studio and use high-end computer graphics. It is a very time-consuming process to create talent, and give it a voice, moves, and a personality.

The Visual and Verbal Layout of Scripts and Storyboards

Every television commercial's verbal story is told through a script; its visual story is seen through the frames of a storyboard. A television *script* is a relatively detailed piece of copy. Its job is to document and organize everything that will be heard, such as SFX, music, and dialogue, as well as any special instructions to the camera, sound and editing crew, the talent, and any information about any important scene changes. Unless you're shooting a Super Bowl ad, today's typical scripts are less detailed. To ensure all options are comprehensively covered, the following section will lay out the variety of available options.

Storyboards Show the Action

Storyboards house the video portion of the commercial, as well as show the crucial timing sequences by frame, between what is said and shown. See Figure 13.1 for a sample blank thumbnail storyboard, showing frames for video and boxes for audio.

The video portions of the commercial are known as *scenes*. Each scene is confined in a *frame*, or the shape of a rounded corner square, plus the rectangle audio box below it. Each scene will depict a significant piece of action or location change. Typically, a 15-second spot uses four to six frames, and a 30–60-second spot uses six to eight frames, to tell the brand's story.

The sounds heard and copy spoken will appear under each video frame, or the portion of the audio or script that corresponds to the video. The audio appearing on the storyboard is an exact copy of the script. The client, as well as everyone associated with the shoot, will be presented with the same version of the storyboard.

Student Name: _____   Name of Television Spot: _____
15 or 30 second spot (Circle One)   Grade: _____

Figure 13.1 Sample blank storyboard.

The storyboard lays out the actionable steps. Since it is impossible to show every scene on a storyboard, you must choose only those that clearly show the conceptual direction and that move the commercial forward. The audio portion of the script needs to showcase great, comprehensive writing skills, which in this case, for students, is more important than having great artistic skills to demonstrate the video aspects of the storyboard.

Television shoots consist of long, exhausting, stressful days and nights. Two or three seconds of footage, shot from multiple angles, and repetitive reshoots thanks to dialogue issues, can take several hours to shoot. Because of this, a detailed script is imperative to keep all the players on the same page, in the correct position, and in the right costumes, so there is no costly down time. If everyone is working from the same script with the same imagery, it is more likely the commercial will shoot on budget and schedule.

Delivery Methods Affect Length

Before choosing a delivery method for your commercial, look to the brief to help determine the best method or combination of methods needed to deliver the key consumer benefit. Consider one, or a combination of the following commercial delivery methods to express your commercial's tone of voice.

- Slice of Life
- Vignette
- Spokesperson

- Testimonials
- Expert Presenters
- Visual Images
- Demonstration
- Creative Comparisons
- Metaphors
- Torture Tests

Slice of Life. This delivery method takes a slice out of the target's life. The slice-of-life approach promotes the brand as a major problem solver. This simple, straightforward format introduces the brand to the target, and ties it to their lifestyle. It moves on to show how the brand can step up and easily solve one or more of the target's problems. It is a great option for an ongoing series of vignettes. The closing informs the target to keep the brand handy to quickly solve a similar problem easily, healthily, or quickly.

Vignette. Vignettes are an ongoing series of related short stories that highlight the key consumer benefit in unique ways. Ties might include one or more reappearing characters, or a specific location, to name just two, that help the brand solve a variety of problems, usually in very creative ways.

Spokesperson. The choice of a spokesperson or animated character representative is critical to expressing the brand's personality and image. The first step will be to decide if the walking, talking, visual representative will be real or imagined. Traits to consider might include age, gender, and an appearance and demeanor that closely matches the

136

target's. Beyond appearance, the creative team will need to determine what the visual representative will sound like. Will the chosen voice lack any distinction, be deep, high, or have an English accent or a New England twang? Each decision made will affect how the brand is perceived. The best visual representative should add in some way to the brand's inherent drama. You need not settle for a single visual representative. Nor does the visual representative need to be seen. An off-screen speaker with a distinctive voice is also an option

Testimonials. If someone has used the brand and they're happy, let them talk about it. Real users are credible and if you're lucky, very colorful and/or eloquent. Trained actors perform reliably and on cue; an untrained individual will need a greater amount of preparation. As a result, many commercials will use actors to speak the words of real users. A common practice, it does require a disclaimer that acknowledges a professional actor(s) is being used in lieu of the actual user.

Expert Presenters. The fastest way to project credibility is to have a scientist, doctor, or engineer back up advertised claims. A celebrity isn't necessarily credible, but they can be used to show status and quality.

Visual Images. Images show the brand alone, in use, or in a setting. They can highlight the brand's personality and tap into the target's imagination. Visuals are a great option for both image and brand building. Ask yourself whether a real or imagined image will define the brand and its use(s)? Will one image work alone or will multiple visuals need to be combined together to create new associations or uses? Image content must be able to deliver both the brand's visual and verbal message.

Demonstration. This show-and-tell delivery method works great on television. Presentation options include:

- Side-by-side comparison. If differences between the client's brand and the competition can be proven, consider comparing the difference(s) and/or unique features.
- Before-and-after comparisons. If you can show how the brand can solve a problem rather than just talking about it, do it. The typical visual/verbal message shows the brand being challenged by a problem it effortlessly solves.
- Product in use. The brand's features and benefits are pushed at the same time the brand is shown actively solving the problem.
- New and innovative uses. A great way for a reinvented brand that has a new unrelated use to showcase changes.

To be credible all demonstrations must be able to prove results. This is a good delivery option if there are any new government stamps of approval or scientific finds, for example. Showing results will always be less boring and more believable than talking about them.

Creative Comparisons. The easiest way to suggest quality is to compare the brand to quality such as a high-performance car or a famous piece of statuary.

Metaphors. Being able to compare a brand to something abstract, for example, alligators to dry skin, is memorable.

Torture Tests. If it has to be durable under extreme or even everyday conditions, then show the results. Showing how any brand performs under adverse conditions will always be a strong selling point.

The Long and Short of Commercial Messages

Budget plays a big role in the length of a television commercial, the most common spots today are 15–30 seconds. If the brand has a lot to say, the client has the option of buying a 30-second spot that can be broken down into two separate, but related 15-second spots. Each spot can deliver a single feature and/or benefit that can be aired in succession. If the two messages are mutually dependent, this split messaging is known as *piggybacking*. Complicated key consumer benefits that require a bit more show-and-tell will find the piggybacking option a great choice.

The Talk and Sounds of Television

Television commercials abound with sounds, some are spoken, created, or set to music. Let's take a quick look at each option:

Talent. Talent refers to those individuals who will deliver the copy or dialogue, and be seen on camera. Off-screen announcers, who are not seen but heard, also fall into this category. The one and only hard and fast rule is that all talent needs to both visually and verbally represent the target, and the brand's image.

Voice-over. When an individual delivers the message off-screen, it's known as a *voice-over*. A voice-over can be used to deliver the entire message or just the closing. The use of a recognizable celebrity voice is a popular choice. It is also less expensive to use a celebrity that is heard, but not seen.

Announcer. An announcer is an authoritative voice for the brand, that is both seen and heard delivering the copy on screen. A spokesperson or character representative make great announcers.

Music. Music is used to set a mood in movies, television shows, and commercials. It tells us what to expect and how to react to diverse scenarios. Music can help express emotions, replace words, or assist in placing the target into a specific emotional state. Mood can also be affected by volume. Music's role in the commercial is as important as the talent and dialogue to tell the story.

Sound Effects. SFX are used in the same way they are in radio, to replicate reality. To introduce the real world into your commercial, there must be noise. The world is full of noises and the sounds we hear should support what is seen and shown, not get in the way of the message.

Assembling the Script and Storyboard

A script is divided into three columns. Column 1 numbers the frames. Column 2 is for all labels, and Column 3 is where dialogue, music, all camera instructions, and SFX are placed. Each piece of information needs to align with the corresponding label. All labels are set in all caps and any special instructions need to be set caps/lower-case and enclosed in parentheses. Dialogue is also set in caps/lower-case and enclosed in quotes. Double space the entire script. Place a half-inch to one-inch of space between columns.

There is no set way to layout a television script and no commonly used set of instructions. The information presented here is just one possible solution. Let's dissect each element that is needed for a comprehensive script in the order in which it will appear on the script.

Opening Up That First Frame

Every storyboard needs to be opened. The initial or opening frame will describe what will be seen in the video portion of the window when the commercial begins. OPEN: (on visual of the Mona Lisa), the next instruction is the camera shot. OPEN is used only in Frame 1. All subsequent frames will use the appropriate frame transition, or the last instruction in the frame, that tells what will be seen in each additional frame.

What Is Seen: Camera Shots

The camera shot is the first instruction seen in each and every frame besides Frame 1, where an opening description of the scene appears. A camera shot's job is to tell the cameraperson how close or far away to be from an image or scene. In my book, *Integrated Marketing Communication From Idea to Implementation*, I break down the diverse variety of commercial instructions for possible use. Refer to the human figure depicted in Figure 13.2 to see what the camera is focusing on. The visual cues are static and would be the same if the camera was shooting a car, food, or a pair of sneakers.

A script can use one or more of the following camera shot options:

ECU (extreme close-up): Chin to top of the head would appear in the shot.
MCU (medium close-up): Throat to top of the head.
FCU (full close-up): Neck to top of the head.
WCU (wide close-up): Collarbone area to the top of the head.
CU (close-up): Chest area to the top of the head.
MCS (medium close shot): Waist to the top of the head.

MS (medium shot): Stomach to top of the head.
MFS (medium full shot): Knees to the top of the head.
FS (full shot): Bottom of the feet to the top of the head.

Camera shots appear in Column 2. They only tell the camera's position, not what the camera is actually shooting. Because of this, no instructions appear across from the camera shot label. On the script, use of abbreviations for the camera shots are acceptable. Since they are labels, be sure to set them in all caps.

Telling the Camera Where to Go: Camera Instructions

Camera instructions deal with camera movement. They can appear anywhere in a frame, depending on when and where the camera needs to move. For example, if every shot will be stationary, or a STILL shot, it need only be stated in Frame 1, immediately following the camera shot. If the camera instruction begins as a STILL, in Frame 1, but changes to a PAN, in Frame 2, the script must say that in Frame 2. If it is forgotten, or mislabeled, the camera will not be in place or be in the wrong place when it is time to shoot. If the camera returns to a STILL in Frame 3, it needs to be notated in Frame 3.

Possible options for camera shots include:

STILL: The camera will hold on the shot, no movement at all.
PAN: The camera will move horizontally left or right from a fixed point. Be sure to tell the camera which way the pan should go: PAN LEFT or PAN RIGHT.
TILT: The camera will move up or down from a fixed point. Again, be sure to tell the camera which direction to go: TILT UP or TILT DOWN.
ZOOM: The camera will move in for a rapid close-up or away to a distance shot: ZOOM IN or ZOOM OUT.
DOLLY: The entire camera will move forward or backward more slowly than a zoom shot: DOLLY BACK or DOLLY FORWARD.
BOOM: The camera will shoot from above, using either a boom or a crane. Used exclusively for overhead views.
TRUCK: The camera will shoot alongside a moving subject: TRUCK SHOT (along the left side and slightly to the back of the car).

The Sounds Heard: Audio Instructions

The placement of audio instructions will depend on when the target will hear the noise or music, and appear before or after a character speaks in a frame. The following is a list of possible audio instructions for use in a script:

SFX: Use SFX alone when a noise is brief:
SFX (One hand clap).
SFX IN: Signals the sound to begin and continue:

Camera Shot Frames

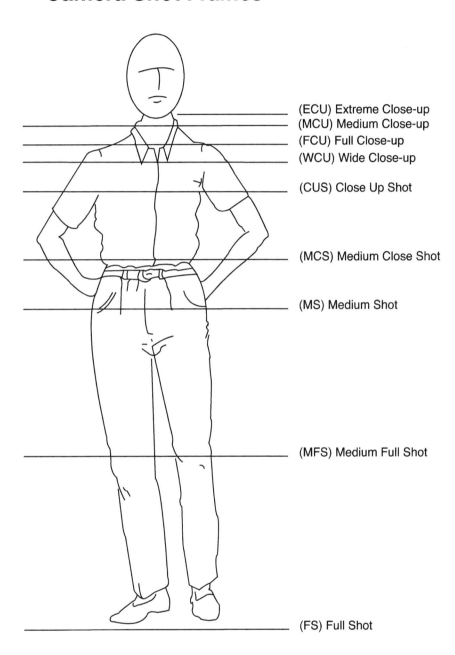

(ECU) Extreme Close-up
(MCU) Medium Close-up
(FCU) Full Close-up
(WCU) Wide Close-up

(CUS) Close Up Shot

(MCS) Medium Close Shot

(MS) Medium Shot

(MFS) Medium Full Shot

(FS) Full Shot

Figure 13.2 The figure shows all the examples of camera shots.

SFX (The crunching of paper) IN.
SFX OUT: Signals the end of the sound effect:
SFX (The crunching of paper) OUT.
SFX UP: Signals for the volume to increase:
SFX (Of clapping hands) UP.
SFX DOWN: Signals for the volume to decrease:
SFX (Of clapping hands) DOWN.
SFX UNDER: Signals for the volume to go under or to decrease
   in volume enough that dialogue can be spoken over it:
SFX IN (Of clapping hands) UNDER.

The instructions are similar for music:

MUSIC IN: Signals the music to begin and continue:
MUSIC ("Twinkle, Twinkle, Little Star") IN.
MUSIC OUT: Signals the end of the music:
MUSIC ("Twinkle, Twinkle, Little Star") OUT
MUSIC UP: Signals for the volume to increase:
MUSIC ("Twinkle, Twinkle, Little Star") UP.
MUSIC DOWN: Signals the volume to decrease:
MUSIC ("Twinkle, Twinkle, Little Star") DOWN.

MUSIC UNDER: Signals for the volume to go under or to decrease in volume enough that dialogue can be spoken over it:
MUSIC IN ("Twinkle, Twinkle, Little Star") UNDER.
SEGUE: Signals there is more than one piece of music being used. A segue is a seamless musical transition between one song to another often used to indicate a change in time, place, or mood:
SEGUE ("Twinkle, Twinkle, Little Star" to "Mary Had A Little Lamb").
MUSIC FADE: Signals that the music needs to fade out.
MUSIC ("Twinkle, Twinkle, Little Star") FADES.

The use of both music and SFX can easily continue through multiple frames or go in, out, or under, in each frame. Remember, SFX bring reality and music can set a mood. Use both judiciously. Too much noise or loud music can dilute the message and annoy.

Tell the Brand's Story: Dialogue

Dialogue as we know includes any spoken word heard on- or off-screen and can appear on the script before or after music, SFX, or camera instructions. Be sure all dialogue is enclosed in quotes and set in caps/lower-case.

VO: (Voice-over) A voice-over is used when the speaker will be heard but not seen.
ANN: (Announcer) An announcer is used when the speaker will be seen and heard.
RUSS: If you are introducing a recurring character whose name will be spoken in the commercial, label the part appropriately.
WOMAN or MAN: If multiple people will be speaking, label their parts separately. If they are not recurring characters and no names are a part of the spoken dialogue, there is no reason to give them a name.

Move the Commercial Along: Frame Transitions

Frame transitions indicate how the commercial will move from one frame into the next. They also describe what will be seen in the next video frame. They are the last instruction in every frame except the last one. The final frame ends the commercial.

Possible frame transitions include:

CUT: Indicates that the picture will change instantly or in the blink of an eye: CUT: (To CU of victim).
DISSOLVE: Indicates the transition will fade out of one picture and into another. An excellent way to show the passage of time. Dissolves do take up a lot of valuable time, so use them sparingly: DISSOLVE: (Show a shadow seen out a window moving from left to right.).

WIPE: Indicates the transition will physically push, or wipe one picture off the screen in order to reveal another. Great for showing a rapid transition from one activity or one location to another: WIPE: (CU of a dirty window to CU of a clean window).
SUPER: Use when one image will sit on top of another image, color, or pattern. The top image is then superimposed on top of the bottom image. Often, the top visual is reversed out, or prints white, over the background image. Supers typically appear in the final frame and are most often used when the logo is placed on top of a background image: SUPER: (Note logo placed on top of the lake).

Below is an example of how a storyboard and script should appear. A script is laid out in three columns. Column 1 is used to label the frames, Column 2 is for labeling instructions, and Column 3 is for dialogue, music, SFX, and any special instructions. Be sure each label lines up to the corresponding information. Labels must be set in all caps; instructions should be enclosed in parentheses. All dialogue should be typed in caps and lower-case, and enclosed in quotation marks. Be sure to double-space the script, place a half-inch to one inch of space between the columns, and use one-inch margins on all four sides.

Frame 1	OPEN:	(on a visual of the Mona Lisa)
	CS:	
	CAMERA:	STILL
	MUSIC IN & UNDER:	MUSIC IN (soft renaissance music plays in the background) UNDER
	VO:	"At Bennett Galleries we cater to master painters and sculptors young and old from around the world"
	FADE TO:	(a modern piece of sculpture)
Frame 2	ECU:	
	CAMERA:	DOLLY (to a close-up of artwork) FORWARD
	CAMERA:	STILL
	MUSIC:	SEGUE (from renaissance music to soft jazz)
	VO:	"We covet those with a modern twist and every artisan in between."
	MUSIC:	SEGUE (from jazz to new age)
	FADE TO:	(the outside of the building)

Frame 3   MS:

MUSIC: SEGUE (from new age to modern)

VO: "At Bennett Galleries, you'll find museum-quality pieces from every genre and era, in every color, shape, size, and material to fit your artistic style."

FADE TO: (pictures of public figures from all walks of life and eras)

Frame 4   CS:

CAMERA: DOLLY (to a close-up of varied public figures) FORWARD

CAMERA: STILL

VO: "For art lovers who are just as timeless."

FADE TO: (people walking around inside the gallery)

Frame 5   MFS:

SFX IN & UNDER: SFX IN (people talking softly in the background) UNDER

VO: "Stop in and look around. Bring in a picture and our curators will help you see how your style investment will look in its new personalized environment."

CUT TO: (SUPER of logo on a black background)

Frame 6   ECU:

VO: "Browse our inventory at bennettgalleries.com. We have your style."

SFX OUT: SFX (people talking softly in the background) OUT

MUSIC OUT: MUSIC (modern) OUT

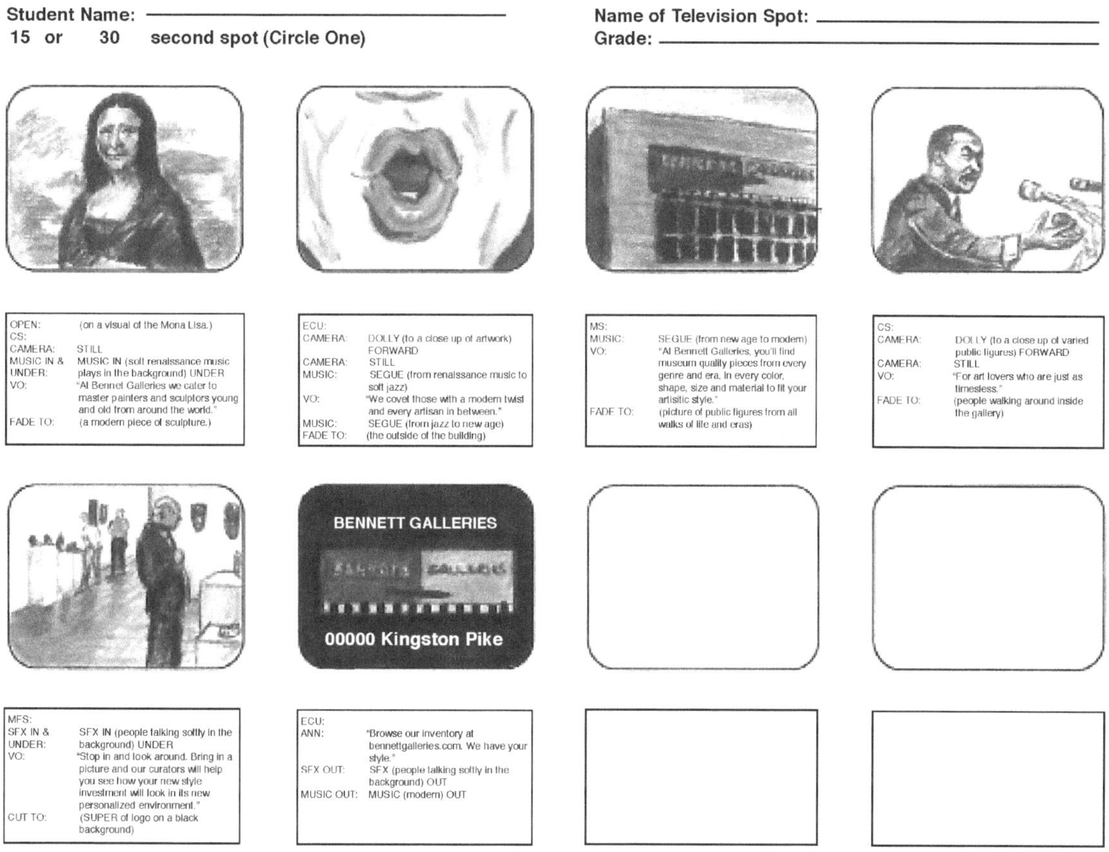

Figure 13.3 Storyboard example. Image courtesy of Reece Crawford, University of Tennessee

Placement of camera instructions, camera shots, or frame transitions must be consistent from frame to frame no matter the concept. When preparing a script for a television shoot, assume nothing. Television is expensive, and requires a larger number of people to complete, so avoid any generalities or short cuts. When in doubt about an instruction, add it to be safe. See Figure 13.3 for a completed storyboard.

Conclusion

Both radio and television have a great amount of influence on who we are as consumers. Radio is the ultimate imagination medium. It is great for building awareness and informing and directing the target to local businesses. Its highly personalized nature helps build a relationship with the target.

Television is a great choice when launching a new brand, maintaining or reinventing an existing brand, building or maintaining awareness, or developing both a brand and a consumer image. Although expensive to use, television advertising can be highly targeted, and with the right message, the use of sight, sound, and motion can attract and hold the target's attention long enough to make an impact.

Bibliography

Blakeman, Robyn. 2018. *Integrated Marketing Communication: Creative Strategy from Idea to Implementation*. 3rd ed. Lanham, MD: Rowman and Littlefield Publishing.

Making It Big and Taking It on the Road: Out-of-Home and Transit Advertising

Chapter 14 Objectives

1. The reader will be able to define the varied types of out-of-home vehicles.
2. The reader will understand how to design the visual/verbal message for these often large and diversely shaped vehicles.
3. The reader will understand the role visuals play when paired with a short verbal message.

Defining Out-of-Home Advertising

Out-of-home (OOH) and digital-out-of-home (DOOH) also known collectively as outdoor advertising refers to any advertising seen outside the home that advertises a product or service. Considered both a traditional and a mass medium, it can be seen in both static and digitally enhanced forms, and typically includes over thirty different types of outdoor and transit vehicles. Publicly placed, they can be found in both urban and suburban locations, in or on public transportation, and along interstate highways nationwide. Personalized or generic messages can be developed for any brand sold locally, regionally, or nationally, but the majority of all out-of-home focuses on local businesses and brands.

Impactful, OOH can reach hundreds of thousands of consumers as they move about their day without disrupting what they are doing. Many need to influence the target quickly, while others appear in places where the target is held captive for the duration of the traffic light, or the ride to and from work. No matter where they are seen or for how long, OOH is unique and can be found everywhere the consumer goes. What makes it unique from other advertising vehicles is that consumers cannot disengage with the message by skipping it, turning it off, throwing it in the trash, changing the channel, or hitting the mute or delete button. Out-of-home advertising is always on.

Once considered nothing more than a road sign, today's OOH has a creative and highly visual voice. These diverse vehicles use size, shape, and often digital enhancement to create memorable visual and verbal messages, which in most cases will be seen and experienced in the least cluttered advertising environments available. Its job is to remind and reach consumers closest to the point of purchase.

Out-of-home is the only traditional medium currently seeing increased revenue. Overall growth can be attributed to the bold in-your-face creative and diverse range of interactive options that 1) help drive consumers to a website or brick-and-mortar location, 2) encourage word of mouth and viral sharing via social media and 3) makes purchasing fast and easy via their smartphone. These interactive and engaging options help modern OOH vehicles attract and hold the attention of today's advertising-avoidant, distracted, and uninvolved audience.

Out-of-home, even before the addition of digital enhancements, has always been a brand's most versatile, largest, and mobile voice. It is one of the few media vehicles that rarely needs to compete for audience attention thanks in part to its big and bold presence that can be seen repeatedly in a fixed physical space. Most unusually, OOH is a loner. It is not content-driven, meaning there is no adjacent content near it to initially draw attention like television, radio, magazine, newspaper and the Internet have; OOH vehicles must do all the work on their own.

DOI: 10.4324/9781003255123-15

The Continued Growth of an Old Titan Is Technology and Creatively Based

Outdoor advertising is an ancient practice. Use can be traced back centuries to venders in Egypt, Greece, and Rome. These cutting-edge independent marketers either painted their advertising onto the sides of buildings or carved them into large rocks that were placed near roads and pathways boasting a heavy amount of pedestrian traffic. To combat any existing literacy issues, shopkeepers would often use visual-only signage that they hung outside their business or market stalls that depicted the types of goods and/or services sold within. Relics of this early visual-only advertising remains today. For example, the pharmacist's mortar and pestle, the blacksmith's, hammer, anvil, and tongs, and the Rod of Asclepius that pointed the way to medical practitioners. As a store locator and reminder device, their purpose has changed very little over the centuries.

What *has* changed is that many of today's vehicles are interactive. OOH is using its very visual canvases to highlight new technologies and new integrated mobile, social, and interactive options to better assist brands with how they interact with their targeted audiences.

This embrace of digital technology goes beyond simply replacing outdoor vehicles with screens. New-age digital options of all sizes are changing how the industry delivers a message. For example, messages can be altered with the flip of a switch by demographic, location, or time of day, and they can show live video and real-time Facebook and Twitter feeds. Smaller vehicles with interactive touchscreens can connect consumers with a brand in highly engaging and thus memorable ways. Newer options allow vehicles to interact with passersby through the use of artificial intelligence (AI), augmented reality (AR), and virtual reality (VR). Beyond simple search and purchase, mobile options might include the use of quick response (QR) codes, Bluetooth wireless applications and near-field communication, or technology that uses contactless communication between devices to share information, such as between smartphones and tablets that can extend a message's reach as passersby film it, photograph it, and share it on social media.

This very adaptive and ageless traditional medium continues to evolve. Whether the design wows with digital enhancements or just cutting-edge creative, modern-day outdoor advertising is a captivating, engaging, and sharable message delivery system that can both stop attention and help start a meaningful conversation with the target.

Big, Small, and Mobile Creative

Most out-of-home advertising is simply but boldly designed. The best designs show rather than tell, with a minimalistic approach. To stand out, the goal is to use bright colors to attract attention and a large, bold visual to assist with memorability. The main copy block is limited to no more than five to seven words plus the logo and slogan or tagline, and directions if applicable. The focus, whether visual or verbal, is on the key consumer benefit.

The very diverse assortment of vehicles is unique to the medium and can be broken down into four basic categories: Outdoor, moving transit, stations, terminals, or shelters, and street furniture. The following lists are certainly not exhaustive but will give you a good idea of the diverse sizes, shapes, and venues where OOH advertising can be seen.

Outdoor includes:

- Outdoor Boards
- Local Business Signage
- Wall Murals

Moving Transit includes:

- Buses (interior and exterior)
- Taxis (interior and exterior)
- Subway Cars
- Cars and Trucks
- Airborne
- In-Flight

Stations, Terminals and Shelters includes:

- Bus Shelters
- Airports
- Bus Stations
- Train Stations
- Posters
- Kiosks

Street Furniture includes:

- Benches
- Bicycle Racks
- Newsstands and News Racks

Let's take a look at some of the more commonly seen creative options.

Big Canvases with Bold Designs

Outdoor boards, or *billboards*, are officially known as bulletins within the industry. These dynamic and creatively diverse monoliths are no longer used for roadway advertising alone. Today's big, loud, and often technology-driven form of advertising is creatively designed, and placed into an assorted array of public places. Its big visual/verbal voice is attractive to brands that feel the public isn't paying attention to traditional advertising messages. Because of the availability of diversified locations, this mass-media vehicle can be a highly targetable advertising option. Where the boards are placed determines what specific neighborhoods, demographics, or ethnic groups can be reached.

These big vehicles must entertain and educate to capture attention, when not located near an intersection where traffic lights help divert and hold the driver's attention, or placed near pedestrian walkways. An outdoor board has only about six seconds to deliver its intended message. This is not the place for lengthy storylines. The best boards have no more than three components: A headline, a visual, and a logo. Since most drivers won't take their eyes off the road and pedestrians will not look up from their phones long enough to catch more than a few words, it is critical to make every word and visual count. This is the challenge to OOH: How do you get your target to look up and engage and/or interact with the message? First, novelty, and second, big in-your-face purposeful visuals will always be more captivating than small visuals confined to a small screen. Because of this, it is important to make a statement that not only intrigues visually, but also encourages some type of action such as searching for more information, sharing via word of mouth or virally, or encouraging an actual visit to a brick-and-mortar store.

Outdoor design is a balance between what is said and shown, while still ensuring the design is pleasing to the eye, attention grabbing, and most importantly, memorable.

The creative challenge associated with all of out-of-home advertising is due to its diversity of size, form, and location. They can be small, medium, large, vertical or horizontal, integrate the surrounding landscape or the monopole or column that holds up the board into the design, have 3D images, or have visuals that extend beyond the live area. The board itself can be altered by tilting it, scrunching it, by peeling away parts, or even leaving sections unfinished, to name just a few possibilities. Finally, for optimal exposure, you will often find multiple boards for a single brand strategically placed along heavily traveled routes.

Outdoor boards come in three different varieties: The standard or static printed bulletins and poster panels, the non-standard spectaculars, and the newer, more colorful, and often interactive digital LED boards.

It is important that each board boldly and creatively promote the brand's key consumer benefit. However, they should not be so visually provocative or overly shocking that they distract drivers. The goal is to creatively and simply inform. Your target no matter their age, occupation, or interests doesn't want to wade through complicated data or metaphors after a long day at work, or while carrying a car load of noisy and excited kids from one activity to another. Its job is to quickly capture attention, with eye-catching visuals, and a thought-provoking and/or informative message. Period.

The best, most memorable boards show a lot, and tell very little. How can you clearly show something without explaining it? Remember, outdoor boards are typically used as a secondary medium that makes them a great choice for raising awareness, brand building, and reminder messages. It is the wrong medium if you need to impart a lengthy or complicated message.

Outdoor Bulletins Are Impactful

A *bulletin* is an outdoor structure typically measuring 14 x 48 feet that is used to display an advertising message that has been either painted directly on the board (although these are rarely used anymore), printed on paper panels, or the more commonly seen vinyl material. These boards can be stationary or rotary meaning they can be moved to varied locations to extend the message's reach. Outdoor boards are one of the largest types of OOH advertising. Located along major interstates, roadways, and along city streets, they can make an impactful statement to both motorists and pedestrians. They're very visible, not only due to their size, but also because they can be customized with extensions, and digital and 3D enhancement, and by incorporating existing landscape features into the design.

Printed bulletins are the most commonly seen standard boards today. Made out of vinyl sheets, they are durable and flexible, and deliver a uniform surface that can feature bright colors and detailed imagery. See Figure 14.1 for an example of a bulletin.

The most elaborate boards are known as *spectaculars*. These large and very creative non-standard structures, often seen in major markets such as New York City or Los Angeles, are custom designed, making them very unique in scope and in execution. To gain maximum attention, they typically employ the use of eye-stopping special effects, such as neon tubing, backlit panels, fiber optics, video screens, message centers, hydraulic movement, three-dimensional sculpted imagery, incandescent lamps, strobes, social media and smartphone interactions, along with an

Figure 14.1 Example of a black-and-white outdoor board, using spot color in the glasses. Image courtesy of Kaylyn Maples, University of Tennessee

assortment of other types of visual graphics. Choice of creative options here is limited only by the local laws and the client's budget.

You Can't Talk Outdoor Boards without Understanding Size

Unlike the very diverse outdoor design options, sizing for these large boards is somewhat standardized. Typical standard sizes include:

* 14'H x 48'W
* 10'H x 40'W
* 10' 6"H x 36'W

Spectacular sizes include:

* 20'H x 60'W
* 16'H x 60'W

When laying out a board in InDesign, you obviously cannot work full size. To determine sizing use either a quarter-inch or half-inch scale. It is always best to contact your outdoor vender to find out what they prefer. Size is also affected by the use of any enhancements such as extensions.

Work within the Live and Bleed Area

Every outdoor board has a live area, in this case the actual size of the board and bleed of at least three inches on all four sides, if using an image or color that extends to the edge of the board. This equates to a quarter-inch bleed when working in InDesign. The industry does not appear to have a standardized bleed requirement so again, be sure to check with the vender for their specific requirements. See Figure 14.2 for an example layout.

Taking the Design Beyond the Board with Extensions

It is possible to extend your design beyond the size or face of the board with extensions. The ability to go up or out with an extension or a three dimensional ad-on offers not only depth but is an attention-getter. Boards can have moving parts, smells, or contextual digital enhancements that change with the time of day,

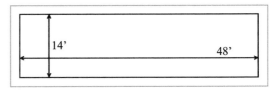

Figure 14.2 This example shows the live and bleed area for a 14 x 48 ft. outdoor board.

the temperature or traffic conditions; still others allow your target to interact with them.

Extensions, also known as top outs, cut outs, extenders, and embellishments, refer to a part of the design that extends beyond the live area of the existing structure. The typically uncommon shapes and additional height are a great way to make your design standout not only from other outdoor boards but also from the surrounding landscape.

Extensions can generally be placed on the top, sides, or bottom of a board. To ensure they can withstand the elements such as wind, rain, snow and ice, it is important the extension be a large, solid piece as opposed to, for example, the thin antennae of a butterfly.

Local restrictions will ultimately determine the overall height of an extension, but typically top placement can be anywhere from 5 feet to 5½ feet, with 2 feet allowable on the sides and 1 foot on the bottom. Finally, if your message feels too cut and dry and your budget doesn't allow for that powerful wow factor, consider incorporating the surrounding landscape into the design. You might consider designing within and around existing power lines, trees, adjacent buildings, or parking lots to make a creative point.

Designing for any out-of-home vehicle can be a challenge thanks to the diverse shapes and sizes, but it never should be dull. Let's take a look at a few of the design rules associated with outdoor boards.

So Much Square Footage, So Little Time to Use It

The board is a quick-read, keep-it-simple-stupid, media vehicle. Because it is most often seen from a car going over the posted speed limit, this is not the place for complex messages. Go with a single visual that both shows and tells your key consumer benefit. The most commonly seen images are photographs, although graphics and illustrations can be stunning and colorful visual alternatives. Outdoor boards are not the place to use graphically obtuse imagery. Show your visual boldly and your type as big as possible to ensure the message is clear and easy to understand.

Layout Options Run Horizontal and Vertical

Most boards have a landscape or horizontal layout but some designs, often due to location, can have a portrait or vertical layout. Format will affect the overall design and placement of components. Overall orientation will also affect the balance of design components. There are no hard and fast rules for working with portrait boards; however, depending on the surrounding landscape, placement of the logo is critical. Better to have trees or cars block part of the image than the type or logo. So know where your board will be seen when working with vertical boards in particular.

Visuals Scream Loudly on Bulletins

The images used on outdoor boards are typically photographs; most are in color but if the design calls for something more dramatic, such as showing abuse, black-and-white images can be a powerful way to show the message. If you need to call attention to one specific aspect of the photograph, always consider using spot color as an option. Images can be cropped, show the entire image, extend off the board, or appear as a three-dimensional image. How your image is shown will depend on the message you are trying to depict. So what size should your image be? To help you envision an image's scalability, use the following simple formula: One inch of imagery size equals one foot of billboard size.

The best designs use a single image; make it large to increase visibility and it will be more impactful than a series of small, disjointed images. Make sure your background is simple and does not interfere or clash with any visual or verbal components or the surrounding landscape.

When possible, use an image of a single person or object. If you must use multiple images, group them together into a silhouette layout style to give the image weight and create a strong focal point. To keep down the clutter, avoid using a photograph of a landscape or a whole building; instead consider using a single architectural detail or single landscape feature. These images are huge, so they need to be of high quality and have a high resolution to ensure they do not pixelate, or visually break up into small colored squares if the resolution is too low.

Determining whether the imagery or type should dominate the design will also depend on what you are trying to accomplish. As a visual society, in many cases a big, bold, visual can grab attention, can say as much as any copy can, and is often more memorable.

Resist the Urge to Repeat Yourself

Space is at a premium in OOH—use it to your advantage. If you use a headline to explain your visual, you're wasting valuable real estate. If your image is not eye-catching, imaginative, and thought-provoking, or doesn't relate to your brand, you waste your target's valuable time and your client's budget. Consumers dismiss so much advertising because it's not relevant or is dull. All great creative teams know it's all about concision, which is critical in OOH. So get to the visual point quickly in the largest and boldest way. Avoid repetition in the copy you do use. If your client is a fitness center and you want to promote the importance of regular exercise, don't talk about it, show an overweight man on the far right side of your board. We see he needs to lose a few pounds because the outdoor board is no longer horizontal it is diagonal. The copy reads: "Time for Silberman's Fitness Center." Now that is show minus the tell. You might have been tempted to show the same guy and say something like "Need to Loose a Few Pounds?" and kept a horizontal board. It's repetitive and not as memorable as showing the weight.

Use Strong Readable and Legible Typefaces

To ensure your message can be easily read from a distance of 50–400 feet, kerning and leading needs to be more open. If you kern and lead your headline in the same way you would for a printed piece, the letters and words would run together when seen at high speeds. Additionally, try to avoid using more than one line of text when possible, it's easier to read at a glance. If the design must use multiple lines, do not use more than two. Watch that ascenders and descenders have enough space that they do not touch. Be careful not to insert too much white space, which would make the headline look like two disjointed thoughts.

How Type Size and Style Affect Readability

The choice of typeface, size, and style can and does influence the readability of an outdoor board. Distance and viewing time require typefaces that are uniform in shape and style to ensure instant letter and word recognition.

Begin by choosing a big, clean, bold typeface that represents the brand's image and the message, without compromising readability and legibility. Be sure to use bright, high-contrast colors that pop and make a statement. Avoid using soft pastels and other similar soft hues. It is also a good idea to avoid using earth tones. These colors have a tendency to blend in with the surrounding landscape.

Make sure the typeface chosen matches the personality of your images. For example, a fun visual requires a fun typeface, while dramatic visuals need to be paired with a more dramatic typeface.

Avoid any typefaces with 1) thin lines, which will optically disappear the farther away from them you get, 2) severely contrasting letter strokes that will lose definition when viewed from a distance, 3) a bulky appearance, which will lose definition between letter forms from a distance, 4) a script, ornate, decorative, or light-weight appearance, as all are illegible at any distance, and 5) all caps or type that's reversed out of the background unless your headline is four words or less. See Figure 14.3 for some good and bad type options.

It doesn't matter whether you use a serif or sans serif typeface, there are enough diverse choices associated with both styles to find one that matches your message and the brand. Whatever the style chosen, it is best to go with a single typeface. Feel free to alter the size or weight to help create both contrast and eye flow by assigning a hierarchy to each verbal element seen in the design. When copy and the visual have to work together, be sure they are not competing for attention and that the type style matches the visual, the message, and the brand's image.

The Short but Creative Work of Copywriting

It might look like copywriters get off easy with OOH, even if the message is copy dominant. However, this is where the copywriter shines. With just a few very cleverly written words, they have to impart the key consumer benefit's message in a unique and quickly digestible way. Whether using humor, drama, or fantasy, outdoor messaging can and does influence consumer decisions. The challenge is to effectively communicate the key consumer benefit with a minimum amount of copy and a maximum amount of visual clarity.

If you're lucky, your board will have a passenger's attention for about six seconds, and the driver's attention for about half of that, so keep your headline to no more than five to seven words minus the logo and slogan or tagline if applicable. No board, no matter its size, when seen by motorists or pedestrians should

have more than ten words. The additional text will be directional, such as the exit number or where to turn. Avoid the urge to place a phone number or web address on the board. No one has the time or the inclination to write the information down. It is only a viable option if it *is* the headline. If you need to use more text, you should not consider outdoor boards as an advertising option.

Whether your target is driving or walking by, the copy needs to memorably amuse, entertain, or deliver a really big benefit. This of course is never easy. It will take a lot of brainstorming and editing to get the copy just right. It will be a little easier if you know what visuals will be used and where the board will actually be located. It is critical the copy relates to the visual but sometimes it can also be helpful if you know where the message will be seen. If you can tie the copy, the visual, and the location together, you have made a tie the target can both see and understand, improving memorability.

Finally, be sure your headline uses short words over longer ones for faster comprehension and, because your message will be viewed from distances of 50–400 feet or more, be sure the text is as big as possible. If the message can be read in three seconds or less, the driver or pedestrian will find it more memorable.

Color Choices

Your choice of color combinations will affect the readability and legibility of your design when seen from a distance and at a high speed. Make sure your color choices have high hue, value, and color contrasts. Remember hue is the identity or recognition of a color, while value refers to a color's lightness and darkness. The higher the contrast the easier the message can be read.

Low-contrast colors should be avoided. For example, complementary colors such as red and green are illegible when used together because they have similar values that can appear to vibrate. Any similar color combinations, whether they appear to vibrate or not, will always have low visibility. High-contrast colors such as yellow and black and high-visibility colors such as blue and yellow are easily viewable at any speed. Below, find a few more high-contrast options listed in the order of strength:

BAD FONT	GOOD FONT
Thick and Thin	Uniform Stroke
Bad Serif	Good Serif
Script	No Script
Too Tight	**Just Right**
Too Fat	**Bold not Fat**
Too Thin	**Thin Just Right**
UNREADABLE	Readable
UNREADABLE	Readable

Figure 14.3 This example shows both good and bad typefaces for outdoor boards.

Black on Yellow	Black on White	Yellow on White
White on Black	Navy on White	White on Navy
Navy on Yellow	Yellow on Navy	Red on White
White on Red	Red on Yellow	Yellow on Red
Yellow on Violet	White on Green	

The use of contrasting colors within the design will not only help focus attention but also help improve retention of your message. When used, backgrounds must also contrast with the colors used in the visual/verbal message and the type. Backgrounds that are too dark or busy can negatively affect both readability and legibility. So it is important to keep the background simple to ensure the foreground isn't fighting for attention. To ensure maximum visibility and impact of a color, place it on a background of a complementary color or those colors from the opposite sides of the color wheel.

A quick way to check contrast is to print out the design and then make a black-and-white photocopy. If both the visual and verbal contrasts are strong, readability and legibility will be strong; if not, rework.

Make Good Use of White Space and Eye Flow

Because most outdoor boards are horizontal, it is not unusual to have to design around spacing issues. To avoid white holes, and ensure the design has good eye flow and balance, you may need to move copy and images around, increasing or reducing elements or adjusting placement until everything fits the space just right. One of the first things to consider is don't crowd your message. Be sure the message has an equal amount of white space around the visual if not a bleed, as well as above and below all verbal components.

Good visual/verbal designs are absorbed in a single glance. There is not a lot of eye flow in outdoor design. The design of a typical board either flows from left to right or from top to bottom, rarely both as in print. Logo placement can pretty much appear anywhere; however, placement in the left corner should be avoided when possible. Ideally, type should not be pushed to the top or bottom of the ad leaving large gaps of white space or white holes. Ads that are well balanced between the visual, the type, and the logo will effectively avoid these badly designed and disruptive blank spaces. To ensure balance, this may take a bit of manipulation; as a fast and loose rule if you've got a vertical visual, set your verbal message up to run horizontal and vise versa.

Don't Forget the Logo

Don't forget to seamlessly merge the logo with the message; you can't sell anything if the visual wows and the target can't see who is selling it. Clients always want the logo to be bigger. There's a reason for this: It's how the they make money. As in all design, be sure to shoot for a large and prominently placed logo that is easy to see and read. Watch your balance of components. If the logo is too small, it will be missed. If it's too big, it distracts from the message. Either way, the result is advertising that fails to deliver a useable and memorable message.

Test Your Design at Arm's Length

You've got a great design. It's clever and it showcases your key consumer benefit. It's simple, and it's colorful and it gets to the

point. But is it both readable and legible? Try the following test to ensure everything works. Print out your board the size of a business card approximately 2"H x 3.5"W. Hold it at arm's length. Can you easily read and understand it in less than six seconds? If not, keep tweaking. Let's take a quick look at a few more of the giant OOH options.

Smaller, Temporary Poster Panels

Poster panels, also known as papers or paper bulletins are smaller in size than outdoor bulletins, and are traditionally created in pasted sections or sheets. These traditionally static boards can typically be found along heavily traveled secondary roads and within community neighborhoods. Their job is to reach local pedestrians and commuters where they live, work, and play.

Traditional construction is similar to hanging wallpaper. Each poster is printed on multiple sheets of treated paper and glued onto the board. The number of sheets used will depend on the size of the board. An effective and inexpensive option, these techniques are giving way to more environmentally sound and faster alternatives. Although many are still composed of treated paper, newer single-sheet posters are replacing traditional paperboards. Printed on vinyl or 100 percent recyclable polyethylene paper, they no longer need to be pasted to the board, making them not only more environmentally friendly but also better able to withstand diverse climate conditions for a longer period of time. Vinyl boards will last up to a year while polyethylene and paperboards will last about 30 days. This short lifespan makes them great for time-sensitive material. They are most commonly used to advertise special sales or promotional events. Posters come in two basic sizes: Junior and standard.

Junior posters, also known as 8-sheet posters, are often used to provide exposure in places where larger standard posters or outdoor bulletins cannot be placed. Sizes range but the most commonly seen size is 6'H x 12'W. They are a particularly good choice if you need to target a hard-to-reach local audience.

Standard posters, often referred to as 30-sheet posters, also vary in size but most commonly measure 12'3"H x 24'6"W. When working in InDesign, bleed for both sizes will be three-quarter inches on all four sides. You can tell posters from bulletins not only because of size but because they are surrounded by a distinct heavy metal frame.

Posters can be either freestanding or attached to the sides of local buildings. Most freestanding boards use a landscape orientation, while those attached to a building can be designed either horizontal or vertical. No matter the direction, board placement is usually just above eye level.

Visual/verbal messages will include at least a logo, a dominant visual and a short message and perhaps a slogan or tagline. Design will follow the rules discussed above for outdoor bulletins. Although posters can have digital enhancements, most are fairly simple and used as a low-cost advertising option. Posters work well as business signage that advertise the location of a business or to promote a product near the point of purchase. All signage can help build brand awareness and/or remind consumers about a brand, or business.

Computer-Controlled Digital Highway Boards

Digital highways signs, also known as digital, LED, or electronic signage, uses computer-based technology to regularly change what's displayed on a screen and are a great choice for campaigns with multiple concepts.

Referring to digitally or electronically enhanced billboards as highway signs is a bit misleading and narrow. Not only does this category include giant boards, but also OOH mediums with smaller digital screens such as posters, bus shelters, and benches, and shopping center signage, to name just a few. Whatever the size, these brightly lit boards display static messages that rotate every six to eight seconds, effectively holding the commuter's attention. Several different messages can be delivered by a single board for one or more brands.

Very artistic, these very bright and large canvases can often be seen on interstate highways from quite a distance. However, to see the board's full rotation most boards are placed near traffic lights that feature a four-way intersection, where drivers are stopped long enough to see a board's full rotation.

Each board can display as many as eight advertisements for different brands on a single board. Brands who use these types of boards in a campaign have the option to use several boards that show the same or different messages in varied locations throughout a city, ensuring that vehicles along the route will see an integrated stream of messages, or choose to take over the entire board.

These highly colorful boards are creative and attractive; they don't fade or take on a tattered appearance after prolonged exposure to the elements. They are efficient—a computer can quickly and easily change signs in minutes. However, there is a downside. These bright, ever-changing messages can cause a driving hazard as drivers focus their attention on the board's continually moving messages. Because of the diverse number of creative options digital boards offer, outdoor can target a larger and more varied demographic than ever before.

How Do Digital Boards Work?
Each board has a small computer attached to it that delivers the advertised message to the screen. The creative team can update the message on these boards remotely, by using a wireless phone network to access the board's computer. Once the art director completes the design on the computer, it can then be uploaded to any number of boards quickly and easily. Because they don't need to go through a printing process, this type of board not only saves time for the creative team, but also offers a huge amount of design flexibility.

There are a few disadvantages to their use. Each board is lit by hundreds of LED bulbs. Unfortunately, LEDs can only be one color at a time, which makes displaying crisp, fine lines and deep shading difficult. Finally, because they typically show several advertisers per board, exclusivity and memorability are an issue.

Design for All Big Boards Is the Same
Design rules follow those for outdoor bulletins: Keep your message short, push a strong visual, use bright colors and easy-to-read type. An additional tip exclusive to digital boards is to avoid using a solid white background; it does not have the same vibrancy as it does on vinyl. Because white is a mixture of color versus an absence of color, it has a tendency to look grey or even muddy.

Tri-Vision Bulletins

Colorful, these digitally controlled and manipulated boards are composed of long, tightly positioned, triangular prisms or strips that turn or flip every seven to eight seconds. Each side of the prism can showcase three different messages from one or more brands. Brands that purchase a single side will see their advertised message revealed on every third turn of the prism. When all three sides are locked in by a single brand, the board can be used to create a message that builds known as *storyboarding*, or display a three-part message. This is a great option if you have more information to deliver than one outdoor board can handle. This very unique type of outdoor board is a big attention-getter.

Placement is typically near stoplights or in locations with heavy traffic to ensure consumers see each message. Design for these colorful boards is identical to outdoor bulletins with one major exception: There are no options for extensions, three-dimensional enhancements, or incorporating the landscape into the design. Tri-Vision bulletins are an excellent option if you're looking for increased visibility in a particular market.

Wallscapes Cover Buildings

Wallscapes are custom designed to fit a variety of unique shapes and sizes. These creative boards are either painted on the surface of a building as a mural, or are printed on vinyl and then attached to a building. Typically placed in high-traffic areas where they can be seen by both pedestrians and motorists, they can provide a powerful visual/verbal message that towers above the streets in prominent downtown business and shopping areas, creating an eye-catching landmark. See Figure 14.4.

No matter the visual content, they are impactful first and foremost due to their often-colossal size. They can be found on high-rise apartment buildings, parking garages, office buildings, hotels, or even attached to scaffolding, to name just a few locales. Many will use more than one building when they appear close together and are the same architectural size, width, and height. Others will use the parking lots below to extend the design. Eye-catching as static designs, they can be further enhanced by adding special effects, such as neon tubing, fiber optics, hydraulic movement,

video screens, three-dimensional extensions, incandescent lamps, and strobes. They are another great option in areas where traditional outdoor boards are limited.

This type of OOH is primarily used to give a company a dominating presence with maximum exposure. They can be used to promote an event, in new product launches, for building brand awareness, or as a reminder vehicle. Because of their custom design, they are often planned for long-term use.

When deciding whether to use a wallscape, it is important to know where it will be viewed. A good design fits in well with the surrounding landscape to ensure it wows rather than annoys. Use the building(s) as a base or canvas to create a unique experience

Figure 14.4 Example of a wallscape advertising the Olympic swim trials. Image courtesy of Robyn Blakeman, University of Tennessee.

Table 14.1 Options for how to determine size for large outdoor vehicles.

Distance in Feet	Examples	Minimal Text Height
5'-50'	Malls, Airports, Retail Lobbies, Offices	1"-2"
50'-100'	Window and Street Display, Drive Through	2"-4"
100'-200'	Posters, Surface Streets	4"-8"
200'-300'	Posters, Surface Streets and Highway Bulletins	8"-10"
300'-350'	Highway Bulletins and Posters	10"-15"
350'-500'	Highway Spectaculars	15"-20"
500'-600'	Highway Spectaculars, Stadiums	20"-24"
600'+	Skyscrapers, Spectaculars, anything set back from the road	24"-40"

Table 14.2 Readable distances for storefront signage.

Letter Height	Best Viewability	Maximum Readable Distance
3"	30'	100'
4"	40'	150'
6"	60'	200'
8"	80'	350'
9"	90'	400'
10"	100'	450'
12"	120'	525'
15"	150'	630'
18"	180'	750'
24"	240'	1000'
30"	300'	1250'
36"	360'	1500'
42"	420'	1750'
48"	480'	2000'
54"	540'	2250'
60"	600'	2500'

for passersby. Designs feature towering visuals often with little more than the logo accompanying them. Some will forgo using the logo and feature the brand's label and perhaps a slogan or tagline. When type does appear it is brief, often no more than three words. Since size is determined by where the wallscape will appear, there are no set sizes for this OOH option.

Table 14.1, taken from a 2017 online article by Clear Channel Outdoor, is a great guide for determining size for large outdoor vehicles.

Local Business Storefront Signage

All the advertising in the world is useless if your target can't find you. The most important signage for any brick-and-mortar business is its exterior signage or name. Every sign, whether elevated (seen by motorists), or seen on a storefront (by pedestrians), should be readable at a glance. Exterior signage can also help your client's business stand out and away from surrounding storefronts, and give their business long-standing exposure.

As with all OOH, keep the message as simple and to the point as possible. Signs come in every shape, size, and material, so make sure your choice of size is readable at the distance you expect your sign to be viewed. See Table 14.2.

Storefront signage is often the target's first impression about a brand. Because of this, it is important that it be functional and informative. So what defines good storefront signage? Let's take a look at a few basics.

Functionality

The first thing to remember when designing signage is scale. Be sure the sign is readable and legible at a distance What looks good on your computer screen can look like a series of disjointed dots and bars that say and show nothing at a distance. Secondly, all signage must relate back to the brand. This can be accomplished with color, materials, imagery, and typefaces. Thirdly, be sure it reflects the personality of the brand, the store, and the experience the target will have when shopping and interacting with sales personnel. Signage is more than a name—it should reflect the attitude and essence of the brand. Exterior signage is the first step to building a memorable first impression.

One way to negatively affect image is to use materials that are not durable. It is important they be able to withstand the local weather conditions so the signage does not easily break or tear. Nothing damages image more than rag-tag neglect. It can also get very expensive for your client to continually have to repair or replace signage that is inappropriate for local conditions. Let's take a look at a few of the most commonly seen types of exterior signage.

Fabric Signs. These can be elegant and very durable. Materials typically include vinyl, plastic, or nylon. It is important that all materials are heavy duty and fade resistant. These types of signs are popular options because of their versatile design options and their ability to be backlit to be more easily seen at night.

Wooden Signs. These types of signs are affordable, simple, and elegant. To avoid being adversely affected by weather conditions shortening their lifespan, they will need to be routinely treated or re-varnished. This type of sign is a great choice if you want your storefront to have a timeless, rustic, or old-fashioned feel. Businesses most likely to use this type of sign include restaurants, boutiques, or upscale retailers.

Glass Signage. Low cost, these signs use the store's window as their display vehicle. These signs are best viewed by pedestrians, so the visual/verbal design can be more ornate. Glass signage is not recommended in places where traffic will be moving at higher speeds.

Punched Metal or Laser-Cut Signage. Very affordable and weather resistant, these clean designs can go modern or retro.

Storefront Metal Signage. These three-dimensional signs are attached directly above the store entrance one letter at a time. They are elegant and depending on the amount of natural lighting can add additional shadowing beneath the lettering, creating added depth and texture, enhancing the design.

Awning Signage. Attractive and clean, these fabric store markers appear above the entrance. The store's name can be placed on the front of the awning or on all three sides increasing visibility. Not only do they lower heating and cooling costs, they are durable and long-lasting. Great for retailers who want a distinctive and welcoming storefront.

Rock or Concrete Signage. Very durable and long-lasting, this option requires a lot of real estate. This type of signage is heavy and permanent, and can either have the business's name carved into the material or have metal lettering attached to it. Either way it's very elegant and expensive looking.

Glass Tubing or Neon Signage. Expensive, bright and colorful, they are easy to see. However, because they are made of glass, they can easily fall prey to adverse weather conditions. Best for businesses that are open late.

Simple Messaging

The best and most recognizable exterior business signs will just reproduce the brand's logo design with perhaps the addition of the slogan or tagline. This is a good idea only if the logo uses a simple visual and/or typeface. If the visual has a lot of small details, it will be difficult to read at high speeds. Consider leaving it off the sign and moving it inside to signage, menus, napkins, cups, receipts, and so on.

Know Your Target Audience

Knowing who the client's target audience is will help determine design choices. For example, if it will be displayed in a multicultural location, it's a good idea to include both English and the appropriate translation, or use visual-only signage. If your target is millennials, they prefer a more colorful graphic look, whereas baby boomers prefer a more simple and streamlined look.

Designing Exterior Signage

When first determining what a sign should look like, make sure you are aware of all the local zoning ordinances that will govern the type of signage that can be used. For example, there may be laws governing size, height, how it can be lighted, and the colors used. It is also a good idea to check out where your sign will be seen. How many other signs are near by? What about the landscape? Is it flat, hilly, or filled with trees? Visibility issues must be designed around to ensure your sign's design stands out in the visually cluttered crowd. Finally, you will need to know whether you need to design an elevated sign, a storefront sign, or both.

Once you know the basics, you need to determine what additional design elements need to appear on the sign. This signage will be viewable 24/7 as a branding tool, so beyond the logo and/ or slogan or tagline, you will want to include any colors or representative typefaces used in other mediums to create an identifiable and harmonious appearance. When possible, if your client's logo is too detailed, their typeface too ornate, or you are restricted by zoning requirements, try to substitute with typefaces and colors that tie as closely as possible with the brand's image.

Signage is a lesson in practical design; its goal is simple: 1) To help consumers locate the store, and 2) get consumers not familiar with the brand to notice you. When designing, remember to make all signage large enough that it can be read from across the street, the parking lot, or the highway. Avoid the readability and legibility traps like using all caps, reverses, and decorative faces, especially if the brand name is long or hard to pronounce. Be sure to use a clean readable typeface with open kerning and leading and colors that are bright, colorful and have a strong amount of contrast. Avoid filling up the space by crowding the edges of the board. Good readable design manages the balance between positive and negative space. Remember, positive space includes content, or the letters and images. Negative space is the blank areas around and between those components. The negative space helps define and give meaning to the positive. Avoid the two biggest design faux pas by paying close attention to the management of the negative space between letters (kerning) and lines of copy (leading). Be sure not to cram so much information onto the sign that it obliterates white space to the point it is not readable or legible from any distance. The amount of white space (white space can be color) surrounding components is as important as other design considerations. As a rule of thumb, 30–40 percent of a sign's usable surface should be left as white space for optimal readability.

Say It Fast: The Message Is Moving

Transit advertising, another form of out-of-home, reaches the millions of people who use public transportation or see public vehicles while moving about on foot, by car, or bicycles, or from their office windows. The diverse array of shapes, sizes, and canvases offers an enormous amount of creative options and challenges. Public transit includes taxis, buses, and trains. Additional options include terminals, stations and platforms, bus shelters, benches, vehicles, and three-dimensional kiosks. Quite simply, any blank surface on any type of moving vehicle, or a space where the vehicle arrives and departs, is a perfect canvas tens of thousands will pass by daily. Transit, like outdoor, is short on advertising space, and thus requires a short, visually dominant message—making it another great support vehicle.

Designing for a Moving Canvas

Design for a moving canvas follows the same rules as outdoor boards. Keep the design simple but bold. It should clearly push the key consumer benefit, be brightly colored, always creative, use a single bold visual. If applicable to the brand, another option is to use the brand's spokesperson or character representative, feature a short headline, if relevant the package design, and/or a slogan or tagline. Because of the unusual variety of shapes and sizes, transit messages need to get to the point in no more than three to five words in most cases. Copy must be set in a bold typeface that is easy to read from distances of up to 500 feet. To increase readability, kerning between letters should be slightly expanded and all caps or decorative typefaces should be avoided to ensure legibility. Images still speak for the brand in transit. Whether to use color or high-contrast black-and-white photographs, spot color, illustrations, animation, or graphic images will depend on your concept and other ads seen in the campaign. Finally, be sure your color choices do not overpower the type or overwhelm the visual. Pop is good, but it should not negatively affect readability and legibility.

CRAP Is Important

A great way to ensure you are using all your design knowledge effectively for any type of medium is to apply the Joshua Tree Principle, developed by Robin Williams in the book *The Non-Designers Design Book*. The principle makes a great quick tip or design check list, especially for OOH and transit design when the goal is to have a clean, readable, often repetitive message that will be seen in diverse mediums and locales.

Straightforward, it is composed of four parts: Contrast, Repetition, Alignment, and Proximity. It can be more easily remembered by its accidental acronym CRAP. If you follow the principle you can easily avoid any design faux pas such as trying to say and show too much, a common mistake seen in OOH. Each principle helps to unite the design's visual and verbal components. Let's take a quick look at each one.

Contrast. Strong contrast is created through visual and verbal differences; avoid similarities when designing. If components such as type, color, size, line thickness, and visual imagery are similar in appearance, then the goal is to make them very different to create more contrasts.

Repetition. Keeping contrast in mind, be sure to repeat visual elements throughout the design. This can include, color, shape, texture, line thickness, type sizes, and line lengths. Repetition of elements helps organize, unify, and harmonize the canvas you are working on.

Alignment. The alignment of every component must be thoroughly thought out. Nothing should be placed arbitrarily on the page, screen, or canvas. Every component needs to be visually connected together. This creates a unified message that is easily read and understood.

Proximity. This principle deals with grouping related objects close together. When several components are in close proximity to each other, they appear to become a single cohesive visual rather than several disjointed thoughts. This helps to organize the message and reduces clutter. Do not feel you have to fill up the space. When components appear to be randomly placed, the design appears unorganized and readability and legibility are negatively affected. Embrace empty space by getting your CRAP in order.

So what types of vehicles will you be designing for? Let's take a look at some of the more creative canvases.

Exterior and Interior Bus Advertising

Bus advertising, because of its large size, can be thought of as a moving billboard. Design should be loud, and entertaining to commuters. Buses are effective advertising vehicles thanks to their large amounts of exterior and interior ad space. Exterior ads reach everyone the bus passes, whether the viewer is walking, driving, or sitting in their office. Interior ads, on the other hand, can catch and hold the attention of consumers who are riding the bus for an extended period of time. Let's take a more in-depth look at each option.

Exterior Ad Design

Exterior bus displays come in five distinct categories: King- and queen-size posters, full bus wraps, "King Kongs," and tail signs. The type of display chosen is based in part on a bus's route.

King-size posters, used by both local and national brands, display the advertised message on both the curb and street sides of the bus. Like all transit advertising, sizes vary by city but the most commonly seen sizes are 30"H x 144"W with a live area of 27"H x 141"W. Queen-size posters appear on the curbside only and usually measure around 30"H x 88"W with a live area of 27"H x85"W. Both king- and queen-size bus posters are either placed inside a frame that is firmly attached to the side of the bus, or printed on self-adhesive, pressure-sensitive vinyl, which is attached directly to the sides of the bus. Backlit kings are also available in certain markets.

Full-size bus wraps sport very creative ads that are attention getting. They are very large designs that colorfully carry a storyline over and around the bus, making use of every available surface, including the doors, windows, and wheels. Made from durable vinyl, these often awe-inspiring designs are both weather and fade resistant and can last up to a year. To ensure viewability from the bus, wraps need to use two types of vinyl: One for the bus's body and the other for the windows. The vinyl used on the windows allows passengers to see out while not compromising the design. The colorful, self-adhesive

vinyl literally molds or wraps itself around the entire bus or part of the vehicle. Seen at eye level, the primary goal of these giant designs is to attract attention with size and originality. One of the most reproduced bus-wrap examples is from the Copenhagen Zoo: The "Snake Bus" shows a very large snake wrapped entirely around a bus that it optically appears to be crushing.

Memorable and relatively inexpensive, wraps are a great option for generating brand awareness and promoting local and national brands and charitable and cultural events. These all-inclusive designs are not exclusive to bus advertising, they can also be used on semitrailer trucks and cars.

King Kongs, also known as ultra or super-kings, measure 108"H x 240"W. Seen on the driver's side of the bus, they partially wrap an ad around the bus's mid-section.

Tail signs are located on the rear of the bus. These smaller, yet no less creative, options have a limited amount of space to work with: 21"H x 72"W. These ads get a lot of exposure to motorists who are trapped behind the bus in traffic. These very popular, creative, in-your-face canvases have become a very special way to highlight a brand or cause. One very creative but simple design from Argentina dog-food brand Tiernitos Dog, shows how much dogs love their food. This very pink ad uses both the back and side of the bus. The back of the ad has the logo and a dog walker who is smashed up against the bus thanks to the four leashed dogs running alongside the bus toward the front where the logo and a bag of the food is shown. This ad does an excellent job showing how good the food is without saying a word. Tail signs also come with an option to wrap over the bus's back window in some cities. For a tail sign, see Figure 14.5, and see Figure 14.6 for placement options.

Figure 14.5 Example of a bus tail sign. Image courtesy of Madison Duncan, University of Tennessee.

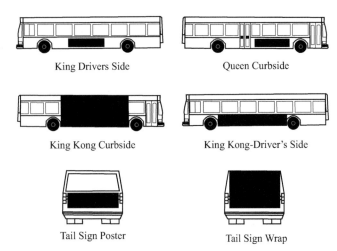

King Drivers Side   Queen Curbside

King Kong Curbside   King Kong-Driver's Side

Tail Sign Poster   Tail Sign Wrap

Figure 14.6 Shows the different bus advertising placement options.

Interior Ad Design

Bus advertising found inside the bus is known as *interior cards* and can take many forms. Top interior bus ads are located in horizontal frames above the window, they can be either backlit or non-backlit, or fitted with car cards. Desirable, front interiors also known as *bulkheads* measuring 33"H x 21"W resemble posters and are placed behind the driver. Ads can also be placed on the ceiling known as Michelangelo's and on the seats.

Repetition is the reason to choose interior cards as a media option. Riders use public transportation to get to and from work. Riders are stuck inside for the duration of their journey, allowing messages to be read repeatedly. Because space inside is finite, advertising clutter is kept to a minimum, increasing memorability.

Diverse in size and shape, interior advertising is just as limited in what it can say and show as the exterior designs with one exception: Brands can buy out the entire interior inventory if needed, creating a *branded bus,* to deliver a more detailed and focused message. Typically printed on heavy, laminated card stock, many interior cards are printed on both sides, so the message can be routinely changed out. Because these cards will be read from a distance of about six feet, make sure type size is around 50–100 point.

Interior advertising can also be a great direct-response vehicle when removable order cards know as *car cards* are added to the message. These car-cards can be saved and at a later time used to request additional information, place an order, or apply a pre-determined discount toward a purchase. Sizes vary by city.

Hold On: Interior Hand Hold Bus or Subway Advertising

Creative ideas can also be extended to those structures that riders without a seat hold onto. These engaging and creative messages can turn a simple horizontal bar into barbells or a vertical handhold into a Barber Pole. No pole to hold onto? How about hanging a watch on a strap you can slip your hand through to see how it looks on your wrist? Design options are limited only by the creative team's imagination and of course the client's budget.

The Target Has to Sit Somewhere: Bus Shelters and Benches

Transit shelters, also known as *street furniture*, are the places where riders wait for the bus making them great for point-of-purchase, event, and promotional advertising. They offer a very creative and often interactive canvas at eye level. Typically placed in high-traffic areas, they attract riders, those passing by on foot, and drivers.

Bus shelters come in many shapes and sizes, but most are partially enclosed, three-sided structures that feature two short sides and a longer back. Designs can use all three sides, the ceiling, or even extend above the enclosed shelter and use the roof. Posters measure 4'W x 6'H, and consist of two identical ads placed back-to-back that are lit by a light box placed in between. These ads can duplicate the same ads used on other transit vehicles to reinforce the message or continue an ongoing theme, begun elsewhere in the campaign. Like most out-of-home advertising, they use a visual, a logo, and perhaps a slogan or tagline to introduce the public to, or remind them about, a local product or service and can be designed in black-and-white or color. Static ads can incorporate multiple panels or use a single stand-alone poster. Digital ads can scroll, allowing a single brand more real estate to tell their story. Brands can even change the shape or design of the shelter to creatively make their point. For example, in Minneapolis, Caribou coffee greeted riders with an interior shelter that looked like the inside of an oven complete with a working heating coil, to push their new hot breakfast sandwiches. The outside of the shelter resembled a stovetop complete with three-dimensional dials. The visual along the back wall showed hot sandwiches baking on a rack. A static poster on the left side filled waiting riders in on the brand with a short message.

Interactive ads can be very helpful and creative. Vitaminwater outfitted bus shelters with USB ports so those waiting for the bus or just walking by could charge their phones. Yahoo pitted neighborhoods in major cities against one another with interactive touchscreens that allowed people to play social games against each other. The winning neighborhood got to host a concert with OK Go.

Shelters also have one or more benches that can be used as an advertising canvas. Always creative, Ikea turned several bus stops into small rooms, complete with a couch for sitting, pillows, a throw rug, and curtains.

Bench advertising need not be confined only to bus shelters. Usable bench surfaces can be found in local parks, restaurants, malls, subways, bus and airport waiting areas, and college campuses, to name just a few. Popular and effective, they are usually found in locations with a large amount of pedestrian traffic. These stand-alone canvases allow unobstructed visibility in any type of weather. Shapes and sizes vary but the most common size is 2'H x 6'W. When designing you can use the whole bench, or deconstruct it and use only a small portion. These highly targetable, low-cost vehicles offer eye-catching imagery that is repetitively seen 24/7.

Although most OOH and transit vehicles say very little, word counts vary wildly for this OOH option, but it is always best to keep the design verbally clean when possible. If it needs a little push to stand out, consider altering the shape of the bench. For example, if you are advertising a deli, instead of showing a simple visual of a sub sandwich, which would be the most common choice, consider turning the bench into the sub sandwich. Add a logo and an address on top and you have a memorable message. Slim Fast used a less-is-more concept when they placed a "Skinny" bench about eight to nine inches wide inside a park. The only message is a small plaque that states it was donated by Slim Fast, but the message is clear: If you can't sit here, you might need to use their product. To ensure the design lasts, bench advertising uses a silk-screened weather-resistant material that is either adhered to the back of the bench or, if required, the entire bench.

Although cool to change up both shelters and seating, it is important to point out that brands that choose to use city property are often responsible for not only upkeep and sometimes even the construction of the vehicles, but of restoring the vehicles to their original states after the campaign is over.

Taxi Advertising Moves the Message Around

Advertising on vehicles—whether taxis, cars, or trucks—can be both creative and informative, no matter the level of detail or size. The most diverse form of vehicle advertising are those messages seen on taxis. Taxi advertising can be bold, static, or technology-driven, no matter where it appears on the vehicle. Exterior advertising can appear on roofs, trunks, windows, as traditional wraps, or support three-dimensional visual enhancements. Interior advertising appears on the back of the front seat and can be either printed or digital.

Advertising appearing on the roof of a vehicle are often illuminated, two-sided panels. These constantly moving canvases have a broad reach and when fitted with a GPS system, can change out depending on where the taxi stops to highlight shopping or restaurants in the area. Other digital options can be displayed on three- and four-sided roof tents that show video and even holograms. Taxi tops generally measure 14"H x 48"W.

Taxi advertising is a great way for local advertisers to promote their message close to their place of business. There are no set rules for vehicle type size. To ensure your ads can be read from a distance of 6–12 feet, use the arm's length business-card test introduced earlier in the chapter: If you can read it you are good to go; if not, increase the size. Taxi-top design can boast copy-only designs, or employ a simple visual and verbal message. No matter which format is used, focus should be placed on the logo and image if applicable and where the brand can be found, so be sure to feature a web address, and/or a phone number or brick-and-mortar address. Static poster designs measuring 17"H x 36"W are also available for the doors and trunk.

Taxis are the only vehicle that supports interior advertising. Some taxis today have video screens that are placed on the back of the front seat. Advertising on these digital screens is still a work in progress. Taxi TV ads can deliver 15-, 30-, or 60-second commercials. The often cluttered, poorly designed video typically runs both local and national brand advertising and promotional information for local events, such as concerts, movies, or current theater productions. Static seatback advertising measures 12"H x 14"W and may or may not be backlit depending on the market.

Moving Truck Billboards

Another form of movable outdoor advertising appears on the backs and sides of semitrailer trucks. These mobile outdoor boards are hired to travel local highways and streets during rush hour, when the target is setting or slowly moving in traffic. They can be either static or digitally enhanced. Static design displays are made out of adhesive-backed masking films or non-adhesive stretch vinyl banners that are attached to specially fitted frames on both sides and/or rear of the truck.

Digitally activated outdoor boards can also move along with commuters in traffic. Designs can be either stationary or digitally scroll or rotate several messages in the same way digital outdoor boards do. These moving displays change every eight seconds, offering up to nine different visual/verbal options. Mobile outdoor boards are great for product launches, event promotion,s and raising brand awareness. They are an excellent way to deliver a targeted message based on the prescribed route or as a promotional tool for mass-marketed brands. Approximate size of a mobile poster is 10'H x 22'W for 30-foot-long trucks.

Subway, Airline, and Train Terminal Posters

Terminal posters are large, typically local ads located in bus, train, or subway stations, or airline terminals. For greater impact many of these posters will be illuminated or backlit. Messages tend to focus attention on brands that visitors can enjoy while visiting a city, or that locals can find near the station or stop. Often the station or terminal posters can be coordinated to match the advertising found inside the vehicles. Sizing will vary by city and location, but the most commonly seen sizes include large posters 36"H x 24"W, medium posters 18"H x 24"W, small posters 11"H x 17"W;

for additional information, be sure to contact the OOH vender for specs.

Airport advertising comes in a variety of formats. Interior advertising can be freestanding, or adhered to terminal walls, windows, columns, ceilings, moving walkways, trams, turnstiles, and floors. Beyond posters, station and terminal advertising might include wall murals, dioramas, floor graphics, and elevator and escalator wraps, to name just a few. It can be placed in diverse locations throughout the terminal including arrival and departure gates, ticketing areas, baggage claims, concourses, retail shops, and VIP lounges. The most common size is 67"H x 46'W. Advertising can also be placed within the airplane on tray tables, overhead bins, within in-flight videos, and on napkins and cups. See Figure 14.7 for an placement on an airport walkway.

Glass floor displays are also common advertising vehicles; these three- or four-sided freestanding units are known as *kiosks* and

Figure 14.7 Example of advertising placed on an airport moving walkway. Image courtesy of Madison Duncan, University of Tennessee.

are used when displaying the physical product is a better way to attract attention than a photographic image.

Rail and subway advertising includes both static and backlit posters appearing on platforms and walkways, entrance displays, station clocks and on special in-car signage. Advertising seen at the station includes one-sheet 46"H x30"W, two-sheet 46"H x 60"W, and three-sheet 84"H x 42"W framed posters that can be found on both subway and train platforms. Advertising seen at subway entrances are known as *urban panels*. Additional options include dioramas and mini-spectaculars that are printed on giant transparencies and backlit to stand out and increase readability and legibility. To increase memorability, advertisers can often buy all or a combination of advertised locations within a station, often referred to as *station domination*.

Many of these ads use advanced technology to grab attention. Today's responsive posters can use artificial intelligence (AI) and facial recognition technology to better tailor a message to consumers passing by, based on gender, age, and even expressions. Privacy is a valid concern with these new posters; however, the few that have been used in the United States do not store or share any collected data.

Other transit options include airborne displays or banners trailed behind small aircraft, blimps, the sails of marine vessels, pedicabs, horse-drawn carriages, bicycles, and racks, to name just a few.

Finally, as in magazine and newspaper advertising, OOH and transit offer cooperative opportunities between local companies and national brands. For example, Bose may advertise noise-cancelling headphones at a discount on tickets, or in the terminal to anyone traveling on American Airlines.

Whether using interactive options, or a traditional in-your-face creative idea, OOH and transit offers an almost unlimited array of creative options. The diverse pallet of flexible formats offers a virtual blank canvas for brands to showcase uniquely disruptive, engaging, and often interactive experiences.

Bibliography

Clear Channel Outdoor. 2017. "Get Creative." Retrieved from: http://clearchanneloutdoor.com/get-creative/.

Williams, Robin. 1994. *The Non-Designer's Design Book*. Berkeley, CA: Peachpit Press.

Direct Marketing: The Old Guard

Chapter 15 Objectives

1. The reader will understand what direct marketing is.
2. The reader will learn how to turn the visual/verbal elements into interactive elements.
3. The reader will understand the role promotion plays in direct marketing.

Direct Marketing and Sales Promotion Incentives

One of the elder statesmen of advertising, direct marketing has been around for a long time. It survives and prospers today because it still offers a service everyone wants—to be more than just a nameless, faceless consumer. It has also become a very creative way to deliver an often interactive message. Although direct marketing is heavily used in digital and broadcast advertising efforts, this chapter will focus specifically on print options.

Direct marketing, also known as *direct response*, along with sales promotion, uses digital (text, e-mail, Internet, social), print media (newspapers, magazines, catalogs, direct mail), and radio and television to reach an individualized member of the target audience with a personalized message. The target's known interests, past purchasing behavior, and demographic, psychographic, behavioristic, and geographic profile, drive content. The goal is to encourage some type of action, such as making an immediate purchase in order to receive an additional incentive. This more customizable approach is the polar opposite of traditional mass media advertising's (newspaper, magazines, radio and television) tactics that attempt to educate a mass audience about a brand's features and benefits. Instead of using a hit-or-miss approach, direct marketing uses purchasing and inquiry information stored in databases to personalize its message on an individual basis, allowing them to address the target by name.

One thing direct marketing and advertising do have in common is the use of promotional offers. *Sales promotion*, also known as *purchase incentives*, entices purchase by offering packaged deals, or exclusive offers; it can also be used to build awareness, encourage trial, and/or reward brand-loyal users.

Direct marketing can offer deeper incentives than traditional advertising efforts because it knocks out the middleman or the wholesaler or retailer, making it easier to sell at a lower price point, and reach the consumer at a time when there are less distractions, making them more receptive to opening and reading the message. Brands who choose to sell directly to their target audience have a greater amount of control over how their brand is promoted. Whether they reach the target through digital or broadcast channels, direct mail, or catalogs, they're able to not only tell a story that defines their image, purpose, and use(s), but can clearly define their place in the target's lifestyle.

Direct Marketing Talks to the Target by Name

When you know exactly who the target audience is and want to talk to them one on one, direct marketing is the way to go. The more the creative team knows about the target, the better they can create a more individually tailored visual/verbal message. This intimate advertising environment makes it easier and more creative when interacting with and talking to the target about situations they can relate to and about a topic or situation they are interested in. The result is a brand's dream, a solid foundation for the development of an interpersonal relationship between the brand and the target. This relationship is needed to build and maintain brand loyalty.

DOI: 10.4324/9781003255123-16

Beyond personalized interaction, interest is also spiked by the overall visual and verbal design. These pieces are often very creative and unique to the brand and are great at grabbing attention. For example, to help a direct-mail piece stand out in a crowded mailbox, you might send pieces that are colorful, visual, oversized, have unusual shapes, pop-up, or even include 3D objects or samples. Consider the difference between receiving a flat postcard talking about the friendly, hands-on service you are guaranteed to receive from your nearby drug store, and one that opens with a pop-up that features the pharmacist and perhaps a discount, game, or contest-related scratch-off card. The former is skimmable; the later is both interactive, engaging, and sharable.

As an added incentive to purchase and ensure a quick response, direct marketing often uses diverse types of sales promotion devices, such as coupons, contests and sweepstakes, samples, and giveaways, to name just a few. Additional perks might include highlighting some of the lowest prices to be found anywhere, the chance to be the first to own, or receive some type of limited-time offer. Other promotions might include the offer of a free gift with purchase or substantial rebates for buying, in response to a direct-mail promotion or catalog offer.

Most forms of direct marketing are not considered intrusive because the target decides what message to respond to, when to respond, and where and how to make further inquiries or make a purchase. Direct marketing is a great vehicle to 1) reach the target in a shorter amount of time, and more effectively, than traditional advertising, 2) introduce a new or reinvented product, 3) remind or encourage retrial, or 4) update the consumer on product changes or additions.

The Ups and Downs of Sales Promotion Use

Promotional offers are typically paired with direct marketing, to give the target some type of gift or incentive to entice an inquiry, such as requesting a catalog, brochure, price list, a sales promotion package, or to stimulate trial, or encourage purchase or repurchase. The goal of sales promotion is to rapidly increase sales or interest through low pricing or other motivation-driven device that is exclusive and available for only a limited amount of time.

What makes sales promotion unique is its intent. For example, while direct marketing brings a brand and message directly to the target, sales promotion sidesteps the message altogether and brings the target to the brand.

Sales promotion techniques are a silent promotional device. The goal, like advertising, is to move the brand now, so the use of many devices are the brand's final chance either before or immediately after purchase, to educate, interact with, and remind the target about a brand.

Although a popular tactic, the use of promotional devices does have a downside. It's easy for brands to get caught in the rollercoaster cycle of promotion, making it difficult to get even loyal users to purchase at a time when there is no current promotion available. Other negative results include the devaluation of the brand to the target over time, overall cost, and an end-of-promotion fall-off in sales. Excessive or unnecessary use of sales promotions can lead to the erosion of brand loyalty, brand image, and eventually brand equity.

To ensure promotions are not overused, the type of promotion used should be based on the brand and where it is in its life-cycle stage. For example, a new product launch, depending on the brand category, will often employ the use of coupons, sampling, bonus packs, or contests and sweepstakes, to promote a trial purchase. A brand in its maintenance stage has a preestablished loyal following on repeat purchases and requires little promotional assistance. A mature brand may make use of multiple types of sales promotion as a way to reawaken interest in an aging brand.

Consumers will no longer accept a one-size-fits-all message as incentive to buy; they want informative, personalized service, from brands that can be adapted to meet their needs and they want something extra for their loyalty. Let's take a look at some of the creative options used by direct marketing and sales promotion.

The Loudest Voice Used in Direct Marketing

After being exposed to all the digital sales vehicles available in your daily life, taking a look at old-school advertising options like sending a physical advertising piece through snail mail may seem like a history lesson on the Dark Ages; however, this is not necessarily the case. Tangible material is memorable, interactive, unusual, and relatively rare, unlike the multitudes of fleeting digital messaging that flood our e-mailbox and phones daily. According to a US survey, as reported in an online 2017 *Forbes* article entitled "Why Direct Mail Marketing is Far From Dead" by Steven Pulcinella, "individuals who were exposed to physical ads experienced heightened excitement as well as a greater subjective valuation and desirability for the items advertised … a significant percentage of millennials like mail. It has an emotional response factor. Gallup reported that 36% of people under the age of 30 look forward to checking their mailboxes every day. What's more, 95% of 18-to-29-year-olds have a positive response to receiving personal cards and letters." This is perhaps a good time to remind ourselves that old school never dies, it's just reinvented.

Direct marketing uses a diverse number and type of contact vehicles, including mass media, the mail, the Internet, social media, and mobile, as well as personal contact. In this chapter, we will concentrate on the most well-known and best-received print option: Direct mail.

Direct Mail: The Granddaddy of All Direct-Response Offers

Direct mail is a highly targetable, and personalized, form of direct response. Consumers respond to and interact with most direct-mail pieces because they specifically address their interests and lifestyles.

Direct mail fulfills many advertising roles. As an informational tool, it can announce, build and shape brand image, reward loyal users, or serve as an enticement device to non-users to try a new or existing brand.

Very interactive, a mailer with multiple and diverse pieces can attract and hold the target's attention, making the interaction more memorable. Do not make the interaction quick and easy. Make sure every piece they open (and hopefully read), offers valuable non-repetitive information about the brand. If a piece with movable parts, or perhaps has something that can be scratched off, are a part of the mailer, it holds attention, creates additional interest, and builds curiosity.

As a media option, direct mail is an informative and creative device. It can be used for any type of brand as a straight advertising vehicle, a sales promotional device, or a combination of both.

A Direct-Mail Kit Is Full of Sales and Promotional Material

Direct mail can be defined as any advertising material sent by mail to a targeted consumer to encourage a sale or further inquiry.

The visual/verbal voice of direct mail reflects a variety of diverse faces, shapes, and sizes. A typical direct-mail kit is not small, and can contain a variety of handwritten notes and postcards. The overall design might showcase, die-cuts, embossing, varied types of folds and perforations, and pocketed folders. Additional content may include brochures, price lists, CDs, calendars, key chains, or menus. More spectacularly creative direct-mail pieces might include three-dimensional designs that incorporate pop-ups or pop-outs, or boast multiple moving parts, sound, or other useable promotional devices, such as water bottles, or pens, to name just a few.

Direct mail, better known as "junk mail," is easily dismissed or tossed because it does not create interest or curiosity or provide any new insights. It's considered junk for two reasons: 1) It arrives unrequested into the target's home, and 2) the whole of the design is junk. You can't change how the pieces arrive, but you can change the interactive quality of the design to ensure it gets opened. A traditional direct-mail kit can arrive with a variety of components, but a typical mailer will include an outside envelope, a personalized letter, an informational brochure, an order form or business-reply card to simplify ordering, and sometimes, a return envelope for mail orders. More elaborate kits might include a take-away, or small promotional item.

A direct-mail kit is a design whole, or a small contained campaign. One piece should not stand out alone; every piece in the kit must work together to create one visual/verbal message. The kit should reflect the key consumer benefit and strategy as defined in the creative brief and use the same tone of voice and reflect the same overall appearance as the other advertising and promotional pieces. The multiple pieces that typically make up a direct-mail kit must be tied together by a key consumer benefit-driven headline style, type style, color, layout, and perhaps the use of a spokesperson or animated character. Let's take a quick look at each of the diverse pieces that make up a direct-mail kit.

The Outside Envelope Is the First Visual and Verbal Step

The design of the envelope is important. Its look, feel, and visual/verbal voice are what will initially entice the target to open the kit or packaged content. Make it creative and colorful, and be sure it boldly states your key consumer benefit in a unique way. You can additionally attract attention by using an oddly shaped envelope or one with a die-cut.

A *die-cut* is very simply the process of cutting a surface (paper) into an interesting customized shape. They are most often used for presentation folders, business cards, packaging, and brochures. The options and shapes are almost limitless. They can be simple offsetting slits to hold a business card, or more elaborate cut-outs revealing images on subsequent pages, or used to change a simple rectangle into a pre-determined image. Although expensive, they are a great way to capture attention or add simple interactive properties to a standard business card or brochure.

The copy seen on the outer envelope of the direct-mail kit is known as *teaser* copy. Its job is to hold the target's attention long enough to build interest and entice them to open and interact with the multiple pieces. If the envelope is initially seen as an interesting piece of design ingenuity, the target's attention will be held. Design direction for the envelop should mimic those used in print. It should have a large, key consumer benefit-driven headline that relates to any color(s), photographs, or graphic images used to "wow" and attract attention. To get the piece opened, the target's curiosity must be tapped into.

Must-Have Promotional Devices

To entice purchase, the direct-mail piece should offer an incentive. The best promotions always offer consumers an additional benefit, such as discount pricing, first-to-own opportunities, upgrades, two-for-one offers, limited-time offers, or coupons, to name just a few.

If working with a smaller budget, create a colorful and expressive key consumer benefit-driven message that is accompanied by some type of interactive promotional device, such as a scratch-off card. If your budget is a bit more fluid, include some type of stimulating mental device that supports the overall message inside. Designs that include a pop-up or other type of three-dimensional image that lifts up and out when the piece is opened is engaging. This is a great way to bring a little personality to a character representative or spokesperson, or give additional credibility to a testimonial from a satisfied loyal consumer. The copy's visual can support the pop-up if written in the visual representatives, or customer's voice. To create even more interactivity consider adding movable pieces that reveal one part of the message at a time, allowing the target to spin a wheel, or open a window or door for perhaps a promotional offer. For exclusive brands, you may want to include some kind of image the target can hold up to a webcam to see an augmented reality (AR) image, or use a QR code the target can take a picture of to unlock an exclusive offer.

The inclusion of any three-dimensional interactive devices will increase the time your target will spend with the overall kit. But if the design is incorrectly targeted, or is not visually and verbally driven by the key consumer benefit, all the fancy inclusions will not ultimately sell the brand.

The Pitch or Business Letter

A direct-mail letter is an introduction. It is usually written by a CEO or company president and addressed to a specific person. The letter's job is to open the sale, give a complete and detailed sales pitch, and close the sale. It tells the target what they should do next, such as pick up the phone, tap an app, or boot up the computer.

If the kit includes a brochure, the letter is used as an introduction to what the reader will find inside the kit. If the kit does not include a brochure, the letter will carry the weight of the sell.

Many pitch letters will specifically include headlines and subheads in order to break the pitch up into individualized sections. You will handle them in the same way as a print ad. Make the headline large and bold, and use bold subheads to break up copy points. Finally, never be afraid to mention price; it's important to the consumer, so don't hide it at the end or in the body copy.

Every pitch and business letter should open by calling the target by name. The overall tone of the letter will depend on the price and type of product being advertised. If the product is reasonably priced, the copy can use a less formal tone. If the brand is upscale or a limited collector's item, the copy should use a more formal tone. Copy should use the same tone of voice as a letter to a friend would employ, so use the second-person pronoun "you" to refer to the target. Whatever tone the copy uses, it is important it inform. Give the target as much information as possible, such as how the brand is constructed, prices, and sizes, as well as how to purchase and/or reach a customer-service representative.

Keep the letter professional looking. Don't use a diverse array of point sizes and weights in the letter. Many direct-mail pieces make this critical mistake, creating a visual/verbal design rich in tacky but low in the ability to attract and hold the target's attention. Use a lot of white space to make the letter appear more formal, no matter what the brand sells for.

The Creative Look and Sound of Brochures

It is not unusual to find a brochure in a direct-mail kit. Brochures bring a lot of class to direct mail, because of their quality paper stock, use of multiple colors, photographs, graphics, and/or illustrations. Brochure copy can be more creative, replacing a pitch or business letter with creatively written copy and spectacular visuals.

A well-written and designed brochure succinctly tells the brand's story in a creatively presented package. Its job is to educate, push the key consumer benefit, and highlight what the brand can bring to enhance the target's lifestyle or business environment. The best designs are original, unique, creative, visual, and relatively copy-heavy. A well-designed and written piece can capture attention and inform both visually and verbally.

A brochure is made up of multiple, folded two-sided panels that can include both copy and/or imagery. Panels can be broken down into front and back covers, interior panels, and depending on size, exterior panels. You can devote entire panels to a different aspect of your key consumer benefit, or even split panels into smaller sections. Let's take a look at how to layout a brochure and its many diverse sections and components.

Laying Out the Brochure

One of the first things you need to consider after you have exhausted all your brainstorming options is how the brochure will be read. This will ultimately be determined by how it will fold. After exposure to the cover, do you want the piece to be opened one panel at a time or will it need to be fully extended to read the entire message? The best way to answer that question is to create a *dummy* folded layout. These thumbnail-size layouts help the designer see how the brochure or self-mailer will be laid out flat when printed, and how the varied types of folds will affect the overall design and visual/verbal message.

Brochures are created from a single sheet of paper and are always designed and produced flat. Because all panels are attached and not laid out singularly, their placement will need to be shown with dashed lines that will not show when printed. It is important to keep the placement of the fold in mind when designing, to ensure no body or detail copy will fall into it which would affect not only readability and legibility but also the overall design. The white space on either side of the fold is known as the *gutter* and should be kept to around a quarter-inch.

Many designs will allow visuals and headlines to cross the gutter and span multiple panels. Although this layout option is popular, it is important to keep a few things in mind. Be sure the fold 1) does not fall across someone's face, 2) does not block a critical component of the brand, especially if pointing out accessories, and 3) falls between, not through, letterforms when possible. Once you have a general idea how the piece will look, it is time to start designing.

Every Panel Plays an Important Role

A typical brochure can have anywhere from four to eight double sided panels. The most commonly seen brochures fall in the middle with four to six panels. Each panel has an important role to play. The front cover screams out the key consumer benefit, the back cover holds detail information and the inside panels tell the

brand's story, and tells the target what to do next. Let's take a quick look at how each panel is used to organize information.

Cover Design

Cover designs can be either visually or verbally driven. The job of a well-constructed cover is to grab attention with a creatively written key consumer benefit-driven headline and preferably one dominant photographic, illustrative, or graphic image. Many covers skip using imagery altogether and focus instead on using type in a more creative and graphic way. This is always a great solution—just be sure you can still read the headline. Additional options include using an abundance of white space, bright colors, or filling the panel with images that bleed off one or more sides.

Interior Panels

The interior panels are where the sell is made. As the brochure unfolds, the first page they will see in most layouts is the inside front cover. This is the panel that sets the tone for why the target needs this brand and what it can do to solve their problem or enhance their lifestyle. This panel should introduce the brand, the key consumer benefit, and the answer to the question "What's in it for me?" The inside center and right panels should flow with a strong storyline that will highlight additional features and benefits, uses, price lists, and have a strong call to action.

If there is a lot of copy, consider using multiple subheads and visuals to break up the long blocks of copy. To create more white space, consider using bullets to make specific points stand out. Don't forget to list the ordering options; let your audience know whether they have to use the enclosed order form, or if they can order online, over the phone, or through an app.

Outside Back Panel

This panel may also contain pricing information, or feature tear-away coupons or order forms, show seating charts, hold a discounted ticket to an event, or show any endorsements or testimonials attesting to what the brand can deliver, before-and-after pictures, statistical information, frequently asked questions, or information on studies conducted.

Brochures have a lot of available space just waiting for the message—in fact, more space than any other medium besides web pages. Use it to sell the brand clearly, informatively, and with a little flash.

Back Center Panel

The center back panel is always reserved for contact and/or mailer information, and a logo and tagline if using one. If you still need more room, consider adding a pocket to any type of fold.

Pockets

Many brochures will have pockets that hold pull-out cards, stacked inside. This is a great interactive addition when you have more information than will fit within your brochure. It also is a great way to highlight specific points by isolating them on their own card. The cards within the pockets are often of differing heights so that they can be more easily removed. Pockets are also a great way to tastefully include coupons, game pieces, scratch-offs, or even small take-aways. Depending on the purpose of the brochure, these pockets could hold a business card, calendar, or refrigerator magnet. See Figure 15.1 and 15.2 for an example of a direct-mail piece with pull-out cards.

Beyond pockets, you may find pop-up pieces, noise-makers, or even be able to smell some type of scent. These are advanced and very interactive design additions and will require working with your production and printing partners to set up and initiate.

Using the panels or pockets to organize what you have to say allows your audience to compartmentalize information as well as help with information flow. Make sure copy flows in an easy-to-follow path across panels. Nothing is more off-putting for a reader than not knowing how to open the piece so they can easily read the contents.

Folds Are a Design Option

The way you choose to fold a brochure will have a lot to do with how you display content. It is important that the visual/verbal content flows in a logical manner, so the target will not miss a well-constructed word or stunning image. All brochures and most postcards and self-mailers are designed on both the front and back of a single sheet of either an 8.5 x 11, or 8.5 x 14-inch sheet of paper. This means a brochure that has a single fold actually has four panels. A two-fold brochure has six panels and a three-fold has eight design-filled panels to work with.

One of the most interesting aspects of brochure design is the amount of folding options that are available for use. The type of fold you choose reflects on the brand, so it is important to adapt the design to the specific shape of the brochure you select. The type of fold employed will depend on your content and, of course, budget. There are nine different types of commonly used folds. Let's take a quick look at each one.

Bi-fold

A bi-fold, also known as a *half-fold*, uses a single sheet of 8.5 x 11-inch paper that is folded in half once either horizontally or vertically, leaving four panels front and back. When opened, the reader will see two main internal panels. The two interior panels are great for highlighting the feature and benefit associated with your key consumer benefit, as well as having enough room to showcase a few visuals. This fold is best used for content that has only one or two product features to push, for new product launches, or for reintroducing a new and improved aging brand. The front cover (1) is the right panel or cover page and the back cover (2) is the left panel. Panels (3) and (4) hold the interior content. See Figure 15.3 and 15.4 for an example.

Current Resident
1234 Smith Street
Knoxville, TN 31930

barksdaycare.com
901-904-0909

**Your Dog Becomes
Our Family**

Figure 15.1 Example of the front and back cover of a mailer. Image courtesy of Tae Hargett, University of Tennessee.

Our Story

Barks and Recreation opened three years ago in an effort to create a unique boarding and day care experience that places the care of each individual dog above all else. At our facility, multiple staff members evaluate every dog that walks through our doors. We pay attention to the specific needs of each dog to ensure their safety, happiness, and health while at Barks and Recreation.

Boarding, day care, grooming, and training are the top quality services that we offer. We have knowledgeable and caring staff members that oversee all of our services and get to know your dogs like their own.

Owners Catie and Mary are certified Pet First Aid Responders and certified Advanced Pet Care Technicians through DogNostics Advanced Pet Care Technician Certification Program. They are well educated in canine anatomy, physiology, health, and handling. They are informed about pet first aid and emergency protocols, pet care equipment, and canine behavior and socialization.

Barks and Recreation is the perfect place for your dog to play, relax, and chow down and we assure you their tails will be wagging the whole time.

Our Services

Figure 15.2 Example of the inside of a mailer, showing copy, images, and a pocket holding pull-out cards. Image courtesy of Tae Hargett, University of Tennessee.

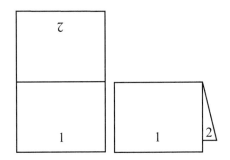

Figure 15.3 Example of a brochure horizontal fold.

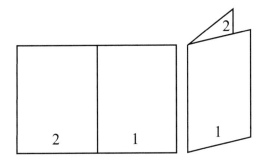

Figure 15.4 Example of a brochure vertical fold.

Tri-fold

A tri-fold is the most common type of brochure used in direct mail. It has two folds that divide an 8.5 x 11-inch sheet of paper into thirds. The right panel folds underneath the left panel. This is one of the most frequently used six-panel folds and is a great choice for almost all types of brands,

since it delivers a perfect balance between visual and verbal components.

The panels fold in on each other to form the finished size. The three panels will not have the same width since you need to accommodate the fold into the center. Panel (3) needs to be slightly smaller around 1/16–1/8 inch to avoid buckling when folded. Note that panel (2) is the back cover. The reader will first see the cover panel; (1) after opening the piece they will see inside panel (1) and (2) and outside panel (3) together, so be sure these two panels have a unifying design. See Figure 15.5 for an example.

Z-fold

The Z-fold is a popular two-fold, six-panel design that is folded back and forth with the final shape resembling a Z. Since a Z-fold can be pulled open to reveal all the panels at once, it is well suited to visual/verbal designs that span the entire brochure, or panels can be used to reveal content one panel at a time. See Figure 15.6 for an example.

Gate Fold

A gate fold also has two folds that divide an 8.5 x 11-inch page into six panels of unequal size. The gate fold is more difficult to work with, so it is not used as often as the previous folds we have discussed. To create this fold, the page is divided into one large panel and two smaller panels. Each side panel measures one-half the width of the central panel. The two side panels then fold in towards the center like a gate. This fold is usually used to target higher-end audiences about a niche brand. Thanks to its more

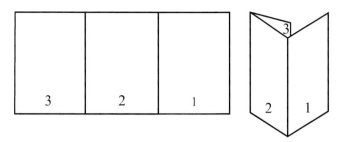

Figure 15.5 Example of a brochure tri-fold.

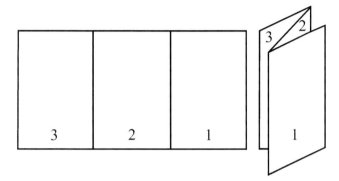

Figure 15.6 Example of a brochure Z-fold.

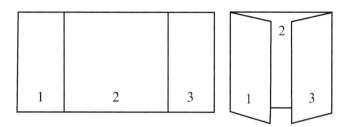

Figure 15.7 Example of a brochure gatefold.

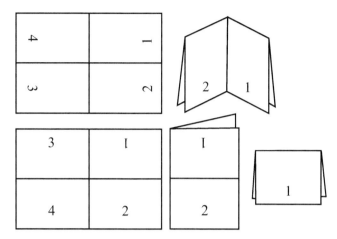

Figure 15.8 Example of a French fold brochure with both a vertical and horizontal fold.

complex appearance, it reflects luxury and the target is thus more likely to keep it rather than throw it out. The inner, larger panel is a great place to showcase visually heavy graphic options that are even more stunning, thanks to the reveal effect of the gate fold. It is also well suited for single brand or graphic-heavy designs. Gate folds have two outside panels. (1) and (3) that each fold towards the middle. See Figure 15.7 for an example.

French Fold

A French fold, or *cross fold* is a bit more complicated two-fold design. It divides a single 8.5 x 14-inch sheet into six panels. This fold is the combination of two half-folds. The sheet is first folded in half horizontally and then again vertically, and is great for graphic-heavy designs that require maps or any brand with a detailed visual/verbal story to tell. Its big size offers up all kinds of design options. Be sure to control the flow of the design with headlines, subheads, and visuals so your audience does not get lost in the multiple panels. These are the types of brochures that can be so graphic and colorful they can be kept and used as posters once they are fully opened. See Figure 15.8 for an example.

Roll Fold

The roll, or *barrel fold* uses a single 8.5 x 14-inch sheet of paper that is folded inward multiple times, so the panels appear to roll in on each other like a cone. Panel (1) and (2) are the same size, but each additional panel gets a little smaller so they can fit inside

each other. A roll-fold brochure is a great design option when you have a lot to say and want to ensure your audience reads the panels in the correct order. An additional use allows you to use a detachable panel that can be used for coupons or response cards. While all brochures can have a perforated or tear-off panel, all but the roll fold removes part of the message when the consumer removes the detachable panel. See Figure 15.9 for an example.

Accordion Fold

An accordion fold, also known as a *fan fold*, has three folds that divide a single 8.5 x 14-inch sheet into eight panels that fold back and forth on top of one another like an accordion or a pleat. Although it looks similar to a Z-fold, an accordion fold uses eight rather than six panels. Each panel is the same size. Some designers make the cover panel slightly larger to make opening easier. An accordion fold forms a W shape when folded. This fold is a great choice if you want to take your target on a step-by-step journey. See Figure 15.10 for an example.

Double Parallel Fold

The double parallel fold, also know as a *double gate fold*, uses a single 8.5 x 14-inch single sheet that is folded in half to create two panels and then is folded in half again to form two parallel

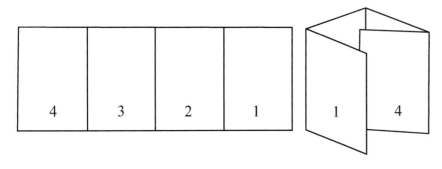

Figure 15.9 Example of a brochure roll fold.

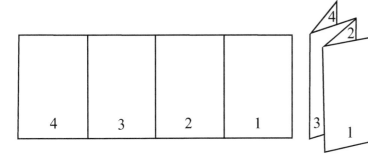

Figure 15.10 Example of a brochure accordion fold.

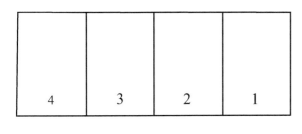
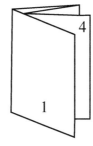

Figure 15.11 Example of a brochure double parallel fold.

folds consisting of eight panels that go in the same direction. For any folds that fold toward the center, in order to avoid any buckling and to accommodate the fold, the inside panels need to be anywhere from 1/16–1/8 inch smaller than the other panels. This fold works well for reference material that your target can use to see varied product offerings. See Figure 15.11 for an example.

Die-cut Fold

Die-cuts are impactful. The basic shape is the same as a Z-fold, the difference is the top of your cover is cut in a diagonal incline, making the front panel smaller than the other two. It reveals the content from the pages below to the reader, when the brochure is closed. The die-cut is used to provide a bit more visual interest to the front cover. If using a die-cut fold, it is important that something interesting needs to peek out. It must also work into the design on its home page. Die-cuts are a great way to have your brochure stand out and appear innovative at the same time. See Figure 15.12 for an example.

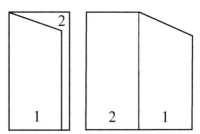

Figure 15.12 Example of a brochure with a die-cut.

Which Paper?

Now that you have your design and folds under control you have one more important decision to make: What type of paper do you want to have it printed on?

Choosing the right weight of paper stock for your brochure is more important than you might think. The flimsier the paper the cheaper it will look and feel. When possible, choose the highest-quality paper your client can afford. Coated paper stocks will give your piece a high sheen, similar to that found in magazines. Colors will be brighter and type crisper. Uncoated stocks often project a heavier weight and can deliver an old-world or more traditional look. Colors will be softer and the typeface chosen will have to be heavier, since the ink will bleed into the paper. Choice will depend on the look and image your are going after.

Reply Cards and Order Forms

These two forms should not be over looked. As a part of the kit, they should also reflect the overall design, perhaps through color and/or typeface, style, or layout. Use a headline to remind the target about the offer and a few lines of copy that sum up any relevant features and benefits. The design must also include space at the very least, for the target's name, address, city, state, zip code, day and evening phone numbers, and an e-mail address. Provide the proper boxes or lines if the consumer needs to make a color or size choice. Be sure the form has enough room to fill in the blanks and uses a type size that is easy to read. Repeat credit-card information here as well as the company's contact information and any shipping instructions.

The size of the response or reply card and whether it is single- or double-sided will vary, depending on the number of items the consumer must choose from and brand details, such as size or color choices.

Finally, although most orders will be placed online, it may seem like an order form is not necessary. However, many people still use them to jot down their order to make purchase easier when they do finally place their order.

The Return Envelope

Yes, they still exist. Whether the target makes use of it or not, every direct-mail kit will typically include a preaddressed, postage-paid envelope. This is where design ends. The return envelope should be plain and show the preprinted return and mailing address, along with a postage bar code and a representative stamp with the copy, "No Postage Needed If Mailed In The United States." It is important the reply card fits easily inside the accompanying envelope without excessive folding or scrunching.

Any direct-mail piece that is poorly designed, no matter how well-written, will never get opened. By working with the basic design parameters, it is possible to design a direct-mail kit that ultimately gets opened.

Individual Direct-Mail Pieces

Beyond a direct-mail kit, some of the most popular, stand-alone direct-mail pieces include postcards, folded self-mailers, catalogs, and boxed mailers.

Postcards. Postcards are a relatively inexpensive and popular direct-mail option. Sizing is diverse and will depend on what needs to be said and shown. Some of the most popular options include 4 x 6, 4 x 9, 5 x 7, 5 x 8.5, 5 x 8.5, 6 x11, and 6 x 8.75 inches. They are great for sending out reminders, a thank you, sale announcements, and coupons. Printed on both sides, the front cover is typically very colorful and/or visual. Since a large portion of the backof the postcard is taken up with mailer information, the cover must convey your message in only a few words. Those with a small amount of copy may also have additional interactive properties such as scratch-off areas that reveal a special offer. A typical scratch off area measures 2 x 1 inches.

Folded Self-Mailers. Folded self-mailers arrive in your mailbox without the protection of an envelope. They are typically created from a single folded sheet of 8.5 x 11-inch paper, or heavier card stock, and can include perforated coupons, and movable and pop-up or pull -out sections. To ensure mailers do not open during mailing. they are either glued shut with a continuous line of glue, spots of glue, or use circular tabs. The design may also close the piece with a vertically or horizontally designed flap.

Catalogs. Catalogs are multiple-page booklets that promote any number of diverse products. Like self-mailers, many will use tabs or glue to keep them closed during shipping. They typically showcase longer copy and multiple visuals. They can be spirally bound, stapled, or stitched. Visuals are large and beautifully photographed. Copy features a headline, a small amount of descriptive copy and a larger, boldly stated price. Orders can be easily made, using any number of options including toll-free numbers, the mail, apps, mobile options, or the Internet. Warranties and guarantees take the worry out of purchasing a product you do not like. Products can easily be returned for a full refund without penalty if the target is not entirely satisfied.

Companies are replacing the big catalogs of the past with *specialty catalogs*. These miniature versions of a larger catalog's specialized content is specifically chosen based on the target's past purchase history.

Boxed mailers are expensive but are a great option if you want to hide promotional keepsakes, samples, or even game pieces inside. Because the offer arrives in a box, it is a great choice for building curiosity and for capturing attention. Typically, the box is plain white, black, or brown. Any text is usually a graphically illustrated logo. These specialty mailers are best used for a niche audience who are already known users of the brand.

Designing Tips for Direct-Mail Pieces

The choice of piece(s) and overall layout used is important because each dictates the amount of copy and images you can use. For example, if the goal is to launch a new brand or introduce new options or uses, you will likely need lengthier copy and multiple images to tell the brand's story. To ensure you have enough space, size will be an important consideration. To further promote the brand, you may also want to include a sample, feature a few interactive options, or introduce a contest or sweepstakes. On the other hand, if your client is a charity, you will need a bit more restraint. To avoid appearing wasteful, you might consider using only black-and-white photography and a lower grade of paper. If you just want to announce a sale or deliver a few coupons, a postcard may be the best way to go.

Because there is so much going on in a direct mail kit, it is important to ensure every piece in your kit gets noticed. The best way to do this is to be sure that each piece is a different size and if possible, uses a diverse selection of colors from your brand color pallet. The most comprehensively designed pieces will reuse graphic or illustrative styles, a photographic theme, or colors from the envelop on the inside pieces.

Simplistic Design

Always go for simple and clean. If you want to add some type of "wow" factor, think graphically or use a bright color palette. Direct mail is first and foremost a sales tool. Make the piece visually appealing and surprise the reader with diverse inserts and well-written copy. It should provide your target with some kind of benefit, a discount, information about a new product launch they have shown an interest in, or details about a special event, to name just a few. Use your type and imagery to create a clear path through the ad that ends with your call to action and logo. Your choice of visuals, whether using photographs, illustrations, or graphics, will help to grab the reader's attention and set the initial tone of the message. The choice of typeface, color scheme, and overall layout must work with your imagery to send a unified message. Let's take a look at a few things to keep in mind when designing a direct mail-kit, self-mailer, or postcard.

Visuals

Memorable design relies on good storytelling and powerful visuals. Carefully chosen imagery increases the likelihood the piece will be read and moves the storyline along. Use as much lifestyle-enhancing imagery as possible. Be sure any images with people in them reflect your target audience. Depending on direction, additional image options might include showing the product alone, in use, or in a setting; these images can easily project a mood or demonstrate how to do something. Illustrations are especially suited to showcasing any statistical information or even simple seating charts.

Choice of imagery should help push your key consumer benefit, reflect the message, the brand's image, and reflect your target's lifestyle and interests. Each piece needs one strong dominant image that will visually speak for the key consumer benefit. Place any smaller images around the main visual or mix them into the body copy. Use of too many of the same, or competing sizes, creates clutter, forcing the reader's eye to roam rather than land on a single important visual.

Make sure visuals appearing inside the piece are sized and when possible cropped in the same way. While it's okay to deviate from this clean but austere look, don't use more than two different crops or sizes. If wrapping text around a visual, make sure to include enough white space around the visual so as to not affect readability and legibility. Use your imagery to focus attention, break up long blocks of copy, and add dimension and interest to the piece.

Remember, images do not have to be confined to individual panels. Both imagery and headlines can span across panels, or slightly overlap into another panel. If you are thinking of putting text on top of your images, be sure the type is bulky enough and placed within a quiet portion of the background, or an area void of imagery, to avoid affecting both readability and legibility.

Typeface

It is easy to ruin a concept and negatively affect readability and legibility if the typeface(s) you use cannot be read. The typeface you choose should not only relate to the brand, but will affect how the target perceives the ad and ultimately the message.

Avoid using decorative faces whenever possible. They are great for accents but not an entire headline. As with all design, it is important to control the number of typefaces used. Stick to no more than two typefaces and be sure they are easily scannable when read. The choice of type style used will depend on your brand, the target, and your concept. You might consider using all serif or sans serif typefaces, or mixing it up by using a strong sans serif typeface for larger text, such as the headline and subheads, and a serif typeface for body and detail copy. Type choice can also be used to create additional contrast on the page by incorporating varying weights and type sizes into the design.

Color

Choosing a color that attracts and doesn't alienate is always a crap shoot. If your brand has a signature color palette, use it. If it does not, how should you go about picking colors? Start by looking to the logo for direction or even the imagery you are using. If money is tight, again consider using a high contrast black-and-white design with a spot of color. Spot color is always elegant and attention-getting, and depending on how that spot of color is used, very graphic.

If you used a lot of color on the cover, be sure to tone it way down inside. Bring colors from the cover or envelope inside to use as accents for such things as bars, charts, page dividers, and headline and subheads. Too much color can become garish and cheap-looking. Push the message inside, not the bold design choices. Two or three well-placed colors will carry the design throughout. If you need more depth, consider adding additional tones and shades from the palette. Color choices will enhance the message visually and can help emphasize specific points. Finally, do not shy away from a minimalistic design. Simple designs are easier to do well, than one that has a lot of color and flash.

Weights, Paper Stocks and Finishes

The look and feel of a direct-mail piece can affect the design and overall response rate, so feel free to play around with the weight of the paper stock the piece(s) will be printed on, its color, and whether or not it will be seen on an uncoated or coated paper stock. The look, feel, and finish of the paper you choose will not only affect the brand's image but the overall print quality of your visuals, type, and folds.

As a rule, heavier paper is stronger, helping any piece with folds stand up to the abuse of multiple page openings. Stock that is too heavy, however, can crack and tear with use. The best weight for pieces with two or more folds is 100# cover. If using a coated stock, 80# cover is a good choice. Paper also affects any specialty techniques you might be considering, such as embossing or debossing. *Embossing* creates a raised image out of the background paper creating a 3D-graphic effect. *Debossing* pushes the image into and slightly below the paper's surface. An embossed surface can have ink or foil added for additional embellishment, or it can be left unadorned, known as *blind*

emboss. A debossed image can also have ink added or left natural, known as *blind deboss*.

Choice of anything above an 80# cover will decrease the amount of detail that can be seen in your embossed element. Postcards are typically printed on 100# cover stock. If it will include a die-cut, a 200# coated cover stock is a great option.

For self-mailers, without an envelope, the thickness has to meet postal regulations. Check with your printer for the best paper stock and weight for your project.

White Space

Like all design, ensuring you're using an adequate amount of white space is critical. White space increases readability and legibility and helps create an elegant and uncluttered-looking layout. Be sure to not fill up the space with unnecessary imagery or an abundance of oversized type. Use white space to enhance the design. The more white space you have, the more elegant, scannable, and clean the piece will look and feel.

Finally, white space fills a very important additional role in self-mailers. If your direct-marketing piece does not arrive in an envelope, it's critical to remember that a big hunk of space needs to be reserved for the address and postal information. Be sure to ask your printer early in the design process for any sizing and placement information.

Direct-Mail Copy That Entices Action

Beautiful images and eye-catching colors can only carry your message only so far. To ensure you educate your target about how your key consumer benefit can enhance their lifestyle, you need to have creatively written copy. What you say will depend on how much space and how many pieces you have to work with. Postcards and envelopes allow for no more than a prominently stated key consumer benefit and offer. Brochures, small product catalogs, or a self-mailer offer more space to tell an intriguing, informational story in a more creative way. Let's take a look at the role of copy in direct mail.

Headlines

Be sure the headline is the first and largest piece of copy on the page and that it screams out both the feature and benefit that make up the key consumer benefit in an interesting and informative way. You might consider using a headline style that asks a question, uses a pun, metaphor or simile, or one that builds curiosity or uses news to both grab attention and entice your target deeper into the piece. An eye-catching headline can be the catalyst needed to elicit your target's attention and get them to pick up the piece(s) and act on the message.

It is important to keep the headline short, no more than five to seven words. If you must add a subhead or a very small amount of additional copy to a brochure cover or envelope, make sure everything comes in at less than 25 words. Be sure anything said on the envelope is repeated on the main selling piece inside the kit.

Subheads

Copy in direct mail is typically longer. Consider using multiple subheads to break up lengthy copy blocks with small informative and creatively written statements that highlight each point you make in the body copy. These multiple subheads can help seamlessly guide the reader through the copy. A good rule of thumb that ensures they can be read at a glance is to keep them to no longer than one sentence.

If you want your headline and subhead to be any color other than black, make sure the color choice is easily legible against any background colors you might be using. Go for contrast—dark colors on a light background, and light colors on a dark background. All body and detail copy should be set in black to ensure readability and legibility is never compromised.

Body Copy

Although it appears you have a lot of space to work with, in most direct-mail pieces, it is still important to get to the point quickly and succinctly. Focus your copy only on your key consumer benefit. Too much information can confuse your reader and dilute your main selling point.

The paragraphs of body copy seen in any direct-mail piece should be concise, yet long enough to educate your target about the key consumer benefit. Copy should help to alleviate any fears or skepticism the target may have. If it does not, the target's hard-won initial interest, created when they first opened the envelope or viewed the cover, will evaporate.

To help support your key consumer benefit, focus on what the brand can do and/or offer, and stay away from any comparisons of competing brands. It is important to back up any facts and benefits with testimonials when appropriate, and be sure your copy focuses on the benefits to the target's interests and lifestyle. Keep the copy light but informative. Avoid using big words that

can easily confuse. Instead, consider using known attention-getting words, such as announcing, discover, easy, exclusive, first, free, guarantee, introducing, know, learn, money, new, now, powerful, protect, proven, results, safe, save, and trust, to name just a few.

A good copywriter must be able to turn an ordinary feature into a unique one, giving it a personality, and perhaps a new twist for an old use. Direct mail is a benefit-driven kind of conversation with the target. Copy must be believable, but creatively written, while seamlessly weaving an imaginative story.

Keep each paragraph to around three to four sentences in length. Long copy can be both intimidating to the eye and boring to the reader. Well-written plot or feature/benefit-driven copy that a reader finds intriguing will be read no matter its length and will initiate an inquiry or produce an order. If you have multiple points to make, consider using bullet points for added emphasis.

The Offer

Every direct-mail piece needs to include some type of compelling offer. The offer needs to not only capture attention but also let your target know what they will receive if they take action within a specified amount of time. Be sure the offer is clear and risk free. Examples of risk-free offers might include money-back guarantees and easy return policies.

Call to Action

Be sure to close the sale. What do you want your reader to do? Make ordering or attaining more information as easy as possible. Make sure the call to action is easy to find and understand. The easier it is for the reader to know what the next step is, the more likely they are to follow through on the offer.

Copy should reference the enclosed order form and provide any additional information about how to purchase and/or contact customer service. For example, if you want them to make a phone call, be sure the phone number is in bold and larger than surrounding copy. If the goal is an online visit, make sure your URL links directly to a landing page that relates to the message. If a trip to a store location is the goal, boldly state the address and consider adding a map and/or a picture of the storefront. Finally, if applicable, let them know that there are operators standing by to answer any questions they may have.

It's important to remember that no matter how well your copy is written, your audience may not be immediately inspired to act quickly. One way to enhance the response rate is to limit quantities or the time the target has to purchase. Always make sure your call to action includes some type of incentive, such as a coupon, or a free sample or gift if they act now or within a stated time period.

Detail Copy

Make sure your contact information or detail copy is clearly stated and easy to find. Because this information can often be lengthy, it is rarely seen inside a brochure or within the body of the pitch letter. Most will be placed on the back center panel or under the salutation, where it is easy to find.

Disclaimers

Some copy and promotions require the use of a disclaimer. These very wordy, legalese types of statements always take up a lot of valuable space concerning terms and conditions associated with purchase, use, or even rules surrounding a contest and sweepstakes. When using them, it's important to make sure that you are adhering to all the rules set up by the Federal Trade Commission for typestyle and readability. Typically, disclaimer copy can be set around eight or nine point. Use the arm's length rule, to confirm readability.

Type Use

Headlines and subheads should be set in bold and can be either centered or set flush left, rag right within a single panel, or run across multiple panels depending on the design. Blocks of body copy need to be no smaller than ten or eleven point with one point of additional leading between lines of text. Type that is too small or pieces that are covered from top to bottom with text are not only unattractive, but are destined to be thrown out. All body copy should be set flush left, rag right unless designed to fit a justified alignment. By adding an indent to each paragraph of copy, you can create more white space within the design.

Proofreading

Proofreading your work is critical—always be sure to proof your piece for spelling and grammatical errors. Make sure the ad flows toward the call to action and logo. Be sure all visuals help to move the storyline along; if they do not, delete them. Next, ask yourself: Does the overall ad design make sense? Are there any places the copy is vague, or unclear, or rambles? Is the key consumer benefit coming across loud and clear throughout the piece? Finally, be sure to verify that all phone numbers are correct and any QR codes or links work.

A Final Look at Sales Promotion

Now that you know the visual/verbal role behind direct mail, let's take a quick look at possible incentives that can be used to entice your target audience to purchase.

The type of sales promotion used must be an extension of the brand's image and the visual/verbal message. The more interrelated the messages across mediums, the easier it is to grab and excite consumer interest. Because of the eclectic shapes, textures, and sizes associated with promotional materials, this is often easier said than done.

Depending on the amount of available surface space, promotional devices should take their cue from print, online, or direct-marketing materials. Always, consider adapting, when possible, the unique headline styles, color combinations, typefaces and styles, or any visual themes used elsewhere. Be sure the logo and slogan or tagline are seen on all sales-promotion pieces. Point-of-purchase or in-store advertising that reflects the overall visual/verbal appearance of other advertising or promotional pieces can assist with brand recognition, should the target forget the product name while shopping. If the goal is to entice the target through trial or gifts and games, then sales promotion is the best outlet.

Sales Promotion Gives Something Back to the Target

Incentives can take many different forms. The most commonly employed include coupons, percent- or money-off promotions, special packaging, contests and sweepstakes, premiums, and/or game boards, in-store displays, and refunds and rebates. When paired with direct mail, the choice of sales-promotion vehicle must reinforce the overall message and reflect the brand's image.

The job of sales promotion is to give the target something for purchasing or for remaining a brand-loyal customer. It must successfully attract first-time buyers, and/or stimulate impulse buys, or entice users of competitors' brands to switch. It is excellent at raising brand awareness through "try me" offers and increasing brand demand through limited-time offers. This is important to all brands, since trial is the first step to obtaining brand loyalty.

All types of sales promotions are consumer motivated. It is impossible to cover all the available design options. But by now you should have enough knowledge to give any sales or promotional piece a strong visual and verbal voice.

There are two basic types of sales promotions: In-store and out-of-store promotions. Some will fall into both categories. The following is a list of some of the most popular.

In-store options include:

- Coupons
- Point-of-purchase (POP) or in-store signage
- Price-off offers or "sales"
- Specialty packaging
- Loyalty programs
- Bonus packs
- Sampling

Out-of-store options include:

- Continuity programs
- Trial offers
- Product warranties or guarantees
- Refunds and rebates
- Special events

In-store or-out-of-store options include:

- Giveaways
- Contests and sweepstakes
- Premiums

Direct marketing talks to the target by name, encourages two-way conversations between the brand and the target, and offers the target an incentive to buy. Personalized messages are written and designed to match the known interests and past purchasing habits of the targeted audience. Direct marketing's unique characteristics give power to the target. They decide when to open a piece, the level of interaction, how or when to respond, the timing of their purchase, and when or if to make a purchase.

Bibliography

Pulcinella, Steven. 2017. "Why Direct Mail Marketing Is Far from Dead." (August 30). Retrieved from: www.forbes.com/sites.../2017/.../why-direct-mail-marketing-is-far-from-dead.

CHAPTER 16

What Makes Internet and Social Media Marketing Work?

Chapter 16 Objectives

1. Readers will understand the role of both Internet and social media advertising.
2. The reader will understand the visual/verbal options available to the creative team.
3. The reader will learn about the varied layout options currently available for both the Internet and social media platforms.

Online Advertising Has Personalized the Advertised Message

Internet marketing, also known as *online marketing*, can be defined as the promotion of a business or brand over the Internet. Reflecting its ever-changing and more personalized environment, Internet marketing is becoming better known as *content marketing*. The Content Marketing Institute defines content marketing as: "A strategic marketing approach focused on creating and distributing valuable, relevant, and consistent content to attract and retain a clearly defined audience—and, ultimately, to drive profitable customer action." It is no longer just about distributing content, it's about delivering truly relevant, useful, and personalized content to the correct target, at the right time, to help them solve their problem on demand, or when and where it is convenient to them. The ease with which information can be gathered makes comparison-shopping easier, faster, and more convenient, so when consumers elect to buy, they are much better educated on product use, quality, price, competitor brands, and/or guarantee or return policies than ever before.

Today's consumers turn to the Internet and/or social media to help with purchasing decisions. When it comes to researching, evaluating, and selecting one brand over another, 24/7 availability and customer reviews have fundamentally changed buying behavior, whether the purchase is made on or offline from our home, office, desktop, tablet, or mobile device.

With that said, as we have learned, traditional media options have not been abandoned, only augmented. When traditional advertising and Internet marketing are used together, known as *cyber marketing*, they are effective at building brand awareness, initiating interactive opportunities, and educating consumers about a brand. When used as an informational tool, the Internet, specifically, is a great place to direct the target to read about tests or medical results, news articles, testimonials and professional advice or tips from relevant experts, or to find current promotions. It is not unusual for many websites to sponsor social media sites, chat rooms, and/or blogs where consumers can interact with and share information with other brand-loyal users.

A website is often the target's first informational impression of a brand or corporation before purchase. The first time the target visits a website, it's like stepping into a brick-and-mortar store. The online visitor will take notice of the furnishings (type, color, layout), how the floor plan is laid out (placement, sizing, navigation, ease of use), and how products are displayed (photographs, illustrations, animation, or videos). A cluttered appearance is a red flag and can easily change a positive image into a questionable choice; a lot of white space and a clean atmosphere gives the illusion of quality and exclusivity. Advertising in any medium, as we have learned, is all about perception and the way the visual/verbal message is delivered. Internet marketing offers up yet another attribute: Interactivity.

Interactive and Engaging Internet Marketing

Interactive mediums, such as the Internet and social media, build relationships between the target and the brand by providing

DOI: 10.4324/9781003255123-17

multiple channels of informational interactivity to encourage target interaction and/or feedback. Engagement is a direct result of this interaction. The content is meaningful enough to engage and hold their attention long enough to inform, follow up with customer service, or make a purchase. This interaction should take little effort or thought on the part of the target and it should always lead them on an informative but structured journey.

It can be a challenge to find ways to make advertising interactive and interesting. To creative teams, interactive means creating and delivering an activity that both attracts attention and informs. To marketers, it is a chance to create opportunities to interact directly with the target.

To accomplish both initiatives, Internet advertising uses many diverse forms of advertising options, such as websites, banner ads, pop-ups, search, pay-per-click, and floating ads. More sophisticated interactive options might include streaming audio and video, webisodes, augmented reality, and interactive television. It can also include more promotional or direct-response options, such as social media and personalized e-mail, or even offer up opportunities to enter a contest or sweepstakes, or a chance to pick up or redeem a coupon. No matter what form(s) it takes, the most successful Internet advertising can also create "buzz" between consumers, also known as *viral* or *word-of-mouth* advertising. This free form of advertising can carry more sales value than any type of advertised message alone ever will. The biggest and most complex Internet vehicle is a website. Knowledge about the design of these online storefronts will lay the foundation for how to design for all other Internet vehicles.

Internet Design Has Its Roots in Traditional Media: Defining Web Design

Design on the Internet is one part print and one part broadcast. Breaking it down even further, it is text heavy with visual accents. At its most complex, the visual/verbal message is delivered using sight, sound, and motion. With that said, Internet design is neither pure print nor broadcast. It of course has its own rules that define its visual/verbal appearance.

A brand website needs to break down and informatively tell the story of a brand and/or company. A well-designed site needs to take the target on an informative and hopefully creative visual and verbal journey that showcases the features and benefits of the brand and what they will bring to the target's life.

To do this well, the creative team will use all the visual and verbal components available to them to inform and engage. Using the same components from print advertising, a website will have headlines, subheads, visuals, body and detail copy, and a consistently viewable logo. Layout will employ almost all of the principles and elements of design, as well as rely on the psychology of color. The basic rules surrounding the use of type will follow those used in television.

Interactive options, exclusive to Internet design, will use the visuals to demonstrate use and/or act as links that can be clicked on to access any augmented reality options, streaming audio and video, or an appropriate webisode or podcast, to name just a few.

Beyond the copy and layout basics, there are many additional aspects the creative team needs to consider, including 1) information architecture, or the order content will appear, 2) user interface, or how components interact within the website, 3) site structure, or what the site will look like, 4) navigation, or how viewers will move around the site, and 5) interactive options.

Websites are a critical part of a brand's identity and are often the target's first interaction with the brand. Because of this, it's imperative for brands to craft a website that reflects the brands and target's self image. The target's first impressions are often planted, nurtured, and developed, based on their initial exposure to content on your brand's website.

Front-End Design and Back-End Production

Web design is a very technical production process, so this discussion will deal only with "front-end" digital design. *Front-end design* refers to the creative teams that imagine and initially create the designs that will then be handed off to the *back-end production designers* who will code and implement the designs. Front-end designers do not need the same in-depth knowledge of code and programming languages as the back-end designers. However, in order to avoid any costly missteps, front-end designers do need to have a general knowledge of what can and cannot be done before designs are sent to the back-end production team . Communication between the front- and back-end teams is a vital part of the design process. The flow of information between the creative teams begins with organization and brainstorming.

Sitemaps

The first critical step is organizing content by developing a sitemap. The *sitemap* is a diagram (sometimes a Word document) that works like a table of contents identifying all the pages on a site and how they will be organized. It will also lay out the overall navigation of the site in a flow-chart format. By organizing content, you can help make a site more user-friendly. Here is where many critical decisions are solidified, such as what pages are included along with navigation decisions and what type of interactive devices will be needed. An important question to keep in mind when creating a sitemap is what will users typically be looking for on the website? A restaurant, for example, will want the menu page to be easily accessible and not hidden behind multiple clicks. See Figure 16.1 for an example of a sitemap.

Wireframes

The next step is the development of a wireframe. Similar to thumbnails, wireframes are simple line drawings that show the placement of both continual and changing content. *Continual content*, or content that will be seen on every page includes page headers and page footers. Page headers sit at the top of every page and most often include the brand logo, navigation bar, and a log-in box. Page footers, located at the bottom of the page, may have copyright information or numbers for page jumps, contact information, about this site, my account, and shopping links. *Changing content* includes visuals, headlines, subheads, body copy, and varied links that will change on every page.

The wireframe does not contain actual imagery, but uses geometric shapes to show placement and the overall structure of the website. For example, image placement will be shown using a box with an X through it. Headlines are typically written out or represented with a sketched-in rectangle. Body copy is represented by straight lines, the navigation bar is generally drawn using lines and boxes, and the logo is often represented with a square or circle.

One of the many reasons for not jumping right into the design of a website is not only about time management and creative options, but also about taking the time to gather valuable insight into both the user experience (UX) and user interface (UI). These two terms are often used together in the industry as UX/UI. *User experience* refers to the "experience," or how visitors will interact with the website, while *user interface* refers to the visual communication between components on the page.

A wireframe will need to be completed for each page specified in the site map. This results in a lot of wireframes being created during the exploratory or brainstorming process. Beyond mere sketches, wireframes will also have a lot of comments describing how certain elements will act in the layout.

Another important aspect the creative team needs to keep in mind is what is known as the "*above the fold*" space on websites. This is the space the site will open to and refers to what visitors will see first without having to click or scroll. The information placed here should identify the site, show navigation options, and will typically have one or more dominant visuals that might have a static display, scroll, or fade multiple visuals in and out. Once a wireframe is chosen, the designer should check with the back-end team to ensure that everything can be coded and implemented correctly. See Figure 16.2 for an example of a wireframe.

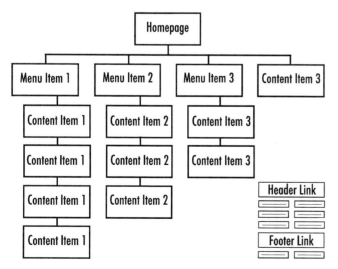

Figure 16.1 Example of a sitemap.

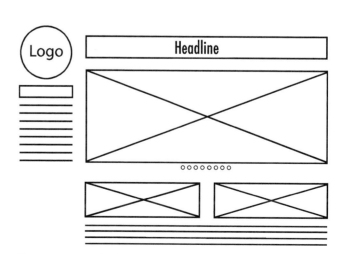

Figure 16.2 Example of a wireframe.

The Design Components That Make Up a Website

Once the sitemaps and wireframes are completed and approved by the client, the design team will determine how each design component will be used to construct the visual and verbal look the site will ultimately have. Let's look at the options.

Color

Color plays an integral part in web design; it can help lead the target through the site and help create consistency between campaign materials. Color is often used on websites to create a visual hierarchy or better user experience. There are four basic color schemes that can be used on a website: Monochromatic (using colors of the same hue), analogous (colors close on the color wheel), complementary (opposite colors on the color wheel), and triadic (colors evenly spaced around the color wheel). Monochromatic color schemes are often the most harmonious and easiest on the eyes. Analogous colors work well together; however, they can often appear to clash. Complementary color schemes typically use only two colors. They can be striking but when overused can overwhelm a design. They are best used when you want something specific to stand out. Triadic color schemes use three colors spaced evenly around the color wheel. They can produce vibrantly colored web pages; because of this they can easily annoy some viewers. The brightness of both complementary and triadic colors will affect people differently, so use them sparingly. To avoid any negative reactions, they should be tested on multiple members of your target group before you commit to using them. In the end, when it comes to picking which colors will be featured on a website, the designer should choose colors that are consistent with the brand's color palette. Remember, different colors not only attract different types of people (review the psychology of color in Chapter 6), they can also alter consumer behavior.

Once you have your color palette set up, pick one color that will dominate the design. Start by looking at your logo and go from there. This color should only be used in a limited number of places—specifically, those areas where you want to attract your visitor's attention with a pop of color, or to those areas that require some sort of action such as a call-to-action (CTA) button. Simplicity goes a long way in web design so don't clutter up the site with too many colors; one or two dominant colors with an occasional secondary or accent color is a good starting point. If you want to add more depth, consider using screen tints of your colors to help with dimension.

Background color, if using one, should not annoy website visitors, or make it difficult to read and understand content by using colors that are too dark or bold. Test out readability and legibility. If the site has a lot of small type, 12 point or less, avoid using a background color. Anything larger will not break up or be difficult to read when placed on top of a color. Start with a light or neutral shade and move up from there. Whether or not to use a background color will depend on the designer and the brand. Although an all-white background is always a safe option, it can often appear too sterile and lack personality.

Type

Typically, a brand will already have an existing typeface(s) they religiously use on other advertising materials. In a perfect world, this would be the same typeface used on the website. However, a typeface needs to be a web-safe face to display correctly on a website which will be seen across different browsers and devices. Frequently, companies are using typefaces on print material that a designer may not be able to use on web pages. Finding a suitable replacement will be needed; just be sure it looks as close to the original typeface as possible. The only thing that should not change is the brand's logo, which is primarily imported as a vector image to the website. Type on websites, especially for body and detail copy, are most often set in a sans serif typeface. Sans serif fonts typically display better on digital platforms and make for a better user experience. Serif fonts are typically harder to read online, especially if placed on a background color. Size is important to readability and legibility in the same way it is in print; however, sizing is unique to the web. Size will of course vary based on the typeface chosen; however, a good place to begin is keeping the minimum type size for body copy to 14–16 point and headlines typically ranging anywhere from 18–36 point.

Along with larger type standards, text on websites need more breathing room than print material. Leading is referred to as *line height* on the web, due to how the back-end code works. When front-end designers are mocking up websites, the general rule of thumb is to use leading that is at a minimum 120 percent of the font size used. For example, if the art director is displaying body copy at 16 point, then the leading would be 19.2. The leading set in InDesign doesn't mean that's exactly what will be implemented through the code (due to how the coding works), but it should look similar. Back-end web designers do have control over kerning when coding a website; however, the code may not be supported on all browsers. Like television, the kerning should typically stay at the default or be slightly more open depending on the typeface used. The more breathing room you can create between line and letter spacing, the easier the copy can be read. Typefaces that have a naturally tight kern should be avoided when designing for the web.

Imagery

Visuals used on the web may be static, animated, or do double-duty as a link. Photographs, illustrations, and graphics add to the user experience of visiting a website along with communicating the brand's story. Visuals used in a website demand attention, but should not overpower the page flow or buttons. The best kinds of images fall into two very specific categories: Story appeal and demonstrative. Images with *story appeal* are best placed above the headline. *Demonstrative* images are best placed within or near the copy. When possible, avoid stock photos, they tend to be very attractive but also tend to be very generic. Be sure every photograph is of the highest quality, and has not been distorted in any way, or appears pixelated. Additionally, when possible show the product in use and be sure the packaging is clearly visible whenever the brand is shown. It is also best to avoid 1) crowd shots—viewers find them boring because they lack a single focus, 2) oversized human heads—they can appear slightly grotesque when we can see every flaw, and 3) historical images—unless your target is enthusiasts. Visuals not only need to be relevant to what is being said, but on the Internet they can also slow down load time, the number one reason surfers abandon a site. Any link should open within four seconds, so if you don't need that image to make your point, leave it out.

Specific steps need to be taken to ensure that images are optimized and showing up correctly on websites. First, all visuals and images that are on a website should be in RGB (red, gree, blue) color mode. The front-end designer should verify this when creating the mock website, along with sending the files to the back-end designer. Images and any animation should be saved as a JPEG, PNG, or GIF and have a resolution of 72 pixels per inch (ppi) minimally. It is also important that all images be named properly, meaning if you download a file that is named stockphoto456.jpg, then the designer should change it to reflect image content and the brand name.

Finally, be sure your visuals have accompanying captions to give relevance to the image. This is a great way to press your main points and spark curiosity to entice your target into the body copy to find out more.

Copy

Writing for the Internet is often handled as if it were a business document—full of facts and little else. This style completely ignores the fact that the target must be both visually and verbally stimulated if their attention is to be held. One of the best ways to engage the viewer is to include creative, interesting, and informational copy. The best way to move the target towards purchase and hold their attention for any length of time, is well-written copy. The same style and tone used in other advertising vehicles should be repeated here. Do not include any copy that does not both tell and move the brand's story forward. Continue to write to your target's interests and lifestyle.

Be sure to not visually overwhelm your target with a lot of copy. Intermix the site with headlines to divide sections, visuals to illustrate copy points, and subheads to help break up long blocks of intimidating-looking copy. For sites with multiple product offerings, be sure each visual is accompanied by descriptive copy and clearly shows the price. Do not be afraid to prominently list prices. Consider making them bold or including them as a part of the page design, as in newspaper. However they are handled, eventual purchase requires they not be hidden. Any links included in the copy should further the target's knowledge about the brand; if they do not, leave them out. When possible, use demonstrations, testimonials, and/or relevant studies to prove a point.

Readability and legibility is as important in web design as it is in print. Make reading the copy as quick and easy as possible. Ideally, lines of text should be no longer than six inches wide, or 45–85 characters including spaces and punctuation, when set in a single column. Anything longer and the eye gets lost as it travels across the page. You also have the option of using one, two, or three columns of copy. Do not use any more than three if you don't want your page to look like a newspaper page. Like magazine design, if you have a lot of copy, be sure to use multiple paragraphs and varied sentence length to break up the gray appearance of multiple long blocks of copy. This is also a good time to work with multiple subheads to break up the page into pleasing proportions. If you need to present a lot of details, consider using bullet points to open up the design and make reading these important callouts easier. Most importantly, be sure to proof the copy several times to ensure there are no spelling and grammatical errors.

Finally, tell the target what you want them to do: Call for additional information, set up an appointment, or make a purchase. If the website is the target's final stop, be sure to make purchasing easy and to provide several payment options.

Layout Options

Keeping visitors on your site involves more than just the products being sold; it is also about ambiance or page layout. Like print, most website layouts are a combination of two or more layout styles. However, in web design, comfort with the site, or ease of use, also plays a big role in layout choices. The following discussion outlines some of the top layout options seen on the web today.

Symmetrical or Single Column

This layout style uses a headline, a dominant visual, and a single column of text directly below it. Most often used on sites with a large amount of text, all visitors have to do is scroll to read the content. This requires additional navigation options, so visitors do not have to scroll back to the top of the page to navigate through the site. This is also a popular mobile display option. See Figure 16.3 for an example of a symmetrical or single-column layout.

Asymmetrical

This layout style works the same on a website as it does in print; the design looks balanced despite its lack of symmetry or equality between its two halves. A relatively new addition to web design, it is believed viewers can scan pages more quickly by helping them to focus their attention on individual components. See Figure 16.4 for an example of an asymmetrical layout.

Grid or Magazine Layout

Sites that have a lot of information to display need to organize components based on a hierarchy of importance to assist with eye flow and equalizing white space. The layout uses a series of varying sized geometric shapes (squares and rectangles) organized into multiple columns. Visuals and text use size and placement to draw the reader in and inform. Remember, not all components are of equal importance; place either visual or verbal emphasis on one item, with all other items getting a secondary amount of emphasis. This very visually complicated layout style should be confined to brands that have a lot of products to display. Varying the size of the grid shapes should help to create a visually pleasing look.

Grid layouts typically have three columns. To break up the page, emphasis is placed on the headlines and images. The most important feature will have the largest head and most dominant visual in the same way it would in print. Both column size and gutter width between columns should remain consistent throughout the design. See Figure 16.5 for an example of a grid or magazine layout.

The "F" or "E" Alphabet

This layout style is based on various eye-tracking studies that say web surfers read a web page in an "E" or "F" pattern. Viewers tend to notice the top, upper left corner and left side of the screen first, with only the occasional glance at the right side. It relies on eye flow to organize and help viewers find and quickly digest content. This layout option is a good choice for brands that need

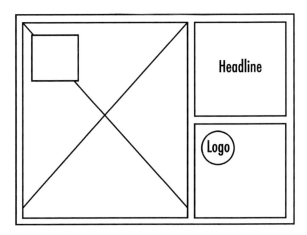

Figure 16.4 Example of an asymmetrical website layout style. Sample layout courtesy of Robyn Blakeman, University of Tennessee.

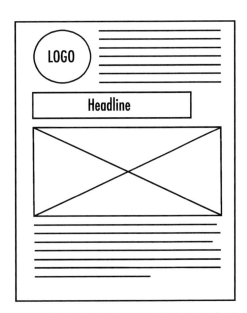

Figure 16.3 Example of a single column website layout style. Sample layout courtesy of Robyn Blakeman, University of Tennessee.

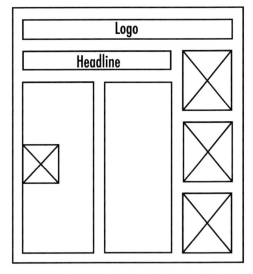

Figure 16.5 Example of a magazine website layout style. Sample layout courtesy of Robyn Blakeman, University of Tennessee.

to present multiple options that can be quickly scanned. See Figure 16.6 for an example of an "E" alphabet layout.

Zigzag

Like the "E" shape layout, the "Z" pattern also follows natural eye-scanning patterns. This pattern uses well-placed visuals, headlines, subheads, the logo, and/or call-to-action buttons and/or boxes to successfully alter traditional eye-flow patterns. It's a pretty simple layout option: Envision a "Z" superimposed on the page. Place the components you want the reader to see first to the left and along the top of the "Z." The eye will automatically follow the shape, but only if it has something of importance to stop on at each junction, ending with a call-to-action button. Placement of the logo or a call-to-action button on the lower right forces the eye back across the page. This layout style is best suited for micro sites or sites with little content. See Figure 16.7 for an example of a zigzag layout.

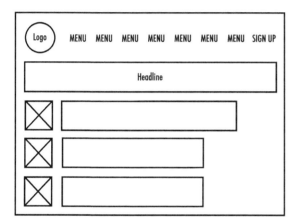

Figure 16.6 Example of an "E" or "F" website layout style. Sample layout courtesy of Robyn Blakeman, University of Tennessee.

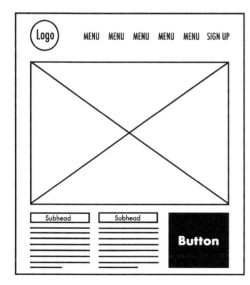

Figure 16.7 Example of a zigzag website layout style. Sample layout courtesy of Robyn Blakeman, University of Tennessee.

Gallery or Grid Cards

Gallery cards hold clickable information. Instead of cluttering up a site with a lot of scrollable copy, gallery cards hide the copy under multiple clickable visuals. These small visuals, often accompanied by a short caption, help visitors locate the content they are interested in by clicking or tapping (mobile) the image. Grids can vary in size, shape, spacing, and number of columns. This layout style is great for sites that need to display a large amount of visual and verbal content that is equal in importance. Pinterest and YouTube are great examples of ways to use this style. To ensure unity on the page, you must have at least six to eight images so they create a pattern; be sure the amount of white space appearing between visuals is consistent. Too much space makes browsing more cumbersome, but more viewable. Less space allows for faster scans and more opportunities to overlook content. For a little more flash, the gallery images can be animated to increase time spent with the message. See Figure 16.8 for an example of a gallery- or grid-card layout.

Split Screen

This layout style uses a single screen that has been cut into two separate but equal segments. This layout style is a great choice for brands that have two equally important pieces of content that you want to showcase at the same time. This is a very static layout style and can often become too predictable and thus boring. One way to spice it up a bit is to incorporate links or animation. See Figure 16.9 for an example of a split-screen layout.

Boxes

This layout style, as the name implies, is boxy but clean. It typically features a larger horizontal box with two, three, or four smaller boxes, usually visuals, aligned underneath. Nick Babich in a 2017 online article entitled "11 Website Layouts That Made Content Shine in 2017" suggests, "connecting the boxes to tell a story. The larg(est) box can be used to showcase products while

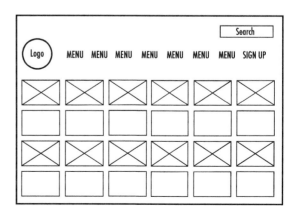

Figure 16.8 Example of a grid card website layout style. Sample layout courtesy of Robyn Blakeman, University of Tennessee.

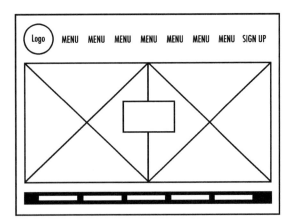

Figure 16.9 Example of a split screen website layout example. Sample layout courtesy of Robyn Blakeman, University of Tennessee.

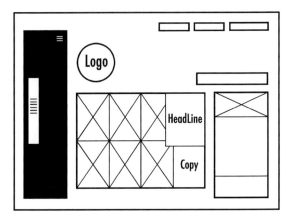

Figure 16.11 Example of a fixed sidebar website layout style. Sample layout courtesy of Robyn Blakeman, University of Tennessee.

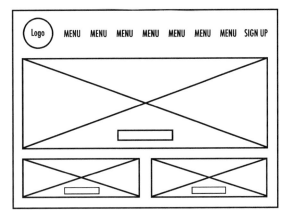

Figure 16.10 Example of a boxes website layout style. Sample layout courtesy of Robyn Blakeman, University of Tennessee.

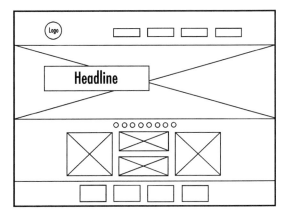

Figure 16.12 Example of a dominant website layout style. Sample layout courtesy of Robyn Blakeman, University of Tennessee.

the smaller boxes can offer further information on the product." See Figure 16.10 for an example of a boxes layout.

Fixed Sidebar Navigation

Since you have to have navigation devices on every page, why not make it a part of the design? This layout style doesn't eliminate the top horizontal navigation bar but instead adds an additional fixed sidebar to the design. These navigational tools are typically vertical and can be placed on either the left or right side of the page and will always remain visible and handy. This option is great for sites that do not require a lot of navigation options. Beyond standard menu items, they typically contain links to news items, social media, contact information, and podcasts or blogs, to name just a few. See Figure 16.11 for an example of a fixed-sidebar layout.

Dominant Visual

This layout style is very dramatic and eye-catching. If you want to capture your target's attention (and you do), feature one dominant image. Used to anchor the content, it can make

a strong first impression and encourage interaction. This is web design's show-*not*-tell layout option. Be sure the visual is relevant to what you want visitors to take away from the site. Videos can also be used to showcase content. This is a great option if you need to make an emotional connection or demonstrate something using sight, sound, and motion. Text is laid on top of the visual in the same way it would be if using a picture-window layout. Be sure copy is placed in a quiet area of the visual and is bold enough and has enough contrast to be easily read and understood. Be sure the image is relevant and of high quality. Don't forget to include an accompanying caption to reinforce the visual relevance. Often interactive, it is not unusual to find a link attached to this visual that will whisk the viewer away to additional content. See Figure 16.12 for an example of a dominant-visual layout.

3D Screenshots

This modern-looking layout style tops the page with a headline and then showcases visuals in unique ways. For example, when the

182

visual is moused over, it might appear to lift off the page, or may even feature a slideshow. This clean but complex layout style is most often used by big brand names that focus on an individual product. See Figure 16.13 for an example of a 3D-screenshot layout.

Thumbnail Gallery

Use this layout style when you have a lot to say but you want to corral the information by topic. Each thumbnail shows a headline, a small amount of descriptive copy, and representative visual. The layout is reminiscent of a manila folder that, when opened or clicked on, will offer up a larger amount of content, and is best used when you have four or more topics you need to bundle. The "thumbnails" are laid out in a grid with an equal amount of gutter space between each content box. This very clean and orderly-looking layout style is best suited for travel sites, blogs, magazines, and financial companies. See Figure 16.14 for an example of a thumbnail-gallery layout.

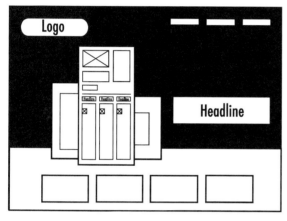

Figure 16.13 Example of a 3D website layout style. Sample layout courtesy of Robyn Blakeman, University of Tennessee.

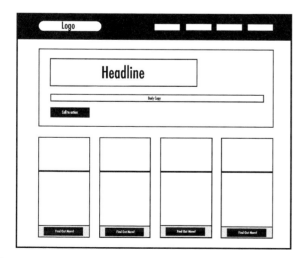

Figure 16.14 Example of a thumbnail website layout style. Sample layout courtesy of Robyn Blakeman, University of Tennessee.

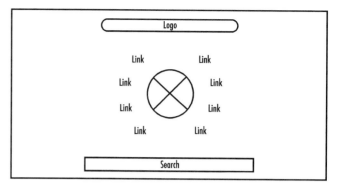

Figure 16.15 Example of a radial website layout style. Sample layout courtesy of Robyn Blakeman, University of Tennessee.

Radial Symmetry

This layout style is rare, but visually interesting. Radial symmetry uses a central point, usually a visual, where relevant type captions equally spaced, circle around or radiate out from the central image. See Figure 16.15 for an example of a radial-symmetry layout.

No matter which layout style or combination of styles you choose, it should ensure content is readable, legible, informative, and creatively presented.

Breaking Down the Parts of a Website

Every site will have specific categories or subject heads where specialized information will be placed. Depending on the website's overall function, these categories will vary between sites. Most sites will include the following categories:

- Home page
- Navigation
- Menu options
- Links
- Text-only format options
- News releases or relevant news items
- Blogs
- Frequently asked questions (FAQ)
- Banners
- Contact or customer service options
- Back button

Home Page

The first page of a website is known as the *home page*. The home page is a brand's headshot and resume; it should introduce, support, or promote the corporation, and/or the brand, and include any information that will strengthen and clarify the brand's identity. The design should directly address and reflect this identity. Typically, a home page will showcase a single dominant visual, a headline, a navigation bar, usually both top and bottom, as well as contact information.

Navigation

Navigation's purpose is to assist users in finding the information they seek. Navigational tools can be either text or graphics that assist the viewer to locate specific topics or sections, and move easily around the site. It is important when working with lengthy amounts of copy and/or multiple pages that the bottom of each page have a list of page numbers the target can click to jump around the page or site. It is important these little links always appear in the exact same place on every page. Buttons labeled "home," "next," "previous," and "help" are the most common navigational tools.

UX and UI designers will have the most input into what type of navigation should be used. Options are typically determined during the site-mapping process. Designers can note on the wireframes what type of interaction will happen when the menu is hovered over and clicked. The design of the navigation options should remain simple and have high contrast from other design elements on the page. It is important that it remain consistent throughout the entire site, all of which should be represented in the approved wireframes.

Menu Options

Menu options are the table of contents that will logically lead the target through the site. These navigational tools ensure the target gets to the specific section of the site they are interested in viewing and nowhere else. These commonly seen links are usually simple graphic bars that are located on the top or left side of the site. To avoid excessive scrolling, it is important there are enough menu options to quickly and easily move around the site.

Links

Simple interactive options, links are a website's roadmap to quickly and easily find information such as FAQs, product testimonials, endorsements, sponsored social media sites, chat rooms, any relevant surveys or tests, and customer-service options to name just a few.

Text-Only Option

Some members of the target audience many not have access to the technology or the patience to wait for image-heavy pages,

webisodes, or streaming audio or video to open. To offset this, be sure to offer a text-only option. A good substitute is to have creatively but informatively written copy that visually paints an imaginative picture for the target. This will also hold their attention if they do decide to click on an image, while they wait for it to load.

News Releases and Relevant News Items

A website is a great place to find additional information about a company and the brands it sells or services it offers. If the info is good and connected to the brand, it should be posted on the website. Positive news or feature articles, and any testimonials, reviews, or awards, help build and maintain image and promote quality.

Blogs

Many websites today contain a blog section for the brand. A blog can serve several purposes; it can be informational, educational, or as a pure entertainment option. The rise of inbound (consumer-to-brand) and content marketing has increased how brands are taking advantage of creating content to specifically attract consumers. Simply designed, website blogs typically contain imagery, and a headline about each post.

Blog interfaces should be easy to navigate. Color schemes should remain consistent with those used throughout the website. If a website does contain a blog (or other information that will be frequently updated), a *content-management system* should be created. A content-management system (CMS) is used by the agency/client to create and manage website content. The back-end developers will be the ones creating this, but the decision should be made early on in the website-design process. The CMS allows the agency/client to update/add information to the website in an intuitive way, rather than having to edit code every time a change needs to happen.

Frequently Asked Questions (FAQ)

Before the target calls or instant-messages customer service, answers to many commonly asked questions can be found in this section. When corralled in one place, the target can quickly find the answers they need to make an informed buying decision.

Banners

Banners are small ads that appear embedded on websites and other digital platforms. With a click of the mouse, a banner can transport a viewer to the sponsored web page. These mass-media Internet vehicles are usually found at the top and on the sides of web pages. In its simplest form, a banner is nothing more than a brightly colored, rectangle, that shows the logo and a small amount of type. *Skyscrapers*, or vertical banners are available, but a rarer option. Banners with a little more "flash" include moving or blinking images that both annoy and attract attention. These types of banners are a strong reminder that just because it can be done with technology, doesn't mean it is a viable creative option. Ignore basic design principle at your peril. It is a very small step from cool animated images to a downright tacky one. The creative team should always be mindful of first impressions and ask themselves how a flashing banner will be perceived by the target.

The colors used in banner ads should remain consistent with the brand's color palette. The brand's dominant color is often used to create emphasis for the button. The logo should always be present in banner ads to promote brand recognition. Copy must be short and pushing only the key consumer benefit due to the banner's limited size. The call to action is typically located on the button and should invite the users to click-through. Visuals should stay simple and recognizable; many viewers will only quickly glance at banner ads. The best typefaces to use are still sans serif and like the website, kerning and leading should be slightly more open. Web-safe fonts are not a concern on banner ads since the ads will be exported as images. See Figure 16.16 for a banner example.

Animation can add to the success of banner ads, but if an animation is used, it should not distract from the central message. Animation can be visually shown in sketches and mock-ups of banner ads.

Contact or Customer Service Options

It is very important there be as many ways as possible for the target to contact a customer-service or technology representative, such as toll-free numbers, instant messaging, or via e-mail.

Back Button

When searching the website for specific information, there are times the target will need or want to return to the previous page. Make it easy to do by including a back button.

Finally, to keep eyes longer on the website, consider offering helpful services such as stock tips, weather forecasts, and sports scores. To make a site appear more personalized, you might also want a feature that welcomes the target back by name or that suggests current brands based on past-purchase behavior they may find of interest. These small but important initiatives often help consumers connect with the brand and increase the chance of an eventual purchase.

Technical Considerations

There are several uncontrollable technical considerations the creative team needs to keep in mind, including file size, resolution, and connection speeds. The size of a file can negatively affect the viewer's experience, so be sure to keep each page, file, and image size to no more than 40–60 kilobytes tops. It is also important to be aware of the monitor resolution the target may be using. It is crucial to choose a resolution that is common to both old and new equipment. Resolution is defined in pixels; the most commonly used include 640 x 480, 800 x 600 and 1024 x 768. A resolution that is on the higher end may not display all visual or verbal elements in the same way.

Another important design consideration is the connection speed of the end user. Not everyone has a high-end computer system or fast Internet access, so it is important to design for both the low-end and high-end viewer. Nothing is more annoying than having to wait for a site to load. Remember, a company's website is its online storefront; it is the first, sometimes only, impression many consumers will have of the brand or company. Graphic-heavy sites take longer to load than copy-heavy sites. Features such as streaming video and webisodes are great for demonstrations and entertainment, but should be kept short, be optional, and have a point.

Diversify Your Internet Presence: Additional Website Options

Creative seen online has grown and matured over the last several decades. Gone are the days of flashing only banners or annoying animation blinking and scrolling for attention in our peripheral vision. Today's advertising options are creative, informational, engaging, and interactive. To ensure engagement, all forms of

Figure 16.16 Example of a banner ad. Image courtesy of Madison Duncan, University of Tennessee.

Internet advertising must be clutter-free because simple ideas are more memorable, and promote some type of interactive component to hold the target's interest long enough to educate. Each medium will follow the design rules laid out for website development. Let's take a look at a few of the most notable options.

Microsites

Microsites are smaller, independent websites that act as a separate entity from the brand's main website. These individual or small groups of web pages act as a separate informational vehicle for the brand. They can be attached to the main website or be a totally separate site. Microsites can be used in a variety of ways to help a brand create the best user experience. Their role may be to highlight points from a current campaign, to target a specific consumer group, to tell a short story, or to encourage purchase. Some common examples are new product launches and exhibitions. Design of microsites follows the same rules as website design; however, they are simpler in design and content and are easier to navigate than a regular website.

Pop-Up Ads

Pop-up ads are separate windows that *pop up* on top of an open web page. These mass-media ads link the target to another site, much like a banner ad. The same design considerations used to create banner ads are used when creating pop-up ads with one major addition—the close button. The close button should be clearly visible and consistent with the industry standard (top right). If you hide the close button, you risk annoying visitors, giving them a reason to make a hasty retreat from the site.

Floating Ads

Similar to pop-up ads, *floating ads* are first to arrive when a website opens and "float" or "fly" over a webpage from anywhere from five to thirty seconds; these entirely block the window beneath and have the ability to take over a viewer's mouse for the length of the ad. These attention-getting but always intrusive (often annoying) ads will try to overcome their strong-arm tactics by featuring animation and/or sound.

Digital Coupons

Digital coupons are a great way to reach your target on the Internet and offer incentives online. Coupons may be redeemed on a website, or in a brick-and-mortar location, for advertised promotions or specially marked merchandise. Online, coupons are designed in the same way as print versions and are used to promote a sale and/or encourage an immediate purchase.

Streaming Audio and Video

Streaming audio and video is the Internet's version of traditional radio and television advertising. A static image or link can be clicked on and played back, creating a great opportunity to highlight testimonials, demonstrations, or to give the spokesperson or animated character a role on the website. It is important to keep in mind that it takes a fast Internet connection to run streaming audio and video combinations; because of a possible slow Internet connection, it is most commonly used not as a primary advertising tool but as an interactive supplement. An art director should sketch out the storyboard in the same way they would for a video or TV commercial. Once the client approves a storyboard, the art director will begin the process of hiring the production team.

Webisodes

A *webisode* is a short, original episodic web program that uses sight, sound, and motion to engage the viewer with branded storytelling content. They are often used to promote brands, introduce music, or publicize news events.

These very engaging forms of branded content keep the target engaged and thus coming back for more. The goal beyond an attention-getting device is to encourage the viewer to visit related YouTube channels, Facebook pages, or any other related touch points associated with the brand. Like streaming video, webisodes will require a storyboard and script before being produced.

Augmented Reality

Augmented reality (AR) places digitally created images over real-world images to create a three-dimensional holographic image. A promotional tool, its main job is to engage the target in another type of interactive activity. To use, the target needs access to a built-in webcam and be able to download a software application or browser plug-in. This is a great option to capture and hold the attention-challenged, distracted, advertising-avoidant target. It offers the target an engaging, interactive, memorable, and shareable experience via either word-of-mouth or virally.

Search Engine Marketing

When brands pay a search engine such as Google, Yahoo or Bing to place their websites first or towards the top in keyword searches, it is known as *search engine marketing* (SEM). This top placement basically improves the chance the site will be clicked on and visited. Sites that employ *search engine optimization* (SEO) will ensure there are relevant links to other sites to increase engagement and further inform. Search engine marketing is tied to the target's interests, making it very effective.

Pay-per-Click Advertising

This advertising option uses simple text-only ads that are strategically placed on multiple popular websites. *Pay-per-click's* only job is to entice the target to click on the ad, where they will be immediately taken to the sponsoring website.

Interactive Television

Interactive television is a mixture of computers, television, and the Internet. Traditional television advertising that features a link lets the target respond directly to a commercial message seen on their television screen by clicking on the link using their remote control or a keyboard. They can then either purchase the item or share information with other viewers, using either their mobile phone, tablet, or via social media.

Interstitials

Interstitials are the ads seen in the main browser between two pages of a website. When the target clicks on a link, these ads will appear. Instead of going to the linked page, there is a quick stop on another advertising page. Upon arrival, the target can stay, and click on any of the additional links that will whisk the target off to the advertiser's web page, or they can wait approximately five to ten seconds to finally be taken to the page originally requested. The click-through rate for these types of ads are very high and are great options to further reinforce the brand's image. Internet advertising in all its guises is only the first interactive step a brand can take to engage with their target; the second is social media.

E-mail Marketing

Another way to electronically reach the target is through e-mail. Like other types of Internet advertising, *e-mail marketing* gets mixed reviews. When the target elects to receive e-mail advertising, it's known as *permission* or *opt-in marketing*. Typically, local retailers use e-mail to announce a sale, distribute a coupon, or some other type of discount. E-mail messages arriving without your permission is known as *spam*.

To keep viewers interested, opt-in e-mails have to be more than just copy. The average reader spends about eight seconds inside the e-mail, once it is opened. So the more fun an opt-in is, the better the chance for viral sharing of the e-mail with friends and family. One of the more creative options is *rich mail*, which is an e-mail ad that can include graphics and audio and video. When the e-mail is opened, it automatically links to an HTML page. Since it is usually opt-in, rich mail has a pretty good click-through rate. E-mails that are relevant and well designed make for a greater user experience.

Design for e-mails should follow the same standards as those laid out for web design. The best designs keep content narrow, when possible on one item. Copy can be longer, 50–150 words, because the target has chosen to receive the information. However, it will not be the copy that initially captures and holds the reader's attention, it will be the visual components, such as color, layout, and imagery. Color specifically can arouse both curiosity and annoy, so choose colors that are already associated with the

brand. It is also important to keep in mind your image-to-text ratio. Generally, you should devote 25 percent of your design space to visuals and 75 percent to text. Tacky is only a few key strokes away—to ensure your email marketing doesn't end up in the spam folder, avoid excessive use of red, of all capital letters, and of large text and symbols, such as exclamation points. Finally, all e-mails should contain a sense of urgency by providing a call-to-action or telling the reader what they should do next to receive the promotion.

A Quick Look at Experiential Advertising Options

Experiential marketing, typically associated with a live event, can be combined with the Internet to create an immersive experience between the target and the brand. Experiential marketing, also known as engagement marketing, uses physical or interactive experiences that set the company or brand apart from competitors by helping to create an emotional attachment to the brand. Although not a new tactic, it has seen a resurgence online, thanks to a multitude of digital interactive options. It is a great choice if you need to attract attention, create engagement opportunities, modernize a brand's image, and/or help make a brand's message more memorable thanks to a created experience.

Jerry Buckley in a March 26, 2020 online article entitled "What Does Experiential Look Like When Everyone is Online and at Home?" tells us that "Experiential storytelling and timelines are in play more than ever in this new online experiential world. Many experiential footprints work well as free-form areas to explore and get lost in, but the online world is typically more timeline-oriented and structured." When you can't or do not wish to go live, there are a multitude of experiential options, such as live broadcasts, Facebook, Instagram, and YouTube Live, as well as AR and personal VR.

Simple but interactive, consider the following example used by Planet Fitness. Thanks to Covid, they had to shut down their gyms. To ensure they did not lose contact with their existing clientele, they offered livestreamed workout classes that allowed their target to work out from home. To attract new gym members, they also offered these workout sessions to inquisitive nonmembers.

Because of its memorable interactive qualities, experiential marketing can be a relatively inexpensive way to build awareness, work as an excellent reminder option, update a mature brand's image, or help to memorably introduce a new brand in the marketplace. If choosing to use some form of experiential marketing, it is important it fits snugly with the brand's image, reflects the current campaign or brand positioning, and reflects the target interests and/or lifestyle. Thanks to its relatively inexpensive options, these online experiential experiences are limited only by the creative team's imagination.

Social Is about Promotion, Not the Hard Sell

Unlike traditional media vehicles, social media encourages a dialogue between the target and the brand as well as between consumers. It is consistently interacted with more frequently, and is more immediate and permanent than any other advertising medium.

A promotional vehicle, it is important to keep in mind that all social media sites are networking sites. This is not the place for hard-sell advertising tactics. Social media, also known as *user-generated content* (UGC) or *consumer-generated media* (CGM) is a great choice for increasing brand awareness, encouraging viral and word-of-mouth discussions, creating interactive opportunities between brand users, giving and receiving feedback, distributing promotional items such as coupons, and promoting repeat visits to both web and social media sites. Social sites are also great brand-building tools, outlets for consumer idea generation, and a means of identifying brand influencers, to name just a few. Additional opportunities include exposure to:

- Diverse promotional offers
- Customer service or technical representatives
- Diverse types of blogs
- Varied reviews
- How-to information
- Humorous or motivational stories
- Imaginative/creative product ideas
- Real time answers to questions
- Music or videos
- Debatable or controversial content
- Influencer posts

Social media is a major contributor to Internet marketing campaigns today. Brands are actively engaging with customers and creating content to increase engagement rates. There is no denying that the most critical factor to creating successful social media content is strategy and relevancy (the right people, the right message, the right time). Well-designed social media messages are vital for increasing the likelihood that users will interact with the message.

Social Media Design Doesn't Have a Lot to Say or Show

Design considerations for all social media platforms should mimic those used for website design. Keep the design simple and clean to ensure readability and legibility, use sans serif typefaces and increased kerning and leading, create a visual hierarchy with size, color, and/or placement, ensure there are strong contrasts, and use visuals only if they move the message forward. To take social media efforts one step further, consider adding some type of video. Sponsored videos allow the target to see the product in use. Visual cues help the target remember the brand at the time of purchase as well as help build loyalty. To promote the sites and build the number of followers, social media apps and hashtags should be showcased on all advertising material.

Because content will often be created for multiple platforms, it is important the creative team know the production standards for each site to ensure the visual and verbal message will post correctly.

Social Media Reaches Consumers from Many Different Venues

Unlike most forms of advertising and promotion, social media, is not forced upon consumers but is used by choice. It is certainly not a medium devoid of brand advertising, but relies most heavily on user-generated content to reinforce the brand's visual/verbal message. Consumers have so many diverse options when it comes to social media that it is impossible to cover them all here. So we will narrow our discussion down to some of the more demographically and psychographically diverse options, including Facebook, Instagram, Pinterest, Twitter, Snapchat, and YouTube. Let's take a brief look at what each one has to offer.

Facebook
Facebook is still a great space for brands to interact with consumers. The majority of companies have brand profiles where consumers can interact with and learn more about the brand. There are two major categories of content views on Facebook—organic and paid. Users view *organic content* though unpaid distribution (friends sharing, page followers) while *paid content* reaches its viewers as a result of advertising. Organic reach is considered more valuable to both the brand and the viewers.

What can designers do to contribute to exceptional content? First, they need to know where the target audience is interacting with the site. A general rule of thumb is that consumers are visiting Facebook on their mobile and tablet devices (there is the occasional exception). Visuals and videos need to not only stick to digital design basics but also create content that looks great on small devices. Short, engaging headlines and descriptive copy are significant to helping users decide if they want to spend more time with the content. Leading and kerning plays a smaller role on social media, since text is shown within the platform. However, if text is included in visuals or video, the kerning and leading should follow the rules for broadcast. Video content will be viewed on the application, but articles will link to the original source, such as through website blogs.

Having a presence on Facebook opens up opportunities 1) to have ongoing conversations with your brand loyal target, 2) to help build brand awareness, 3) to promote new brands, 4) to get feedback on current brands, and 5) for distributing varied types of sales promotions that encourage word-of-mouth and viral sharing, and initial purchase or repurchase of the brand.

Getting the target to repeatedly visit a brand's pages requires content that is less about the hard-sell pitch and some coupons, and more about being an active part of something exclusive, useful, and meaningful, such as the chance for access to exclusive content, insider tips, and information, and the chance to be the first to hear about upcoming brand launches, and/or play a meaningful role in providing feedback or ways to improve overall brand performance.

Advertising Options for Facebook and Instagram

Facebook offers a variety of advertising formats to successfully deliver the brand's message. Options range from ads with simple visual and/or verbal components to more complex and creative long- or short-form videos that are viewable on every device. Like other social media outlets, Facebook is constantly changing the types of ads brands can purchase for use. Currently, there are eleven major ad formats used by both Facebook and Instagram, including video, image, collection, carousel, slideshow, instant experience, lead generation ads, offers, post-engagement, event responses and page likes. Let's take a look at the specs for a few of the more creative options:

Video. Sight, sound, and motion will always attract attention— use them when you need to both show and tell something. Videos can run anywhere from 1 second to 240 minutes. For a more immersive experience, they also offer 360-degree videos. These videos provide a more interactive experience when users turn their device or drag their finger over content. Since research has found that most people view content with the sound off, it is important to use captions. Keep your text to no more than 125 characters. If the video is used as a link, your headline should have no more than 25 characters and the link description be no more than 30 characters. No matter which ad format is used, it is important that all images appear with the highest available resolution possible.

Image. This format is a great choice if you want to drive consumers to the brand's website with beautiful imagery. The best file types include JPEG or PNG with a recommended resolution of 1080 x 1080 pixels. Text recommendations will follow those used in the video format.

Collection. This popular mobile option creates interest by displaying an array of products sold by a brand that are personalized for each targeted consumer. Imagery can include static images or video that offer up a full screen experience. Headlines are limited to 25 and text to 90 characters or less.

Carousel. This ad format allows you to feature up to ten images or videos within a single ad, each with its own link. The ability to show so many visuals allows for more immersive storytelling that can be confined to a single image, or can be developed across multiple images. This format allows for longer headlines of 40 characters and text of 125 characters or less with captions for links topping out at 20 characters. See both video and image formats for additional specs. See Figure 16.17 for an example.

Slideshow. An inexpensive alternative to video, a slideshow format can tell the brand's story in detail, no matter the end-user's connection speed.

Instant experience. This format pretty much offers it all for mobile viewers: Full-screen visuals either static or video, swipe-through carousels, order forms, the ability to quickly view a brand's inventory and highlight lifestyle images with tagged brands. This format can be combined with almost all Facebook ad formats.

Offers. This is the format to use if a brand wants to give away promotional items. Offers can appear as a static visual, a video, or a carousel.

Event responses. Through static visuals or video, this option is used if you need to promote an event and drive responses.

Instagram

Instead of posting a boring cell-phone picture on Twitter or Facebook, Instagram gives the photographer a chance to apply one of their digital filters to it, transforming the image into something memorable and visually unique. Best used as a promotional tool, Instagram can help build new and existing brands and increase consumer trust. For small business owners, brands shown on the site can increase chatter and sales leads. It is also a great place for brands to employ user-generated content through photo contests.

Instagram has several ad options (identical to user options) such as photos, videos, carousels, and stories. Content on Instagram is uploaded via the platform and has a specific size, and resolution specs that match those used in Facebook. Instagram and Pinterest both use organic and paid options for marketers. See Figure 16.18 for an example.

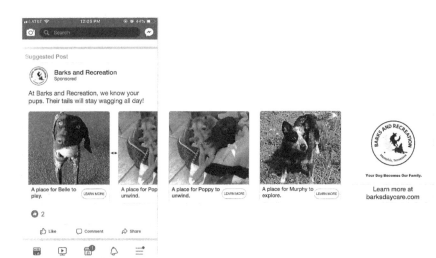

Figure 16.17 Example of a Facebook carousel ad.
Image courtesy of Tae Hargett, University of Tennessee.

Figure 16.18 Example of an Instagram ad. Image courtesy of Emily Harris, University of Tennessee.

Pinterest

Pinterest is a place to "pin up" photographs. This very visual bookmarking site allows viewers to share personal images or videos of images found online. As an advertising tool, it is a great way to show uses, options, or sponsored events. Like Facebook, visitors can "like" a pin, and follow or comment on a pin. To be successful, these mini-virtual showrooms must either solve a problem for the target and/or entertain them.

Pinterest has several options for advertising, such as promoted pins, promoted video pins, promoted carousels, and promoted app pins. Very simplistic and understated in appearance, promoted pins features a visual and descriptive copy. Promoted videos have very little copy; their job is to inspire consumers to engage their imagination. Promoted carousels can show up to five images allowing brands to showcase multiple brands or tell a more immersive story. Promoted app pins show multiple visuals and a small amount of copy. This ad format's job is to encourage consumers to download an app. Overall appearance and specifications follows Facebook and Twitter.

Twitter

Twitter is all about making a comment in 280 characters or less, although most advertisers still follow the old 140-character rule. Learning to write concisely and pointedly is a Twitter strength. Hashtags, pinned tweets, and social media influencers all help a brand increase sales, boost brand awareness, and improve customer service.

Twitter's ease of use makes it a popular vehicle for promoting more in-depth, word-of-mouth discussions. Additionally, one of its most important attributes to marketers is the insight into public opinion.

Thanks to the addition of visuals, content is even more shareable; the same digital design principles used on Facebook should be used for Twitter visuals. Like Facebook, Twitter has organic and promoted (paid) content. Videos will play on the Twitter platform, while content will link to external sources. The only design difference for Twitter is the suggested image size. Designers should check current recommended standards from the company (this changes with updates occasionally).

Constantly changing their offerings, Twitter currently offers ten different ad formats including plain-text Tweet, image-website card, image-app card, promoted video, single-image Tweets and GIFs, multi-image Tweets, video app card, video website card, conversational ads and direct message card. Let's take a quick look at the varied options:

Plain-text Tweet. Simple and to the point, this format allows 280 characters. For every link included in the copy, it will reduce the allowable character count by 24 characters.

Image-website card. This format uses a dominant visual and 50–70 characters. Image size is 800 x 418 pixels and acceptable file types include PNG and JPEG.

Image-app card. The only difference between this format and image-website cards is the available 280-character option.

Promoted video. Typically, video options run for 2 minutes and 20 seconds, with special dispensation given to larger brands to request an increase up to 10 minutes. Headlines or titles can be up to 70 characters with descriptive copy appearing under the video at 200 characters. File types include MP4 or MOV.

Single-image Tweets. Most commonly seen on mobile, single-image tweets can show up to 280 characters. Recommended file types include PNG, JPEG, or GIF, with an image width and height of 600 pixels.

Multi-image Tweets. Also common to mobile, theses mimic the single-image Tweets with the exception of their ability to show up to four images. Recommended file types include PNG and JPEG.

Video app card. Really the only difference to promoted videos is an option for downloading an app.

Video website card. Instead of a static visual, this option employs video. The specs for this ad option matches promoted videos and the format follows that of image app card.

Conversational ads. This ad format uses images or videos but also includes a call-to-action button with customizable hashtags. The goal is to encourage users to forward the message to their followers, further expanding the brand's reach. Specifications include Tweet copy of 280 characters and hashtags of 21 characters. Headlines can be 23 characters long and thank-you text can have up to 23 characters. Video, if used, follows the specs for promoted videos; image size should have a width and height of 800 x 320 pixels. Appropriate file formats include JPEG, PNG, and non-animated GIFs.

Direct message card. This format features a single large image, either static or video, and 280 characters. Its defining feature is the ability to chat with a brand ambassador. The call-to-action button will take up 24 characters and can feature an emoji. Specifications for video follow promoted videos and image-website card.

Twitter can be employed to improve and maintain relationships, to create an ongoing two-way dialogue between buyer and seller, or as a promotional tool. Its main focus is on interaction and building a brand's current target audience, initiating, building, or maintaining brand awareness, and encouraging the target to visit a website or brick-and-mortar-location.

Consumers who follow brands on Twitter want pre-promotion updates on brands before the launch, to be kept up to date with new technology or innovations, to get coupons, freebies, or trial offers, and to get advance notice on upcoming sale offers.

Snapchat

Snapchat, similar to Instagram is photo and video based. The same digital design considerations are needed for Snapchat. However, Snapchat has a different set of ad options available to advertisers, such as snap ads, 10-second videos with a swipe-up option, lenses, allowing viewers to make modifications to images, and filters, or customized overlays. The biggest difference between Snapchat and other social media options is that it pushes the use of augmented reality within its platform. Designers should check the Snapchat guidelines for additional help on specifications. Front-end designers should also check with back-end developers when designing interactive elements for Snapchat such as lenses.

YouTube

As an advertising vehicle, YouTube is a relatively inexpensive way, beyond initial production costs, to consistently entertain, educate, and influence the target, often without hard-sell advertising tactics. Many spots let the viewer know in an unobtrusive way who is sponsoring the video.

There are three basic types of YouTube Video ads: True-view ads, preroll ads, and bumpers. True-view ads are the standard type of video ad found on YouTube. They come in two types: Video discovery ads that show up on YouTube's home page, and In-stream ads that play before you watch the video you have selected. These ads often offer a skip option after the first five seconds. Preroll ads cannot be skipped and can run before, mid-roll, or after the main video. Each ad can be 15–20 seconds in length. Bumpers are the shortest of the offerings, running at just six seconds. These spots run before a viewer's chosen video.

Like television, the creative team will need to develop both a storyboard and script for ads seen on YouTube. Specs for ads vary (some have regional regulatory standards) and designers should check with internal teams on what needs to be built. The ultimate goal is to have the video go viral, where the target shares the creative content with their friends. There is really no way to guarantee any video will go viral, but to help it along, there should be no advertising sales pitch. However, it does have to be, if possible, all of the following—entertaining, creative, unique, and engaging—to encourage viewers to share it repeatedly with others within their social network.

Depending on the vehicles chosen, design for Internet vehicles can run the gamut from complex to relatively easy. The goal of all Internet marketing is to attract the target to the message with well-designed, informative, and entertaining content. Because all Internet and social media advertising is elective, it is important to remember that advertising will not reach the target unless they decide to interact with it. Because of this, it is important to keep both the design and content continually refreshed and reflective of both the brand and the target audience to ensure repeated interaction.

Bibliography

Babich, Nick. 2017. "11 Website Layouts That Made Content Shine in 2017." Retrieved from: http://theblog.adobe.com/11-website-layouts-that-made-content-shine-in-2017.

Buckley, Jerry. (2020). "What Does Experiential Look Like When Everyone is Online and at Home?" Retrieved from: www.emcoutdoor.com>blog>2020/03. March 26, 2020.

Content Marketing Institute. 2017. "What is Content Marketing?" Retrieved from: https://contentmarketinginstitute.com/what-is-content-marketing/.

CHAPTER 17
What Makes Mobile Work?

Chapter 17 Objectives

1. Readers will understand how mobile's interactive options help drive the target to the web or social media.
2. The reader will understand mobile's visual and verbal options.
3. The reader will understand the varied screen and app design options.

Always on Mobile

Mobile advertising, also known as *mobile-in-app*, the advertising seen specifically on smartphones, or *mobile geofencing*, location-based mobile advertising that reaches the target near or at the point of purchase, is a very sophisticated, technology-driven advertising vehicle that takes advantage of developing mobile capabilities by reaching out to the millions of consumers who see their smartphone as an extension of their personal and business personas. It's always-on, always-mobile, and always-accessible attributes make it a very attractive advertising vehicle for all types of brands. For consumers, it is the go-to device to easily get what they need when, and wherever they need it.

Mobile's major advantage is its ability to open up a channel between the brand and its target, by offering a diverse amount of personalized options. Smartphone use has completely changed not only the way consumers access information but also their consumption behavior.

Because these small screens can go with us everywhere, this creates both challenges and opportunities for the brands that use them. Successful mobile advertising must 1) deliver relevant and creative content that encourages the target to opt-in to receive messages, 2) deliver visual/verbal messages, and promotional and entertainment options that can be used across multiple and diverse platforms, and 3) find multiple interactive opportunities for branded entertainment to both educate and engage.

Options for reaching and interacting with the target are diverse and include (though are certainly not limited to) augmented reality, search, text messaging, banners, audio and video, animation, interstitials, coupons, location-based mapping capabilities, and gaming.

Creatively, whether a brand's mobile media advertising uses advanced technology, or features all copy, visuals, or video, it is important to push a personalized, relevant, and creative message.

Mobile Phones Make Life Easier

Mobile phones play a role in almost everything we do today. They have become one of the major ways consumers access the Internet, shop, play games, seek out entertainment options, connect with friends, and check out both the news and the weather, to name just a few uses. As consumers' constant companions, it has made reaching the target at the right time, with the right message, a whole lot easier for marketers. Not only is mobile consumers' primary search tool but, thanks to its built-in GPS (global positioning system) capabilities, the target can easily receive timely and geographically useful ads. Mobile's ability to reach those who have opted-in to receive messages, gives it the ability to reach the target with messages they are interested in. For example, they might receive a timely lunch deal or coupon from a nearby restaurant, or while traveling down an aisle at the grocery or drug store, when standing outside, a movie theater, the cleaners, a bookstore, or at a car dealership or toy store, to name just a few. This ability to access up-to-the-minute deals and the ease of instant purchasing are a driving force behind the success of mobile advertising. Mobile is a very diverse medium that can send, receive, educate, and personalize a message. Content sent to the target is relevant, timely, and often immediately advantageous, making the visual/verbal message appear as a brand loyalty reward rather than annoying spam or junk mail.

DOI: 10.4324/9781003255123-18

Strategy Is Built around Use

Thanks to the short attention spans and reduced patience levels of today's consumers, mobile advertising has to make the most of the first three seconds of the target's exposure to the message count. Be sure to give them what they came for immediately, before they click out and move on to another site that is easier to peruse and/or navigate. To ensure they stop, look, and/or listen to the ad, it must be pertinent, address their individualized interests and needs, and embrace the KISS principle (Keep It Simple Stupid)—or your message will be ignored, with your target happily remaining ignorant about what your brand has to offer.

Strategically, to ensure engagement and interaction with an ad, be sure the ad is correctly targeted. This means knowing your target and how they use their device. What do they search for? How do they buy? When do they use their device and where do they typically consume content? Placement, or where an ad is encountered, is also important. For example, mobile is especially successful when paired with social media since most do not find *native advertising*, or advertising that fits seamlessly into the user experience, intrusive. As a result, ads that are correctly targeted, informative, and creatively executed are more likely to be immediately shared with social contacts, increasing both the brand's reach and overall awareness.

To strategically ensure engagement, focus on using more images and less text, make the message a quick read by using larger text that can be easily scanned, consider where the target is when reading the ad and use it to your advantage, for example, simple ads for walking or waiting for the bus, longer video formats or interactive options when riding the bus. Avoid clutter, don't make the target hunt for information, be sure the website and ads load quickly and that any information surrounding the key consumer benefit leads off any visual and/or verbal stop.

It is imperative the search for information or the shopping experience be intuitive and as easy and quick as possible. For example, when a potential consumer sees a mobile ad for shoes, be sure when they click on the shoes it takes them directly to that specific shoe's landing page and not the brand's mobile webpage where they will have to waste time trying to refind the shoe, a cumbersome chore many will not bother with. Another option that does not disrupt the user-experience is to provide in-ad interactions that do not require moving the target to an additional landing page.

It is also important to provide some type of promotional incentive with the ad. The promise of free stuff or discounts is an effective way to get mobile users to respond to an ad. Finally, be sure to provide a tap-to-call phone number; this is the quickest way to help them find additional information, get questions answered and/or place an order.

Why Mobile Advertising Is a Good Strategic Investment

First, research has shown that consumers interact with diverse types of information more often from their smartphones than from their desktops; secondly, because the consumer is on the move, they are more likely to make an immediate purchase using their phone than they would when setting at their desktop. Because of this, an effective mobile advertising strategy is essential for a brand to compete in today's marketplace. It is an efficient way to not only reach the target but also engage with the target. It is interactive, offers 24/7 availability, and is an excellent choice when a brand wants to deliver an entertaining and always informative experience for the target.

Brands employing mobile will find it a great promotional device for increasing brand awareness, building or strengthening brand loyalty, and/or encouraging interaction. It is also a great vehicle for increasing both recall and response rates, increasing Internet traffic, pushing real-time promotions, encouraging visits to sponsoring websites, and making a quick and easy purchase. Apps that work over time delivering useful information, video or promotional material, or offer a game or two, will always be more attention-grabbing and memorable, creating multiple opportunities for word-of-mouth or viral sharing. Before we take a look at web options, let's take a more detailed look at the design options available for in-app designs beginning with the varied format options.

Design for the Mobile Screen

There are basically two kinds of mobile ad categories: Mobile web ads and mobile in-app ads. Mobile web ads are located in mobile web browsers in the same way they are in traditional web browsers. In-app ads, on the other hand, are seen inside the mobile apps consumers download. Formats include both video and display and offer creative teams a wide range of advertising options. The choice to use simple text and/or visuals or more sophisticated options will depend on the brand, the target, and the overall outcomes, or the reason for advertising.

In-App Display Ad Formats

Very diverse, in-app display formats offer creative teams a flexible way to reach their targeted audience. These formats typically deliver content that is tailored to the app as well as the target's interests. Most will include a visual, headline, and small amount of descriptive and/or actionable copy. The most commonly seen options include banners, text messages, push notifications, text and video, interstitials, native, rich media, and augmented reality.

Banners

Mobile banners paired with text links were the first form of mobile advertising and are still the most common. Banners are small rectangular boxes that can be either static or animated and found either at the top or bottom of the screen. The basic banner will show one or more of the following: A visual and/or verbal logo, a visual, a headline, and a link or call-to-action button. The most successful banner ads have a high amount of brand recognition. Big brands can make the most of a small space because they don't have to say much beyond a logo and tagline. Banners are a simple, inexpensive advertising choice that most consumers consider both crude and annoying. To make the interaction more memorable and worthwhile, be sure to offer some type of take-away, such as a coupon, recipe, game, or information on a contest or sweepstakes.

Banners are considered a passive, non-intrusive form of mobile advertising because they do not interrupt the user experience. Because of this, it also causes "banner blindness," where consumers are so used to them they don't actually see them.

Designs should be simple, subtle, and eye-catching, and devoid of any garish distractions. The best designs avoid using overly bright colors, an inordinate amount of text, or oversized and/or mediocre visuals. Messages should focus on the key consumer benefit and feature a clear and concise call-to-action. Measured in pixels, standard-size banners measure: 320 x 50, or 300 x 50 pixels. See Figure 17.1 for an example of a top placement banner.

Text Messages

Also known as Short Message Service (SMS), this is a simple, commonly employed form of mobile advertising. Its job is to dispatch both ads and promotions via text message that can conveniently reach the target at or near the point of purchase. These messages will often include a link where the target can download a promotion, or read about special sales exclusive to brand-loyal consumers. Brands that use this simple form of reminder advertising will find it flexible, measurable, convenient, and affordable.

Push Notifications

A push notification is a short mobile alert that is sent to a smartphone from an application to deliver important information to a mobile user who has opted-in to receive them. The goal is to not only inform in a creative way and encourage engagement, but to capture those short attention spans with a logo and a small amount of actionable copy.

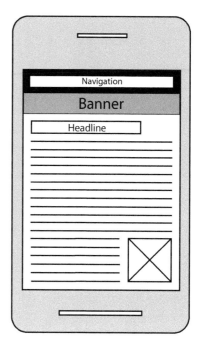

Figure 17.1 Example of a mobile banner.

Text and Video

Officially known as Multimedia Messaging Service (MMS), these are ads sent only to those who have opted-in to receive them. MMS builds onto the simple text message by adding images such as audio/video and photographs, illustrations, or graphics that can often be sent and watched in real time.

Interstitials

An interstitial ad is a full-page rich media ad that loads between page views on a site. These highly visual interactive ads appear during a content break within the app, such as when the app is loading or after the app is closed. The goal is to encourage the target to download the site's native app. These ads are brief and most display for no more than ten seconds. Almost all will have a skip or close option, or include a countdown clock showing how much time is left before the ad closes, and all require the user to click or swipe to navigate content. It is best that sites use no more than one per session, because they can easily annoy. The most popular interstitial sizes are 320 x 480, or 480 x 320 pixels. These ads are often colorful, attractively designed and can feature animation, photographs, or graphics, and a small amount of informational copy. See Figure 17.2 for an example of an interstitial.

Native

Diverse in size and form, native ads fit comfortably into app content. The goal is to ensure the ad fits seamlessly into the app's "native" content without interrupting the user experience. Though similar in appearance to banner ads, they

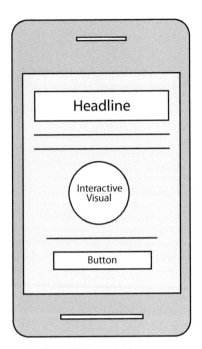

Figure 17.2 Example of a mobile interstitial.

Figure 17.3 Example of a native mobile layout.

don't take up additional screen space or automatically fill the screen space when opened. Users can still browse content while viewing the ad, but because of its native look and feel, it is not disruptive. Placement of native ads are contextually appropriate, making them very effective. For example, you might find a native ad for pet food placed in the middle of an article on pet nutrition. Viewers tend to treat the ads as additional content in their information flow, making them more likely to click on the ads.

Native ads mimic the look of the viewable content and can include text, visuals, and/or video. Because these ads are not considered intrusive or seen as a traditional advertised message, they do not affect the user's experience or user loyalty. Sizes vary but the most commonly used size is 320 x 480 pixels. See Figure 17.3 for an example of a native ad.

In-App Mobile Video

Popular, mobile video ad formats can successfully deliver engaging content that highlights a more in-depth level of storytelling. A typical video can run anywhere from 15 to 30 seconds, and can be tapped on to play or set up to automatically play when viewed. It is important these videos are of high quality, offer up meaningful information, and are placed at a natural junction in the target's interactive journey so they do not frustrate them and cause them to click out. Additionally, since most mobile viewers initially view video without the sound on, it is advisable they do not open up with the audio blasting. It is best to give your target the option whether to turn the sound on or not.

Video content can be either passive or informative in nature, containing no interactive options, or using an active format that allows viewers to click buttons on overlays and video player frames. Interactivity can be increased when videos use click-to-call or share-with-a-friend options.

Sizing deals with the overall aspect ratio of an image or the proportional relationship between its width and height. You will commonly see it shown as two numbers separated by a colon, as in 4:3 or 5:3. What does it mean for creative teams? It very simply converts to 4 x 3 or 5 x 3 inches. This is important to know because there are many different mobile and tablet screen sizes that video will need to be adapted for. You may also see sizing stated in terms of pixels—a full-screen vertical ad measures 320 x 480 and a horizontal ad measures 480 x 320. Laid out using storyboards in the same way as a television commercial, the most commonly seen forms of in-app video includes interstitial video, outstream video, and instream pre-roll ads:

> *Interstitial Video Ads*. Interstitial video ads are full-screen videos that pop up during any type of break within the app, such as after completing a game. These attention-getting ads fill the screen and are an ideal option for delivering a detailed storyline.
>
> *Outstream Video Ads*. These ads are placed within content such as between images or paragraphs of copy. They are not activated by tapping but play automatically when the ad becomes viewable on the user's screen. Since it takes

the decision making away from the viewer, they post high viewability rates.

Instream Pre-Roll Video Ads. These popular videos can play before, during, and after a video seen within the app's native content.

Rich Media

Rich media can be either an interactive or non-interactive ad that includes one or more of the following: Streaming audio and/or video, animated GIF, or some type of user interaction that requires input other than clicking or tapping, such as an accelerometer, camera, or GPS, to name just a few. Because of its advanced options, these ads tend to be very creative, interactive, memorable, and sharable. Sizes include XXL expandable—320 x 50 pixels, XL Expandable—330 x 50 pixels, Square Banner—300 x 250, and Full Screen Interstitial—320 x 480 pixels.

Quick Response Codes

One of the easiest ways for brands to share rich media content is through quick response codes. Quick response codes (QR) are another way mobile can be used to attract and hold attention, educate, and entertain. These simple little graphic squares hold an enormous amount of information. Activation requires two steps: 1) Photograph the code to immediately receive a text message, and 2) click the link. From there, the target will be taken to a web or social media site to see relevant images or videos, to download a coupon or recipe, view a webisode or podcast, view additional nutritional information, play a game, request a sample, or participate in a contest or sweepstakes. Available options will vary by brand.

For the consumer to consider the code relevant, it must include information that is unavailable at the point of purchase, for example, brand reviews, and product attributes, such as height, weight, range of colors, alternative uses, and purchase options, to name just a few. This commonly seen symbol can appear on almost any type of print or digital vehicle. Because of this, almost any type of brand, service, or promotion, can employ them, making them a viable advertising option. See Figure 17.4 for an example of a quick response code.

Figure 17.4 Example of a QR code.

Mobile Augmented Reality

Mobile augmented reality (AR), unlike that found on websites, is used more as an informal device than an entertainment one. Like other forms of mobile advertising, the goal is to capture and hold the target's attention longer by creating a memorable, interactive experience with a brand. Smartphones and tablets can bring images alive by using the built-in camera to overlay copy and/or advertising content on top of real-world objects.

Brands that incorporate AR in their advertising can extend the brand's visual/verbal message with unique and creative experiences that the target can share virally or through word of mouth.

The best mobile strategy is to include a combination of layout options to ensure the target finds and interacts with the one they most prefer. That is why a combination of display, video, native, along with interactive options are the most effective ad choices for reaching the target with a delivery method they are sure to interact with.

Social Media

Another sure-fire way of reaching a large number of the target audience is to combine mobile advertising with social media. The diverse sites available to consumers today are highly targetable. This very personalized way to reach the target allows brands to tap into the target's lifestyle and interests in a very meaningful way. When messaging is both informative and creative, it can also be easily shared with others creating strong word-of-mouth and viral opportunities.

Because both mobile and social media cater to an immersed audience, they are a perfect coupling, with research showing a higher return on investment than many other mobile advertising options. Native advertising is particularly effective when the two are paired together.

Type Design on the Go

As we have learned in previous chapters, type choices play a huge role in determining not only the level of readability and legibility but also the overall user experience. Using a typeface that is too small, too light, too decorative, or incorrectly kerned and leaded, can cause the reader or viewer to turn the page or click out. Let's take a look at the specialized rules surrounding mobile type use.

Typeface

Type may arguably be one the most important components of UX design. If the type isn't readable and legible, viewers will exit a site and/or app quickly. So it is critical to choose the right typeface and size, and employ the correct amount of leading and kerning. Web Designer Jeffrey Zeldman in a 2015 online article entitled "The Year In Design" tells us that "90 percent of design is typography. And the other 90 percent is whitespace," meaning the choice of typeface and overall layout of that space rule user experience. Since what you say digitally will be seen on diverse screen sizes, it's important to remember that what reads well at desktop size also has to scale down and be equally as readable and legible on a mobile device.

As discussed in Chapter 16, if a brand's typeface is not available online, you will want to choose a typeface that matches the brand's typeface and style as closely as possible. With that said, some of the most readable and legible mobile typefaces include Arial, Courier, Garamond, Georgia, Helvetica, Times New Roman, and Verdana. If you need a more unique-looking typeface, ask yourself the following: How many weights does it come in to ensure contrast on the screen? Is readability good based on the typeface's open x-height? Will the typeface scale well when viewed on multiple devices?

Finally, never use more than two typefaces in your design. Be sure they complement each other in look and style, such as x-height and character width. Avoid typefaces that don't have a diverse set of characters. For example, always compare how an uppercase "I", lowercase "l" and the number "1" appear when seen beside one another; they can often be almost indistinguishable, as with Myriad Pro. Also do a side-by-side check of the letters "r" and "n". Be sure you can differentiate each letter to ensure they don't mimic the letter "m" when placed to close together. Each of these readability and legibility issues slows down the reader. See Figure 17.5 for a Myriad Pro type example.

There are currently two categories of typeface used in mobile design: Custom and native. Custom typefaces are those chosen by the creative team that reflect the brand's image and concept. Native faces are those built into each platform, for example, iOS uses San Francisco and Android uses Roboto, and the differences between the two are negligible. San Francisco comes in two different styles: San

Figure 17.5 Example of Myriad Pro, showing letterforms without a distinct set of characteristics.

Francisco Pro Display, which is best used for any type sizes displaying 20 points or 26 pixels, or larger, and San Francisco Pro Text for everything else. Although you don't have to use a native typeface, it does offer the most reliable results across platforms. The choice to use a custom or native typeface will be up to the creative team.

Benefits of using a native typeface over a customized one include 1) faster download times, 2) they work across a wide selection of supported platforms, screen sizes, and resolutions, and 3) better readability and legibility at varied sizes. The downside of using either of course is the lack of customization for the brand.

Mobile Faux Pas

When choosing the best typeface(s) to use, be sure to stay away from any that are overly decorative or condensed. You don't have to ditch them completely, but just use them in small amounts. Due to size, it is also a good idea to avoid using any reverses except for call-to-action buttons. However, thanks to their larger size, it is permissible for headlines to be reversed out of visuals or background colors. Avoid under all circumstances placing body copy on top of anything other than a white background. The use of all caps, often considered a no-no in design, is an acceptable type design option in mobile, because most heads are short and sweet.

Type Size

Once you have determined which typeface(s) to use, you will next have to determine size. Determining type size in mobile design is a bit more complicated than other digital or print vehicles and will depend on the device used. Unfortunately, mobile needs to adjust for iOS and Android specifications, which of course are different. iOS sizes are based on point (pt.) size, Android devices use scalable pixels (sp.) or "sips" for short, and the mobile web uses pixels (px.). Not a big learning curve for the creative team since they will be turning it over to the back-end mobile designers.

The following type sizes are just a guideline for determining the optimum sizes for headlines, subheads, body, and detail copy.

iOS

- Headlines, 34 pt.
- Subheads, 30 pt.
- Body Copy, 17 pt.
- Detail Copy, 10–13 pt.

Android

- Headlines, 20 sp.
- Subheads, 17 sp.

- Body Copy, 14–16 sp.*
- Detail, 12 sp.

*The best size for body copy will depend on copy length. Use 14 sp. when you have a great deal of copy and 16 sp. when using smaller amounts of copy.

Finally, because space is limited on smartphones, it's important to vary both type size and weight to ensure an optimal amount of contrast on the screen and ensure an optimal reading experience. Although viewers can pinch or zoom to see content more easily, you don't want your target to take too many additional steps. For example, type that is too small requires zooming and text that is too big requires additional scrolling.

Leading
Leading should not be too tight on a small screen. The best rule of thumb is that your leading should be 150 percent of the type size. Copy that is single-spaced uses a line height of 100 percent, or spacing equal to the point size. Spacing of 1.5 uses a line height of 150 percent, or spacing equal to 1.5 times the point size. Copy that appears double-spaced uses a line height of 200 percent, or spacing equal to twice the point size. A good rule of thumb concerning the amount of white space to apply between components and paragraphs is to look at the headline size. For example, if the headline is 34 pts. high, the amount of space between the head and body copy should be 34 pts. You don't want the leading to be to open, which would require the viewer to swipe multiple times to see any content appearing below the fold, or the copy hidden by the opening screen's viewability size. The more they must swipe to view content, the more their patience is tested. If you're unsure of what to use, test it out for readability and legibility.

Kerning and Tracking
Since it is okay to use all-cap headlines in mobile design, it means you will have to pay more attention to kerning between letterforms. You don't want to get too tight, affecting readability and legibility; you just want consistent spacing. Tracking for body copy should be limited. The easier way to control spacing is by character count. For example, for body copy, the standard recommendation is to have no more than 30–40 characters to a line. This leaves enough white space in both the left and right margins to make reading easy.

Alignment
The best alignment for mobile body copy is flush left/rag right. Although all type can be set in this alignment style, to break up the page and increase white space, headlines and any subheads can be set center on center.

Call-to-Action Links
Make sure they stand out. The best way to do this is to place them in a colored box and be sure they are big enough to tap on.

White Space
As we have already learned, white space keeps a design from looking cluttered and improves both readability and legibility. As in all design, the amount of white space to be managed falls between lines of text, within the margins, around components, and between paragraphs. It is important to understand that an abundant use of white space also gives a site a more modern appearance, makes tapping easier, and keeps accidental clicks to a minimum. See Figure 17.6 for a mobile example.

Color and Contrast for Small Screens

Color is just as important in mobile design as it has been in all the other mediums we have covered thus far. Since mobile tends to be a more visual medium, there is a lot you can say with the color palette you chose for your overall design, images, and text. Because of this, it is important when placing headline type on top of a visual or dark color, for example, that the contrast be strong so as not to adversely affect readability and legibility. To minimize a cluttered look, try to keep this overlapping of color-saturated elements to a minimum, if not avoiding it all together.

Choice of color palette should begin with the colors currently being used by the brand. Keep the number of colors used to no more than two. Give the design contrast by using varied tints and shades of your main color and by altering the size and weight of the typeface(s) used. Contrast is also affected by environment. A design viewed indoors under artificial light can more easily reflect even the subtlest contrasts. Outdoor lighting on the other hand, can make it much more difficult to view what's on the screen clearly if the design lacks strong contrasts.

Visuals Sometimes Have to Say It All

Thanks to the quality of today's mobile screens, visuals often will talk for the brand. The use of high-quality visuals is crucial, so be sure they are not distorted or pixelated in any way. To ensure this, be sure to display your visuals at 100 percent of size; in other words, don't overly enlarge or reduce them.

Mobile no longer needs to rely on tiny thumbnail images that only gave a viewer a small glimpse of the product. With just a click,

Created by Awesomed

Figure 17.6 Example of Instagram mobile ads. Images courtesy of Kaylyn Maples, University of Tennessee.

today's mobile shopper can easily see a detailed image of what they are buying fill their entire screen. Design options that heavily feature visuals include 1) image-led landing pages, 2) search results featuring large scrollable images, 3) image-only browsing, 4) click-to-enlarge imagery, 5) image-only product screens, 6) slide shows, and 7) static imagery with accompanying video.

Because you don't have a lot of room, be sure to only use images that are relevant to what you want your target to know. Since users respond to visuals faster than text, it is important the visual has something to say. It must clearly help move your storyline along; if it does not, leave it out.

The choice to use photography, illustrations, or graphics is a contextual one. Photography is a great way to showcase details, reflect reality, and tell a more complicated story. Illustrations and graphics are a great choice for showing more abstract concepts. The choice of imagery used directly reflects the concept employed; if you're talking about it, making a comparison or demonstrating use, show it through photography. It is best to limit the focus to a single item when possible, avoid crowd shots, and use images that are singularly focused. If you want to create a more imaginative storyline, use graphics or illustrations. Don't crowd any type of image. Be sure there is an ample amount of white space surrounding it to help make it stand out even more.

Finally, it is important to understand that a well-executed product image is what actually sells the brand. Copy is helpful,

but consumers need to see what it looks like in order to imagine wearing it, or seeing it in their home.

Be sure your primary image is visible above the fold; don't make your target scroll, or have their first impression of your brand be of a partially viewable visual.

As we have learned, visuals are often your brand's first impression. They must be of high quality and of enough interest to your target to entice them to click on the imagery. Once clicked on, that image will take them to a landing page. A *landing page* is a single web page that opens after the viewer clicks on a search result or online ad. The best ones stop attention, demand an action, and get a conversion. These pages typically focus on a single call-to-action and showcase clean design and simple navigation. The best landing pages are developed around the user experience and nothing enhances this experience more than imagery. What they see will reflect their overall impressions of the brand and the site. Mobile is very much a show-don't-tell vehicle, so make sure your imagery talks to the target about something they are interested in. The images don't have to say it all, but they should reflect the overall message. Be sure they are correctly placed within the design. The more important the visual to the main storyline, the more dominant it should be. Supporting visuals should be smaller, so the layout does not appear cluttered or slows down loading time. Be sure the main visual grabs attention. The more unique, or emotionally powerful in appearance, the more memorable it will be.

Headlines, Subheads, and Body Copy the Mobile Way

Headlines still rule in mobile and still are responsible for screaming out the key consumer benefit. The largest piece of copy on the screen, they can be set in bold and with initial caps to stand out, or for the first time in all caps, since most mobile headlines are short and sweet. The goal is to keep them no longer than three to five words in length.

Technically, there are no subheads in mobile, just varying sizes of headlines. A good rule of thumb is for any secondary headlines to be about half the size of the headline to stand out from the body copy. They can be bold, but because of their small stature avoid using all caps.

Mobile copy needs to be captivating but succinct; there is not a lot of room for long, visually descriptive storylines. Good copy, no matter its length, should quickly connect the brand and the benefit it provides to the target's lifestyle to encourage the target to read on. The more abbreviated the copy, the more clever and colorful what is said needs to be. You can't say it all without testing the patience of your viewer, so cut anything that is not relevant without sacrificing clarity. If something is needed to help them make a decision, leave it in. To make scanning easier, think about using bullet points to make reading faster. Don't ramble on; keep sentences and paragraphs short. No one wants to scroll for days through a long block of copy to figure out what you are trying to say. Focus copy on the key consumer benefit. It is especially important to keep headlines short, for example, a ten-word headline can end up being six to seven lines long, and you do not want your target to have to scroll just to finish reading it.

The more compelling the copy, the more likely it is to persuade the target to take an action, such as purchase. Copy must clearly state the key consumer benefit and include a dominantly placed call-to-action. The more engaging the copy, the more likely the target will go through the series of visual and verbal steps required to complete the desired call-to-action.

This may seem a given but be sure to use a single-column format. There is no room for multiple columns, and they can be confusing and junky-looking when encountered.

Since mobile is a scaled-down retail ad, be sure it features the price prominently, along with any purchase options such as sizes or colors. It is also important to prominently feature any incentives offered above the fold to encourage purchase.

Incentives are a proven way to get conversions. They can be anything from offering free shipping, a coupon, or showcasing limited time offers. The key is to not hide them in the ad. Make sure they are large and appear either in the headline or an overhead subhead.

Be sure the call-to-action is prominent and simple. Place as much white space around the button as possible and place it in a central location to ensure it can be easily seen. You can draw more attention to the button if it is placed in a contrasting color that stands out from the background and surrounding imagery. The text placed on the button also is important—think action-oriented, such as "Learn More" or "Buy Now."

Finally, every ad needs to include detail copy, especially contact information, to assist the target with quickly getting an answer to any additional questions they may have. To encourage a quick purchase, be sure to include a streamlined order form, which is easy to fill out.

What Can Go Wrong?

In short, pretty much everything—but there are a few things you can look out for to ensure a positive user experience for the target.

- *Keep Typefaces to a Minimum*. It is okay to use a native typeface. If you want a more expressive look, consider going custom. Just remember less is more, don't use too many typefaces, sizes, or colors that will only end up cluttering up your design. Consider using a custom typeface only for emphasis.
- *Less is More*. Use only what you need to attract attention and visually and verbally get the message across. Keep the layout intuitive; you don't want the target to click out because they are overwhelmed or frustrated by inconsequential information.
- *Consistency Counts*. Don't try to be clever by changing up call-to-action buttons or navigation options. We are creatures of habit, and repetition keeps things moving. Anything consumers have to relearn takes time; they may not want to invest. As in all design, be sure to keep the layout, color, and tone of the copy consistent.
- *Key Consumer Benefit*. Push it first. Understanding the hierarchy of what you want to say will help ensure the viewers respond in the way you want them too. The dominant visual and/or verbal message you want to push can be further emphasized with type size, color, visual scale, and placement.

- *Navigation*. Be sure all links and call-to-action buttons work and are easy to find and click on.

The Mobile Web Is Not Your Desktop's Web

The visual and verbal look of a mobile webpage is vital to the success of any mobile strategy. Webpages designed specifically for desktop will look very different on a mobile device. Desktop sites are typically too heavily encumbered with text and visuals to be optimally reproduced on a smartphone. To avoid chasing off the target with an overwhelming amount of clutter which is hard to read and navigate, the design needs to be simplified.

Research shows that more and more consumers are turning to their smartphones over their desktops for web searches. Because of this, many businesses are moving toward mobile-first development, where software developers design a brand's website to visually and verbally look optimized on a smartphone screen. A mobile-first site will use a greater amount of white space, minimal text, place a greater amount of emphasis on visuals, and highlight an immediate call-to-action option that features some type of incentive. A streamlined design is not only accessible on a number of mobile devices, but is easy to read and navigate, and produces a more positive experience between the brand and the target.

When developing a website specifically for these mobile vehicles, keep the following in mind: 1) Mobile users read less than desktop users, so keep the delivery simple, 2) be sure load times are as fast as possible—consumers have less patience on mobile devices than on desktops, and 3) prioritize usability with call-to-action (CTA) buttons that are easy to find and tap.

Designing for the Mobile Web

Design choices for mobile rely on 1) how and where the device is used, 2) connectivity issues, 3) screen sizes, and 4) the number of device features, and their limitations. Mobile phones are used for more than making a simple call; users can send and receive texts and e-mails, search the web, and play games. Let's take a quick look at some of the mobile webs diverse properties.

The Simplified Mobile-Friendly Web

Websites seen on a smartphone's small screen must be mobile-friendly or easy to use. All content, images, videos, and texts

must be viewable under varied conditions. At its most complex level, mobile-friendly means using all the bells and whistles that come on a smartphone to deliver an effective and positive user experience.

For the design of a mobile website to be successful, it must understand not only the type of visual/verbal content that will be displayed, but how it will be employed across devices, and of course, its smaller viewable size. The question of how much content to bring over from a brand's traditional website will depend on how the target will use the site.

So the first thing the creative team needs to think about before designing a mobile website is: How does the target use the web? What features do they search for? What type of device will they use to view the site?

Understanding how the site will be used by the target is critical. Most will use the mobile web to find something they need or want *fast*, such as to make reservations, view a menu, check pricing, or get directions. Because of this, the design needs to not only make information easy to find, but it should also limit the number of taps it will take for the consumer to find it to no more than three.

It is also important to know what features are important to the target and what features they find frustrating when using mobile websites. Do they prefer informative text or visual options, video demonstrations, or will they interact with some form of rich media content?

Finally, what type of device(s) do they use when accessing the mobile web? This places an enormous emphasis on context. *Context* is all about the environment in which content is viewed. Since most consumers use their device on the go, speed and ease of use will be a priority, as will be the need for designing a graphic yet straightforward and stripped-down site that focuses on a streamlined experience. Understanding overall use will help the creative team determine what needs to be included on a site and what can be left out.

Thanks to the diverse types of mobile phones, to save time and money it is advisable to start out with a design that can work on as many different types of devices as possible. Do not get too creative with either content or overall look of the site. An appearance similar to what the target would see on a desktop version will avoid confusing the target.

Designing Your Website for Multiple Screen Sizes

Designing with multiple screen sizes in mind is a key factor in the delivery of a mobile website. It is critical that the design focus on the overall user experience. It is the look and ease of use that determines whether the target will stay on a site or click out in frustration. To address the diversity of sizes, creative teams can choose between using either a responsive or adaptive design.

Responsive design automatically reacts to changes in screen size by adjusting the placement of both visual and verbal design elements to ensure they fit in the available space. This type of design is very fluid, meaning users can access and peruse a site no matter whether they are using a desktop, laptop, tablet, smartphone, or watch. For this to work seamlessly, responsive design requires a strong layout and an in-depth knowledge of how the target consumes information.

Alternatively, *adaptive design* uses multiple fixed layout sizes, making it not only more expensive but more time-consuming to produce. It is not unusual for a layout displayed on a mobile website using adaptive design to look entirely different from its desktop version. This happens because the creative team has chosen to use a different layout for each mobile screen rather than allowing one design to automatically reposition itself for multiple devices. Today, teams using adaptive design typically end up developing up to six different layouts to fit the most commonly used screen widths: 320, 480, 760, 960, 1200, and 1600 pixels.

So which design style works best? Well that depends on how much control you want to have over the final design. Responsive design is easier, cheaper, and takes less time to develop. However, the brand loses control over the final look of the design by screen size. Adaptive design will typically ensure the best user experience according to which device the target is using. Where responsive designs flow between devices, adaptive design offers custom-made design solutions.

Are Brand-Centric Apps Necessary?

There are two ways to end up on a brand's site, through a web link or via an app. Apps require brand-loyal members of the target group to take the extra step of downloading the brand's app or application. If you want to create a more personal and focused experience, apps are a great choice. An app is warranted if a large number of the target audience will go to the site directly and often. If they arrive at a site via a shared link, an app would be repetitive since they will visit the site whether they have downloaded the app or not.

Designing for a New Digital Medium

The visual/verbal design for mobile devices will closely mimic those learned in the discussion of traditional desktop website

design covered in Chapter 16. In this section, we will cover only the significant differences that must be considered when designing for the mobile web. Creating a user-friendly experience is critical when designing for mobile. Users expect pages to match the integrity, quality, and performance the brand projects elsewhere.

Let's start out by looking at the differences between desktop and mobile sites. There are five main differences between the mobile and desktop experience.

Probably the most important difference is the minimal amount of space there is to work with when designing for mobile. Say and show only what is needed to inform quickly. When laying out the design, be sure to keep the site simple, clean, and optimized for use on a mobile device. Mobile sites will offer a lot less information than that found on a traditional website. All buttons, links, copy, visuals, and videos will need to be resized to be usable. Size limitations, especially for smartphones, require all designs to use a layout. They are not only easier to read but are adaptable to readability in both portrait and landscape modes.

Secondly, and certainly not surprisingly, visitors are not as focused on a mobile site in the same way they may be when visiting a desktop site. Mobile users may be distracted by what is going on around them, or they may be multitasking. Interaction must be quick to hold their attention. Visitors to a site are not going to wait longer than three seconds for a site to open, so it is important to consider how a page behaves when loading, how rich media performs, and the waiting times between transitions. Additionally, to decrease download times, avoid using background images, keep the design simple, avoid using unnecessary visuals and graphics when possible, and give visitors an option to view any video content.

Always keep in mind that mobile web users are typically in a hurry. They are searching for something very specific that fulfills an immediate need. It is critical that navigation be kept simple. One click should drop the viewer off where they want to go.

If a visitor is interested in finding out more information or making a purchase, be sure order forms are easy to use. Sites that require viewers to fill out forms need to use a more simplified version than those found on a traditional website. First and foremost, keep them short. This is important, since half the page will be taken up by the on-screen keyboard. When longer forms are needed, break them up into multiple pages that take up only half the screen. Place a clearly visible, "next" button at the end to avoid the need to excessively scroll. Other easy-to-use options might include using radio buttons and lists that can be tapped in order to pick preselected options. Be sure any data entered or page screen viewed is savable for use in later visits, or readable at a later time by the target. It is also helpful to show the user a step they made has been accepted. You can do this by giving them some type of feedback when the function is complete, such as showing the button indent or by highlighting a box around it.

Finally, something rarely considered is battery life. Both smartphones and tablets have limited battery life and ramped-up processors, so the more the processor has to work, the shorter the battery's lifespan. Big drainers include location-based features, animation, and other varied types of rich-media enhancements.

Website Type Sizing

Type sizes for the mobile web are measured in pixels (px.). If you are designing a website that can be viewed on a smartphone there is only one rule: Your body copy can be no smaller than 16 px. Anything smaller on iOS browsers, for example, will automatically zoom in on the left side of the text, often blocking out the right side, and requiring the user to take the extra step of zooming out to see additional content. The following sizes for components are given only as a starting point; as in all design, type size will be reflected by the layout and overall concept. Guidelines for headline and subhead use are based on the level of importance given to the information.

> Headlines: 32 px.
> Subheads: 18–26 px.
> Copy: 16 px.
> Detail Copy: 12–14 px.

Navigation *Must* Be Easy

Do not forget about navigation devices; they should be easy to find and intuitive to use. The use of what's known as "sticky" headers and footers keeps navigation options in the same place throughout the site, making it easier for viewers to find what they are looking for. Be sure to put all call-to-action and search devices at the top of the site above the fold. It is important to remember that the opening page will be the first visual and verbal impression the viewer has of the site. It is also the stop that encourages them to go deeper into the site by clicking on some type of informative button.

The placement of navigation devices will depend on content. More comprehensive sites may place a menu link at the top and navigation buttons on the bottom of the screen to alleviate any unnecessary scrolling. To save valuable viewing space, still others may partially hide the menu until the user taps on it. Links can be

text only, or have an accompanying visual. Since scrolling cannot be entirely eliminated, it is simpler if it goes in a single direction, usually vertical. If you must include a horizontal swipe option, be sure it is clearly marked with an arrow. Simple visual instructions ensure nothing gets missed.

Drop-down menus are another option to help ensure the target can accomplish everything they set out to do when visiting the site. Most menus are located on the top right-hand side of the screen and remain hidden until tapped on. They help keep a site clean by keeping certain actions out of sight until needed. To make the small navigational buttons even easier to tap, increase the amount of white space around them. Small buttons and big fingers are not compatible. Be sure there is enough space to tap options, so the viewer is not frustrated by being taken to a place they don't want to go.

The acceptable tap size of any link (width and height) can range from 28 to 34 pixels, depending on the device. In its Human Interface Guidelines concerning navigation, Apple explains "that anything tappable should be the size of a fingertip," which translates to around 44 points wide x 44 points tall. A text link appearing within copy will also vary by device but usually measures around 14 pixels high.

Sites have a diverse number of navigation options to employ beyond tapping, such as double tapping, dragging, swipe to scroll, pinch to zoom in or out, and press and hold. It is important to remember when deciding the type of navigation device to employ, that simple and traditional will usually be the safest way to go, as it eliminates the need to learn new and often unnecessary techniques.

A Little Bit on Tablet Design

Tablet design is similar to designing for a website. First and foremost it must be easy to use, informative, and showcase relevant visual and verbal content. Go for clean and simple—battery time is limited.

Design must take into consideration that the target will use desktop, mobile, and tablet interfaces differently. For example, research shows that tablet users. unlike desktop and mobile users. prefer to swipe horizontally.

All design for digital devices is affected by resolution, screen size, and speed, so a one-size-fits-all space does not apply. For example, a tablet user prefers a full version of the site, but does not want to spend a lot of time zooming and pinching to continually see content.

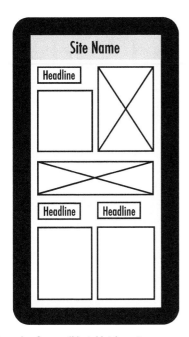

Figure 17.7 Example of a possible tablet layout.

Table 17.1 Table sizing options

Banners:	728 x 90 and 300 x 250	
Interstitials:	Half Page: 300 x 600	Full Page: 1024 x 768 or 768 x 1024
Native Ads:	728 x 90 and 300 x 250	
Video:	768 x 1024 or 1024 x 768	

offer the option to share any visual/verbal aspects with others via e-mail or social media. Many newspapers and magazines that are available on tablets also offer video options. See Figure 17.7 for an example of a tablet layout.

Tablet layout options match those used for the Internet. The major difference is sizing. Table 17.1 shows sizing options.

Mobile continues to dominate how consumers not only interact with a brand, but how they shop and ultimately purchase. Creative teams should always seek to design useable, cutting-edge, memorable and high-performing ads and sites. Designs that are clean, visually stimulating, easy to navigate, and optimized specifically for small screens, will hold the target's attention longer, and encourage repeat visits, shared experiences, and purchase.

Tablet design should use simple, clean user interfaces with large, well-spaced, easy-to-find navigational options. Visual/verbal elements that are set up in horizontal columns are preferred over vertical ones.

Tablets, like Internet design, blend print and digital qualities together. For example, layout follows a print format and type choice a broadcast format. Tablet users are looking for immediacy, but also want to be able to easily "turn" pages, have a clearly designated final page, and the ability to see several, but not all, stories or categories at once. All digital aspects should be able to update users in real time, use diverse multimedia options, and

Bibliography

Apple. "Human Interface Guidelines." Retrieved from: https://developer.apple.com/design/human-interface-guidelines/ios/visual- design/adaptivity-and-layout/.

Zeldman, Jeffrey J. 2015. "The Year in Design." Retrieved from: www.zeldman.com/2015/12/24/the-year-in-design/.

CHAPTER 18

Campaigns, and Visual and Verbal Uniformity across Multiple Mediums

Chapter 18 Objectives

1. The reader will understand the role a campaign plays in delivering a comprehensive brand message.
2. The reader will learn how to develop a continuously uniform visual and verbal message across mediums.
3. The reader will learn how media choice affects both target choice and design decisions.

Putting All the Visual and Verbal Pieces Together: Campaign Development

Everything you have learned so far about design will come into play when developing a brand's advertising campaign. A *campaign* is a family of ads that deliver a synergistic, strategic, and cohesive collection of planned messages. It will use one unifying visual and verbal message that can be seen across multiple mediums or be contained within a single type of medium that promotes a single idea—your key consumer benefit.

Coordinated visual/verbal development is the backbone of any advertising campaign. Coordination requires that advertising seen in all media has a single message, driven by the key consumer benefit, and uses the same tone of voice, strategy, and common imagery. The coordination of these visual/verbal components ensures the message is louder and more memorable than any individual message could alone. It also guarantees that a cohesive, consistent message reaches the target. Messages that lack cohesiveness across multiple mediums are not memorable and they can confuse the target about what the brand actually stands for.

A brand may develop a campaign for any number of reasons but the most common include 1) initiating or building on existing brand awareness, 2) the launch of a new brand, 3) improving name/brand recognition, 4) promoting a new brand use, and

5) showcasing a reinvented or improved brand. Development for any of the above requires the use of a diverse array of media vehicles that not only reaches the target with the right message in the right media, at the right time, but also engages and informs, as well as promotes trial and/or feedback with interactive devices, such as taste tests, free trial samples, or coupons, to name just a few.

Informationally, the key consumer benefit will lay the foundation for the development of the campaign. Although it is possible for a key consumer benefit, if clearly stated and properly targeted, to uniformly fuse campaign pieces together, it cannot, however, create a lasting visual/verbal identity by itself. Creatively, to increase memorability and strengthen uniformity not only between ads but also between media vehicles, a campaign must also rely on the use of any number of repetitive visual and verbal cues, such as layout styles, typefaces and type styles, visual imagery, spokespersons or character representatives, color palette, package design, logo size and placement, headline and body-copy style, slogan or tagline, and/or a jingle.

Creating a uniform set of messages does not necessarily mean copying and pasting a visual and/or verbal component directly from one medium into another. Although single components can be successfully recycled between ads to create consistency, such as using the same headline attached to different visuals, it is often more attention-getting if copy and images build and expand from a consistent interpretive theme that is seen across mediums.

From a design standpoint, it doesn't matter whether a campaign's role will be a complex introduction or reintroduction of a brand, or a series of simple reminder ads. It is the creative team's job to isolate a multipurpose visual/verbal direction between what is said and what is shown, no matter how long or short the content, or its overall size and shape.

Finally, the development of a campaign is both expensive and time-consuming to produce, typically taking anywhere from

DOI: 10.4324/9781003255123-19

90 days to a year to complete, depending on the amount of research done to help determine what needs to be accomplished, the simplicity or complexity of the overall visual and verbal design, the brand's life-cycle stage, and the overall strength of the competition within the brand category, to name just a few key factors.

Creative Teams Need to Know a Lot More Than Copy and Design

As you have already learned, creative teams need to have a lot of knowledge about how to write and design for the diverse types of mediums used in advertising today. But before thinking about creative solutions, it is important for the creative team to know as much as possible about the target audience, the client's brand, and the competition.

First, it's important to remember that all advertising messages revolve around the targeted audience. The more knowledge you have about them, such as demographics, psychographics, behavioristics, and known geographic location, the better the creative team can customize the visual and verbal message to enhance the target's lifestyle or solve an existing problem.

Secondly, make sure you understand your brand's attributes, capabilities, and limitations. Ask yourself how is the brand currently perceived within the brand category? How does its current image affect what needs to be accomplished? Does the brand's image need to be strengthened or corrected? How many features does the brand have? How is it manufactured? Is it the same, similar to, or completely unique from competing brands? What is the quality of materials used, and how is it reflected in the price, packaging, store layout, and so on? The strength of the concept and overall design aesthetic will rely on your overall knowledge of the brand.

It is also important to know whether the brand offers some kind of actual benefit that competitors either do not have, or is not advertised as important. Savvy consumers today have multiple ways to gather brand knowledge together and compare product attributes, making purchase decisions about more than just price, or a creatively designed or produced visual and verbal message. Ultimately, they need to find a viable solution to a real problem they have. They want to know why they need this brand over competing brands? What problem can it solve? Are there any benefits of ownership? Is it easy to use? Where can it be purchased? What does it cost? Does it reflect my personal image? Knowing the answers to the questions before the target can ask

them will make the brand appear more relevant or helpful than the competition's brand.

Finally, to ensure the brand stands out both creatively and informatively, you must also know as much as possible about the brand's immediate competitors. Ask yourself what is different about your client's brand as compared to the competition? What is similar? Are manufacturing or overall results better, similar, or worse than your brand? What is the competition's reputation and/or image in the marketplace? What is their current slogan or tagline, concept or theme, and is there a noticeable difference between brands? Does the competition offer any additional accessories, or multiple colors or sizes? How long has the competition been in business? What are the performance differences between brands?

Knowledge is priceless when building a visual/verbal concept that must stand out from competitors' brands. Use this knowledge to build the brand's visual and verbal voice and overall image, and determine how the brand should be positioned. Once your research is complete, it is time to determine what media vehicles will best reach the targeted audience.

Reviewing the Promotional and Media Mix of Design

Before the concept is solidified and imagery and copy developed, the creative team needs to know about both the promotional and media mix the campaign will employ. The more they know about where the message will be seen and/or heard, the easier it will be to exploit each vehicle's attributes and deliver a unified visual and verbal appearance that fits snugly into each format.

As previously discussed in Chapter 1, the promotional mix includes any combination of public relations, traditional advertising, direct marketing and sales promotion, out-of-home and transit, Internet and social media, mobile, or alternative media options.

The media mix breaks the promotional mix down into specific media vehicles, such as newspaper, magazine, radio, television, direct mail, Twitter, event marketing, gaming, and so on. The use of a *concentrated media mix* places all advertising efforts into one medium, while an *assorted media mix* employs more diverse types of media vehicles. The type of media vehicle(s) employed will depend on budget, overall objectives, and the target audience to be reached.

To show and/or tell the brand's message effectively, the creative team needs to know where the ads will be seen and/or heard.

Once the creative team has digested the research and tentatively outlined the media options, the next step is determining the overall ties that will bind the individual ads together.

Looking for Uniformity in Campaigns

The typical campaign has three interrelated components that can directly affect concept development and appearance: Campaign uniformity, and visual and verbal uniformity.

Campaign uniformity means that the visual/verbal message is consistent across diverse types of media vehicles. *Visual uniformity* means that all images have a distinct look or style. This happens when typefaces, layout style, visual images, representative character representatives or spokespersons, slogans/taglines, and brand color combinations are exhibited on all pieces.

Each visual element employed should help the target see or experience the brand and the benefit it will bring to their life. Visual images can show the brand alone, in use, in a setting, or place it directly in the hands of the target. The types of images, layout style, and typeface chosen should help bolster the ad's visual/verbal tone of voice. Color choices should work to set a mood, and the purposeful placement of components within an ad can help define the overall brand image.

Visually when possible, try to do something unusual or unexpected. The most creative ads, no matter the budget or medium, say or show something unexpected. You might astonish with a unique visual or turn of phrase, or might find a way to combine the visual and verbal treatments together to form a unique graphic image.

If the brand has no distinguishing features or uses from that of competing brands, then the visual and verbal concept will have to set it apart. Brainstorm to develop and define a creative and unique approach that not only sets the brand apart based on intangibles, such as reputation, but also aids in further defining or strengthening its image. Another option to overcome repetitive features between a brand and its competitors might require a "big idea" that promotes a repetitive feature as unique. That should definitely get the creative juices flowing.

Maybe your brand of running shoes is not only good for a runner's feet and/or overall performance but also has a small pocket built in, perfect for holding a house key or small amount of money. If it is helpful and unique enough, your target will wear the shoes any time they need to be hands free.

Verbal uniformity is all about using a universal tone of voice to push the key consumer benefit across multiple media vehicles. The verbal elements, such as headlines, subheads, body copy, slogans or taglines, and jingles, should create a cohesive and consistent tone of voice throughout the campaign and across all media. A campaign's verbal message should be so intertwined that the consumer gets the feeling of continuity of thought from one ad to the next.

The choice to use a diverse promotional mix that spotlights the same verbal tone of voice and visual appearance increases its memorability with the target, and will help position the client's brand as different from competing brands.

The campaign's visual/verbal foundation will emerge from the creative brief. Before any concept moves forward towards final development of the visual and verbal message, it must encompass and accomplish each of the following:

- The campaign concept is driven by the key consumer benefit in the form of either a big idea or unique selling proposition (USP).
- Strategically, every ad must both visually and verbally work together to accomplish the stated objectives.
- It is imperative every message used in the campaign speaks directly to the target about how the brand can solve their immediate problem.
- All visual/verbal messages no matter the media, employ the same strategy and tone as laid out in the creative brief.
- The overall visual and verbal concept is expressed through one or more of the following: A key consumer benefit-driven idea, layout and/or headline style, visual theme, typeface and style, and/or color use.
- The campaign's overall visual/verbal identity is clearly recognizable in all advertising and promotional pieces, no matter the size or shape of the media vehicle.
- To set the brand off from the competition, the overall concept needs to create and successfully promote a unique brand identity.

The more knowledgeable the creative team is about what needs to be accomplished before the start of the design phase, the more the brainstorming phase will be about unearthing unique, memorable ideas.

To help you determine whether your campaign is consistent across all media and has all the required elements, see Template 18.1 for a campaign checklist taken from *Integrated Marketing Communications from Idea to Implementation* that will help you ensure you have included everything you need to ensure a successful campaign.

Template 18.1 Campaign design checklist

1. _____ Does each ad clearly state the key consumer benefit?
2. _____ Does the campaign's message talk to the target in a language and in a way that holds their attention?
3. _____ Does the campaign's message address and answer each stated objective in the creative brief?
4. _____ Is the relationship clear between the key consumer benefit, the headline, the body copy, and the visuals?
5. _____ Does each ad or promotion's visual and verbal image match the tone, approach, and appeal stated in the creative brief?
6. _____ Does the layout style chosen reflect the strategy and overall visual and verbal style?
7. _____ If a jingle was created, do the music and words reflect the concept and overall strategy?
8. _____ Is the concept as strong visually as it is verbally, no matter what medium it appears in?
9. _____ Is the concept unique to the brand, and does it clearly position itself away from the competition?
10. _____ Does the copy's tone of voice match that stated in the creative brief?
11. _____ Does the first paragraph of the body copy continue the key consumer benefit discussion begun in the headline?
12. _____ Does the middle paragraph(s) of the body copy give enough information about the brand to understand what it is, what it does, and how it will affect the target's lifestyle or solve their problem?
13. _____ If using a support statement, did you remember to include it in the body copy?
14. _____ Does the copy close with a strong call to action?
15. _____ Is detail copy included in all ads to make shopping or ordering easier?
16. _____ Is the message clearly consumer or product focused, as laid out in the creative brief?
17. _____ Do the visual components match the strategy?
18. _____ Do the verbal components match the strategy?
19. _____ Do the visuals match the image created in the headline and copy?
20. _____ Is the logo clearly seen in every message?
21. _____ Does the slogan or tagline appear in every message and in the same position above or below the logo?
22. _____ If specific color combinations were used in the ads, do they uniformly appear in every message?
23. _____ Is the typeface and style consistent in every ad?
24. _____ Is the layout style evident and the tone apparent in every ad?
25. _____ Is the headline size and body-copy length as consistent as possible in every ad?
26. _____ Is the logo and tagline or slogan as consistent in size and placement in every ad as possible?
27. _____ If using a spokesperson or character representative, are they seen or heard in every ad?
28. _____ Is the cropping and image size of visuals as consistent as possible in every ad?
29. _____ Did you use the white of the page judiciously?
30. _____ Is there one visual or verbal dominant element within the ad?
31. _____ Does the package's design match the brand's image?
32. _____ Does the campaign reflect a long-term focus, with enough time built in to educate and build consumer loyalty?
33. _____ Are there interactive components built into the campaign?
34. _____ Does the promotional mix reflect the target's lifestyle and interests?
35. _____ Does the campaign have one clear benefit, a distinct appearance, and one tone of voice that is apparent across all media?
36. _____ Is the visual/verbal relationship so strong that if the campaign were thrown into a vat with a thousand other campaigns, the target would be able to pick out the brand's specific series of ads?

Managing the Details for Uniformity

So far we have dissected the design process down into relatively large chunks of information, such as the psychology of color use, and the visual and verbal reasoning behind the choice of type and layout styles. In-depth knowledge about foundational design is critical to the development of any ad or campaign. But what sets a good designer apart from a great designer is their ability to hone in on the smaller, less immediately noticeable details. Paying close attention to detail is particularly critical to maintaining a consistent visual/verbal identity across multiple media vehicles. Let's spend a few minutes on campaign minutiae detection and control.

Beyond what the imagery shows, all visuals must be similarly sized, cropped, and displayed. For example, if the visual is attached to the side of one ad, it is important to try as closely as possible to maintain that look across vehicles. Images should have a consistent theme. This means if you use animals in one ad, they must be used everywhere; they don't have to be the same animal but they should come from the same genre, such as wild animals versus domesticated animals. If using a character representative or spokesperson, be sure they are seen and/or heard consistently. If using a border treatment of some kind, reuse it everywhere when possible.

Details are just as important to maintain when space is at a premium. If your brand has a lengthy tagline or detailed logo design, you may have to simplify it to fit the available space. For example, the logo may need to go from a detailed graphic to a type-only format. Just be sure to never alter the typeface or placement of the tagline or slogan to the logo.

Typestyles should be consistent across mediums, and headlines, subheads, body copy, and logos should be the same size and similarly placed when possible. If your headline is displayed using initial caps, it is important to use initial caps on every headline. Be sure all body copy and headlines have a consistent tone of voice across all vehicles and are kerned and leaded uniformly. And maybe most important of all, watch for grammar and spelling errors.

via multiple media vehicles, and a unified visual and verbal message.

Good copy, no matter where it appears, will always rely on the following:

1. A strong key consumer benefit-driven headline that stops attention and delivers relevant information of interest to the target. The best headlines are simple, informative, and creative, and lead the target to take some type of predetermined action. It can be direct, educational, and emotional; it can ask a question, or surprise with a thought-provoking pun or metaphor. The creative team can decide to use the same headline throughout the campaign, explained through a diverse use of visuals, or use multiple headlines. The key is to ensure they all have the same aesthetic sound, look, and feel to ensure continuity between the ads.
2. Nobody wants to read copy that just sells, but everyone loves a good immersive story. Copy that is consumer focused and tells a beneficial and relatable story will get read. Be sure the copy matches the tone of voice used by the headline.
3. Be sure your copy is scannable, or quick and easy to read. Use multiple subheads to break up longer or difficult copy.
4. The entire ad needs to push and creatively develop the key consumer benefit. The "what's in in for me?" question needs to be thoroughly answered by placing the target into a situation they can relate to with the brand.
5. Be sure every ad in the campaign leaves the target wanting to know more about the brand, so they will feel compelled to take some kind of action. That action might be doing additional research or simply making a quick purchase.
6. All ads need detail copy that makes contact with the brand or its representatives fast and easy.

A Campaign's Verbal Storyline

A campaign needs to tell an ongoing story about the brand. To do that, the next step is to develop a compelling verbal storyline. One of the first things the creative team will need to decide is whether the campaign will need to tell a simple one-dimensional story, or use a more complex multi-dimensional story built around the key consumer benefit. A one-dimensional story will simply introduce or elaborate on the key consumer benefit using a repetitive headline style and/or visuals. A multi-dimensional story will let the key consumer benefit develop slowly across the promotional mix, using a diverse but cohesive set of copy and visuals. The story can be developed all at once using multiple ads, or over a specific set of time using a series of ads that are strategically released one-by-one. The goal is to creatively inundate your target with an immersive storyline

Not All Campaigns Have the Same Job to Do

Because brands need to accomplish different types of goals with their advertising efforts, the creative team can pick and chose from four distinct varieties, including national, service, corporate, and retail. Let's take a look at each one:

National Campaigns. These campaigns can be seen across the country and tend to use a diverse promotional mix. National campaigns are expensive and most often used by large established brands with big budgets.

Service Campaigns. Services like healthcare, insurance, or banking are services everyone needs and uses. Because of this, it is important to convince the target your service is the best option. Most service brands are not unique in any measurable way, so you often have to create importance. Break down the experience for the target, for example, quality customer service is important to everyone, as is quick responses to claims initiatives, to name just two. The goal is to make services offered by the competition seem lacking. It is not unusual for the advertised message to directly offer a solution to a problem the target is having. Depending on the brand, service campaigns need to instill a strong sense of quantifiable attributes, such as security, trust, and reliability.

Corporate Campaigns. Corporate advertising, also known as institutional advertising, is basically advertising for an entire company or organization rather than specific brands. The goal is to build an image or even address a specific issue, such as green initiatives. Building goodwill with constituents, the community, and the target is priceless. It is an important step to building brand equity.

The most expensive type of corporate advertising is the need to repair its reputation to their targeted audience. Beyond cost, it is also a very time-consuming process to re-prove itself in order to build back consumer loyalty.

Retail Campaigns. Retail campaigns typically advertise a store rather than individual brands. Advertising efforts can focus on price, reputation, and sometimes both. Reputation often centers around prices and merchandise sold, whether found at Bergdorf Goodman, Macy's, or Target. Each will promote the quality of the merchandise differently. Some will focus on price, others on personalized service, image and/or reputation, avoiding any discussion on price.

Brand-intensive retail campaigns rarely stand out with cutting-edge creative, since they need to push a lot of price-focused merchandise. However, a well-structured ad with as much white space as possible speaks volumes about quality, customer service, and so on, even if price is the star of the visual/verbal message. Price-prominent ads require constant change, so a sense of urgency is always present. The goal is to get the target into the brick-and-mortar store and move merchandise, whether the sale lasts a weekend, a week, or a month.

Retail campaigns have a lot to do. They need to attract attention, create interest, boldly show prices, push a diverse number of brands, highlight any promotions, and of course encourage purchase. These types of campaigns never stop selling, from the signage outside to the store layout inside.

Every contact point the target will see or interact with while shopping needs to express the campaign's visual/verbal voice. These informative contact points are numerous, and clearly visible throughout the store; consider the following:

- Interior displays or kiosks
- In-store signage
- Window displays
- Window signage
- Shelf and rack announcements
- Presale advertising or direct mail announcements, with or without coupons
- Credit card stuffers
- In-store credit card promotions
- Promotional buttons, name badges or any type of uniform worn by sales personnel
- The colorful wrapping tissue and coordinated shopping bags or boxes used to package up purchases
- Receipt coupons
- Table tent promotions for restaurants
- Menus.

These are just a few of the promotional options that brands both large and small can successfully employ to build image through their communication efforts. See Figures 18.1 through 18.10 for a campaign example.

Lucy In The Sky With Diamonds.

Because beer isn't groovy enough.

WiLD HONEY
RECORDS
Modern music. Real records.
WildHoneyRecords.com

Figures 18.1 and 18.2 Examples of in-store posters.

Sing Us A Song, You're The Piano Man.

Chopsticks doesn't count.

Figure 18.2 Continued

[Figures 18.1–18.10 Show a campaign that uses graphics and lyrics from popular music past and present to promote a local vinyl music store. Images courtesy of Emily Harris, University of Tennessee.]

Media Choice Affects Design Decisions

For a campaign to be considered successful, it will take more than just a good idea and a coordinated look. It will require a consistent and relevant visual and verbal message, media vehicles that are sure to be seen by the target, and more than a little bit of old-fashioned luck.

Historically, almost every campaign launch relied on traditional media like television and magazines to reach their intended target. Modern campaigns are inventive, highly personalized, and may never employ a traditional vehicle, relying instead on vehicles that are more personalized to reach the target, where they are, and with what they care about, such as the Internet, direct mail, sales promotions, and mobile or social media outlets.

Today, the rules dictate that a campaign employ media vehicle(s) that research has proven the target uses. Messages need to stop

When you walk into Wild Honey Records you get the best of the past and the present, the nostalgia of vinyl with the selection of modern albums and artists. You're guaranteed to find your favorites in our wide selection of vinyl, CD's, and cassette tapes. Not only can you come enjoy our variety of vinyl, but you can also meet other music lovers at our live shows featuring local Knoxville bands and artists. By recieving this mailer, you have been given premium access to this month's upcoming Wild Honey sessions. Thank you for being a member!

December Lineup
- **Moccasin Cowboy**
  12/8 - 8:00pm
- **Filthy Blondes**
  12/16 - 7:00pm
- **Gag Me**
  12/23 - 5:00pm

Figures 18.3 and 18.4 Examples of a direct mailer, showing the front/back and inside copy and graphics.

Modern music. Real records.

WildHoneyRecords.com
@WildHoneyRecords

1206 Kenesaw Ave.
Knoxville, TN 37919

Manny Sample
1234 Great Street
Knoxville, TN 37916

Figure 18.4 Continued

Figures 18.5 and 18.6 Examples of newspaper ads.

Figure 18.6 Continued

and engage the target with interactive devices, such as QR codes, interactive mobile devices, and coupons, to name just a few of the options available to today's advertiser.

Beyond the creative message it is important to consider when will the message be seen and how often? What media vehicle(s) will be employed to deliver the message and when? How many messages will be available to the target? Will multiple messages be available to the target at the same time? The answers to these questions will help determine the type of visual and verbal message employed.

Every media vehicle chosen needs to say something important about the key consumer benefit and, by default, the brand. If any

aspect of the visual and verbal message is lacking, it can confuse your target and undermine the brand's image.

Whether or not to reuse any visual or verbal design element will depend on the media vehicles delivering the campaign's message. If you have a lot to say, the Internet, direct mail and magazine ads are a few excellent media options. Other choices like television or video clips may offer only 15–30 seconds, but sight, sound, and motion effectively captures attention. Vehicles like most out-of-home or mobile options have to get the same message out in only five to seven words, or at most a couple of sentences. The key is to be sure every ad, no matter its size, is visually and verbally interesting, can be easily scanned, delivers relevant and thus interesting information,

Domo Arigato, Mr. Roboto.

Does anyone have a robot charger?

When you walk into Wild Honey Records you get the best of the past and the present, the nostalgia of vinyl with the selection of modern albums and artists. Not only can you come enjoy our variety of vinyl, but you can also meet other music lovers at our live shows featuring local Knoxville bands and artists. Next time you need your new music fix, stop into Wild Honey Records. We are located just two miles west of UT campus, come and find your vinyl.

Modern music. Real records.

WildHoneyRecords.com
@WildHoneyRecords

Figures 18.7 and 18.8 Examples of magazine ads.

and clearly indicates what action the target needs to take next.

Campaign Messages versus Single-Shot Messaging

During a campaign's lifetime, there may be incidences when a single-shot ad will be needed. This could happen due to overstocks or the need to clarify information; no matter the reason, the key is to be sure the ad uses the same imaging and messaging devices used in the original campaign. You don't want it to appear like an anomaly in what was an orderly pattern.

The need for reoccurring visual/verbal ties is what sets a campaign apart from single-shot messages. When an advertised message has no relationship with other brand advertising currently, or previously seen, it is known as a single-shot message. You cannot have synergized messaging in a single ad seen only once, or even the same ad seen once in a while. The same ad running over time does not constitute a campaign, because it lacks a recognizable identity, is not memorable, and cannot alone reinforce or build brand image.

Single-shot ads are not memorable to a distracted, advertising-saturated target. To ensure the target gives your visual/verbal message more than a glance, it must be seen in multiple mediums and have a consistent message. It's this repetitiveness that moves a message from the target's short-term to long-term memory, where it can be called up the next time the target purchases.

Hello From The Other Side.

Who? Please stop calling.

When you walk into Wild Honey Records
you get the best of the past and the present, the
nostalgia of vinyl with the selection of modern
albums and artists. Not only can you come
enjoy our variety of vinyl, but you can also meet
other music lovers at our live shows featuring
local Knoxville bands and artists. Next time you
need your new music fix, stop into Wild Honey
Records. We are located just two miles west of
UT campus, come and find your vinyl.

WiLD HoNeY RECORDS
Modern music. Real records.

WildHoneyRecords.com
@WildHoneyRecords

Figure 18.8 Continued

Budget Restraints Do Not Rule a Good Idea

Good ideas are what drive a campaign, not its budget. Students of advertising often mistake large campaign budgets with creativity and success, while assuming those with smaller budgets will lack ingenuity and engagement aspects, ultimately causing them to fail. Untrue. A great idea has nothing to do with a hefty budget; it has everything to do with the creative team's interpretation of the key consumer benefit. A larger budget does have more creative bells and whistles, but without a great idea that talks to the target about something they care about, in a language they will respond to, it will fail.

Great creative ideas are not the best advertising solution for every brand. In fact, unique ideas are best suited to well-known brands that simply need to remind, not sell. With that said, to be successful, ads don't need to excite or surprise. Creatively, they just need to be genuine. Every brand will have different reasons for developing a campaign. For example, some brands need to announce who they are, how they are used, or educate on how they are unique within the brand category. Some campaigns will be copy heavy others will have little to say and a lot to show. Beyond the key consumer benefit, a look at the brand's life-cycle stage will help determine what needs to be said and/or shown. The brand itself will also help guide the creative team. For example, simple food items will have less to say than new, technology-based items. Good ideas are based on creatively applied knowledge.

wildhoneyrecords
Sponsored

Come into the store today to join our members club! #FindYourVinyl

20   50 Comments   15 Shares

👍 Like   💬 Comment   ➤ Share

Figure 18.9 Example of a Facebook ad.

Figure 18.10 Example of a shopping bag.

Making the Message Last and Last

Successful campaigns have longevity. Brand image is built over time, as are lasting relationships with the target. Because of this, a campaign's consistent visual/verbal lifespan needs to outlive any competitor's messages. Small changes or additions to a brand, like new flavors or sizes, are not good reasons to change or launch a new campaign. Consistent messaging builds consumer trust.

Campaigns that are on-target and on-strategy do not need to compete with a competitor's constantly changing message. Change should only be an option when the brand or company makes significant changes, or wants to modernize its image. Today's campaigns change routinely affecting memorability, and the time it takes to build loyalty. Continual repositioning or ongoing comparisons to competitors can negatively affect the target's image of the brand. Brands that are patient and consistently and methodically work at building loyalty based on brand consistency, even customer service, or performance, will find competitors' ever-changing messages less of an issue to holding the target's attention and building and maintaining, brand equity.

How long a campaign is used will depend on how many storylines can be adopted. Those that last for years never tell the same story twice. You do not want your target to get bored with repetitive messaging. To stand out in a world of multiple media options, disinterested targets, and almost immediate product parity, it is important for campaigns to have an ever-evolving storyline delivered in unique and creative ways. When a campaign does change course, it is imperative that any changes be integrated into the campaign incrementally over time, avoiding any abrupt directional changes that can confuse or even anger loyal brand users. Changes will be less noticeable if slogans or taglines, or any character representatives or spokespersons, are maintained.

The goal of all campaigns is to bring uniformity to the creative message. The biggest advantage of a well-targeted, well-designed, multimedia campaign is the ability to deliver the brand's message at the right time to the right audience with a coordinated, multifaceted visual and/or verbal message that successfully educates, informs, and entertains every time the ads are encountered. When placed in diverse media the target is sure to see, it creates repetition and increases the likelihood the ad will be remembered and acted upon.

Bibliography

Blakeman, Robyn. 2018. *Integrated Marketing Communication: Creative Strategy from Idea to Implementation*. 3rd ed. Lanham, MD: Rowman and Littlefield Publishing, p. 125.

Pitching, Approvals, and Deadlines

Chapter 19 Objectives

1. The reader will understand what a pitch to clients entails.
2. The reader will understand the client's role in the ad approval process.
3. The reader will understand why deadlines are critical to media and design decisions.

Client Direction and the Agency Pitch Process

The purpose behind every advertising agency pitch is to determine whether the agency understands a brand's current advertising problem, and can deliver a viable solution with enough creative ingenuity to give the brand a significant point of difference between it and other brands within the category.

Covering a lot of ground, a typical pitch must state the objectives to be accomplished, the target to be reached, the advertising problem to be solved, the media to be used, and the visual and verbal solution that will help to deliver the intended results. It must also demonstrate the agency's ability to find and promote a significant difference between the brand and competitors within the brand category, that will ultimately enhance the brand's image and create awareness.

Brands look for a new agency for any number of reasons: Slow sales, dysfunctional relationships between the brand and the current agency, costs, overall return on investment, distrust, the need for a new visual and verbal direction, new and diverse media specialization, and/or the move to the use of in-house agencies, to name just a few.

Competitive, a brand will typically request pitches from three to five agencies, although there could be more depending on the size of the new business. Diversification helps the client gain a more well-rounded idea of options and insights into their current advertising needs.

The overall development of a pitch is always an exhaustive and intoxicating mix of creative ingenuity and explosive frustration. Although time-intensive to prepare, deadlines are always too short. Agencies may have anywhere from a couple of weeks to a couple of months to prepare a unique way to creatively solve the client's advertising problem and stand out from competing agencies.

Who Is in Charge of Dazzling the Client During the Pitch?

Having the correct cast of characters in place for the pitch is critical. It is important those presenting are not just the agency's heavy hitters, or the high-ranking account and creative personnel. Today's clients want to see and meet the actual team members that will be working on their account. Modern-day interaction between the client and the agency is as much about building a relationship as it is about offering up a viable solution to their advertising problem. The strongest, and often the most long-lasting business relationships are built on credibility and trust. So it is important the client not only pick a team they both respect and won't mind spending a lot of time with, but that can also show a strong return on investment.

The number of people to include in a pitch will typically depend on the size of the client. Pitches to a large brand with a big budget, such as Kellogg's or Nike, will require a more formal pitch, where each member of the account, media and creative team will present. Depending on client needs, specialist teams, such as those responsible for public relations, direct response, web development and social media, to name just a few, will also present. Pitches to smaller brands will typically include one or two key people. Theses pitches tend to be more informal and may for

DOI: 10.4324/9781003255123-20

example, take place over lunch. No matter whether the pitch will be formal or informal, the key is to bring the experts needed to solve the client's advertising problem.

Preparation for the Perfect Pitch: Breaking Down What Needs to Be Accomplished

The pitch process will begin as all advertising does, with an internal deconstruction of the pitch brief known as a *request for proposal* (RFP) supplied by the client. An RFP outlines their needs, wants, and expectations. The agency will use the RFP, basically a streamlined creative brief, to outline direction. If an RFP is not supplied, the agency will develop a creative brief internally.

Before the creative team can begin any brainstorming sessions, they will need access to any research gathered and information on media direction. Before moving on to finalized super comps, all ideas will need to be approved by the account management team and the creative director in charge of the pitch. Once a final direction is solidified, the team will move on to finalizing both the copy and layout for any print and/or digital options, as requested by the client. This is a very busy and stressful time for the creative team. Timelines are short and the days and nights are long. The more ideas need to be reworked, the more taxing and frantic the "pitch mode" or pace becomes.

The Steps to Preparing a Pitch Deck

Once each team has completed their assigned sections, the next step is the development of the pitch presentation. This will begin with all the teams regrouping to discuss direction and create a brief outline of what the presentation of the pitch should say and show, followed by the development of a pitch or presentation deck. A *pitch deck*, typically created using PowerPoint or Keynote, introduces the agency to the client and outlines the agency's solution to their advertising problem.

The best pitches will tell a captivating story. They do not bore with facts, delivered in a monotone voice, but entice with a storyline that weaves the facts, or the agency's solutions into a plot the client can relate to. Difficult concepts and tedious statistical data can be simplified when placed in a setting, shown in use, or used to demonstrate a direction.

Well-organized pitch presentations that revolve around a storyline follow a detailed presentation formula. Each deck should open by introducing the characters (the agency and team) and the three key points the team wants to make, based on the problem set up in the RFP. The plot or middle section should introduce the conflict or villain (the problem), and show and tell ways the hero (the creative solution) can overcome obstacles (competitors, target attitudes). The ending will wrap up the three main points and how they will help the brand overcome any hurdles. Let's take a more detailed look at each section.

Step 1: The Opening

The opening, also known as the *upfront*, is the time for the agency to toot its own horn. Start by thanking your audience for the opportunity to present. Next, introduce the team that will be working on the brand on a daily basis; you might have a slide that not only showcases their skills but personality. This will help to not only develop a rapport, but show the client you have the right people in place. This should be followed by a brief highlight of past and present work. Keep this portion of the pitch brief but concise.

The opening will set the tone for the entire pitch. Never start with dull facts, or an apology because technology wasn't working, or you were late. Instead, set up your story, deliver a startling fact or ask a thought-provoking question, which ties the solution to the client's advertising problem. You might also consider making some kind of provocative statement to capture attention, such as "consumers don't care about your brand." A statement like this will require you to sell the solution quickly but compellingly. It is always best to abstain from opening with a joke unless you are really good at telling one. There is nothing worse than you being the only person laughing.

Next, succinctly outline the parameters set up in the RFP. This will help show the client you fully understand their current needs. To streamline the pitch, the team will need to break down their solution into three main points, as an audience will only remember three points. Introduce each of your three points in the beginning, dissect and explain them in the middle, and summarize them at the end, or closing. Back up this discussion with any qualitative and/or quantitative research the agency has gathered.

Step 2: Tell a Story

Here is where you will weave your solutions to the three main points presented in the opening, into a story rather than just dryly pitching an idea. Presentations that are plot driven will have a clearly articulated beginning, middle, and end. Set up the problem and then slowly and systematically deliver the solution to the problem.

Stories, especially ones with some type of relevant interactive devices, are memorable because they engage more parts of the brain. A good storyteller can take the viewer on an informative visual and verbal journey. Bullet points do not excite, or hold attention. But a good tale with interesting twists and turns can break down all the boring statistics and turn them into something visually exciting, useful, and tangible.

Every compelling story must address and answer who, what, when, where, why and how, using both stimulating visual imagery and the spoken word. The presentation slides should not overwhelm your audience with excessive text and statistically driven charts and graphs. Instead, you should build a believable level of drama that arcs with a suspense-filled presentation of your solutions. Steve Jobs, Apple founder and a brilliant master of the suspense-filled pitch, believed, "every new business pitch should do three things: Inform, educate and entertain." If you can do this succinctly, you will hold your audience's attention for the duration of the presentation.

Be sure to create a strong protagonist or hero. This could be the brand, or the agency's visual and verbal solution to the client's advertising problem. Every hero must overcome some type of obstacle, so you will need to introduce a compelling villain. The villain or antihero can be a direct competitor, the target audience's impression of the brand, or it can be the problem to be solved. The tension that is created between the problem and solution can help you to persuade the client to look at the problem differently and help them better understand how the solution originated.

Be sure your solution includes some type of surprise or hook. Whether introduced at the beginning of the presentation pitch or in the summary, delivering something the audience does not expect will hold attention. This surprise is the unexpected twist you will often find in fiction or movies.

Step 3: The Creative Solution

This is the challenge solved, or the hero to the rescue. Now is the time to present ideas that creatively and uniquely solve the client's advertising problem as stated in the RFP. Each creative piece and media choice can dazzle, but if it cannot demonstrate how it can solve the client's advertising problem, it's only sizzle, with no substance. If the creative solution went a bit off brief, now is the time to explain why. This is where many new business pitches are lost. The team was unable to articulate their understanding of the client's problem and tie it back to the solutions presented.

Step 4: Closing and Summary

To ensure your audience didn't miss anything important, be sure to close the presentation by summarizing the three main points that were introduced in the opening moments of the presentation and fleshed out in the middle. Summarize how the hero, your agency, slayed the villain, the competition, and how the brand will emerge triumphant and live happily and profitably ever after, thanks to your heroism.

Step 5: Q&A

Open up the floor for questions. Be prepared before the pitch for as many questions as possible. The team can decide in advance who will answer what questions and which kind of questions can be tag-teamed. There will be times when you will be hit with an unexpected question; if this happens, give yourself time to think, by restating the question in a way that favors your agency and solution.

In the end, there is no quicker way to lose the battle between multiple agency pitches than to bore your audience. The ability to beat out the competition is as much about excelling at what you do as it is about presenting your agency's essence in a creative, intelligent, and organized way. The best pitch presentations are a mixture of eye-pleasing slides, an informative show-and-tell approach, and confident presenters. It is critical your presentation not only inspires trust in your work, but showcases knowledge and overall experience that will lead the client to chose your agency to lead their marketing efforts.

PowerPoint Should Be Considered a Design Tool, Not Just a Presentation Tool

Most presentation pitches are created in PowerPoint or Keynote. Both are simple to use and sure to open on any device. In the right hands, these two presentation programs can turn a pitch deck from a slide show into an impeccably designed and visually stimulating work of art. Well-executed and engaging presentations can help make your agency pitch stronger and more memorable. Let's take a look at the steps needed to develop a persuasive presentation.

Laying Out the Slides
How clearly information is arranged on each slide reflects organization and hopefully clarity. The first step to determining what will be said and shown is to create a storyboard and script.

As we have learned, good presentations often mimic other good storytelling outlets, such as television, movies, and novels.

If showing copy points, be sure to limit each slide to expressing a single idea, in a single sentence or less. Too much information delivered at one time not only looks tacky, but can be confusing, and almost always forgettable.

A storyboard will help ensure a logical flow of information, and overall cohesion, as you write and design. Use no more than ten slides; anything more will not be memorable, and overly lengthen the pitch.

As with all types of storytelling mediums, pacing is critical. A storyboard helps set up the problems to be solved, or opportunities to exploit. Start out explosive and then slowly descend down to the specifics. Mix in the detailed slides with simple dramatic moments, by showing a single dominant image, a quick video clip, or even adding to the drama with music. This will help to keep your audience engaged throughout your presentation.

Keep the Layout Simple

Use text only to highlight your most important points. Every visual needs to punctuate a concept or thought you are presenting. They are not there for visual interest, but visual explanation. Every image needs to succinctly move along your presentation storyline. Visuals should be used to support the spoken word and/or replace the written word. They can be experienced. Imagery can tap into the viewer's imagination, demonstrate one or more uses, or simplify a concept. So show, don't textually tell, when possible, to make each point stronger.

For a great show-and-tell example, we can look to Steve Jobs again, who was a master storyteller and presenter. When he first introduced the MacBook Air, he concisely summed up its look in a single sentence, calling it, "the world's thinnest notebook." To demonstrate how slim the MacBook Air actually was, he showed a photograph of the computer fitting inside a traditional manila envelope. What more needed to be said or shown?

The Visual and Verbal Look of a Pitch Deck

As in all design for multiple pieces, you are going for a unified look. Each slide should be a part of a unified family, not an individual expressionist. To ensure strong branding, be sure each slide has a consistent look and tone of voice. To ensure consistency, be sure to:

1. Place only one key point per slide. State each point in a single sentence.
2. Make your main points obvious. Consider using a strong, informative headline to set up each slide. Ask yourself: What is the point I'm try to convey with this piece of information? How does this information connect back to the problem and set up the solution? What is the key take-away for the audience?
3. Promote each point with a visual. Let a single dominant visual tell your story whenever possible. Visuals make information or concepts easier to digest. If it can't be stated or emphasized with a visual, rethink your presentation script.
4. Always use high-quality images. Make sure every image uses a high resolution—300 ppi or higher. Be sure choice moves the presentation forward.
5. Always stay away from clip and stock art images; they are not original ideas.
6. Be sure to never stretch or skew an image to fit in a desired frame and avoid excessive use of visual effects such as shadows, reflections, arrows, and moving or blinking accessories.
7. Work with diverse types of photographic crops. If you have a lot to show, visuals can be cropped a multitude of different ways. Think of confining images in multiple circles, squares, rectangles, triangles, polygons, collages, letter shapes, or even as a part of a brushstroke. Shape will be determined by how many visuals you have and content of the presentation.
8. Use no more than two typefaces in the presentation. If you need differentiation, consider adjusting the weight and/or size of the typeface.
9. Use typefaces creatively. Be sure they match the message behind the presentation or consider using the client's existing typefaces, brand colors, photographic style, and/or any unique shapes that match the brand or packaging.
10. Be sure all text is readable and legible from anywhere in the room where the presentation will take place.
11. Bold sans serif typefaces always work well visually.
12. For titles, use at least 32–44 point type. Keep bullet points to no smaller than 28 point.
13. If you must use a lot of text, aim for about twenty words or less per slide.
14. Don't be afraid to combine thick and thin typefaces together. Big, bulky typefaces are a great way to call attention to copy points or slide titles. Additional options might include bleeding the letters over the edges of the slide or running titles vertically along one side. The best typefaces to use are

ones with minimal swishes and swirls. Decorative typefaces work best if the copy is relatively short.

15. Always use present tense, active voice, and descriptive words.

16. Avoid using all caps, reverses, and italics. As previously discussed, these are all difficult to read. Use a traditional upper- and lower-case look to ease readability and legibility issues.

17. Be sure more than one person has thoroughly proofed the presentation for any grammar and/or spelling errors.

18. Use strong color contrasts on your slides to ensure information pops, and attracts and holds attention. Additionally, if placing type on a color or tinted background, be sure there is strong contrast between it and the typeface.

19. Consider using bright colors that scream "Look at me!" Clever combinations of color can hold attention. If you remember the chapter on color psychology, you know color can conjure up a diverse array of emotions. Use a small palette of no more than three to four colors, and reuse them throughout the pitch deck.

20. Watch out for balance, text alignment, white-space use, and page margins.

21. Consider uniformly diversifying the look of each slide. Not every slide needs to use a horizontal format. Feel free to mix horizontal and vertical layouts to create interest and avoid repetitiveness. Just be sure to do it consistently.

22. Intersperse the deck with interactive options when possible. Consider adding handouts, packaging options, mock-ups, or even an old-fashioned flip chart to encourage discussion. Distribute tactile materials to hold attention. Going more boldly, the creative team might consider creating an app that the audience can temporarily download, or showcase an interactive option on your website they can view, in order to interact with any additional, but relevant, information.

23. Chart up any statistical information you need to show. To make it more memorable, understandable, and visual, consider corralling this type of information into some type of visually informative graph, chart, or infographic. Consider the following options. A *line graph* is best used when you need to track changes or trends over time. A simple *bar graph* uses rectangular or horizontal boxes to compare statistical information between different groups. A *pie chart* is best used when you need to compare parts of a whole. A *pictogram*, or *infographic*, is an image-based type of bar graph. Instead of using numbers, it uses pictures to represent numbers. For example, to show ages or participants, you could use small, repeatable images of people. Finally, if you really want to creatively attract attention to statistical information, banish the traditional bar graph and pie chart from your visual repertoire. To ensure your data is seen and is memorable, use real-life visual objects. People

respond to images consisting of recognizable objects. So if you want to show the amount of money to be made, deliver up stacks of money on a platter, literally. You might also want to consider using alternatively sized cloud formations, mountain ranges or trees, building blocks, polygons, squares, or even use a stair-step approach full of angles and curved imagery, to showcase data points.

To ensure your presentation is unique, always design each pitch deck like a new ad campaign, complete with its own visual and verbal continuity.

Getting Your Pitch Ducks in a Row: Preparing for the Pitch

Everyone reacts differently to the prospect of speaking in front of any size crowd. If you are one of the many who fight nervous jitters, here are a few ways to corral your churning stomach before stepping up to speak:

1. Practice makes perfect. Rehearse, rehearse, rehearse, and don't stop, until you feel confident about your part in the pitch. Keep it simple by always using a conversational approach. Over-memorization can make a pitch seem stiff. If you understand your solutions to the problem, there is no need to stick to a tightly worded script. With that said, be sure not to ramble—stay on point and hammer it home, and then move on.

2. Role playing. Do a little role playing to prepare, or consider watching yourself in the mirror, or have a friend videotape you to highlight your visual/verbal style.

3. Energy is enthusiasm. Channel all that pent-up energy into enthusiasm about what you have to say. Enthusiasm is infectious.

4. Arrive early. By arriving early, you will have time to relax a bit before hitting the presentation stage.

5. Look around. Spend a little quality time in the room where the presentation will take place. The more acquainted you are with your environment, the more comfortable you will feel.

6. Breathe. A few deep breaths can relieve a lot of nervous energy.

7. Smile. A big smile increases endorphins, helping to replace anxiety with an aura of confidence.

8. Appropriate pauses. When you are nervous, it's easy to race through your part in the presentation. Pauses also make a presentation feel more like a conversation than a monologue, so slow down. There are typically three times you want

to pause during a presentation: 1) Before and after you deliver an important piece of content, 2) before and after a transition between talking points, and 3) between the beginning, middle, and ending closing points. Be sure not to fill pauses with wasted noises or words such as um, ah, or ya know. These are wasted words. A good silent pause can attract attention, so don't fill it.

9. Speak clearly. Show off your personality and passion for the project by speaking clearly and animatedly. Vary the tenor of your voice and alter the speed with which the information is delivered.

10. Dry mouth. Anxiety often causes dry mouth, so be sure to have a bottle of water with you. You do not want to stumble over your own tongue because it's stuck to the roof of your mouth.

11. Don't fear anxiety. Anxiety can actually help keep you in the moment. Embrace that nervous energy and use it to land the account.

Finally, try not to let the unexpected throw you. In a 2016 online article entitled "Acing the Pitch: How to Pitch New Clients," Neil Tortorella quotes Dave Willmer, former executive director of The Creative Group: "Presentations are close friends with Murphy's Law; if they can go wrong, odds are, they will." So be sure to always have at least one backup of the presentation. It's always a good idea to bring your own adapters and clickers, even if the client assures you they have everything you will need. If you are blessed with an unexpected power outage, be sure you can continue with the presentation without the benefit of PowerPoint and always bring hard copies of everything.

If You Need to Pitch It, There Is a Way to Say It

There is no one way to make a pitch. However, to help you find your voice, Meg Prater in the 2018 online article, "The 8 Types of Presentation Styles: Which Category Do You Fall Into," suggests eight different types of presentation styles. The best advice is choose the one that best fits your style and personality. Let's take a quick look at each one.

Visual Style. This style focuses on the visual, rather than bulleted points. If you are an especially good speaker and you can make your points, without the prop of a PowerPoint slide or bullet, this style is for you.

Freeform Style. If you are a great storyteller and absolutely hate PowerPoint presentations, consider this option. For every missing bullet point, the speaker uses a compelling story to illustrate the point. This is particularly successful if you need to make a presentation quickly and are well versed in the content.

Instructor Style. This presentation style allows the speaker to deliver relatively detailed information using figures of speech, voice moderation, metaphors, body language, and visual aids like PowerPoint. It will look and sound a lot like one of your professor's lectures, thus the name. Content should be delivered in a set and logical order. Any visuals used, will support the topic and keep the audience engaged. This type of presentation style is great if you're thrown into the pitch process at the last minute and have a relatively limited knowledge of the subject matter.

Coaching Style. This style is for the energetic, inspirational, and charismatic speaker. They can use their voice and body language, role-playing, and audience participation, to help make their point, as well as effectively connect with, and engage with, their audience.

Storytelling Style. This style is all about engaging through anecdotes and examples the audience can relate to. Stories always engage, and the best ones are always closely tied to the subject matter, making them more memorable. However, this type of presentation style can burn up valuable time because it relies on you tying each story to an important point you are trying to make.

Connector Style. The connector-style presentation allows the speaker to connect with listeners by tying their wants, needs, and lifestyle choices, back to the speaker's. By making a valuable connection between the speaker and listener, you can tell a story based on experience. These presenters generally use body language and encourage interaction during the presentation from the listeners. By allowing intermittent participation, you will appear not only knowledgeable, but approachable, and open to suggestion.

Lessig Style. When you are short on time, this is the presentation style to choose. It requires the presenter to address each slide within 15 seconds. Slide text is usually synchronized with the speaker's words. Using both text and visuals, the rapid pace of this type of presentation style keeps the audience interested and engaged.

Takahashi Style. This presentation style uses large, bold text that dominates each slide. Each word is followed by one or two descriptive but concise sentences. If you hate using PowerPoint or Keynote, this is a big step out of the box.

When placing your personality into the presentation you cannot only deliver a memorable pitch, but you help to make a connection with the audience.

Mannerisms That Annoy and Distract

When all eyes are on you during a presentation, body language can speak volumes. During every presentation you should always use controlled facial expressions and hand movements to effectively communicate important points. If you overuse them, they can become a source of distraction for your audience and they may find themselves concentrating more on your squint and fist pumps than on what you are saying. Controlled body language is also a great way to show off your confidence as a presenter. A few of the most commonly made mistakes include:

Hand Movements. Use your hands wisely, don't clasp them together, or use them to fidget with a hang nail, or to tap anything. Any type of repetitive hand movement makes you appear nervous and less than confident. Alternatively, when you stuff your hands in your pockets you appear dismissive, meek, or unsure.

Grouchy Stance. Whenever you cross your arms, you look aggressive, bored, or inattentive. It is a defensive posture that will not help build a rapport with your audience. A better stance is to keep your arms open and slightly away from your body, as though you are about to give someone a hug. This open gesture is more welcoming and gives off an aura of confidence.

Darting Eyes. When you avoid eye contact, by checking your watch or looking at the wall or an empty chair, it appears dismissive and rude. Eyes that are constantly on the move give you a shifty appearance as well as implying insincerity, insecurity, and disinterest. Instead, be sure to look at each audience member for at least two to three seconds before moving on; any longer, and it's uncomfortable for the receiver.

Slumping. If your posture is not upright, you appear to lack confidence. Go for a comfortable but neutral position. For example, if standing, be sure your back and shoulders are straight. The same goes if you decide to sit during your section of the presentation.

Bodies in Motion. Be sure not to pace back and forth, and do not fidget or make any quick gestures or repeated motions. Movement is important, so that you don't look rooted in place or robotic, but just be sure to make each movement purposeful.

Jumpy Legs. Don't jiggle them, or rock back and forth. Shifting legs make you appear uncomfortable and restless.

Grumpy Face. Your face and its open or closed appearance will determine how the audience feels about you. Don't forget to smile. Make it natural, and be sure not to frown when making a point. The minute you step up to the podium, smile. If you are standing or sitting with a group, waiting for your turn to speak in front of an audience, be sure to smile every time one of your co-presenters makes an important point.

Slide Reader. If you want to appear dismissive, disinterested, and unprepared, turn your back on your audience and read directly from your slides. Your audience can read the slide; if you repeat it, it's not only boring, but redundant. PowerPoint slides are not a cheat sheet for you, but there to help your audience better understand what you are saying. Instead, consider keeping a hard copy of each of your slides in front of you, so you can be eye-to-eye with your audience throughout the presentation.

Jargon. Never use jargon, rhetoric, trade, or pretentious language. Always speak plainly and to the point.

Nervous Gestures. Don't fold or hold onto any paper, pencil, pen, or marker, touch your face, finger your jewelry, run your hands through your hair, scratch anywhere, or clear your throat excessively. Be sure to not repeatedly lick your lips or swallow, or aggressively move toward the audience, continually bob your head, lean on the podium, if there is one, or excessively repeat the same emphatic gesture. Nervous habits are distracting. While practicing your presentation, get team members to point out these nervous mannerisms before it's too late.

What Should You Look Like: What Does Your Attire Say about You?

You are not only presenting your solutions during a pitch, but yourself. Begin by taking a good hard look, first at your mannerisms, and then your appearance. Never look wrinkled or disheveled. Look for any spots on your tie or blouse before leaving for work. Business casual or even jeans can be considered acceptable, but I would check with your creative director before assuming casual will work.

How you dress reflects how your message is received. What you wear to the presentation can often be as important as the presentation itself. First impressions can not only set the tone of your presentation but your relationship with the client. If your audience is sitting there wondering what you were thinking when you chose that shirt, jacket, or shoes, they will not be listening to what you have to say. So it's important to get your audience focused on the message, not focused on the messenger's clashing colors.

The safest bet is to always dress more stylishly and professionally than your audience. Wear comfortable and practical pieces. If you look confident, you will project confidence.

Unlike other members of the team, creatives don't have to be quite so buttoned down; no one expects this, and it may make you appear too conservative or even uptight. Men may want to consider a plain jacket, or a simple shirt and tie boasting a bolder print, and khakis. Women may consider wearing a mis-matched but coordinated top and pants, a flowing skirt and jacket, and even a few larger pieces of jewelry. Be sure everything fits and is not too large or form-fitting.

Always avoid impractical accessories, anything too revealing, casual, scruffy or distracting. You want your ideas to stand out, not your lack of business fashion savvy.

Presentation Length: Don't Bore, Leave Them Wanting More

It is important to get a clear presentation schedule from the client, so you know how long the team will have to make their presentation. According to Berman and Blakeman in their book, *The Brains Behind Great Advertising Campaigns*,

> it's critical the team create a timeline that synchronizes the presentation's various visual/verbal elements to fit within that time frame. A good timeline should dedicate 15 percent of the allotted time to the introduction, 75 percent to the middle or body of the presentation, and 10 percent to the conclusion. If allowing for questions at the end of the presentation, an additional 10 percent will need to be deducted from the middle of your pitch.

You never want to go over your allotted time. You do not want your audience missing an important point because they are looking at their watch, or their mind is starting to wander.

Working with a Client's Personality Quirks

All clients are different. Some are introverts, others extroverts. Some are easy-going, while others are easily perturbed. Some are better communicators than others. All have different knowledge, tolerance, and work-ethic levels. So how do you adapt? The first step is to get to know them—begin building trust and credibility. The more you know, the easier it will get to anticipate their needs. Learn how to avoid unpleasant disagreements and how to negotiate through their level of tolerance for change and

surprise. One of the most common reasons for client/agency contention involves the misunderstanding of their needs or the miscommunication of their perceived needs.

The truth is many clients don't know what they want from their agency. Many problems center around communication issues. Clients want agencies to 1) know their business almost as well as they do, 2) communicate constantly—surprises are rarely welcomed, 3) have a strong creative and media strategy, 4) manage and use consumer insights, 5) accomplish more with a smaller budget, and of course, 6) show quantifiable results.

The Tedious Approval Process for Existing Clients

There are only two absolutes in advertising—that changes will happen during both the internal and external approval processes, and that they will happen at the last minute. The creative team does not have the final approval of any idea, copy, or layout. Internal (account) and external (client) approvals are required for all creative output for all mediums, before they are published, printed, posted online, or shared on social media.

Necessarily, internal and external approvals ensure the quality of the work not only meets both the agency's and client's standards but is also soundly on-strategy and on-target.

Before any idea or finished piece(s) can go to the client for review or approval, it will first need to be discussed internally with the creative director, and then again with the account manager in charge of the account. It is up to the creative team to ensure everyone understands the idea, how it evolved, and how it addresses the client's communication goals. It is critical the team be able to back up how the idea accomplishes the objectives, talks to the target, and strategically pushes the key consumer benefit, in other words, how the brand will differentiate itself from competitors. This does not, unfortunately, guarantee all feedback will be positive. An account manager from New York City sums up the process saying, "Creative teams, can at times be extremely precious with their work and either ignore or are offended by constructive criticism from the account team during the development stage." Constructive or not, the creative team will always believe strongly in their ideas. Because of this, they will often, to varying degrees of success, continue to negotiate direction. Win or lose, there will be always be changes that will need to be immediately made before it can be presented to the client.

There are three times an existing client will need to approve a design: 1) When a new concept direction is needed, 2) after the super comps are completed, and 3) before the ad is printed or uploaded.

Presenting New Concept Directions to Existing Clients

Once internal approvals to the copy and layout are complete, the entire concept will have to be sold externally to the client. Depending on what the agency was asked to do, the account manager and perhaps a member of the creative team may pitch anywhere from three to five ideas to the client. These pitches could be formally or informally presented to a single individual or to a panel of client representatives. The goal is to get the client and/or their team to approve a direction immediately to ensure the project meets any predetermined deadlines.

Once a design direction is approved, the account manager will bring any and all changes, corrections, and/or additions back to the creative team. The next step is to complete the final ads.

Presenting the Final Design

Before any preparation for printing or production can begin, the client must approve the final copy and layout. This final step in the creative process can often be a very stressful and frustrating one for the creative team. "If they [account management] can't defend or champion our ideas, the creative process can often seem like a big waste of time," an art director from Dallas lamented. An account supervisor from Richmond counters with "There is so much back and forth and drama that we keep them [creative] from ever being a part of. We fight for the work long after that one-hour meeting. We are always looking to be the best advocate for the work even when you aren't there. And getting clear, actionable feedback is never easy, so when we give it to you, know that at least five conversations had to happen to get it to you."

No matter how good the account team is, or how much client input there initially was, it is unlikely any ad or series of ads will ever be approved by the client without additional changes. Some changes are small and insignificant; others are major and very significant, and will require a great deal of work to complete. When the final round of changes (there could be more than one) is complete, the ad(s) will need to be signed off on by the creative and art director, the copywriter, and the account manager before going back to the client for final approval.

Although often tedious, it is critical the creative team always be open to client feedback. Involving them in the creative process at each stage ensures everyone understands how the idea is evolving and how it will be executed, both visually and verbally.

The external review process can often be slow if more than one approval is needed. If only one person on the client side has final authority to approve the ad(s), the process can be relatively quick. When both the internal and external teams have approved the design(s), they will move into production. Once the production process is complete, the ad(s) will need to be signed off, once again by both teams.

Understanding the Importance of Deadlines

Most design and production deadlines are nonnegotiable. Missed deadlines for any reason, for any type of medium, will not get produced, on time and on budget. Outside specialists, printers, and media outlets, to name just a few, have had time or space purchased or budgeted for. So whether the ad is completed on time or not, it will still cost the client money and noticeably disrupt a campaign's cohesive message.

There are big consequences to missed deadlines, so no deadline is ever missed. If for some reason they are, people's jobs will be on the line. Your unprofessional actions can have a devastating domino effect, so show your professional responsibility by getting work done well, and on time. This is how you build a reputation as a reliable, trustworthy creative team member who can deliver strong creative solutions within a set period of time.

To avoid springing any unnecessary surprises on the client, it is important that the creative team adhere to the creative brief as closely as possible. Unexpected idea directions not supported by the creative brief, account management, and/or the client can often expect to see considerable last-minute changes made to the final design. A surprised client tends to become a difficult client, and will often not only second-guess direction, but try to manipulate the visual/visual solution back towards the creative brief. Clients don't fear unique creative solutions—they fear how it will affect both brand image and loyalty.

Today's Streamlined Approval Process

The approval process of yesteryear required the account manager to physically drive the ads over to the client's office or use a courier service to deliver them. Everybody waited until they were returned to make any necessary changes. If a second round of changes were needed, they would have to make a repeat journey to the client for final approval.

Today, thanks to the computer, the approval process is more streamlined, less time-consuming, and more collaborative, under most circumstances. The online review and approval process offers a higher level of engagement between the client, the account manager, and creative team. Gone are the days of hard-copy reviews.

The introduction of easy-to-use desktop publishing tools allows for online proofing by the client. Additionally, real-time discussions, and more advanced video conferencing has made it possible for the client to take a more active part in each stage of the design process. Existing clients, unless requested, no longer must wait to see design options in a formal pitch; they can now actively engage with, and influence the campaign's development.

Collaboration early and often creates less uncertainty on the client's part, which often results in smaller and fewer changes. No matter how many client approvals are required, thanks to the advent of a fully online review and approval process, all members of the client and agency teams can tweak, and ultimately approve the designs from anywhere in the world.

Whether presenting a new pitch to a future client or new ideas to an existing one, creative teams will always need to passionately sell the sizzle of a big idea and capture the essence of the brand.

Bibliography

Berman, Margo and Robyn Blakeman. 2009. *The Brains Behind Great Ad Campaigns*. Lanham, MD: Rowman and Littlefield Publishing, p. 209.

Prater, Meg. 2018. "The 8 Types of Presentation Styles: Which Category Do You Fall Into?" (September 25). Retrieved from: http://blog.hubspot.com/sales/types-of-presentation-styles.

Tortorella, Neil. 2016. "Acing the Pitch: How to Pitch New Clients." Retrieved from: www.howdesign.com/design-business/clients/ace-your-design-pitch.

Glossary

Adaptive design	Mobile content that uses fixed layout sizes, making it not only more expensive but more time-consuming to produce.
Analogous colors	Three colors that sit next to each other on the color wheel.
Art	Imagery creative with expressiveness and imagination.
Ascenders	The part of a letterform that extends upward and away from the body of a letter, such as b, k, h, d, and i.
Assorted media mix	Employs more diverse types of media vehicles in a campaign.
Back-end production design	The outside agency production team that will code and implement the website designs.
Balance	A principle of design that ensures an ad appears balanced or equalized.
Banners	An announcement sales device used in newspaper advertising. Usually seen at the top of the ad.
Baseline	The invisible line type sits on.
Big idea	A type of key consumer benefit where creative ideas set the brand off from the competition in order to solve the brand's advertising problem.
Bleed	The area that extends beyond the trim in magazine design.
Blind deboss	A debossed surface that is left unadorned.
Blind emboss	An embossed surface that is left unadorned.
Body copy	The smaller, storytelling text in an ad.
Brainstorming	The creative process used to find multiple visual and verbal solutions to an advertising problem.
Brand	The name, term, sign, symbol or design, or any combination, that is intended to distinguish one brand from another in the same brand category.
Brand equity	A company's or a brand's reputation in the marketplace.
Brand image	A brand's personality, as compared to other brands within the brand category.
Brand loyalty	Refers to the relationship between the brand and the target.
Branded bus	A single brand buys all the advertising space on a city bus.
Bulletin	An outdoor structure that is used to display an advertising message.
Callouts	Includes a couple of lines of descriptive copy, a small headline, and one or more prices that are connected to a visual by a small line.
Campaign	A family of ads that deliver a synergistic, strategic, and cohesive collection of planned messages.
Campaign uniformity	The visual/verbal message is consistent, no matter the media outlet.
Changing content	The content on a website that changes out for every page, such as headlines, subheads, visuals, body copy, and links.
Character representative	An imagined, animated brand representative who will represent the brand in all forms of media.
Clip art	Free, publicly available, line-art drawings that can be used without permissions.

Color	One of the elements of design that creates a mood and can mean different things to different people.
Color palettes	Also known as color schemes, these are harmonious color combinations.
Color wheel	Helps an art director to understand how colors mix, match, or clash.
Complementary colors	Colors that sit opposite each other on the color wheel.
Concentrated media mix	Places all advertising efforts into one medium.
Concept	Refers to your thoughts and ideas on how you can creatively solve the client's advertising problem.
Content	Refers to the varied visual and verbal components seen in the ad.
Content management system	Manages website content.
Content marketing	An approach focused on creating and distributing valuable, relevant, and consistent content to attract and retain a defined audience.
Context	The environment in which mobile content is viewed.
Continual content	The content that will be seen on every page of a website.
Contrast	A principle of design that creates visual interest between components on the page using size, value, tone, color, shape, or texture.
Cooperative advertising	Two or more individual but compatible clients have paired up to share the cost of the advertising.
Copy break subheads	Informative, small headlines, used to break up long blocks of copy.
Cover wrap	An ad that takes over the front page of a newspaper ad. Seen above the fold.
Creative brief	An internal agency document, the creative brief evolves from the client's marketing plan. Its job is to lay out for the creative team the communications plan of attack.
Creative team	A team of individuals, which typically include a creative director and one or more art directors and copywriters.
Cropping	The removal of any unnecessary part(s) of an image.
Cybermarketing	A combination of traditional advertising and Internet marketing.
Database marketing	A highly targetable, personalized, and measurable form of direct response.
Debossing	A technique that pushes an image into and slightly below a paper's surface.
Demographics	Defines the target audience by their sex, age, income, marital and professional status, education, and number of children, as well as other relevant factors.
Descenders	The part of a letterforms body that projects downward below the baseline such as with the letters g, p, and j.
Detail copy	The smallest copy on an ad, that informs about location, hours, credit cards accepted, and so on.
Die-cut	The process of cutting the surface (paper) into an interesting customized shapes.
Dimension	The overall shape, or the roundness or flatness, of an object.
Direct response	Televised ads that involve the target in the message process by asking them to do something, such as make a purchase.
Display	A style of loud, decorative typefaces that have an unusual or irregular appearance.
Display ads	Newspaper ads that feature both visual and verbal elements.
Dominance	A principle of design: One element within an ad needs to dominate the layout.
Duotone	Gives a black-and-white photograph a wash of a second color.
Dummy	A thumbnail layout that shows how a folded piece will both lay out and look.
Elements of design	The visual elements we see in a design, that include line, shape, volume, texture, value, and color.
Embossing	A technique that raises an image out from the surface of the paper, creating a 3D effect.
Extensions	Also known as top-outs and cut-outs, extenders and embellishments refer to a part of the design that extends beyond the live area of an outdoor board.

Eye flow	A principle of design, involves arranging an ad's components in such a way as to create a predetermined path for the reader to follow.
Font	Refers to all the upper- and lower-case letters, numbers, and punctuation for a specific typeface.
Form	Refers to how the visual and verbal components will be organized within a design.
Formal balance	Imagines a line that runs down the center of an ad, where every element that appears on one side of the ad is duplicated in size or shape on the other.
Frame	The individual audio and video portions for television are confined in a frame.
Frames	Also known as borders, frames are placed around an ad, defining its edges.
Freelancers	Outside independent creative, media, or research contractors hired by an agency or brand to handle overflow work.
Freestanding inserts	One-page, full-color coupon ads, that are inserted into newspapers and your mailbox.
Front-end design	Refers to the creative teams that imagine and initially create the designs for web pages.
Geometric shapes	Refers to the shapes of circles, squares, triangles, or rectangles.
Gestalt principle	A set of theories that deal with visual perception.
Gradation	A principle of design that refers to the gradual and orderly step-by-step change in color, tone, or size.
Graphic	Uses a combination of visuals and/or shapes and type to colorfully, symbolically, and uniquely represent an idea or concept.
Greeking	Also known as placeholder text, greeking is illegible copy, consisting of letters, numbers, punctuation, and paragraph breaks that is used to temporarily represent copy.
Gutters	The white space appearing between columns of typeset copy.
Halftone	The line screen added to a black-and-white photograph.
Headlines	The largest piece of copy on the page or screen, that screams out the key consumer benefit.
Home page	The first or opening page of a website.
Horizontal cooperatives	Two clients have budgets that are equally distributed, giving each sponsor equal exposure in a single ad.
Hues	Can lighten, darken, or mute a color.
Illustration	A drawing, painting, or digitally created image that uniquely informs and visually represents a brand or concept.
Implied texture	Texture you can only see and not feel.
Informal balance	Deals with optical weight, but each side uses different-sized images to reach balance.
Infomercial	Long commercials, usually 30–60 minutes.
Inherent drama	Something the creative team needs to find in a brand during brainstorming sessions, to make the brand interesting to the target audience and stand out from competing brands.
Inset graphic border	A decorative border that is set noticeably smaller than the printable size of the ad.
Interactive television	Allows the viewer to click on a link appearing on the television screen.
Interior cards	Horizontally aligned advertising frames, located inside and above a bus's windows.
Interstitials	Ads seen in the main browser, between two pages of a website.
Kerning	A computer term used to describe the numerical amount of white space appearing between typeset letterforms.
Key consumer benefit	A combination of a brand feature and its corresponding benefit to the target, that is the central focus in every ad.
Kiosks	Three- and four-sided glass advertising floor displays.
Landing page	A single web page that opens after the viewer clicks on a search result or online ad.
Layout styles	The different ways components can be laid out on a page or screen, which include big type, grid, circus, copy-heavy, frame, Mondrian, multipanel, picture window, rebus, silhouette, symmetrical, asymmetrical, repetition, anomaly, and concentration.

Leading	A computer term used to describe the numerical amount of white space appearing between lines of typeset text.
Legibility	The ease with which an ad can be understood when read quickly.
Letter spacing	A design term used to describe the white space appearing between letterforms.
Life-cycle stage	The age, or amount of time, the brand has been available on the market.
Line	One of the elements of design, a one-dimensional stroke that has a defined beginning and end.
Line art	A simple black-and-white line drawing with no tonal qualities.
Line height	A computer term that refers to the amount of digital leading.
Line screen	In printing, the resolution must be able to convert to the proper line screen needed for a print medium.
Line spacing	A design term used to describe the white space appearing between lines of hand-drawn text.
Live area	The safe area type must be confined within for magazine ads.
Logo	The identifying symbol for a brand.
Media mix	Breaks the promotional mix down into specific media vehicles, such as magazine, television, direct mail, Facebook, the Internet, and so on.
Mobile geofencing	Location-based mobile advertising that reaches the target near or at the point of purchase.
Mobile-in-app	Also known as mobile advertising.
Modern	A style of typeface that can be very forward-thinking, trendy, and futuristic looking.
Monochromatic	A single color scheme.
Monotone achromatic	Color scheme that employs all the tints and shades falling between black and white.
Native advertising	A nonintrusive form of mobile advertising that fits seamlessly into the user experience.
Negative/positive space	A principle of design that refers to occupied and unoccupied spaces.
Niche marketing	The division of target groups into smaller, more specialized segments, for the purpose of focus marketing.
Organic content	Facebook users' view of content through unpaid distribution.
Organic shapes	Any shape that is not geometric.
Orphan	A single word, or the last line of a paragraph of copy, that appears at the top of a second column of type.
Outdoor boards	Also known as billboards, outdoor boards are large, out-of-home boards used to show advertising near the point of purchase.
Overline subhead	Appears above the headline and is used as a teaser, or to make an announcement.
Paid content	Reaches its social media viewers as a result of advertising.
Pantone matching system	A system for mixing special colors.
Perforations	Small cuts placed around coupons to make them easier to tear off and use.
Permission marketing	Also known as "opt-in marketing," refers to members of the target audience who elect to receive e-mail messages from brands.
Photo illustration	The combination of photographs and illustrations to create a single, more graphic and interpretive image.
Photo shoot	A photo session led by the art director, where the brand and/or actors appearing in an ad are photographed.
Pictogram	Also known as an infographic, a pictogram is an image-based type of bar graph.
Piggybacking	Used in television or radio advertising, when a 30-second commercial is split into two 15-second spots.
Pitch deck	Used in new business pitches to introduce your agency to the client and outline the agency's solution to their advertising problem.
Points	Very small measurement devices, used to determine the overall size of a typeset letter.
Positioning	Refers to how the consumer thinks about a product or service, and rates it against the competition.

Postproduction	The editing of a commercial.
Preproduction	The development of the commercial script, storyboard, budget, and hiring of on-air talent, director, and production crew.
Primary colors	Red, yellow, and blue.
Principles of design	The visual guidelines that govern the way the elements are used within the layout, or the arrangement of the elements as a whole.
Product placement	The deliberate placement of a brand into a television commercial, video, or movie.
Production	The actual shooting time of the television commercial.
Promotional mix	The communication options that will be used to reach the target with an advertised message, employing any combination of public relations, advertising, direct marketing, sales promotion, digital, guerrilla marketing, and alternative media.
Raster images	Images seen in Photoshop that are composed of pixels.
Readability	The ease with which an ad can be read quickly at a glance.
Realistic imagery	Realistic imagery is educational, focusing on specific facts, uses, or lifestyle enhancements.
Rebranding	Takes place when a brand's look needs to be modernized, or rehabilitated after product failure or scandal.
Repositioning	Takes place when there is a need to alter the target's views of the brand.
Request for proposal (RFP)	A pitch brief supplied by the client to help the agency prepare their new business pitch.
Responsive design	Mobile content that automatically reacts to changes in screen size.
Retail advertising	A term used for mediums who sale direct to the consumer.
Return on investment (ROI)	The amount of money made versus how much money was spent on advertising.
Rich media	An e-mail ad that can include graphics and audio and video.
Roughs	Also known as layouts, roughs are quickly drawn, full-size ideas, used to simulate how the final ad will look.
Sans serif	A sturdy style of typeface that has no thin lines attached to the letterforms.
Scenes	The visual aspects of a commercial or video.
Screen tints	Also known as "shades," screen tints are an inexpensive way to offer depth to any one color.
Script	A style of typeface that mimics handwriting.
Scripts	The copy sheet of what will be said and seen, used in radio, television, and video.
Search-engine optimization	Sites that include relevant links to other sites to increase engagement.
Search-engine marketing	When brands pay a search engine such as Google to place their websites first or toward the top in keyword searches.
Secondary colors	Green, orange, and violet.
Serif	A style of typeface that has delicate lines that protrude from letterforms.
Shade	A color created by adding in black.
Shape	One of the elements of design comprised of both length and width, having two-dimensional boundaries and which can be created using lines, color, value, and texture.
Sitemap	The first step in organizing content for a website design.
Skyscrapers	Vertical banners seen on the Internet.
Slogan	A statement usually found either above or below the brand logo, that expresses a company or corporate philosophy.
Social TV	The use of social media while watching a television program.
Sound effects	The noises heard in radio, television, and video.
Spam	E-mail messages sent without the permission of the target.

Spectaculars	Large, custom-designed and creative outdoor boards.
Split complementary colors	Uses three, rather than two, colors.
Spokesperson	A real person, celebrity or not, who represents a brand in all forms of media.
Spot color	Black-and-white photographs that use a spot of color to highlight the brand, packaging or logo.
Standard rate and data system	Gives to production artists information about line screen and bleed, before sizing and determining resolution.
Station domination	A single brand can buy all, or a combination, of advertised locations within a subway station.
Stock art	Existing photographs of all varieties that can be inexpensively purchased and used in an ad.
Storyboard	Shows the visual and verbal portion of a television commercial or video.
Structure	A principle of design: Nothing is randomly placed—each component has a controlled or thought-out appearance.
Subheads	The second largest piece of copy on a printed or digital screen. Used to expand on what the headline is saying.
Super comprehensives	Also known as super comps, these are a finished design executed on a computer.
Super-families	Type families that are specifically designed to complement each other, making pairing easier.
Supplemental advertising	See "Freestanding insert."
Support statement	Highlights one feature/benefit combination that directly supports or further advances the key consumer benefit.
Symbolic imagery	Uses an indirect approach to connect the brand with the meaning given them by the advertising.
Tagline	A statement usually found either above or below the brand's logo, that highlights a campaign's direction.
Tactile texture	Used in three-dimensional design, where you can actually reach out and feel the texture.
Target audience	Also known as "target market," this consists of those individuals that research has determined will most likely use or buy the brand.
Teaser	Copy placed on the outer envelop of a direct-mail kit.
Tertiary colors	Also known as "intermediate colors," these include red-violet, and blue-violet, red-orange, yellow-orange, yellow-green and blue-green, and are created by mixing a primary and a secondary color together.
Tetradic colors	Also known as "double complementary colors," tetradic colors use four colors arranged into a rectangle, or two complementary opposing pairs, on the color wheel.
Texture	One of the elements of design that refers to the surface or visual feel of a visual.
Text wrap	The way type is designed to wrap around an image.
Thumbnails	Small, proportionate drawings that are used to get brainstorming ideas down on paper.
Tint	When white is added to a color, to create a light hue.
Tone	Created by mixing in both black and white, resulting in a grayer color.
Tone of voice	Also known as "tone," this determines the personality and the overall visual/verbal voice and/or style of the advertised message.
Triadic color	Three colors that are evenly spaced around the color wheel.
Trim	Refers to the size of the ad, and where a magazine ad will be trimmed after printing.
Typeface	Refers to the given name of a typeface.
Type alignment	The way type is aligned on the page or screen.
Type style	The overall shape of a typeface, such as serif or sans serif.
Underline subhead	Also known as the "main subhead," this appears below the headline and explains in more detail what the headline is saying.
Unity	A principle of design, also known as "harmony," unity ensures all visual and verbal elements in an ad work together, to send a cohesive single message.

Unique selling proposition	One type of key consumer benefit that is unique to a brand, or that will promote a commonplace feature/benefit combination as unique.
Urban panels	Advertising seen at subway entrances.
User experience	Refers to how visitors will interact with a website.
User-generated content	Also known as "consumer-generated media," user-generated content is the visual/verbal sharing of thoughts and ideas by the target on the Internet and social media sites.
User interface	Refers to the visual communication between components on the page or screen.
Value	One of the elements of design that highlights details or textures through the use of contrast, or lights and darks.
Verbal uniformity	Takes place when all creative pieces promote one idea or key consumer benefit.
Vector images	A type of image file that does not need pixels to reproduce an image, typically created in Illustrator.
Vertical cooperatives	A shared ad, where one sponsor pays more and plays a larger or more prominent role in the ad.
Viral	Advertising shared between groups on the Internet or social media.
Visual uniformity	All creative materials have a unique appearance or style.
Volume	One of the elements of design, visuals that have a three-dimensional appeal consisting of length, width, and depth.
Wallscape	Custom-designed outdoor boards designed to fit a variety of unique shapes and sizes.
Weight	The thickness or thinness of a typeface's body style.
White space	A principle of design, the white of the page that is used to emphasize and organize the elements within it, as well as bring order to chaos.
Widow	A single word, or possibly two short words, that appear at the end of a paragraph or column of text.
Wireframe	Simple line drawings that show the placement of both continual and changing content on a website.
Word of mouth	Face-to-face discussions about a brand.
X-height	Refers to the body height of a typeface's lower-case letters.

Index